M000307820

Beginning to Be a Jesuit

Instructions
Pour
le Noviciat

Les Instructions communes à Tous.

Instruction première

De l'Ordre du jour

Reglement Exterieur

Les jours ordinaires, les jours de fête, les jours de jeûne, les jours de Récréation, & les jours qu'on repose, l'ordre du jour n'est pas le même.

Ordre pour les jours ordinaires

A 5h. le lever, on couvre soulit, ou visite le St. Sacrement & la Ste. Vierge, & on repasse sa méditation s'il reste du temps.

Beginning to Be a Jesuit

Instructions for the Paris Novitiate
circa 1685

Patricia M. Ranum
Translator and Editor

The Institute of Jesuit Sources
Saint Louis

Number 26 in Series I:
Jesuit Primary Sources in English Translation

All rights reserved

© Patricia M. Ranum 2011

The Institute of Jesuit Sources
3601 Lindell Boulevard
St. Louis, MO 63108

tel: 314-633-4622
fax: 314-633-4623
e-mail ijs@jesuitsources.com
www.jesuitsources.com

Library of Congress Control Number: 2010938194

ISBN   978-1-880810-75-0 (cloth)
        978-1-880810-76-7 (paper)

Cover illustration: The novitiate as depicted on the Turgot-Bretez map of 1739 (Ranum collection)

For

François de Dainville, S.J.

Pierre Delattre, S.J.

Henry Fouqueray, S.J.

and Pierre Moisy

Dicebat Bernardus Carnotensis nos esse quasi nanos, gigantium humeris insidentes, ut possimus plura eis et remotiora videre, non utique proprii visus acumine, aut eminentia corporis, sed quia in altum subvenimur et extollimur magnitudine gigantea.

John of Salisbury, *Metalogicon* (1159)

Bernard of Chartres used to say that we are like dwarfs on the shoulders of giants, so that we can see more than they, and things at a greater distance, not by virtue of any sharpness of sight on our part, or any physical distinction, but because we are carried high and raised up by their giant size.

Illustrations

Frontispiece Instructions pour le Noviciat
(Bibliothèque Mazarine, manuscript 1793, page 9)

Figure 1 The Novitiate as depicted on the Turgot-Bretez
map of 1739 (Ranum collection)   34

Figure 2 Martellange's drawing of the Hôtel de Mézières, 1630
(courtesy of the Bibliothèque nationale de France)   35

Figure 3 Gaspard Mérian's engraving of the Novitiate
as seen from the rue du Pot-de-Fer, circa 1650
(Ranum collection)   36

Figure 4 The Novitiate church and two floor plans by
Martellange dated 1630: left, the ground floor
with its high altar and side chapels; right, the upper
level with its side galleries and rear loft (courtesy of the
Bibliothèque nationale de France)   37

Plan 1 The ground floor of the Novitiate residence   38

Plan 2 The "noble story" of the Novitiate residence   38

Plan 3 The uppermost story of the Novitiate residence   39

Table of Contents

Preface: John W. Padberg, S.J.   ix

Introduction: Patricia M. Ranum   1

Editing principles: Patricia M. Ranum   41

Instructions pour le Noviciat   44

    Avertissement   44

    Les instructions communes à tous   50

    Table des trente-quatre instructions   204

Instructions for the Novitiate   45

    Notice   45

    Common instructions for everyone   51

    Table of the thirty-four instructions   205

Appendix 1

    Les Tons   206

    The Tones   207

Appendix II

    Schooling and Courtesy: Orest Ranum   210

Selected Bibliography   221

Index   225

Preface

The first ten members of the Society of Jesus had all been students at the University of Paris. Ignatius of Loyola, the first superior general of the Jesuits, greatly appreciated the education he had received in Paris. In 1540, the very year of the official approval of the Society by Pope Paul III, Ignatius sent a group of Jesuit recruits to study there. The Society almost immediately began to flourish in France and increasingly enjoyed royal support even if the monarchs were sometimes exigent in their demands on the Society.

The Jesuits also regularly encountered a great deal of opposition, principally from the University of Paris and from the parlement. The university was hostile to the Society's educational endeavors and to some of its theological positions. The parlement was rife with Gallican views regarding the rights of the French church in its relations with Rome. And later both university and parlement became increasingly supportive of Jansenism and its hostility to the Society.

The Jesuit "province" of France was established in 1552. A province is a group of Jesuits engaged in the works of the Society in a particular geographical region under the direction of a provincial superior, appointed by the general superior in Rome. As the number of Jesuits and their works grew, four other provinces followed: Aquitaine in 1564, Lyon in 1582, Toulouse in 1608, and Champagne in 1616. By 1630 there were seventy-two Jesuit houses in France, fifty-eight of which were colleges educating more than thirty thousand students.

Concomitant with that growth, the provinces established novitiates or houses of formation that over an initial period of two years introduced men aspiring to membership in the Society into how to begin to be Jesuits. The novitiate with which this book deals was founded in Paris in 1610. As noted in the Introduction that precedes the text and translation of the rules for that novitiate, its establishment took place in "a period of devotional fervor that began around 1600," the start of what has been called "the great century of French spirituality."

The sources of that spirituality were manifold. They included the impulse toward Catholic reform, specific currents of thought and activity, outstanding personalities, and circumstances of time and place. All of these drew on a revival in the frequent reception of the sacraments and in the devotional practices and ways of living the Christian life.

To mention only a very few of the outstanding French personalities in the spiritual life of that seventeenth century, we might list Francis de Sales and Jeanne de Chantal, founders of the Visitation nuns; Pierre de Bérulle, who introduced the Oratory into France; Vincent de Paul, founder of the Congregation of the Mission and, together with Louise de Marillac, of the Daughters of Charity; Jacques-Bénigne Bossuet, orator and bishop of Meaux; and François Fénelon, educator and archbishop of Cambrai. Among the Jesuit writers and "directors of souls" in that century were men who then and later had a marked influence on the spirituality of both Jesuits and of society at large. Again to mention only a few: Jean Suffren, preacher, writer, and royal confessor; Claude la Colombière, preacher and promoter of devotion to the Sacred Heart of Jesus; Vincent Huby, founder of the first

Jesuit retreat house; Louis Lallement, master of novices and director of the tertianship, the last period of Jesuit formation; Jean-Joseph Surin, writer on mystical theology; and the great preacher, Louis Bourdaloue.

Many are the works that have been written on such men and women and on the movements and the institutions that contributed to the richness of the spiritual currents of that century. Not least have been the scholarly monographs and popular treatments of Jesuit spirituality during that time. Three items make the present work, translated and edited by the distinguished historian, Patricia Ranum, a unique contribution to the study and understanding of Jesuit life and spirituality during that century. First, the book presents a "primary source" text in the original French language of the seventeenth century and, on facing pages, an English translation that faithfully reproduces the substance and the nuances of that text. Second, the translator and editor has contributed both a wide-ranging introduction to the work and detailed footnotes throughout the text that clarify the meaning and deepen the understanding of the activities in which the novices were engaged and the attitudes or inner dispositions that were to accompany those activities. In addition, the understanding of that context is deepened by the appendix, "Schooling and Courtesy," by another distinguished historian of the period, Orest Ranum. The third special, and perhaps most important, characteristic of this work is that it makes available to us a direct and detailed look at specific activities that went into the initial formation of members of the Society of Jesus in France during that period. This set of instructions sets forth, not what Jesuits may have thought and written about such initial formation, but what they actually did in those first two years of Jesuit life. These three characteristics all contribute to making this book an extraordinarily valuable work.

John W. Padberg, S.J.
Director
The Institute of Jesuit Sources

Introduction

The *Instructions*
for the Jesuit Novitiate of Paris

Patricia M. Ranum

The manuscript

Manuscript 1793 of the Bibliothèque Mazarine in Paris, *Instructions pour le Novitiat*, is a rather small, unimpressive volume. It measures just under seven by nine inches (170 mm. by 217 mm.), and it contains 210 numbered pages.[1] Its inexpensive late-seventeenth-century rough suede binding (known as *la peau retournée*) was typical for registers and other record books. The suede has faded to a rusty brown, but it was once a vivid purple. The four margins of each page are ruled with red pencil (*réglées au crayon rouge*). The binder trimmed the margins, especially the top ones, thereby eliminating not only some page numbers but also the first line of a Latin inscription on the title page.[2]

That the pages are not dog-eared, suggests that this was a master copy kept in reserve,[3] not one of the copies that novices aspiring to the priesthood were expected to read monthly from start to finish. (Novices preparing to be temporal coadjutors,

---

[1] These page numbers are shown within square brackets in both the French text and the English translation. It is these bracketed numbers (and not the number of the page where the text appears in the printed book) that are cited throughout this introduction. A translation into German of ms. 1793 was done by Hermann Stoeckius, *Untersuchungen zur Geschichte des Noviziates in der Gesellschaft Jesu* (Bonn: Falkenroth, 1918). I wish to thank the Bibliothèque Mazarine for authorizing the present transcription and translation of the manuscript.

[2] There is evidence that the bookbinder tampered with the outer sheets of the manuscript, and that a few minor modifications were made in the nineteenth century. At some point one or two outer sheets were removed; a fragment of this paper has survived around one of the sewing holes. As a result of this loss, the sewing threads are unusually loose. One of the missing pages clearly had writing on it: while the ink was still wet, two letters on a missing page were transferred to the previous page, which survived and now serves as the front end paper. (The letters are illegible.) In addition, the first surviving page bears an indentation: "7," followed by an illegible figure and a "4," doubtlessly a catalog number written in pencil on the previous page, now lost. In the nineteenth century, a small leather label bearing a title was glued to the spine of the book, and a large handwritten title in very black ink was added to the almost blank right-hand page at the start of the volume. I am indebted to Isabelle de Conihout of the Bibliothèque Mazarine for sharing these insights.

[3] If this particular copy had been read month after month by four novices, would not manifest errors or lapses (for example, the missing words on pp. [5], [11–12], [79], and [93–94], as well as the inversion of *supérieur* and *inférieur* on p. [177]) have been repaired? Does not the presence of these lapses suggest that once copies had been made for the novices, this little purple book was placed on a shelf and was only occasionally consulted by the superiors for whom, and by whom it had been written? And that once the the novices noticed the lapses in their copies, a superior authorized their repair ([1]), but that no one took the time to repair the lapses in the master copy?

who are mentioned only in passing in the manuscript, presumably had a separate set of instructions more pertinent to their vocation. It probably was read to them, since many would in all likelihood have been illiterate.) The Instructions permit some inferences to be made about the daily routines, until the time when another scholar deepens our knowledge.

Stylistically, the prose is the opposite of sententious. There are none of the complex sentences so characteristic of learned treatises, where a typical sentence can consist of sixty or even seventy-five words linked by commas, semicolons, and colons. True, there are a few run-on sentences, but in the main the sentences are straightforward and direct, and the vocabulary is relatively small. An effort was clearly being made to communicate a body of very specific rules, and to do so with a minimum of words and no rhetorical flourishes.

Although the manuscript is undated, it contains clues that permit a relatively precise dating. First of all, the handwriting of the anonymous copyist manifestly dates from the second half of the seventeenth century. So does the quite modern spelling. (That is not to say that the person who made this copy of the *Instructions* did not sometimes lapse into archaic spellings more typical of his youth.[4]) These modernisms conform to a guideline stated in the *Instructions*, to be observed by all who belong to the Society, young and old:

> As for spelling, one copies something from a nicely printed book
> in modern French; and while copying it, one should apply oneself to
> observing not only how all the words are written, but also all the periods
> and commas, how they are placed, and where one should use capital letters
> and lower-case letters. ([136])

In the *Instructions* we see these religious not simply imitating recent spelling, but also using the accent marks that were increasingly being employed in elite publications.[5] Taken together, spelling and accents strongly suggest that the *Instructions* date from the 1680s,[6] and that they were copied out by a man in his fifties, not by a novice.

From oral rules to written ones

The introductory pages of the *Instructions* state why the manuscript was drawn up. The conduct of novices and fathers alike had long been shaped not only by Ignatius

---

[4] For example, amid modern spellings such as *ici* and *ni*, archaic *y*'s of the first half of the century creep in: *employ, infiny, icy, ny, quoy, aussy,* and so forth. These *y*'s could still be found in books printed in the 1670s and 1680s, but by the early 1690s they had virtually disappeared from both published texts and personal correspondence.

[5] In the manuscript, the *estre*'s of previous decades have given way to the *être*'s that had become routine by the 1660s. Even more, the copyist employed the sort of mid-word accents that came into use during the 1670s: *expressément, fidélité, inférieurs, obéissance,* and so forth.

[6] There can be no doubt that the manuscript post-dates 1671, because there is an allusion to "Saint" Francis Borgia ([74]). He was canonized in 1671.

Loyola's written *Constitutions,* but also by a body of rules and regulations that met the specific needs of the Paris Novitiate.[7] Seven decades after the founding of the Novitiate, these regulations were perhaps being observed too mechanically, with little attention to the inner meaning of the humbling activities that were part of a novice's day. Worse still, because the regulations were partly written and partly oral, they were causing discord within the house.[8]

A committee of "very wise persons" was therefore created, to revise the existing instructions ([182]). Imagine the hours of talk that accompanied this move from near orality to an acceptable written document! We do not know who ultimately assumed responsibility for the revisions, but this individual referred to himself twice, in the first person, "I" ([129], [203]). Was the rector himself speaking? If so, which rector? Father Pierre Dozenne, who served as rector from 1682 to 1685? Or Father Henri Guymond, who directed the Novitiate for ten years, September 1685 to September 1696?[9]

The committee did not discard the existing instructions and start over; it used them as a point of departure. The unidentified author could therefore assert that the *Instructions* "contain nothing new." He realized, however, that it was essential to move from orality and memory, to a written handbook that would make the regulations truly authoritative:

> Many things have been added that were being practiced without being written down. Now that they have been written down, no one will forget them, conduct can be perfectly uniform, and no one will henceforth dispute what one is obliged to do or not to do. ([2])

As a major innovation, each regulation would henceforth have two facets, the "outer" regulation itself, and the "inner" lesson to be learned by obeying that specific rule. Or, as the author put it:

> Each instruction, be it general or specific, will distinguish between two things: that which, so to speak, forms its body, and that which forms its soul. The body of the instruction is what is ordered concerning the time

---

[7] In 1889 (and despite the 50-year hiatus caused by the suppression of the Society in France in the 1760s), the rules and regulations that form the underpinnings of the *Instructions* survived and were shaping almost every aspect of daily life at the novitiate in Pau. See Michael H. Dziewicki, "A Glimpse into a Jesuit Novitiate," published in both *Blackwood's Edinburgh Magazine* (1889), 146: 366–80, and *The Living Age* edited by E. and R.S. Littel (1889), 182: 805–15. (Both versions are available online through Google Books.) For a summary of the numerous regulations that provincials of the late sixteenth century were expected to take into account, see A. Lynn Martin, *The Jesuit Mind, the Mentality of an Elite in Early Modern France* (Ithaca: Cornell University Press, 1988), 107–10.

[8] For the oral versus the written in seventeenth-century educated circles, see Françoise Waquet, *Parler comme un livre, L'oralité et le savoir (XVIe–XXe siècle)* (Paris: Albin Michel, 2003). For the increasing importance of written rules in the seventeenth century, compare [1–4] of the *Instructions* with Waquet, 152–54 and 162–63; and for how the written rules of the Jesuit *Ratio* shaped the orality of speech-making, see Waquet, 167–68.

[9] *Les Établissements des jésuites en France depuis quatre siècles,* directed by Pierre Delattre, S.J. (Enghien: Institut supérieur de théologie, 1940), 3:1318.

and the manner of doing each action. The soul is the inner spirit with which everything that is ordered must be done, the motives that should animate one's action, the pious and solid considerations with which one can busy oneself and sustain oneself while doing it. ([6–7])

This attention to the inner spirit of the rule had been lacking in most of the old Instructions, he noted. Reflections on the inner meaning of each regulation were therefore "judged the most necessary to add to these Instructions" ([7]). Consequently, each of the thirty-four specific instructions in the manuscript comprises an "outer regulation" about how the activity should be conducted, and an "inner guidance" that will help novices advance along the ways of God.[10] By observing these outer regulations and by making the inner guidance associated with them an integral part of their own actions and devotions, in the space of two years a novice would begin to learn to be a Jesuit.

No brief summary of the contents of the *Instructions*, no outline of the thorny path along which a novice was supposed to make his way in the course of those two years, must be allowed to preempt what the *Instructions* themselves state! Rather, the next section of this Introduction suggests some general points that readers may wish to keep in mind, as they work their way through the *Instructions* and are awed by the multitude of rules over which an aspiring Jesuit risked stumbling day after day.

Learning to be a Jesuit

Like the disciple who, "leaving all things," followed Jesus, a novice who entered the Parisian Novitiate left his family and its possessions, and he relinquished the social class in which he had been raised. He was no longer the son of an aristocrat, a judge in the Paris Parlement, a shopkeeper, a craftsman. He was no longer a street-savvy Parisian or a provincial bumpkin. He was now a "very humble and very obedient servant in Our Lord and novice of the Society of Jesus," a position of which he was reminded every time he signed a letter ([177]). Be it elegant or uncouth, the behavior he had learned from his parents, his brothers, his uncles, and his friends had to be put aside: he would henceforth emulate the civility, the demeanor, and the discourse of the Jesuit fathers who had been entrusted with the heavy responsibility of training novices, most of whom were still adolescents. After two years at the Novitiate, obedience to the

---

[10] Here are a few examples of how the two parts of a given instruction worked in tandem. Instruction 21 discusses the bedchamber. The outer regulation begins: "In the bedchamber one should scrupulously keep silence"; the inner guidance begins with a sentence that parallels this image: "We should view our chamber as the tomb in which we have voluntarily shut ourselves up for Jesus Christ." Instruction 18 discusses writing and spelling. The outer regulation begins: "In the order of the day there is a half hour set aside for learning to write well, and a quarter hour for learning to spell." Again, the inner guidance begins with a parallel thought: "Others are inconvenienced when someone does not write at least legibly." The longer instructions are built upon multiple parallels of this sort.

content of the *Instructions* should have become second nature for the novice: he would be now thinking and behaving like a Jesuit. That was as it should be, for the material in the *Instructions* was applicable for the rest of one's life in the Society.

True, the minuteness of the detail might give the impression that these rules for novices could scarcely apply to mature Jesuits and must be peculiar to the Paris Novitiate. That conclusion would be misguided. The manuscript is a precious example of Jesuit pedagogy. It is grounded on a corpus of general or "common" rules dating back to the early days of the Society, rules that were observed by Jesuits throughout the world. The manuscript breaks these rules down into a mass of very pointed regulations, on the premise that "these [more] particular regulations can scarcely be too detailed" ([1]). Every regulation in the *Instructions* is within the grasp of the most exuberant adolescent, or of the rustic but intelligent and devout youth whom someone had discovered in the provinces and had sent on to Paris.

Each bedchamber at the Novitiate contained a copy of the *Instructions*. Throughout their novitiate, novices were expected to read these regulations monthly, from start to finish ([7]). In addition, from the very beginning of their novitiate, they became acquainted with the common rules of the Society, which were regularly read aloud in the refectory. Upon leaving the Novitiate, the young men presumably no longer needed to consult the detailed regulations in the *Instructions*. Rather, for the rest of their lives as Jesuits, and irrespective of the house where they were residing, they would refer to the common rules that were read aloud monthly in the refectory.

Take, for example, the thirteen "Rules of Religious Decorum" (*Regulæ Modestiæ*) composed by, or in great part attributable to Ignatius. Along with the Summary of the Constitutions and the Common Rule, these rules of decorum were read aloud each month in the refectory of all Jesuit houses, wherever they might be. Rule 2 states that "the head should not be moved around thoughtlessly, but only when there is need, and then it should be done with dignity. If there be no need, it should be held erect, slightly inclined, but without leaning to either side." In the *Instructions* this rule takes the form of an admonition to novices to avoid "leaning their head to one side or sticking out their neck while praying to God," or "looking over their shoulder . . . to see what is going on" ([149]). Rule 3 states that "the eyes, for the most part, should be kept lowered, and should not be immoderately raised, or allowed to rove from side to side." In the *Instructions* this becomes: "One will not let one's eyes wander" during exhortations ([48]); "the eyes should not dart lightly here and there, to see what one's neighbors are doing, or what is happening on the other side of the refectory" ([83]); "it is necessary to have one's eyes absolutely lowered to one's glass while drinking" ([84]); and "letting their eyes dart about lightly or fixing them on the floor, instead of positioning them at a suitable distance," demonstrated a singular lack of modesty on the part of a novice ([149]). Rule 5 reads: "Wrinkles on the forehead, and much more about the nose, should be avoided. The serenity of the countenance will thus be a reflection of serenity of soul." For novices, this rule of decorum is transformed into reminders to

refrain from displaying distress and looking "as if one were straining too much" ([173]), especially if one plays chess, when "it is necessary to be careful not to look as if one were straining too much" ([189]). Rule 8, which stipulates that "clothing should be kept clean and worn in a manner befitting a religious," is elaborated upon in Instruction 22 on modesty and in Instruction 23 on cleanliness. Rule 12, which stipulates that "If many are together, they should keep the order prescribed by the Superior, and walk in groups of two or three," provides the underpinnings for Instruction 16 and its lengthy discussion of how "bands" are to be formed during recreation, and also for Instruction 31, where the same principles apply when walking through the city and suburbs. And on and on, rule after rule.

The *Instructions* also contributed to the building of an *esprit de corps* in the novices, by introducing them to the great Jesuits of the past.[11] Brief allusions to the humility of one or another father, or his devotion for the Blessed Sacrament gave the youths in Paris examples to emulate. Eventually they would learn more about these saintly men, perhaps through quiet personal reading ([63]), perhaps through listening to excerpts from books about the fathers that were read aloud in the refectory ([96]).

A certain number of the instructions in the manuscript are based neither on long-standing Jesuit rules nor on Jesuit hagiography. They tend to be practical and teach the youths how to live in a community: for example, how to make their beds (Instruction 23), how to clean and dust a room or a hallway (Instruction 9), and how to wash dishes or serve at table (Instruction 15).

Although many of these practical instructions were doubtlessly applicable to Jesuit houses across Europe, some of them have a distinctly French flavor, especially the ones that prepare the novices for the day when they will find themselves among lay people, be it in Paris, be it in the provinces. Instruction 14 is especially French, because it goes into considerable detail about table manners. (The text does not say so, but the manners being taught at the Novitiate are those of an administrative and courtly elite.) Pages [131–32] and [195] offer suggestions about how to conduct oneself in society, especially when one's host proposes a game of chance.

In sum, the *Instructions* represent a first step to obeying the rules of the Society of Jesus, presented to young people through unambiguous examples.

The manuscript also lays out a daily schedule that governs not only the spiritual activities at the Novitiate, but the routines of daily life as well. Novices have little free time, and virtually no time alone. They memorize together, they practice spelling and

---

[11] The *Instructions* cite inspirational remarks by Jesuit fathers and recount anecdotes about them. Longer versions of these materials are found in biographies written by French Jesuits that doubtlessly were available at the Novitiate. The anonymous author of the *Instructions* did not quote from these passages, however; he used his own words. Among the biographies written by Jesuits where these sayings and anecdotes can be found are Francisco Cachupin's life of Luis de La Puente (1652), translated by Nicolas Roger, S.J. (1663); Dominique Bouhours's life of St. Ignatius (1679) and his life of St. Francis Xavier (1682); Jean Adam's and Antoine Verjus's lives of St. Francis Borgia (1672); and Daniello Bartoli's life of Vincenzo Carafa (1652), translated by Thomas Le Blanc, S.J. (1653).

composition together, they scrub and clean the rooms of the residence together, they recite litanies together, they pray together, they visit the Blessed Sacrament together. In pairs they carry food from the city market, and as a group they assemble to point out one another's faults.

The Novitiate on the rue du Pot-de-Fer

The *Instructions* depict the Novitiate as a highly disciplined institution. It literally attempts to run like clockwork; it obliges everyone to read the new written-out regulations monthly; and it is administered by a strong rector without whose permission nothing even slightly out of the ordinary can be done.

The different segments of this daily schedule were marked out audibly by two devices. The first was the tower clock (*horloge*), whose bell informed Novitiate and neighborhood of the hours that passed. It appears to have had a technologically advanced mechanism, with a face showing quarter hours, but perhaps not minutes, and a bell that sounded not only the hours but perhaps the half and quarter hours as well. The second device was the hand-operated bell located near the refectory of the Novitiate: it sounded the "little rings" mentioned throughout the *Instructions*. A close look at the daily schedule set forth in Instruction 1 ([9–17]), reveals that, more often than not, the ringing of this bell did not coincide with the quarter hours shown on, and perhaps rung by the tower clock.[12] It was this rudimentary device that constituted Time for the Novitiate and that determined the movements of fathers, brothers, and novices throughout the day. Working in tandem, the two manners of announcing the time are described as being a "clock that rings seven or eight times each hour" ([129]).

A modern-day historian has called tower bells the "public voice" of the early-modern secondary school, the *collège*:

> The bell – the inevitable bell – installed in some tower or attic of the schoolhouse . . . tolled the children in and out, sending them and their masters to class, lunch, recess, study hall, assembly, public lecture, and home at last in the evening. This bell was the public voice of the new *collège*. The bell signified that discipline had been established. Order reigned.

---

[12] Most of the "little rings" (*petits coups*) were sounded shortly before or after the quarter hour shown on the clock face, but a few coincided with the quarter or half hour ([10], [69]), and once a "little ring" was rung on the hour ([46]). This bell clearly was rung by hand, because the manuscript says *on tinte*, that is, someone rings the bell ([69]). If the tower clock sounded the hours and quarter hours, then the hand-operated bell appears to have occasionally coincided with these automatic rings. The overall impression gained from the *Instructions* is that, irrespective of how frequently or infrequently the tower clock might have rung, the novices chiefly heeded the hand-operated bell. A refectory bell is mentioned ([183]); and novices serving in the refectory were entrusted with an hourglass (*sablier*, "*sable*") that permitted them to measure the time spent there and before the fire ([103], [105], [126]). For the Society's fascination with clocks, see Catherine Pagani, "Clockwork and the Jesuit Mission in China," in John O'Malley, S.J., et al., eds., *The Jesuits II: Cultures, Sciences, and the Arts, 1540–1773* (Toronto: University of Toronto Press, 2006), 658–78.

The public's orders had been handed to the trusted principal; and he in turn now regulated the lives of the *enfans de la ville* [children of the town] with the steady pealing of his bell, whose sound reached into neighboring streets and hastened the steps of stragglers in the morning.[13]

One of the most famous *collèges* in the realm was the Society's Collège de Clermont (in 1682 its name was changed to Louis-le-Grand), a short walk from the Novitiate. There, as at other Jesuit colleges, throughout the day bells were "sounded for retiring for sleep, for taking meals, and so forth."[14] Throughout the *Instructions*, we find the Novitiate using bells of one sort or another, in a strikingly similar manner.

Impelled by the combined "public voice" that sounded from the clock tower and the institutional voice of the hand-rung bell, novices moved from one room to another, from one activity to another. Going to and fro in this manner served a dual purpose: "This sequence of separate and varied actions is very useful for preventing boredom," noted the author. "But the principal aim is to learn to break one's own will" ([17]). To which can be added a third purpose, one so self-evident that the author did not mention it. Save for a few delicious minutes before the fire or near a stove, novices spent the entire day in unheated, drafty rooms. Keeping active warded off hypothermia.

From their rising at four in the morning until the candles were extinguished seventeen hours later, novices moved through the buildings in accordance with patterns imposed on them by the written regulations and the "little rings" of the bell. Without some notion of the layout of the buildings, we can scarcely understand the physical and psychological demands that the *Instructions* placed upon these youths. Indeed, the Novitiate was a veritable stage-setting for what amounts to a written-out choreography that sent youths in soutanes up and down stairs, off to the loft over the church entrance, and along hallways and walkways, as they carried out the "sequence of separate and varied actions" designed to "break their will."

Let us therefore become better acquainted with the Parisian Novitiate.

The creation of the Novitiate

Expelled from France in 1594, the Society of Jesus was permitted to return a decade later. Its return to Paris coincided with the emergence of what has been called a "generation of saints," a period of devotional fervor that began around 1600 and continued into the 1640s, and that led to the creation of numerous convents and

---

[13] George Huppert, *Public Schools in Renaissance France* (Urbana, Chicago: University of Illinois Press, 1984), 77.

[14] The *Constitutions of the Society of Jesus and their Complementary Norms* (St. Louis: Institute of Jesuit Sources, 1996), 176 [436]; and 176 [435] for how bells signal the "regular order of time for study, prayers, Mass, lectures, eating and sleeping, and so on."

monasteries on land along the southern outskirts of the city that had once been used for vegetable gardens.[15]

The Society, too, hoped to create a new house, a seminary to train the young men who were being turned away by the rectors at Rouen and Nancy; but the prices of property in the suburbs were soaring. Then, in April 1610, a group of devout laymen and women acquired the Hôtel de Mézières, a noble residence built some thirty years earlier. They were acting for forty-year-old Hélie du Tillet, baron of la Bussière and *seigneur* of Nogent, who wished to remain anonymous. It cannot be ruled out that Hélie's older brother Jean, *greffier civil* (civil registrar) in the Parlement, played a role in this purchase. Be that as it may, Jean was later given the glory that his brother had shunned. Hélie and Jean's first cousin, Madame de Sainte-Beuve, née Madeleine Luillier, conducted the negotiations in Hélie's stead.

The du Tillets de la Bussière were a respected family that had boasted two archivists for the Crown, one of them a bishop. Since the late fifteenth century, the position of *greffier civil* had passed from generation to generation of du Tillets. Upon their father's death, the office of *greffier* was passed to Jean du Tillet, while the barony of la Bussière went to Hélie, who acquired offices as "councilor" and *maître d'hôtel ordinaire du Roi*, a position he held until 1621. (Their brother Séraphin had become a Capuchin, probably in the early 1590s.) The 24,000 *livres* that Hélie paid for the Hôtel de Mézières were the equivalent of the full purchase price for the office of councilor at the Châtelet of Paris, and just short of half the cost of a lay councilorship in the Parlement of Paris.[16]

These devout lay people gave the house to the Society, "repairs" were quickly made, so that the "buildings would be compatible with the usages of a religious

---

[15] Orest Ranum, *Paris in the Age of Absolutism* (University Park, PA: Pennsylvania State University Press, 2002), chap. 8; René Pillorget, *Nouvelle Histoire de Paris: Paris sous les premiers Bourbons, 1594–1661* (Paris: Diffusion Hachette, 1988), especially 473–509, 537–77; and Joseph Bergin, *Church, Society and Religious Change in France, 1580–1730* (New Haven: Yale University Press, 2009), *passim*.

[16] The *Instructions* provide an important clue to the identity of the self-effacing "M. du Tillet": he was no longer alive circa 1628, when litanies were founded in his memory ([135]). Jean did not die until 1648, but Hélie clearly died in the early 1620s. To be specific, he was still alive in 1621; but by April 1624 Jean had inherited the barony and was adding "*baron de la Bussière*" to his title of *greffier*. As for Jean's possible involvement, Henri Fouqueray, S.J., *Histoire de la Compagnie de Jésus en France* (Paris: Bureaux des Études, 1922), 3:124–27, reproduces the account by Mère Pommereu, *Chroniques . . . des Ursulines* (Paris, 1673), where "M. du Tillet" is described as both *baron de la Bussière* and *greffier* in the Parlement of Paris. Elsewhere in his study (3:364), Fouqueray talks of "Jacques du Tillet" and cites Léon Charvet, *Étienne Martellange, 1561–1641* (Lyon: Glairon-Mondet, 1874), 93. Charvet's identification is highly suspect, because Jacques du Tillet, a councilor in the Parlement (he was Jean and Hélie's uncle), had become a Carthusian prior to 1592. For the sixteenth-century du Tillets, see Donald R. Kelley, *Foundations of Modern Historical Scholarship* (New York: Columbia University Press, 1970), 215–33; and Elizabeth A.R. Brown, *Jean du Tillet and the French Wars of Religion* (Binghampton: Medieval and Renaissance Texts and Studies, 1994), to whom I am most grateful for opening to me her research files on the family. For Mme de Sainte-Beuve, see Barbara Diefendorf, *From Penitence to Charity* (Oxford: Oxford University Press, 2004), 125–30, 184; for Hélie in 1621, Eugène Griselle, *État de la maison du roi Louis XIII* (Paris: Éditions

community," and the Novitiate opened that July. The *hôtel* stood in an undeveloped area not far from the Luxembourg Palace. The residence and its gardens occupied the left portion of the rectangle shown in figure 1, a detail from the Turgot-Bretez map published in 1739.[17] In this illustration, this rectangle is demarcated on the left by the rue du Pot-de-Fer (today's rue Bonaparte), along the top by the rue Honoré-Chevalier, to the right by the rue Cassette (site of the convent of the *Filles du Saint Sacrement*), and along the bottom by the rue de Mézières.[18]

Several plans drawn by Brother Étienne Martellange, the architect for the Novitiate, reveal that the fathers initially entertained the possibility of tearing down the Hôtel de Mézières and beginning anew.[19] In the end, the *hôtel* was retained and modified to fit the Society's needs. For example, a window in the kitchen was turned into a door that opened onto the courtyard. Throughout the structure, the heavy ceiling beams that stretched from one side of the building to the other, and that were so typical of the late sixteenth century, almost certainly were retained. Surviving drawings show that most of the fenestration so typical of that period was not modified. As in most noble residences, the rooms of the *hôtel* ran the entire depth of the structure, from street to garden. There were no hallways; instead, one moved from room to room via a series of opposite and parallel doors in enfilade, situated just behind the street elevation. As a result, privacy was almost nonexistent. Gaining

de documents d'Histoire, 1912), 13; and for the purchasing power of the 24,000 *livres* paid for the Novitiate, Robert Descimon, "The 'Bourgeoisie seconde'; Social differentiation in the Parisian Municipal Oligarchy in the Sixteenth Century, 1500–1610," *French History*, 17 (2003): 388–424, especially Table 3; and for an overview of the history and development of the Novitiate, and its activities over the decades, *Les Établissements*, 3:1307–19.

[17] Armed with passes from Michel-Étienne Turgot, *prévôt des marchands* of Paris, Louis Bretez and his staff measured and sketched every building in the city, street by street, and entered every courtyard. Although they omitted details such as chimneys, the map is considered very reliable. See Alfred Fierro and Jean-Yves Sarazin, *Le Paris des Lumières d'après le plan de Turgot (1734–1739)* (Paris: Réunion des Musées nationaux, 2005), Introduction. Martellange's floor plan is recognizable in Jacques Gomboust's distorted bird's-eye representation of the Novitiate (*Plan monumental de Paris*, 1652), as well as in François Blondel and Pierre Bullet's *Plan de Paris* (1676), which copied Gomboust. When Bretez's rendering of the Novitiate is compared with Martellange's floor plans of the 1630s, only one significant discrepancy has been noted: the segment immediately to the right of the stair tower is one window too narrow.

[18] The detail from the Turgot-Bretez map (it is in the lower left-hand corner of plate 12) happens to be oriented so that it can be superimposed mentally on Martellange's layout (which is the basis for plans 1, 2 and 3). As a result, north is at the bottom; and although the facade of the church is to the left in the illustration, it did not face west at all, as churches usually do, but east.

[19] See, for example, Hd 4b, 172 and 175. These two plans, and the others discussed in this introduction, are mentioned in Jean Vallery-Radot, *Le Recueil de plans d'Édifices de la compagnie de Jésus conservé à la Bibliothèque nationale de Paris* (Paris: Bibliothèque nationale, 1960), henceforth abbreviated "V-R," followed by the number he assigned to each plan. (For example, Hd 4b, 175 can also be cited as V-R, no. 568.) The drawings at the Bibliothèque nationale de France (Département des Estampes) that depict the Paris Novitiate bear the general call number Hd 4b, followed by the appropriate folio number. The full identification of these two plans is therefore: BnF, Estampes, Hd 4b, 172 and Hd 4b, 175. For a brief biography of Martellange, see Pierre Moisy, *Les Églises des jésuites de l'ancienne assistance de France* (Rome: Institutum Historicum Societatis Iesu, 1958), 1:107–31.

access to a room at the other end of a wing meant walking through a succession of bedchambers and drawing rooms.[20]

The Novitiate buildings

The Society of Jesus transformed these enfilades of doors into hallways (*galeries*). This was done by constructing partitions parallel to the street, from one enfilade door to the next, along the public side of the building. These partitions are easily identified on plan 1, which is based on Martellange's plan for the ground floor[21]: they are thin walls such as those that enclose the little "domestic" chapel and the kitchen.

Doors inserted into these partitions created a chapel, an enclosed kitchen, and, on the upper floors, numerous "chambers" (*chambres*, that is, bedchambers) plus a room where the rector could converse privately with novices or visitors. Not only could these rooms henceforth be shut off from passers-by, there were now clearly demarcated thresholds that must not be crossed without permission from a superior ([148]). Each room received light from the windows in the courtyard elevation.

The original enfilade of doors was retained in the three large "halls" or community rooms (*salles*) where the novices assembled, and also in the ground-floor room "for speaking with laywomen" (*pour parler aux séculières*). As a result, these rooms were deeper than most of the other rooms. They also were brighter, since no hallway robbed them of half the available light. To move from one end of the building to the other, one went along the nearest hallway and, upon arriving at a community room, passed through one of the enfilade doors, walked across the room to the next door, and entered the next hallway. Any activity that required closed doors, and that was conducted in one of these community rooms, could potentially block the entire hallway for the duration of that activity.

---

[20] For illustrations of late-sixteenth and early seventeenth-century houses, inside and out and from street to rooftop, see Jean-Pierre Babelon, *Demeures parisiennes sous Henri IV et Louis XIII* (Paris: Le Temps, 1965). See especially, beamed ceilings, 202, 221; doors in enfilade, 191, 226–27; and noble stairways, 99, 102–103, 105.

[21] The plan, Hd 4b, 192 (V-R, no. 569), dated 1634, is the point of departure for the three plans that accompany this introduction. Plan 1 uses a scan of Martellange's drawing. The walls were kept, but his labels were redone and a few additional labels were added, among them an ornamental arrow whose fleur-de-lis points north. No plans of the upper floors have survived, so the ground-floor plan was re-scanned and modified, to create plans 2 and 3. Into these plans, elements mentioned in the *Instructions* were then inserted. This introduction will look at each element in turn. No attempt was made to adjust the staircases: thus the tower steps are not on the right-hand side of the stairwell in plan 2, as they probably should be. Several little door-less rooms with no attribution were preserved and were repeated in all three plans. The basic layouts of the two upper stories vary little from the layout of the ground floor. This is as it should be, because the use of heavy beams stretching from one side of a room to the other obliged architects to stack their bearing walls and their fireplaces one atop the other. This widespread architectural practice can be seen in Babelon, *Demeures*, 70, 104, 157, 187; and in Gaignières's multi-story representation of the Hôtel de Guise, published by Ch.-V. Langlois, *Les hôtels de Clisson, de Guise et de Rohan-Soubise* (Paris: Schemit, 1922), 309. Gaignières's plans served as a point of departure for Patricia M. Ranum, "« Feindre des poutres pour faire simettrie aux vrayes »: la rénovation de l'hôtel de Guise, 1666–1667," *Histoire et archives*, 10 (2001): 5–60.

In 1631, construction began on a church dedicated to Saint Francis Xavier. To show the physical relationship between the church and the Novitiate building, Brother Martellange made a detailed drawing of the garden elevation of the old *hôtel* as it was in 1630 (fig. 2).[22] In the right half of the drawing, the curved outline of the planned church apse is visible on the ground; a tall cross marks the position of the altar. The three-story wings to the right and left of the tall stair tower survived the construction project, but the low arcade, the little house, and the tower at the far right of the drawing were subsequently pulled down and replaced by a sacristy and a room to receive laymen (plan 1). By 1634 the Novitiate building extended from the stair tower and the rooms adjacent to it, all the way to the rue du Pot-de-Fer.

The principal benefactor for the church's construction was François Sublet de Noyers, a prominent royal official and collaborator of Cardinal Richelieu. As royal superintendent of buildings, Sublet arranged for Nicolas Poussin, one of the greatest painters of the day, to return for a time to Paris from Rome. Over the high altar of the Novitiate church hung one of Poussin's most important works, the *Miracle of Saint Francis Xavier*, which Sublet commissioned in 1641.[23] (It is now in the Louvre.)

Gaspard Mérian's mid-seventeenth-century engraving shows the rue du Pot-de-Fer (80, rue Bonaparte) and the church façade with its Vignola- or Gesu-style volutes (fig. 3).[24] To the right of the church, rises the residential building of the Novitiate, running along the narrow rue de Mézières.

Mérian's engraving, like Martellange's drawing, reveals that although the church was built of stone, the residence was made of red bricks intermixed with limestone quoins that ran up each corner, a style typical of late-sixteenth- and early-seventeenth-century Parisian architecture.[25] The engraving also shows the trees of the Novitiate garden, rising behind the wall to the left of the church. When the drawing was made, that corner contained a square garden with an X-shaped path where novices could stroll. (It is visible in the bird's-eye view of the Novitiate in Jacques Gomboust's

---

[22] In this drawing, did Martellange truncate the right-hand part of the *hôtel* in order to simplify the overall effect? Or had that wing really not been completed? If the latter, then the three future community rooms (*salles*) did not exist, and the Society extended square rooms into the rectangles shown on plans, 1, 2, and 3. The former option appears the more plausible, because other drawings by Martellange, dated 1634, show the building stretching along the rue de Mézières to the rue du Pot-de-Fer (for the illustrations, see Pillorget, 502–503, where the Novitiate church of St. Francis Xavier is identified as being dedicated to St. Louis, the patron saint of the church at the professed house, on the other side of the city).

[23] *Les Établissements*, 3:1310; Isabelle Pantin, *Les Fréart de Chantelou* (Le Mans: Création et Recherche, 1999); and Orest Ranum, *Richelieu and the Councilors of Louis XIII* (Oxford: Clarendon, 1963). See also the note on p. 224, below.

[24] For the church, see Moisy, *Les Églises*, vol. 2: plates XXIII D, LV A, LXXIV B, LXXV B, and LXXXI A.

[25] In the depictions of the Novitiate that illustrate this introduction, details sometimes diverge, especially as far as the height of a specific building, the position of a chimney, or the pitch of a roof are concerned; but for the basic layout of the establishment, there is a reassuring consistency from

engraved *Plan monumental de Paris*, 1652.) This square garden would become the site of the sodality chapel discussed later in this introduction.

The old stair tower of the Hôtel de Mézières is visible on both the Turgot-Bretez map (fig. 1) and Martellange's drawing (fig. 2). So is the refectory, situated in the structure with ground-floor arcades at the left in Martellange's drawing, and visible in Bretez's rendering, just behind the rounded apse of the church. These same elements appear on plan 1.

Mérian's depiction of the buildings along the rue du Pot-de-Fer reveals that two doors, a narrow door for pedestrians[26] and a door wide enough to admit vehicles, provided direct access to the residential part of the Novitiate. Through the pedestrian door the novices left the house, in pairs or as a group. By contrast, lay persons attending devotions such as the daily late-afternoon litanies, used the main door of the church.

The distribution of space: a proposal

Novices could see little of the world beyond the walls that surrounded the Novitiate. House elevations that overlooked someone else's property were generally windowless,[27] so it is unlikely that occupants of the private houses at the right end of the large rectangle of land shown in figure 1 could peer into the Novitiate. As for the novices, they presumably saw only blank walls and roofs, rising above the wall at the back of their garden. Nor were they supposed to peer out from the hallways that ran along the street. (They were, however, permitted to dump dust and sweepings out those windows.) The young men rarely left this rectangle of walled-in land. Once a week, two of them would accompany Brother Gardener to the central market and carry back the produce he had purchased; sometimes a pair of novices would walk across the city to the professed house adjacent to the Society's church of Saint-Louis, on the other side of the Seine; and every two weeks, all novices, accompanied by a few fathers or brothers, would quietly set off on foot, pass through one of the customs barriers that ringed the city, and spend the day at a Jesuit property near the village of Montrouge, some three kilometers due south of the Novitiate.

Martellange's church was an integral part of the Novitiate. It was physically connected to the L-shaped residence by covered walkways (*galeries*), some of them

the earliest illustration to the latest. Above all, these illustrations are consistent with the plans in BnF, Estampes, Hd 4b. Martellange's ground-floor plan, Hd 4b, 192 (adapted as plan 1), corroborates much of the evidence provided by the illustrations. For pictures of buildings with limestone quoins and bricks, see Babelon, *Demeures*, 18, 29, 68.

[26] This door is not shown on Martellange's plan dated 1634. It has been tacitly added to plan 1, but without the little gatehouse shown by Mérian.

[27] True, the Turgot-Bretez map (fig. 1) shows windows on the upper floors of the refectory wing, overlooking someone else's property. When the *hôtel* was built, it had no neighbors, and none apparently were anticipated. These windows constituted the "public" side of the wing, hence my decision to mark the indispensable hallway along that side in plans 2 and 3. On the Parisian building code, see O. Ranum, *Paris*, 125–26.

two stories high. One of these two-story walkways ran behind the wall on the rue du Pot-de-Fer, all the way to the church. Then, as a single-story "slated" gallery (*galerie d'ardoise*),[28] it continued past the sacristy and on to the refectory. By its mere existence, this cloister-like gallery served as a formal, and psychological, separation between the residential building and the garden. A two-story segment of this walkway can be seen along the left edge of the Turgot-Bretez map (fig. 1), near the word "*Pot*."

Irrespective of the activity or devotion in which a novice was participating, he usually could reach the assigned place without going outside, and therefore without removing his house slippers and putting on his shoes. For example, if he was on an upper floor of the refectory wing and wanted to go to the ground floor of the church, he could go down a spiral staircase at the garden end of that wing, then follow the slated gallery to one of the two doors that opened into the church (plan 1). If he was at the other end of the Novitiate, he could descend a larger, rectangular staircase, all the way to the ground floor, then enter the adjacent covered walkway. Or if he was heading for the loft (*jubé*) shown over the church door in the right-hand plan of figure 4, he could proceed along the upper level of that walkway and enter the loft.[29]

Kneeling in this loft, with only the tops of their heads visible from below, novices attended the Mass said at nine o'clock on feast days; and from there they visited the Blessed Sacrament five times each day. Some devotions took them to the sanctuary of the church: the daily celebration of Mass at six in the morning (seven o'clock on holidays), and the daily recitation of the Litanies of the Virgin at four o'clock. At such

---

[28] The *Instructions* mention a "slated" gallery adjacent to the garden ([68]). The roofs of these galleries (presumably covered with slate) are visible in the bird's-eye depiction of the Novitiate in Jacques Gomboust's engraved *Plan monumental de Paris* (1652). His rendering is quite misleading: these relatively narrow walkways appear to be as wide as the residence buildings.

[29] Neither Le Pautre's nor Marot's drawing of the inside elevation of the Novitiate church (Moisy, *Les Églises*, vol. 2, plates LV A, and LXXIV B) shows this loft (*jubé*), yet it clearly existed. The *Instructions* refer to an elevated space known as the "*jubé*," from which the kneeling novices could look out and visit the Blessed Sacrament ([72]). This space was large enough to contain all the novices when they gathered there, to be present at the second Mass of the day ([13–14]). That is to say, Martellange's floor plan for the church (fig. 4), which we know was 15 m. wide (49 ft.), makes it possible to calculate the dimensions of the *jubé*: it was just under 10 meters wide (approximately 32 ft.) and 5 m. deep (16 ft.). When each kneeling novice is allocated a bit more than a meter square of floor space (say, roughly 3.5 ft. by 3.5 ft.), there proves to have been ample room for as many as 40 novices to kneel without touching one another. On either side of the nave there were also 3 arched galleries or *tribunes*; but since each gallery was only 2.5 m. deep (8 ft.) and 4 m. wide (13 ft.), at most 8 persons could kneel there. In other words, these side galleries can scarcely be the *jubé* to which the *Instructions* repeatedly allude. The 2 galleries near the high altar offered a view onto the Blessed Sacrament below. (Moisy calls them "*oratoires*," hence the abbreviation "orat." on plan 2.) These oratories doubtlessly were allocated to the fathers, who are said not have exceeded 10 in number. For *tribunes* and *oratoires* in general, see Moisy, especially 1:323–25, 396–99, 476–77, 484–87. Moisy (1:396) reasons that the galleries over the entry doors of Jesuit churches were intended for organs or musicians, or else were used by the public. This may have been a widespread practice, but it was not the use to which the *jubé* of the Paris Novitiate was habitually put. The novices carried out some of their devotions in this loft, but lay people worshiped in the church proper ([181]). One can only speculate about whether musicians sometimes performed from the loft at the Novitiate, as they did at the church of Saint-Louis.

times, especially if it was raining, they moved along the ground floor of the covered walkway, to the sacristy and the door that opened onto the apse of the church.[30] Protected from the elements, they could assemble in this walkway, then process as a group toward the sanctuary, which was separated from the nave by a balustrade (fig. 4, left-hand floor plan; plan 1; and page [25] of the manuscript).

The fathers used these same walkways, of course; but they probably were the only ones permitted to move through the upper story of the hyphen-like structure that linked the midpoint of the residence wing to the church (fig. 1). Plan 2 shows this structure, but since the *Instructions* do not allude to it, no attempt was made to subdivide the considerable space it enclosed.[31] The hyphen began at the heart of that story, adjacent to the rooms with crosses where the fathers most likely lodged; and it ended at a little gallery or oratory that looked down onto the sanctuary of the church, from which the fathers could discreetly visit the Blessed Sacrament on the high altar directly below. They also had exclusive use of the large stairway in the clock tower, the novices being restricted to the smaller staircases at each end of the L-shaped residence.

Within this complex of community rooms, bedchambers, hallways, and protective walkways, novices spent the two years of their probation, not only deepening their vocation but learning to interact in a civil manner with one another, with their superiors, and with any lay persons they might encounter.

Novices, fathers, brothers: spaces and hierarchies

What follows is an overview of evidence pulled together from a variety of sources. It ought not displace the text of the *Instructions*, which is far more interesting

---

[30] Martellange's plan for the church (fig. 4) diverges slightly from a later floor plan that was incorporated into plan 1. The little door at the curve of the apse became a window, and the window became the door exactly opposite the sacristy.

[31] The structure was approximately 85 ft. (27 m.) long and 32 ft. (10 m.) wide. Was it a gallery where the fathers could walk and meditate, as the novices did in the garden or monks did in a cloister? For this type of gallery, see Monique Chatenet, "Un lieu pour se promener qu'en France on appelle galerie," *Bulletin monumental* of the Société française de l'archéologie, 166 (2008): 5–13, a special issue entitled "La galerie à Paris, XIVe–XVIIe siècle." Brother Martellange created a vaulted gallery for the Jesuit college at La Flèche. Constructed above a covered walkway similar to the one that ran behind the street wall at the Paris Novitiate, the gallery at La Flèche connected the wing where the fathers lodged to the "fathers' oratory" (*tribune des pères*) that looked down onto the high altar of the church. For Martellange and the gallery, see the floor plans provided by Camille de Rochemonteix, S.J., *Le Collège Henri IV de La Flèche* (Le Mans: Leguicheux, 1889), 1:74; and 2:22, plus the frontispiece to vol. 2, which shows the covered walkway on the ground floor. In the 1690s, the gallery at La Flèche was decorated with large paintings depicting the life of Henri IV (Rochemonteix, 1:152–55). It cannot, of course, be ruled out that the hyphen-like structure at the Novitiate was not a gallery at all, but was subdivided into a row of bedchambers with a hallway along one side. If so, this hyphen could have contained 5 rooms, each approximately 16 ft. (5 m.) on all sides, plus a space that facilitated access to the little gallery or balcony ("orat." on plan 2) that opened onto the sanctuary.

and complete. By its very nature, this broad tableau is subjective. It represents one individual's attempt to find coherence in the details packed into the thirty-four separate but interrelated compartments that form the *Instructions*. On some points, other interpretations doubtlessly are possible.

The novices

The word *frères* ("brothers" or "brethren") recurs throughout the *Instructions*. In all but a few instances, it denotes the novices, the young "brethren" who intend to become priests.[32] Although the manuscript says nothing about the social and geographical origins of the novices, it provides strong evidence of their youthfulness: some of them are still too "small" to draw water from the well, and too "young" to fast ([56], [196]). The manuscript also refers to novices who are preparing to be coadjutors (*coadjuteurs*), doubtlessly "temporal" coadjutors who are not going to enter the priesthood and who characteristically "exercise themselves in all the low and humble services, . . . although they may be employed in more important matters in accordance with the talent God may have given them."[33] The "boys" to whom the novices sometimes read aloud ([148]) were neither novices nor students at the nearby College. Clearly illiterate or marginally literate, they probably came from poor but upright families and ran errands or did light chores in the kitchens or the garden, in return for room, board, and some basic instruction in reading and writing.[34]

Nor do the *Instructions* provide precise information about the number of novices. The manuscript does, however, tell us that there were nine bedchambers, each supervised by a "senior" novice (*ancien*). From time to time, as many as three

---

[32] *Frère*, and its plural form *frères*, refers to the two lower ranks at the Novitiate: the novices and the temporal coadjutors. (The latter, who had already taken their vows, were not destined for the priesthood.) Members of both groups were individually addressed as "Brother" in English and *Frère* in French. The French used the plural *frères* for novices and coadjutors alike; but until recently, English-speaking Jesuits employed two distinct terms in the plural. Several novices who were preparing to become priests were called "brethren," while several temporal coadjutors were known as "brothers." Now and then a detail in the *Instructions* reveals how *frères* should best be translated: "coadjutor brothers" (*frères coadjuteurs*), "novice brethren" (*frères novices*), or "brother novices who will be coadjutors" (*frères novices coadjuteurs*). When there is no descriptive adjective to suggest the category to which a "brother" belonged, *frères* has been translated "brethren," because the *Instructions* were primarily addressed to novices planning to become priests. There are a few exceptions to this distinction between "brethren" and "brothers": on the front flyleaf, and again on p. [135], we find the formula "our dear brethren" (*nos chers frères*). Superiors employed these words to denote a cross section of the Society as a whole: fathers, temporal coadjutors, novices. *Frères* is used in a similar broad sense in an evocation of the day when novices will have taken their vows and will be called upon to shoulder administrative responsibilities such as writing official letters ([137]).

[33] *Constitutions*, 49 [114]; see also 26 [13], 49 [72], and 74 [148].

[34] One wonders how many of these boys eventually became temporal coadjutors of the sort described in reports dispatched to Rome. Their "ingenuity, judgement and prudence" might be rated as "good"; their "administrative talents" would probably not exceed what one would expect "for their rank"; and their "perfection in letters" was unlikely to rise above "zero." Thus reads the report for Antoine Charpentier, a temporal coadjutor who cared for the sick at the College in 1655,

of these chambers might be unoccupied ([170]). An early plan for the Novitiate had envisaged a new wing with a succession of "rooms for four novices."[35] Was the senior novice one of the four? Apparently so. Although hypothetical, the dimensions and shapes of the rooms on the two upper stories (plans 2 and 3) suggest that each chamber housed four novices.[36] The maximum number of novices at any given time would therefore be thirty-six. This is the exact number of two-year novices at the Novitiate in 1639.[37]

The *Instructions* are more informative about the clothes worn by the novices.[38] They dressed in a button-less soutane that was held closed at the collar by a clasp and at the waist by a belt or "cincture" (*ceinture*) just under two inches wide. From the cincture hung a rosary. Under the soutane, they wore "linens": a loose white shirt that came down to the knees and did double duty as a nightshirt, and knee-length drawers (*caleçon*), probably dyed black. Long black stockings completed their underclothing. The linens were changed a least weekly, as were any dirty outer garments ([154]). This fact, combined with other comments in the *Instructions* about the importance of keeping clean, reveals that the novices were being raised to a level of cleanliness that was perceived as promoting good health but that probably focused more on looking clean than on actually being clean.[39]

Whenever they stepped outside the Novitiate buildings, even if it was only to pace back and forth in the garden as they memorized texts, the novices donned a long cloak or "mantle" (*manteau*) and a black hat with a wide flat brim that contrasted markedly with the stylish upturned, curving brims preferred by more worldly religious of the day. Soutane, hat, sturdy black shoes, and mantle constituted a novice's "city clothes" ([191]). Coadjutors stood out from novices who were preparing for the priesthood,

---

and then was transferred to the professed house of Saint-Louis, where he served as porter (*janitor*, "doorkeeper") and purchaser (*emptor*). Although Brother Charpentier could both read and write, he had not completed the full college *cursus*. Nor had Brother Florentin Dalibert, who likewise was literate and whose grades were similar. Rome, Archivum Romanum Societatis Iesu, Franc. 15, triennial catalogue for 1675, p. 4, no. 38, and p. 39, no. 25.

[35] Hd 4b, 175.

[36] The rooms blocked out on the two stories over the refectory (plans 2 and 3) are approximately 13 ft. (4 m.) wide and not quite 20 ft. (6 m.) deep. These rooms lend themselves to a division into 4 equal rectangles of floor, each approximately 6.5 ft. by 9 ft. (2 m. by 3 m.). Into each rectangle must be fitted the single bed, the prayer desk, the lightweight chair, and the stool mentioned in the *Instructions*. With the bed along the wall, the prayer desk and stool next to it, and the chair at the foot of the bed, the better part of the rectangle is occupied. These calculations do not take into account the wardrobe to which the *Instructions* allude. In short, there was no room for a fifth occupant.

[37] *Les Établissements*, 3:1311. The *Instructions* contain a corroborating clue about the number of novices. When warming themselves before the fire, they grouped into "3 or 4 bands," each composed of "8 or 9 novices" ([124–25]). This suggests a maximum of 36 novices at any given moment.

[38] For an overview of Jesuit clothing, see Giancarlo Rocco, ed., *La Sostanza dell'Effimero: Gli abiti degli Ordini religiosi in Occidente* (Rome: Edizioni Paoline, 2000), 460–63.

[39] On perceived cleanliness, see Daniel Roche, *La culture des apparences, une histoire du vêtement, XVIIᵉ–XVIIIᵉ siècle* (Paris: Fayard, 1989), 150–68; and for clean shirts, hygiene, and modesty, 154.

because their soutane was about five inches shorter than that of a future priest, and their cloak was shorter than their soutane.

Novices dressed somewhat differently indoors. For example, they could wear a robe (*robe*) over their soutane in the manner of a modern-day academic gown, to fend off the cold of the high-ceilinged, unheated, drafty rooms where temperatures could drop below freezing in winter. The *Instructions* shed little light on when one garment was to be preferred to the other, and when both were required.

Inside the buildings, novices covered their heads with a "birette." (The invented term *birette*, which has been retained in the translation, may have been inspired by the French word *barrette* and the Italian word *berretto*, both of which denote the supple, beret-like brimless cap shown in late-Renaissance portraits.) The birette set the novices apart from the fathers who, indoors, wore a rather tall, three-cornered head-cover that the French called a "bonnet" (*bonnet*).[40] In short, we must modify our modern vocabulary and our way of thinking when we read the *Instructions*. In the 1680s, a Jesuit priest did not wear a "biretta" when saying Mass; he wore a "bonnet." A novice wore a "birette," but that head-cover did not resemble the modern biretta.

Novices wore slippers indoors and were forever putting on their shoes when obliged to set foot outside. In addition to helping keep the floors cleaner, slippers muffled the sound of some three dozen pairs of feet, hastening along hallways and climbing or descending stairs. To do household chores, the young men covered their soutane with a duster (it was called by an invented name, *nuptiale*, doubtlessly from *nubo, nupto*, whose primary meaning is "to cover"); but to wash dishes, they wore an apron. Since their daily cleaning chores inevitably sent them into the garden to fetch the appropriate materials, even before consulting the assignment list, the duster-garbed novices would put on their shoes and hats. When they walked to the central market, they likewise wore their duster and soutane, plus their hat and shoes.

Finally, if the *Instructions* are taken literally, each novice was entrusted with a skeleton key (*passe-partout*, literally, a "go everywhere") on a leather strap. Or is the term *passe-partout* yet another bit of jargon that denotes an object that literally went everywhere with the novice, perhaps a little pouch or carrying case suspended from a strap? To call attention to this ambiguity, the translation reads "go-everywhere."

The superiors

Boys and novices alike were supervised by an undetermined number of fathers

---

[40] The seventeenth-century novice's *birette* should not be equated with the modern biretta, with its three "horns" or "wings" that jut asymmetrically from the crown of a four-cornered hat. Nor did seventeenth-century Jesuit fathers wear that sort of biretta. Engravings reveal the extent to which their *bonnet* differed from the modern biretta. The seventeenth-century head-cover was made from three identical pieces of cloth that, when stitched together, formed a "horn" at the peak of each seam. Sometimes the seams were prominent, but sometimes they resembled tapes that join at the center of the crown. See Alfred Hamy's Jesuit portrait gallery at www.digitalmarquette.cdmhost.com.

whom the *Instructions* group under the general term "superiors" (*supérieurs*).[41] Weighty decisions were entrusted to Reverend Father Rector, who simultaneously directed the Novitiate and served as master of novices. The *Constitutions* describe the sort of man who was selected to be the rector of a college or a novitiate:

> Care should be taken that the rector be a man of great example, edification, and mortification of all his evil inclinations, and especially a man of proven obedience and humility. He ought likewise to be discreet, fit for governing, experienced both in matters of business and of the spiritual life. He should know how to blend severity with kindness at the proper times. He should be solicitous, stalwart under work, a man of learning, and finally, one in whom the higher superiors can confide and to whom they can with security delegate their authority. . . .

> He should watch over all his subjects with great care, and guard them against difficulties from within or without the house by forestalling the difficulties or remedying them if they have occurred, in a way conducive to the good of the individuals and to that of all. He should strive to promote their progress in virtues and learning, and care for their health and for the temporal goods both stable and movable. He should appoint individuals discreetly, observe how they proceed, and retain them in office or change them as he judges appropriate in the Lord.[42]

Father Rector's chief assistant was Father Minister, who was responsible for material issues. He is described in the *Constitutions* as a sort of "vice-rector or master of the house, who should provide for everything necessary for the common good."[43]

These two administrators were assisted by fathers who heard novices' confessions, said Mass, and led the daily recitations of the litanies. Beneath this group labored at least seven temporal coadjutor "brothers," some of them bearing titles that were an amalgam of French and Latin words pertaining to their function in the House. Brother Admonitor (*Admoniteur*, "he who warns of faults") made sure that the *Instructions* were closely followed. Brother Manuductor (*Manuducteur*, "he who beats time with his hand") oversaw schedules, determining, for example, the exact time to set off for the weekly shopping expedition to the central market.[44] Brother Pantryman (*Crédencier*, "he who supervises the *crédence* or cupboard") oversaw the pantry where utensils were stored, and he perhaps had other duties involving stocking and distributing food

---

[41] According to *Les Établissements*, 3:1311, there were never more than 10 "priests" at the Novitiate. It asserts that the Rector was assisted by the Minister, the Bursar, the *Socius* of the Master of Novices, and a few elderly priests who heard confession. (Does this maximum of 10 "priests" include the 7 administrative "brothers" to whom the *Instructions* specifically allude?)

[42] *Constitutions*, 174 [423] and [424], about the rectors of the colleges.

[43] *Constitutions*, 176 [431].

[44] Was this "Brother" a coadjutor? Or was he, as in mid-twentieth-century America, the "chief novice" who, during his six-month term of office, conferred daily with the Master of Novices and oversaw the daily schedule of the novices?

supplies. Brother Housekeeper (*Propretaire*, "he who is entrusted with keeping things clean") struggled to confine mud to the "cleanliness room" so that it would not invade the premises. Brother Sewer (*Couturier*, "he who sews") not only mended clothes in the sewing room, he also took charge of the possessions of novices who were setting out across the city to the professed house of Saint-Louis. And so forth. These rather exotic titles, like the invented term for groups of three bedchambers, and the invented names for some of the items worn by novices, are testimonials to a strong *esprit de corps* at the Novitiate. The residents not only spoke Latin but, when communicating in the vernacular, they employed a vocabulary that would have baffled most outsiders.

Spaces, activities, hierarchies

Specific rooms or areas were allocated to each physical and devotional activity. This reflected the hierarchy of household activities that was shaping the layout of Parisian residences in general.[45] These allocations of space appear to have reflected hierarchies within the Society itself.

The ground floor (*rez-de-chaussée*) of the typical stately residence was primarily devoted to physical concerns: kitchens, store rooms, guard rooms, and places to receive tradesmen or visitors of modest social origins. When the Society moved into the Hôtel de Mézières, the fathers thought along the same practical lines. For example, just as the noble who had built the *hôtel* would have received non-noble outsiders in ground-floor rooms, so laywomen and laymen were received in ground-floor rooms, each gender in a specific room. Activities that ministered to the body and its well-being were installed in ground-floor rooms (plan 1), as in a typical noble residence. These service rooms consisted of the dispensary and adjacent pharmacy, the kitchen and pantry, the refectory, and the "cleanliness room" where muddy shoes were cleaned and damp mantles were hung.[46] There was also the Hall of Saint Joseph, a community room where the novices warmed themselves before the fire. Fireplaces were quite scarce in sixteenth-century residences.[47] In fact, there were only two fireplaces on the entire ground floor of the Novitiate, one in the kitchen and one in this community room. The *Instructions* suggest that the upper floors, too, were basically unheated. Being cold was a penance sent by God, and enduring it became a virtue ([157]).

Down the L-shaped hallway from the Hall of Saint Joseph were the kitchen and the refectory. Although the refectory technically ministered to the needs of the body, it was a place for both bodily and spiritual activity. Each novice periodically

---

[45] For the evolution from vertical to horizontal floor plans, see chaps. 6 and 7 of Annik Pardailhé-Galabrun, *La Naissance de l'intime* (Paris: P.U.F., 1988), and for day-to-day concerns such as heating, cooking, and sleeping, chaps. 8 and 9.

[46] Hd 4b, 192 (V-R, no. 569) calls it "the place to hang things" (*penderie*). This must be the "cleanliness room" (*propreté*) mentioned in the *Instructions* ([58]).

[47] For fireplaces (or the lack of them) and for stoves, see Pardailhé-Galabrun, 332–37.

waited table in the refectory or washed dishes in the kitchen and nearby pantry: on these occasions, the novices doing kitchen duty would eat at the second sitting or "table," along with any latecomers. Three times each day, novices and fathers ate in common in this large room,[48] while someone read aloud from the pulpit. Prior to each meal, novices washed their hands and faces in a basin reserved for that purpose. They were also supposed to wash their hands upon leaving the refectory, an important consideration in an era when good table manners permitted a liberal use of the fingers.

The *Instructions* reveal that novices and fathers alike were served a simplified version of the three- or four-course meals being served to the upper classes. (Also in emulation of the upper classes, novices were being taught to use a fork, not their fingers.) There is, however, a distinct difference between meals at the Novitiate and those served the upper class: so that nothing would be wasted, bread crumbs and untouched food were carefully collected, to be used in another dish.

Loaves of bread, or slices of bread were brought in first, and throughout the meal novices and fathers served themselves. The meal proper began with either a soup eaten from a two-handled porringer, or a "first course" (*entrée*) served in a large bowl or platter. The nature of this first course is not specified, but in upperclass families it generally consisted of meats with sauces, eggs, stews, cooked or creamed vegetables, patés and cold meat pies. Removing only those serving dishes that had been emptied, the novices who were waiting table next brought in the main course on "cutting boards" (*planches*) laden with roasted meat, poultry, or fish that had been cut into individual "portions" (*portions*) in the kitchen. Known to the elites as the "roast" (*rôt*), this main course was often accompanied by a salad. When everyone had finished, the novice-waiters began to clear the tables ("un-serve," *desservir*), so that they could bring in the final course, the "dessert" (*dessert*). Indeed, French civility required, and still requires, that all dishes, condiments, and utensils employed during the meal be removed before dessert can be served. Dessert generally consisted of fresh or cooked fruit, cheeses, meringues, or small cakes or biscuits.[49]

The refectory was also the scene of two potentially humbling activities. A rhetoric exercise known as "the Tones" was conducted there; and it was in the refectory that novices publicly declared the faults, the *culpae,* they had committed.

The original owners would have called the next story of the Novitiate residence the "noble story" (*étage noble*). This story typically housed the principal reception

---

[48] Not counting the "little room" at its end, the refectory was 57 ft. (17.5 m.) long and almost 25 ft. (7.5 m.) wide.

[49] This translation of the *Instructions* carefully avoids the word "entree," which in the United States refers to the "main course." In France *entrée* still denotes, as it did in the seventeenth century, the "first course." For meals among the elite, and the terminology used in the seventeenth century, see Florent Quellier, *La Table des Français, une histoire culturelle (XVᵉ–début XIXᵉ siècle)* (Rennes: Presses universitaires de Rennes, 2007), 90–97, and also his "analytical index," 262–70.

rooms and the noble's bedchamber, with its imposing curtained bed. The decorations on its walls and ceilings would therefore have been nobler than anywhere else in the building. The large stair tower was an integral part of this noble effect. Stairwells of the late sixteenth century usually boasted stocky turned balustrades and a thick handrail, the ensemble either sculpted from stone or carved from solid walnut. The stair treads were generally made of impressively large limestone slabs or massive heart-of-oak planks. When the Society moved into the *hôtel*, it reserved the noble staircase for the fathers. A likely explanation is that their lodgings (marked with crosses on plans 2 and 3) were adjacent to this staircase, some on the noble story and some on the uppermost one.[50] Novices were forbidden to go up or down this stairway ([117]), although they were allowed to pass through the enfilade doors on each side of a landing, in order to move from one end of the building to the other.

What might the fathers' lodgings have been like?[51] The death inventories of a certain number of religious have been studied by French historians, but these documents do not specifically involve the Novitiate or other houses of the Society. The sources suggest that a religious who was low in the hierarchy of an institution tended to be assigned a small, numbered room that opened off a hallway.[52] One can therefore surmise that the temporal coadjutors who supervised the more menial aspects of communal life, slept in such rooms. (Plan 2, which is from necessity hypothetical, shows four such narrow, contiguous rooms, each marked with a cross.) Priests teaching in non-Jesuit colleges tended to occupy two or three rooms: a bedroom, a *cabinet*, and sometimes a small antechamber, while the administrators of those colleges lodged

---

[50] My reasoning about the distribution of rooms in plans 2 and 3 is strongly influenced by the fact that the novices resided at the two extremities of the L-shaped building. This effectively leaves the central portion of the two upper stories to the fathers and the coadjutor brothers. Where else could they have resided?

[51] Keeping in mind that each room had to have least one window, lodgings were marked off for the "10 priests" mentioned in *Les Établissements*, 3:1311, with each priest occupying a private room. (Crosses indicate the sleeping space allocated to each Jesuit.) Two of these lodgings had to be apartments, one for the rector and one for the minister. Both are equal in size, although the rector's apartment should, in principle, have been larger than the minister's. The probable locations of these apartments were determined by the fact that there almost certainly would be fireplaces in the rooms directly above the ground-floor kitchen. The hierarchy of sleeping rooms and apartments in plans 1, 2, and 3 mirrors the hierarchy of lodgings shown in the La Flèche plan reproduced by Rochemonteix, *Le Collège de La Flèche*, 2:22. There, approximately half the "fathers" occupy long narrow rooms; the other half occupy square rooms that are twice as big; and, adjacent to the central stairway tower, are several large "chambers," the largest one possessing a big fireplace. At the Novitiate, space also had to be found for 3 curitories, each consisting of 3 adjacent bedchambers ("1, 2, 3") capable of housing 4 novices each. There also had to be chambers for coadjutor novices, presumably adjacent to those of the other novices. In the end, everyone could be squeezed in; and if some or all of the space in the dormered attic was allocated for sleeping quarters (as was the case at La Flèche), any problem about where to lodge coadjutor brothers and menials such as the "boys" ([148]) is dispelled.

[52] Pardailhé-Galabrun, 207: at the Seminary of Saint-Nicolas-du-Chardonnet, a religious lived in just such a room, "on the first hallway, number 5." The cell-like rooms in the upper stories of the seventeenth-century Jesuit retreat house of Serres (commune of Valady, Aveyron, France) are emblazoned with numbers.

in apartments with as many as five rooms.[53] By contrast, at the Jesuit college at La Flèche almost all the priests occupied individual bedchambers (*chambres*), some of them square, some of them rectangles only half as large. Two of the largest bedchambers at La Flèche were part of very small apartments: that is, the bedchamber opened directly onto an adjoining room, rather than onto a hallway as most bedchambers did. Taking La Flèche as a model, quite modest apartments for Father Rector and Father Minister were inserted into plans 2 and 3. Each apartment boasts a large room with a fireplace, a bedroom through which a visitor need not pass, and an antechamber lighted by a small window high in the hallway partition. Father Rector would have used the larger room as a space for talking privately with novices and discussing not only the faults they had committed or the doubts that might be tormenting them, but much more importantly, their spiritual lives and their progress in understanding the Society, their progress in prayer, and so forth. (Instruction 28 gives an idea of the subjects discussed.)

Humility and lowliness aside, civility demanded that Father Rector be able to receive, with all the honors due their rank, a prelate, a nuncio, a superior in the Society, or a nobleman with longstanding ties to the Society. The hallways constructed along the street side of the building had diminished the elegance of many rooms; yet remnants of the original stateliness would have survived to create an ambience worthy of a prestigious guest. During such a visit, all the rules of civility would have been observed, including conducting the visitor up the staircase with the appropriate ceremony and ushering him into a room that was warmed by a fireplace and furnished with chairs appropriate to every social level: an armchair for the highest-ranking individual in the room, an armless chair for a person of slightly lower rank, a stool for someone of still lesser importance. Everyone else stood.

In the very heart of this story was the Hall of Our Lord, a community room where all novices assembled daily. There they would recite the texts they had memorized. And there, on the final day of each month, a memory exercise known as *Sententiæ* would be conducted.[54] The fathers occasionally took their recreation in this community room; and when they did, the hallways on both sides of the community

---

[53] Pardailhé-Galabrun, 208, the "principal" of the Parisian Collège of Cambrai had 5 rooms, the *procureur* of the college had 7 rooms; and a professor at the Collège d'Harcourt occupied numerous rooms scattered about the building.

[54] The activity called *Sententiæ* was doubtlessly similar to the competitions held at the Jesuit colleges, where "competition or exercise will find a place sometimes in the correction of errors that one rival has caught in the other's speech; sometimes presenting in turn whatever they practiced in the first hour; sometimes in distinguishing and fashioning figures of speech; sometimes in stating and applying the rules of rhetoric or letters or poems or history; sometimes in presenting the more difficult passages of authors and explaining the difficulties; sometimes in investigating issues in an ancient culture and matters that belong to the field of scholarly learning; sometimes in interpreting hieroglyphics, symbols, Pythagorean doctrines, apothegms, adages, emblems, and riddles; sometimes in declaiming, and in similar activities, at the teacher's discretion," *The Ratio Studiorum, The Official plan for Jesuit Education*, translated and commented upon by Claude Pavur, S.J. (St. Louis: Institute of Jesuit Sources, 2005), 162 [386]. For *sententiæ*, see Francis Goyet, *Le sublime du 'lieu commun,' l'invention rhétorique dans l'Antiquité et à la Renaissance* (Paris: Champion, 1996), especially chap. 6.

room were out-of-bounds for novices. The *Instructions* mention at least one stove. This technological innovation appears to have been installed in this community room: the fathers sometimes warmed themselves there ([118]).

The less prestigious parts of the residence building were allocated to the novices. Their lodgings were situated on the periphery, not in the heart of the L-shaped building. The staircases available to them were also peripheral. Because novices could not go up and down the clock-tower staircase, they were continually walking from one end of the building to the other, simply to reach a stairwell that would take them to another story of the residence. In fact, when the fathers were taking their recreation in the Hall of Our Lord on the noble story, rather than pass through that particular community room to reach their destination at the other end of that story, novices were expected to climb up one flight, move along the hallway, pass through the Hall of our Lady, continue on along the next long hallway, and finally, at the other end of the building, go back down to the noble story ([118]).

The novices slept in one of nine bedchambers, each occupied by four people. Each chamber was supervised by a senior (*ancien*) who served as role-model and advisor. The chambers were grouped, by three's, into curitories (*curitoires*, another coined word), hence the indications "1, 2, 3" on plans 2 and 3. Each curitory opened onto a hallway with the same name. There was the Curitory (and the hallway) of the Blessed Martyrs, where the chambers were named for three Japanese martyrs, Blessed Goto, Blessed Miki, and Blessed Kisai. The chamber of Blessed Goto clearly was the most prestigious chamber occupied by novices, for its senior had considerable decision-making powers. There was also the Curitory (and the hallway) of the Angels, with chambers named for Raphael, Gabriel, and Michael. The third curitory, not always occupied, was the Curitory of the Apostles. It consisted of chambers honoring Saint Matthew, Saint Thomas, and Saint James.

Each curitory had been assigned a specific stairway. Residents of the lesser-used Curitory of the Apostles (presumably situated on the uppermost story, rather than on the noble one) used the "big stairway" at that end of the building. The other two curitories were located at the opposite end of the Novitiate, over the refectory. The Curitory of the Martyrs occupied the equivalent of the noble story, a position in the hierarchy of stories that was commensurate with the superior position of the senior of Blessed Goto. The Curitory of the Angels was directly above it, on the uppermost floor.[55] Novices from these two curitories used the "small garden stairway" that spiraled down to the ground floor. That they could do this, means that L-shaped hallways had been constructed on the two upper stories of the refectory wing, permitting them to move from the heart of the building all the way to the end of that wing. (Hence the hallways shown along the outer wall in plans 2 and 3.)

---

[55] Page [118] of the manuscript contains an important clue to the locations of the three curitories: it places the Curitory of the Martyrs on the noble story, and in the refectory wing.

Within a chamber, each novice appears to have been allocated approximately one-fourth of the floor space, a rectangle approximately six feet wide and nine feet long.[56] They slept in curtained beds, with straw ticks in lieu of mattresses. (Was the choice of filling intended as a mortification of the young men's pride? Most Parisians, from modest shopkeepers and artisans, all the way up to nobles and government officials, slept on mattresses stuffed with wool.[57]) Symmetry of placement was the rule of the day, down to the bed curtains pulled aside at a precise angle ([24]). Near his bed stood the novice's personal prayer desk (*oratoire*), equipped with a cubby for storage. Kneeling on the rail of this prayer desk, the novice spent an hour each morning and a half hour each afternoon, in the meditative, contemplative prayer known as *oraison*.[58]

Close at hand, a lectern rested on a stool, permitting the prayer desk to be transformed into a reading stand for the novice, now seated on the stool. In addition to sleeping and praying in this chamber, novices recited some of their lessons aloud there, as a group. Near the window or the light source, they would form a circle with the chairs that were kept at the foot of each bed. Each chamber contained a "small library,"[59] basic equipment such as scissors and a whiskbroom, and a wardrobe (*armoire*) where the occupants stored their few possessions.

Novices assembled in one or another community room or "hall" (*salle*) for group activities such as the conference, the exhortation, and the colloquy that expanded upon the exhortation, or to recite memorized texts or prepare the next day's meditation. Seated on benches and grouped by chamber or curitory, they were supervised by a

---

[56] See above, n. 36.

[57] Pardailhé-Galabrun, 276–78, 280, 282. Poor folk, servants, and children slept on straw-filled ticks; but most beds consisted of frames filled with horsehair, topped with a straw tick and, on it, a mattress stuffed with wool.

[58] The *Instructions* describe the *oraisons* as sometimes followed by an "examen of the prayer," *examen de l'oraison*; sometimes by a "recollection," *récollection*; and sometimes by a "meditation," *méditation*. In the seventeenth century, the *oraison* almost certainly took one of two forms. It was meditative prayer that emphasized a composition of place, a consideration of a truth of faith, or a commandment or a virtue, as in the meditation on the "Three Classes or Types of Men," in Loyola's *Spiritual Exercises*, nos. 149–57, which begins with "the usual preparatory prayer" and moves to a meditation on attachment to wealth. Or else it was contemplative prayer, in the sense of inserting oneself imaginatively in some scene from the Scriptures, actively "looking at," "regarding," "engaging the person or persons involved" (for example, St. John Baptist, the Virgin Mary, the Apostle Peter, Jesus), speaking to them, asking how one might respond to their needs, and so forth, as in the "Contemplation on the Incarnation," *Spiritual Exercises*, nos. 101–109, where "the usual preparatory prayer" is followed by a contemplation, in the soul's eye, of the Trinity, Hell, and the Annunciation. Each of the above Exercises ends with a "colloquy," that is, a verbal exchange between the worshiper and the personages he had contemplated or meditated on in the *oraison*. The "examen" was an examination of what worked, what didn't work, how a person responded or felt about what he was meditating on or contemplating, what distractions he encountered, how he dealt with them, and so forth. The "recollection," or review of the week's *oraisons*, was reserved for Sundays, feast days, rest days, and the walk through the countryside to the house at Montrouge.

[59] *Bibliothèque* can mean "books," "a bookshelf," or a "library" in the fullest sense of the word. The expression "little library" ([145]) probably denotes a small collection of books kept on a simple shelf. There was also a "library" ([144]), which I have assumed did not have a room all its own, but was stored in a locked cabinet in one of the community rooms, or perhaps in the hyphen-like structure.

senior. Each community room was named for a member of the Holy Family. On the ground floor was the Hall of Saint Joseph, also known as the "great recreation hall." It was very dark and probably rather damp, because there were no windows along the street, and only three windows on the courtyard side. Coals would be brought there from the kitchen, to light a fire so that the novices could briefly warm themselves. Above the fireplace hung a crucifix. Memorized texts were recited one story up, in the Hall of Our Lord, and one or another litany was occasionally recited there. During inclement weather, the fathers would take their recreation in this community room, and they would warm themselves there in winter. (The *Instructions* say nothing about where they took their recreation on fine days.) In the Hall of Our Lady, on the uppermost story, the Litanies of the Holy Name of Jesus were recited, catechism was conducted, and the *Imitation* or some other "little meditation" was read aloud. This community room was also the site of the criticism sessions known as "the exercise of charity." The two upper community rooms appear to have been smaller than the "great recreation hall" of Saint Joseph: a bedchamber presumably had been created at one end of each.[60]

The Novitiate church was, of course, the place where Mass was said, where visits were paid to the Blessed Sacrament, and where novices learned to serve at the altar. Fathers and novices alike gathered in the church daily, at four o'clock in the afternoon, to recite the Litanies of the Virgin that drew laymen and laywomen to the church. Novices were expected go to the loft (*jubé*) over the church door five times each day, to visit the Blessed Sacrament: after rising at four in the morning; shortly after ten o'clock, when they had finished the day's memorization; shortly before one in the afternoon, after reciting the litanies of the saints; after the daily late-afternoon recitation of the Litanies of the Blessed Virgin; and at half past five, when evening prayer was finished. From this perch they could gaze at the Blessed Sacrament without being seen by worshipers in the church below.

Lastly, there was the garden, where vegetables probably were emphasized over flowers. Indeed, from mid-August to early November the garden may have provided some of the produce consumed at the Novitiate. During their daily cleaning duties known as the "bodily exercises"[61] (as contrasted with the "spiritual exercises"), novices would go to the garden to fill watering cans at the well or at the water trough adjacent

---

[60] The Hall of St. Joseph was approximately 49 ft. (15 m.) long by 25 ft. (7.5 m.) wide. That it is described as "great" or "large" (*grande*) suggests that partitions had been raised inside the Hall of Our Lord and the Hall of Our Lady, to create bedchambers adjacent to the stairwell, as in plans 2 and 3. This would have shortened each community room by approximately 16 ft. (5 m.), transforming it into a near square.

[61] The "bodily exercises," *exercices corporels* (the two hours of daily housekeeping tasks assigned to the novices, also known as the *manualia*) constitute one panel of a devotional diptych: the activities of the body versus the activities of the spirit (that is, the *exercices corporels* versus the *exercices spirituels*, chief among the latter being Ignatius Loyola's *Spiritual Exercises*). Throughout the *Instructions*, these "bodily exercises" are presented as acts of devotion that complement the "serious exercises," the "exercises of devotion" on which the novices spend the better part of each day.

to the Retreat where laymen stayed. Early in the morning on feast days the novices would gather in the garden for the Office of Our Lady. And in bands of three or four, they would walk up and down the garden paths, carrying out devotional or educational obligations, or striding back and forth as they conversed during what was considered "recreation." If the weather was fine, the group colloquy was held in the garden. Be the weather fair or be it foul, it was in the garden that novices memorized texts or recited the rosary. Under no circumstances were they permitted to seek shelter beneath the arbor, the slated gallery, or the arcades of the two little lodgings that constituted the sodality Retreat. In addition, when laymen were in residence at the Retreat, novices were not permitted to walk along the garden path that ran past these arcades. In other words, they could not stroll in the shade of the chestnut trees on a warm day. That was perhaps all for the best, because it was strictly forbidden to pelt someone with a chestnut ([122]).

The Retreat: when the *Instructions* were drawn up, laymen were coming to this little house with increasing frequency. For two decades, the land along the rue Honoré-Chevalier had been given over to the activities of a sodality, and to the retreats that were an integral part of its devotional program.

The Congregation of the Novitiate

In the early 1660s, the Society of Jesus created a chapel for a Marian sodality known as the Congregation of the Novitiate. One of the group's devotional activities consisted of retreats to make the Spiritual Exercises; but not until the 1680s would these retreats become the centerpiece of the lay activities conducted at the Novitiate.

The Congregation and its Chapel

This association of lay persons was not a recent creation, it dated back to the earliest days of the Novitiate. Nor was it unique: in the 1660s there was at least one very prestigious Marian congregation at the church of Saint-Louis, several congregations for the students at the College, and still another congregation at the Novitiate. (Two princes of the House of Lorraine and several Parisian curates belonged to the Congregation of the Novitiate.)

Father Jean Crasset, the driving force behind the Marian congregations at Saint-Louis, pointed out that in large cities there often were a dozen or more congregations, each created for a specific social group:

> The Congregation embraces all social conditions. There are congregations for ecclesiastics, for the nobility, for people in the legal professions, for lesser nobles, for merchants, for artisans, for servants: no one is excluded, since the distinctions drawn among these social conditions in large cities are not made in order to exclude anyone, but solely in order to be able to

instruct each person more conveniently, according to his capacities and his profession, and to have him practice the devotions that are the most suitable for the life he is leading.[62]

Integration, that is, the amalgam of various social ranks into a single organization, was avoided, owing to what amounted to a pedagogical strategy that would "instruct" the faithful as effectively as possible. The goal was to raise people of all social levels to a common level of devotion, but one's social condition determined how that common level would best be attained.

Congregants not only read devotional books and listened to the Word of God, they actively strove to be virtuous in thought and deed:

> There one receives the sacraments; one learns how to pray [do the *oraison*]; one recites the Divine Office; one says public and private prayers; one mutually stirs each other up, both by word and by example, to practice all the virtues; if one wishes, one gives alms, which are distributed by the members themselves to the shamefaced poor, to prisoners, and to the sick; one learns to make, from time to time, saintly retreats, to regulate one's life and prepare oneself, in a Christian way, for a good death.[63]

Circa 1660, having acquired the field in the center of the rectangle shown in figure 1, plus two small houses on the rue Honoré-Chevalier, the Society decided to turn the field into a large garden, and to build a chapel for the "Congregation of the Novitiate of the Society of Jesus" on the site of the old garden. The architectural plans were completed in May 1661.[64]

---

[62] "La Congrégation embrasse toutes les conditions. Il y en a pour les ecclésiastiques, pour la noblesse, pour les personnes de robe, pour celles d'épée, pour les marchands, pour les artisans, pour les serviteurs, personne n'en étant exclu, puisque la distinction que l'on fait de chacun de ces états dans les grandes villes n'est pas pour donner l'exclusion à personne, mais uniquement afin de pouvoir instruire plus commodément chacun selon sa capacité et sa profession, et faire pratiquer les dévotions qui sont les plus convenables dans la vie qu'on a embrassée," Jean Crasset, S.J., *Histoire abrégée des Congrégations de la Très-Sainte Vierge*, ed. A. Carayon, S.J. (Paris: Ruffet, 1863), 72. Carayon's edition is basically Crasset's *Des Congrégations de Notre Dame érigées dans les Maisons des Pères de la Compagnie de Jésus* (Paris, 1694). Crasset also published a collection of hymns, some of them set to popular tunes, *Cantiques spirituels pour toutes les grandes festes de l'Année* (Paris, 1689). A register signed by members of the congregation at Saint-Louis, 1631–1676, testifies eloquently to the elevated social status of its members (Archives nationales, Paris, MM 649). A manuscript entitled "Hommes illustres de la Congrégation de la Vierge, maison professe des pères de la Compagnie de Jésus, à Paris," sheds light on the devotional and educational activities pursued by its members, from 1660 on: Crasset, "so famous for his writings," is mentioned on p. 214 (Bibliothèque Mazarine, ms. 3335). For the congregations at the College, see *Les Établissements*, 3:1170–72. I did not find similar records for the Congregation of the Novitiate.

[63] "On y fréquente les Sacrements; on y apprend à faire l'Oraison; l'on y récite l'Office divin; on y fait des prières publiques et particulières; on s'y excite mutuellement et par paroles et par exemples, à la pratique de toutes les vertus; on y fait si l'on veut des aumônes que les confrères apportent eux-mêmes aux pauvres honteux, aux prisonniers, aux malades; on y apprend à faire de temps en temps de saintes Retraites pour régler sa vie, et pour se préparer chrétiennement à une bonne mort," Crasset, *Histoire abrégée*, 63.

[64] This plan, Hd 4b, 173 (V-R, no. 173), bears the inscription: "Plan et Elevation de La Congregation du noviciat de la Compagnie de Jesus à Paris, may 1661."

The chapel was a handsome, symmetrical structure with a mansard roof and dormers. (Its roof can be glimpsed in figure 1, see page 34, just behind the belfry of the Novitiate church.) The spacious ground-floor chapel boasted a stylish coved ceiling.[65] Along the street, there were only three narrow windows; but on the other side, four large arched windows opened onto a formal garden. Beyond this courtyard garden, and beyond a decorative fence that separated these lay people from the Novitiate proper, could be glimpsed the greenery of the new garden where the novices walked. Congregants reached their chapel by passing through the church.

The chapel, and the acquisition of the plots of land that had made it possible, marked a major change in the activities being conducted on the rue du Pot-de-Fer. Except for the large new garden, the Novitiate itself appears to have remained unchanged after 1661. By contrast, the Congregation gradually expanded, until it occupied most of the strip of land along the rue Honoré-Chevalier (fig. 1).

Thus it came to pass that, when the *Instructions* were drawn up circa 1685, two quite separate entities were going about their respective devotional lives behind the high walls of the Novitiate. The degree to which these two entities interacted remains a matter for conjecture, because the *Instructions* refer neither to the Congregation nor to its chapel. The manuscript does, however, allude to the Retreat situated in the large garden; and when it does, it is to emphasize the need to maintain a strict physical separation between laymen and novices.

The location of the Retreat is shown on an architectural plan made some years after the completion of the Congregation chapel, probably in the late 1660s or early 1670s. Although the plan focuses on buildings to be constructed at the intersection of the rue du Pot-de-Fer and the rue Honoré-Chevalier, adjacent to the Congregation chapel,[66] it also shows a two-room structure described as the "exercitants' house" (*maison des exercisans*). This plan reveals that neither this small house, nor the new structures adjacent to the chapel, had doors opening onto the street. Lay people entered the Novitiate through the church, then proceeded through the gardens to the Retreat. Six windows wide, the Retreat is the little building with six ground-floor arches opposite the letters "*ciat*" of *Noviciat* on

---

[65] The chapel was approximately 21 ft. (6.5 m.) wide and 54 ft. (16.5 m.) long, roughly half the size of the Novitiate church, which was 31 m. long and 15 m. wide. Above the entrance door of the chapel was a loft (*jubé*), and behind the altar a small sacristy and a privy. At each end of the building, a flight of stairs led to a bedroom that was two windows wide. To each of these two bedrooms was appended a small *cabinet* with a view of the garden. These apartments presumably were intended either as guest apartments, or as apartments for the elderly priests associated with the Novitiate.

[66] Hd 4b, 174 (V-R, no. 573). The plan does not show the use to which the ground floor was put; instead, it shows the story above, which consisted of a large common room with seven doors. Three of the doors opened onto the antechamber and private stairway of a four-room apartment with two bedrooms. Two of the remaining four doors opened directly onto a small bedchamber, and the other two onto the private stairway and *cabinet*. These rooms, with their lack of privacy, seem unsuitable for retreats. Were they guest quarters? Or perhaps, after January 1682, lodgings for Father Le Valois and his assistants?

Turgot-Bretez's map (fig. 1).[67] In other words, as late as 1670, a maximum of two exercitants could withdraw to the relative isolation of these two lodgings, to make the Spiritual Exercises.

While construction was being completed adjacent to the Congregation chapel, the Novitiate as a whole was attracting attention, owing to the illustrious guests who attended solemn religious services, sometimes in the church and sometimes in the new chapel. Among these guests were Queen Marie-Thérèse, Louis XIV's consort; Jean III Casimir, a one-time Jesuit and former king of Poland[68]; François Harlay de Chanvallon, the new archbishop of Paris; and Madame de Guise, Louis XIV's extremely devout first cousin.[69]

The 1680s at the Novitiate

In January 1682, Father Louis Le Valois came to the Novitiate, to organize retreats similar to those he had been conducting in the provinces for nobles and gentlemen. The first retreat was held two months later, in March 1682. These retreats were the culmination of the Jesuit program that had been expanding ever since the 1660s and that used programmatic instruction suitable for each social group's level of learning. The undertaking was extremely successful: during the twelve months of 1682, 20 exercitants came to the Novitiate to make the Spiritual Exercises; in 1687, 199; in 1688, over 200. Louis XIV was so pleased with the results that in 1685, the

---

[67] The dimensions of this little house are roughly comparable to those of the most modest house in Pierre Le Muet's *Manière de bâtir pour toutes sortes de personnes*, first published in 1623 and reproduced in O. Ranum, *Paris*, 124. The Retreat house consisted of two rooms, each with a private staircase and a privy under the stairs. Each room measured approximately 12 ft. by 15 ft. (3.6 m. by 4.5 m.), slightly larger than Le Muet's principal bedchamber, which was 11 ft. by 12 ft. (3.3 m. by 3.6 m.). The height of the ground-floor arcade of the Retreat can be estimated, thanks to Le Muet's plans and the elevations of the Congregation chapel. From floor to ceiling, the sacristy was approximately 12 ft. high (3.6 m.), a little bit taller than Le Muet's ground floor, which measured just over 11 ft. (3.3 m.). Thus the arcades of the Retreat were presumably about 11 ft. high. Figure 1 suggests that other little houses were subsequently built to the left of the original "exercitants' house" (there was no house there when Hd 4b, 174, was drawn, circa 1670); and that the "rental houses" (*maisons de louages* [*sic*]) to the right of the original Retreat house were either torn down and replaced or modified to match the other segments of the Retreat. Judging from the Turgot-Bretez map, the Retreat eventually consisted of 8, or perhaps 9 little lodgings connected by a cloister-like arcade and benefitting from a perspective that opened onto the garden but faced north. The *Instructions* suggest that these houses were known known as "St. Ignatius" and "St. Xavier" ([68]).

[68] In 1671 Jean III Casimir withdrew to the Novitiate to make the Exercises, *Les Établissements*, 3:1312.

[69] Sources clearly distinguish the chapel from the church. The *Gazette de France* informed its readers that, in November 1670, the queen had attended mass in the "chapel of the Novitiate"; in March 1672, King Casimir attended the annual "solemnity" for the Annunciation "in the chapel of the Congregation," and he did so in the presence of "an audience composed of prelates and other persons of high nobility"; in December 1672, the archbishop celebrated mass in the church for the Feast of St. Francis Xavier; and in November 1676, Isabelle d'Orléans (better known as "Mme de Guise"), who had played a pivotal role in converting a protestant woman to Catholicism, came to the Novitiate church with her musicians, who simultaneously celebrated the woman's conversion and the Feast of St. Cecilia with an oratorio by the Guise composer, Marc-Antoine Charpentier. For Mme de Guise, see Patricia M. Ranum, *Portraits around Marc-Antoine Charpentier* (Baltimore: the author, 2004), 336–43, 404–25; and for Charpentier and the Jesuits, 227–40.

year of the Revocation of the Edict of Nantes, he made a gift to the Novitiate of 1,000 *écus* (3,000 *livres*). Other benefactors hastened to follow his lead.[70]

This, in brief, was the state of affairs at the Novitiate during the 1680s, when the *Instructions* were drawn up. Preparing novices and ministering to lay people making the Spiritual Exercises were now physically separate activities, each conducted on its half of the property.

Separate activities? It appears that during the two years of their novitiate, novices were expected to restrict their interaction with lay people, even their closest relatives, and that they did not participate in devotions at the Marian chapel, nor in the activities for lay people that were conducted in the Novitiate church. Indeed, the *Instructions* are silent about whether the novices played any role in teaching Christian doctrine in general. As for the printed gazettes, they refer primarily to special devotions in which illustrious princes or prelates participated, and they are mute about devotional activities that the Novitiate may have sponsored for humbler Parisians, and about whether the novices participated in them in any way.

In the face of so many silences, this Introduction cannot end with a formal conclusion that weaves all the loose threads together. The threads refuse to be woven. In place of a formal conclusion, let us therefore look at the "good instructions" (*bonnes instructions*) that a female linen-seller received at the Novitiate over the course of a half century, and how she viewed the Novitiate, the novices, and the reverend fathers of the rue du Pot-de-Fer.

"Good instructions"

During the 1640s little Étiennette Charpentier began attending classes at the Novitiate. What she would later describe as the "good instructions I have received there since childhood" probably began as catechisms for children and continued as classes for adults, perhaps taught during Advent and Lent. As she grew to womanhood and developed into an astute and respected shopkeeper, she kept returning to the Novitiate to deepen her understanding of Christian doctrine.

Étiennette was far from learned, but over the years she acquired thirty-three books, most of them probably devotional. We know the titles of four of these publications, and two of the titles are suggestive of the "instructions" she was receiving at the Novitiate.[71]

---

[70] *Les Établissements*, 3:1313.

[71] Only the top book in each pile is identified. Thus we find "seven volumes of books in-4° bound in calf, including the *Meditations* of de La Puente" (*sept volumes de livres in quarto reliez en veau dont Meditations de Dupont*), and "seventeen other volumes of books in–12°, including the *Imitation of Jesus* in verse by Corneille, bound in red morocco, and the others in [brown] calf" (*dix-sept autres volumes de livres in douze dont Imitation de Jesus en vers de Corneille relié en maroquin rouge, et les autres en veau*). Of the other two books, one was an "antique" folio volume called the "Lives of the Saints," a title too general to permit identification. The other book was about Holy Week and its liturgy, "La Semaine sainte." Once again, no specific publication can be singled out. The books are listed in the inventory drawn up after her death, Archives nationales, Paris, Minutier Central, XXIII, 399, inventory, April 5,

One book was a red morocco-bound copy of the *Imitation of Jesus Christ*, paraphrased and put into French verse by the Jesuit-educated poet Pierre Corneille. In other words, Étiennette was reading Thomas à Kempis. Of course, owning Corneille's version of the *Imitation* does not necessarily imply a link to the Novitiate; but the *Instructions* tell us that the novices frequently read the *Imitation* ([13], [191]). Above all, throughout the 1650s the emblem of the Society of Jesus was an integral part of the title pages of edition after edition of Corneille's translation, as if to inform purchasers that this publication was approved (and used?) by the Society. Did Mademoiselle Charpentier purchase this volume because it was repeatedly mentioned at the Novitiate?

As for the second book, its link to the Society is undeniable. She owned the *Meditations on the Mysteries of our Holy Faith*, by Luis de La Puente, S.J., almost certainly the three-volume edition translated by Jean Brignon, S.J., and published in Paris in 1683. In other words, around the time that the *Instructions* were being drawn up, the linen-seller acquired a treatise that had been written early in the century by a Spanish Jesuit. He is mentioned in the *Instructions* ([74], [194]).

Mademoiselle Charpentier's "instructions" continued until at least 1707, when she drew up her last will and testament. Having referred to the modest sums that God had permitted her to earn by blessing her labor, she continued:

> I give and will to the Jesuit reverend fathers of the Novitiate of the Faubourg Saint-Germain the lump sum of two hundred *livres*, in gratitude for the good instructions I have received there since childhood and ever since, very humbly begging Reverend Father Rector of the aforesaid House to recommend me to the reverend fathers and novices of that House, for their blessed sacrifices and prayers, and to have them take communion once on my behalf.[72]

The bequest focuses on the Novitiate, rather than on a specific father or novice. That is to say, she wills the money to the "House" where the reverend fathers reside and

---

1709. For illustrations of the title pages of Corneille's translation that incorporate the Jesuit emblem, see Avenir Tchemerzine, *Bibliographie d'Éditions originales et rares d'auteurs français* (Paris: Plée, 1930), 4:129–39; and for printed versions of the *Imitation* and Jesuit devotional texts, see Henri-Jean Martin, *La Naissance du livre moderne* (Paris: Éditions du Cercle de la Librairie, 2000), 389–99.

[72] The daughter of a master scribe, Mlle Charpentier surely was not referring to being taught how to read and write: she had learned that at home, although as her bequest shows, she had not excelled at spelling: "Je supplie sa divine majesté de conduire ma main afin de ne rien faire contre la charité chrestiene dans la disposision du peu de bien qu'il [Dieu] m'a fait la grase de gagné en benisant mon travail. . . . Je donne et legue aux reverands peres Jesuites du novisiat du faubour St Jarmain la somme de deux cents livres une fois payée en reconoisans des bonnes instructions que j'i ai receu dès mon enfance et depuis, supplian tres humblement le reverent pere recteur de ladite maison de me recommander aux saints sacrifices et prieres des reverands peres et novises de ladite maison et de vouloire les fere communier une fois à mon intantion," Archives nationales, Minutier central, XXIII, 399, testament deposited on March 22, 1709; and P. Ranum, *Portraits*, 53–62, for Étiennette's biography (she was the eldest sister of Marc-Antoine Charpentier, composer to the Jesuits throughout the 1690s), and 227–40 for her family's longstanding ties to powerful Jesuits. Her summaries of Church doctrine, stated in the preamble of her will, are really quite standard: see Jean-Paul Poisson, "Foi et au-delà dans les clauses religieuses des testaments déposés au sénat de Savoie au XVIIIᵉ siècle," in *Notaires et société* (Paris: Economica, 1990), 2:419, 439–41.

go about their devotional and instructional activities. She asks Reverend Father Rector, as director of the House, to oversee the execution of this bequest; but carrying out her wishes will be the responsibility of all the fathers and novices. In a sense, these men in soutanes are the Novitiate; their faces and their names change every few years, but the Novitiate remains the same. (She could scarcely have imagined that the Novitiate would be closed a few decades later.) She therefore requests that, at one of the morning Masses celebrated daily in the Novitiate church, the entire community take communion on her behalf.

When Étiennette Charpentier wrote that paragraph, she must have been reliving the many times she had attended one or another of the two daily devotions in which the entire Novitiate community participated: specifically, the Mass that was said at seven in the morning on feast days, or at six on ordinary days ([10], [13], [25]), and the recitation of the litany every afternoon at four o'clock ([11], [13], [132]). In other words, a tableau appears to have been unfurling before her mind's eye, a tableau that can be deduced from clues in the *Instructions*, including an allusion to women.

In that tableau, three dozen novices and a dozen or so Jesuit fathers and brothers solemnly file into the sanctuary and take their place inside the balustrade. Farther back in the church are the "devout . . . people [who] come here to pray," the "people from outside who are present," the "people taking communion," the people to whom the novices "owe edification" by reciting the texts as distinctly and clearly as possible ([43], [73], [133]). Étiennette is perhaps among those who take communion. After the morning service, people generally do not linger, for they, like the novices, have a busy day ahead. By contrast, people are less rushed in the late afternoon. At the end of the four o'clock litanies, a woman who regularly attends these devotions approaches two novices. She exchanges a few words with one of them; he struggles to come up with an edifying reply. His "companion," acting as his "guardian angel," stands nearby in silence ([180]). The bell rings for evening prayer, and the novice and his companion hasten out the side door, in the direction of the residence ([181–82]). The woman turns and walks slowly toward the door that opens onto the rue du Pot-de-Fer.

"Good instructions," "edification," "outsiders who are present," "communion," figures dressed in black whose youthful faces are briefly glimpsed by the lay people attending the morning or the evening service. Young men who soon will be reverend fathers themselves and who, in that role, will celebrate Mass, give communion and hear confessions, catechize the young, instruct the faithful about the mysteries of the faith and about how one can begin to imitate Jesus, and who will perhaps train novices. Season after season, decade after decade.

It is in this broader chronological setting that the grateful linen-seller's bequest should be read. It is likewise in this broader chronological setting that the *Instructions* should be read. If they are, they will not be mired in the 1680s and confined within the high walls around that rectangle of land on the rue du Pot-de-Fer. In the 1680s, the *Instructions* were deemed "useful for advancing us along the ways of God" ([3]). They are no less useful today.

Figure 1 – The Novitiate as depicted on the Turgot-Bretez map of 1739

Figure 2 – Martellange's drawing of the Hôtel de Mézières, 1630

Figure 3 – Gaspard Mérian's engraving of the Novitiate as seen from the rue du Pot-de-Fer, circa 1650

Le Nouiciat des Iesuistes à la Ville S.Germain
Des Prez.

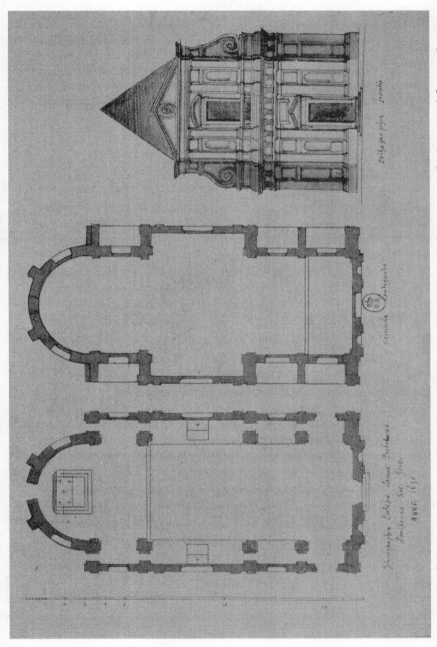

Figure 4 – The Novitiate church and two floor plans by Martellange dated 1630: left, the ground floor with its high altar and side chapels; right, the upper level with its side galleries and rear loft.

Plan 1 – The ground floor of the Novitiate residence

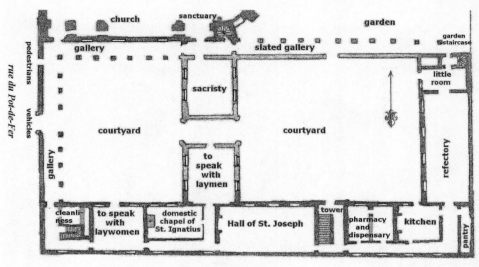

Plan 2 – The "noble story" of the Novitiate residence

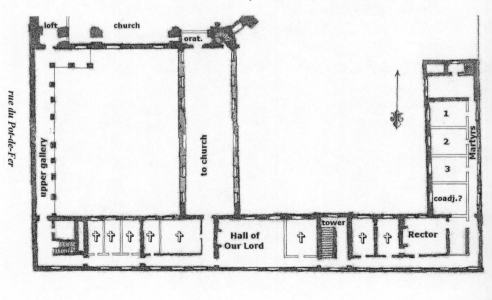

Plan 3 – The uppermost story of the Novitiate residence

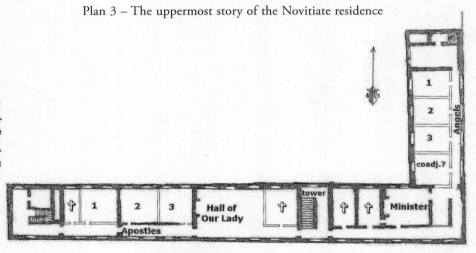

Editing Principles

Patricia M. Ranum

The French text

The principles currently observed by the École des Chartes of Paris served as my guide to editing the *Instructions*.[1] That is to say, since the manuscript clearly was written after 1650 and is not an autograph, an edition that faithfully reproduces the original abbreviations, accentuation and punctuation would be inappropriate. Where accent marks were omitted from the French version, or point in the wrong direction, or are superfluous today, the accentuation has therefore tacitly been modernized. Making this editorial decision was easy, because the Jesuits of the 1680s were striving to be as modern as possible. Equally easy was the decision to be guided by the appearance of the original text, despite constraints imposed by formatting side-by-side printed pages with parallel paragraphs. To this end, the right margins have not been justified, the printed headings evoke the headings in the manuscript, and italicized small capital letters imitate the large italic script employed for references to God, Jesus, and so forth. The three dots that follow a few of the quotations are original and suggest that the author was intentionally leaving a quotation incomplete. (These dots have been preserved in the translation, as well.)

The original spelling of the French manuscript has been preserved. Modifying the spelling ever so slightly, in order to eliminate variants (for example, *réfectoir* instead of the more common *réfectoire*, *ortographe* instead of *orthographe*, or *icy* instead of *ici*) would not only have eliminated the evidence upon which I base the dating of the manuscript, it would also have created a stylistic homogeneity that is not in fact there. Except where a comma or a semicolon was required for clarity, the original punctuation has been respected. Quotations and paraphrases of conversations posed a special problem, which was resolved as follows: Latin quotations are shown in italics, without quotation marks; statements in the vernacular that are put into someone's mouth are set off with single quotation marks.

The pagination of the original manuscript is shown within square brackets. It is these bracketed numbers, not the page numbers of this printed version, that are cited throughout the volume. Readers should think of these bracketed numbers as representing the page turns they would make when perusing the little handwritten book.

---

[1] *L'Édition des textes anciens, XVIᵉ–XVIIIᵉ siècle*, ed. Bernard Barbiche and Monique Chatenet (Paris, 1990), especially 15–21.

Two sorts of editorial emendations were made: 1) where a letter or a word was omitted and its absence could potentially affect the meaning of the phrase, the missing element was inserted within square brackets; 2) serious misspellings or confusions of meaning based on the sound of a word are corrected inside square brackets, after the indication "*read.*" Words crossed out by the copyist were retained in their crossed-out form, so that readers can judge whether they represent the sort of change of mind one often finds in early drafts, or whether they should be chalked up to momentary distraction.

A system of capitalization was devised especially for this edition. Certain nouns are capitalized, because they tend to be capitalized in the original: for example, *nos Frères*, or *nos Pères*, expressions that designate one or another rank of Jesuit. For another, very compelling reason, this edition also capitalizes some concepts or activities, not only because they tend to be capitalized in the manuscript, but also because capitalization helps distinguish these terms from the identical word employed in a less specific way. For example, a rosary, *chapelet*, as an object, is lower-case, but *Chapelet* refers to the devotional activity of praying the rosary; *charité* denotes an act of charity, but *Charité* refers to a rather painful exercise during which the novices criticized one another's conduct; *faute* denotes a fault in general, but *Faute* refers to the exercise of publicly declaring one's faults (*culpæ*); *maison* refers to a house such as the country house at Montrouge, but *Maison* denotes an institution belonging to the Society of Jesus, in most cases the Novitiate; *exercices* denotes either devotional activities in general or the two daily periods of assigned housekeeping tasks known as the "*exercices corporels*" (*manualia*), but *Exercices* is reserved for the Spiritual Exercices that were an integral part of Jesuit devotion; and so forth. Since capitalizing nouns in this way was a common practice in the late seventeenth century, these capitalizations add a bit of visual "flavor" to the text.

Many of the italicized Latin passages that stud the manuscript prove to be mosaics. That is, verses from different books of the Bible are strung together into a long sentence that reinforces the point being made by the anonymous author. Now and then, a phrase from a Church Father or from an apocryphal text crops up amidst these excerpts from the Scriptures.

The anonymous author's Latin was carefully checked against my tattered copy of the *Biblia Sacra, Vulgatæ editionis, Sixti V. Pont. Max. Iussu recognita, et Clementis VIII. auctoritate edita*, printed at Lyons by Pierre and Benoît Bailly in 1676. This edition was published only a few years before a committee began drawing up the *Instructions* for the Paris Novitiate. Our Jesuit's citations prove to be extremely accurate, and he himself turns out to have been adept at linking one bit of Biblical text to another. Still, there are occasional differences between the text of the *Biblia Sacra* of 1676 and the way he quotes those texts in the *Instructions*. Should we explain away these differences and assume that they are mistakes resulting from carelessness or faulty memory? Or are these differences intentional? To permit readers to judge for themselves, the notes to the French version show the Latin of the *Biblia Sacra* of 1676.

Details about the manuscript itself, explanations of terms, identifications of individuals, and citations of paraphrases or of likely sources for anecdotes, do not accompany the French text. They are found in the notes to the English translation.

The English translation

The translation stays as close as possible to the original French. I especially resisted the temptation to add variety and find other ways to say "one should" (*on doit*) and "it is necessary" or "must" (*il faut*). The author of the *Instructions* did not use these expressions lightly or interchangeably. "Should" conveys the hope that the novice will eventually find within himself the fortitude to obey the rule; but "it is necessary" and "must" make it very clear that breaking that particular regulation at any time would be a rather serious fault.

The bracketed corrections scattered through the French version have been tacitly woven into the English translation. Punctuation has been adapted to English practices. Capitalization is patterned after the system created for the French text. The pagination of the original manuscript, shown within square brackets in the French version, has been inserted into this translation, thereby facilitating comparison of the two versions. As with the French version, it is these bracketed numbers, not the page numbers of the printed translation, that are cited throughout.

The notes to the English translation shed light on the manuscript itself, and on the different activities at the Novitiate. They also identify people and propose likely sources for anecdotes or sayings that do not involve Jesuits. The author of the *Instructions* clearly was not inventing the anecdotes about Jesuits, the pithy sayings by Jesuits. Indeed, variants of these anecdotes and these sayings can be found in the numerous "lives" that were published in France during the seventeenth-century. However, rather than quote from these books verbatim, our Jesuit relied on oral tradition and told the story in his own words.

Double quotation marks surround the translations of the Latin texts that are quoted in the French version; and, as in the French version, single quotations surround statements put into someone's mouth. Most of the passages within double quotations come from the Douai-Reims translation of the Vulgate, available online at www.newadvent.org. Less often, the passage comes from the Church Fathers, and I was able to find a published English translation. (For the sources of the passages surrounded by double quotations, readers should consult the notes to the French version.) Where the anonymous Jesuit's Latin diverges from an established text, the English translation has been modified accordingly. If no translation could be found, I turned to Dr. Georg Luck, Professor Emeritus of Classics at the Johns Hopkins University, to whom I am very grateful. I also wish to thank Françoise Hildesheimer and Françoise Waquet for advising me about passages where the French text was ambiguous.

Il est expressément défendu de faire dans ces Instructions aucune correction, rature, addition, ou autre marque sous quelque prétexte que ce soit. Si on remarquoit quelque chose qu'on croiroit avoir besoin d'explication, on s'adressera directement au révérend père Recteur, sans qu'il soit permis de communiquer ses doutes à aucun de nos chers Frères. [1]

Laudent, honorem et gloriam

Instructions
Pour
Le Novitiat

Custodite et facite ea quæ præcepit Deus vobis: non declinabitis neque ad dexteram, neque ad sinistram.[1] Deuteronomie, chapitre 5, verset 32.

Avertissement

Dans la Préface des *Constitutions*, saint Ignace déclare que, outre les *Constitutions* mêmes et les règles tirées des *Constitutions* qui sont parmy nous comme des espèces de loix, parce qu'elles regardent le Corps en général et qu'elles doivent s'observer en tout temps, en tout lieu, et par tous ceux qui sont de la Compagnie, il sera nécessaire de faire d'autres règlemens plus particuliers, pour s'accommoder aux besoins propres de chaque lieu, de chaque temps, et de chaque employ.

Il avertit ailleurs que ces règlemens particuliers ne sçauroient entrer dans un trop grand détail, et qu'on est obligé de les observer avec la même fidélité que les règles générales et communes à tous.

C'est donc pour entrer dans les vues du saint Fondateur [2] et pour obéir à ses ordres que de tout temps on a fait, surtout dans les Maisons d'épreuves, des Instructions qui pussent diriger les novices, et les conduire comme par la main à tout ce qu'ils avoient à faire selon leur âge, leur état, et leurs besoins présens.

Celles que l'on trouvera icy n'ont rien de nouveau, sinon qu'on a ajouté à ce qui étoit déjà écrit beaucoup de choses qui se pratiquent sans être écrites. Étant écrites, personne n'en perdra la mémoire, la conduite pourra être parfaitement uniforme, et l'on ne disputera plus sur ce qu'on est obligé de faire ou de ne faire pas.

---

[1] Deuteronomy 5:32, *Custodite igitur et facite, quæ præcepit Dominus Deus vobis: non declinabitis neque ad dexteram, neque ad sinistram.*

---✦✦---

It is expressly forbidden to make any correction, cross-out,
in these Instructions for any pretext whatsoever. If one should n
believes needs explaining, one will speak directly to Reverend
not permitted to communicate one's doubts to any of our dear

Laudent, honorem et gloriam[2]

Instructions
for
the Novitiate

"Keep therefore and do the things which the Lord God hath commanded you: you shall not go aside neither to the right hand, nor to the left," Deuteronomy, chapter 5, verse 32.

Notice

In the Preamble to the *Constitutions*, Saint Ignatius[3] declares that, in addition to the *Constitutions* themselves and to the rules based upon the *Constitutions* that among us are like laws, because they concern the body of the Society in general and because they must be observed at all times, in all places, and by all those who belong to the Society, it will be necessary to draw up other regulations that are more particular, in order to adapt to the specific needs of each place, each time, and each task.

He warns elsewhere that these [more] particular regulations can scarcely be too detailed, and that one is obliged to observe them with the same fidelity as the general rules that are common to all.

It is therefore in order to partake of the views of the saintly Founder [2] and obey his orders, that, especially in the Houses of probation, Instructions have always been drawn up to guide the novices and, so to speak, lead them by the hand to everything they had to do, according to their age, their estate, and their current needs.

---

[1] Inscribed on the verso of the title page by a different hand. The use of the expression "our dear Brethren," which is generally reserved for texts in which a superior (a rector, a provincial) addresses all or some of the members of the Society, suggests that this brief note was penned by a superior.

[2] The first line of this motto was cut off by the binder.

[3] In the 1530s Ignatius Loyola (1491–1556) gathered together as "friends in the Lord" the companionship that became the Societas Iesu. The Society was approved by Pope Paul III in 1540, and in April 1541 Ignatius was chosen as the Society's first superior general. From then until his death, his major work was the writing of the *Constitutions* of the Society. He was canonized in 1622. See *The Constitutions of the Society of Jesus and their Complementary Norms* (St. Louis: Institute of Jesuit Sources, 1996) for Ignatius's work on the *Constitutions*, xv–xx; and for the text of the Preamble, 56, 58.

que ces Instructions ne soient ny des constitutions, ny des règles,
raison que nous venons d'aporter, cependant nous ne sçaurions bien
er ny nos règles, ny nos *Constitutions* sans observer nos Instructions.
utre que saint Ignace dans ses *Constitutions* authorise les supérieurs à en
faire, et qu'il oblige les inférieurs à les suivre, comme nous l'avons dit,
beaucoup d'autres règles ne sçauroient se garder qu'autant qu'on sera fidelle
à garder ses [read: ces] Instructions:

1° Toutes les règles sur l'obéissance veullent que nous obéissions à nos
supérieurs en tout ce qu'ils peuvent [3] nous ordonner pour notre avancement
spirituel, sans qu'il soit nécessaire qu'ils nous en fassent un commandement
exprès. Un seul signe de leur volonté doit suffire pour nous faire obéir.
Pouvons-nous douter ou que nos supérieurs veullent que nous gardions nos
Instructions, ou que nos Instructions ne soient utiles pour nous avancer dans
les voies de *Dieu*?

2° Nous avons une règle qui nous ordonne la plus grande abnégation de
nous-mêmes, et, autant qu'il se pourra, une continuelle mortification en toutes
choses. Les Instructions ne sont guères qu'une application de la règle, et elles
nous apprennent quand, et en quoy, c'est qu'il la faut pratiquer principalement.

Nous ne serions pas religieux, et nous n'aurions point de règles, qu'il nous
faudroit encore observer la plupart de nos Instructions par le droit naturel,
supposé que nous fissions certaines actions, nous serions obligés de les bien
faire. Nos Instructions nous apprennent à faire nos actions d'une manière
digne de *Dieu*, et de l'état que nous avons embrassé par son ordre. Enfin,
si nous avons quelque zèle pour notre perfection, nous devons avoir une
affection particulière à bien garder nos Instructions; car notre [4] vie n'est
vraiment parfaite, qu'autant que sont parfaites les actions ordinaires qui
la composent. Les actions extraordinaires reviennent trop rarement, pour
qu'elles puissent composer ce qui s'appelle l'état habituel de notre vie. Ce sont
donc nos actions les plus communes et les plus fréquentes qu'il faut songer
principalement à perfectionner, et c'est à quoy tendent toutes nos Instructions.

Aussy à quoy peut-on d'avantage attribuer la haute sainteté à laquelle
arrivèrent en si peu de temps nos Louis, Stanislas, et Berchmans, qu'au
respect infiny qu'ils eurent toujours pour ces sortes de règlemens et à la
religieuse exactitude avec laquelle ils les observèrent. Soions asseurés qu'en
marchant par le même chemin et du même pas qu'eux, nous arriverons en peu
de temps au même terme qu'eux; mais si nous nous écartons de leur conduite,
outre que nous ne deviendrons jamais bien vertueux, il est encore à craindre
que nous n'en venions jusqu'à perdre notre vocation même, et se pourroit-il
rien de plus funeste?

On n'a jamais vu sortir du Noviciat personne qui eut une grande fidélité
aux Instructions, ou bien ce fut par infirmité. Tous ceux qui en sortent
autrement, les négligent [5] et puis les méprisent, ou bien les méprisent et puis
les négligent. Ceux qui ont le malheur dans la suite de leur vie de quitter la
Compagnie, ou ne les avoient pas observées au Novitiat, ou bien regardant ces

The instructions found here contain nothing new, except that, to what had already been written, many things have been added that were being practiced without being written down. Now that they have been written down, no one will forget them, conduct can be perfectly uniform, and no one will henceforth dispute what one is obliged to do or not to do.

Although these Instructions are neither constitutions nor rules, for the reason just stated, we nonetheless could not follow either our rules or our *Constitutions* well, without following our Instructions. Beside the fact that Saint Ignatius, in his *Constitutions*, authorizes superiors to draw up Instructions, and obliges their inferiors to follow them, as we have said, many other rules can only be kept to the extent that one faithfully keeps these Instructions.

1. All the rules concerning obedience want us to obey our superiors in whatever they might [3] order us to do for our spiritual advancement, without it being necessary for them to give us an express command. A single sign of their will should suffice to make us obey. Can we doubt that our superiors want us to follow our Instructions, or that our Instructions are useful for advancing us along the ways of *God*?

2. We have a rule that orders us to observe the greatest self-abnegation and, as much as possible, a continual mortification in all things. The Instructions are scarcely other than an application of the rule, and they teach us when, and in what way, the rule should principally be practiced.

Even if we were not religious, and we did not have any rules, we would still have to observe most of our Instructions by natural law, on the supposition that if we did certain actions, we would be obliged to do them well. Our Instructions teach us to carry out our actions in a manner worthy of *God*, and of the estate we have embraced by his order. Finally, if we have any zeal for our perfection, we should have a special affection for following our Instructions well; for our [4] life is only truly perfect to the extent that the ordinary actions that form it are perfect. The extraordinary actions occur too rarely for them to form what is called the habitual state of our life. It is therefore our most common and most frequent actions that we must chiefly think about perfecting, and it is to this that all our Instructions lead.

Also, to what else can one attribute the high holiness attained, in so short a time, by our Louis,[4] our Stanislaus,[5] and our Berchmans,[6] if not to the infinite respect they always showed for these sorts of regulations, and to the religious exactitude with which they observed them. Let us be assured that, by walking along the same path and in step with them, in a short time we will reach the same outcome as they; but if we deviate from their conduct, in addition to the fact that we will never become very virtuous, it is also to be feared that we will go so far as to lose our vocation itself, and could anything be more woeful?

No one who showed great fidelity for the Instructions has ever been seen to leave the Novitiate, unless for bodily infirmity. All the others who leave, neglect the Instructions [5] and then scorn them, or else scorn them and then neglect them.

---

[4] Aloysius Gonzaga, a Italian-born Jesuit, beatified in 1605 and canonized in 1726.

[5] Stanislaus Kostka, a Polish-born Jesuit, beatified in 1605 and canonized in 1726.

[6] Seminarian John Berchmans, a Fleming, died in 1621 and was canonized in 1888.

règlemens comme des pratiques de novices, ils les oublièrent dès qu'ils se virent plus en liberté. Cependant on ne nous les donnent icy qu'afin la plupart de dir qu'elles [*read*: qu'afin que la plupart d'elles] servent de direction dans la suite, et cela s'étend à tous les articles de la suitte qui ne [re]gardent pas spécialement le lieu où nous vivons aujourd'huy. Il n'y a presque aucune action qui, pour être bien faite, ne doive se faire dans les Collèges et les Maisons, comme au Novitiat. C'est icy une raison de s'accoutumer de bonne heure à les faire comme l'ordonne nos Instructions. Nous travaillons pour tout le temps de notre vie, et dès que nous aurons acquis de bonnes habitudes, rien ne nous coûtera.

On ne parle point de ceux qui, non contens ou de mépriser, ou de négliger les Instructions, seroient cause encore, par leurs discours et par leur maxime relaschée, que d'autres les négligent ou les méprisent. Outre [6] qu'ils se rendroient coupables envers *Dieu* d'un grand nombre de péchez, et peut-être de l'âme même de leurs Frères qu'ils auroient détournés de leur devoir et endurcis dans l'imperfection, et de plusieurs âmes que leurs Frères, étant des saints, auroient gagnées à *Dieu* dans la suite, ils ne doivent attendre du Supérieur que les châtimens les plus rigoureux. On peut ménager pendant quelque temps un membre qui n'est qu'inutile au corps, mais c'est une mauvaise compassion de vouloir conserver un membre cangrainé [*read*: gangrené]: il pourroit corrompre les autres; il faut le retrancher impitoiablement et au plus vite.

Il y a au Novitiat des instructions communes à tous, et il y a de particulières pour ceux que l'on charge de certains petits employs. On trouvera les premières dans ce livre, et les autres se demanderont chaque fois qu'on sera chargé de ces petits emplois, ou à ceux qui cesseront d'être en semaine, ou à notre frère Admoniteur. De plus, dans chaque instruction, soit commune, soit particulière, on distinguera deux choses: ce qui en fait le corps pour ainsi dire, et ce qui en fait l'âme. [7]

Le corps de l'instruction, c'est ce qui est ordonné touchant le temps et la manière de faire chaque action. L'âme, c'est l'esprit intérieur avec lequel il faut faire tout ce qui est ordonné, les motifs dont on doit animer son action, les considérations pieuses et solides dont on peut s'occuper et se soutenir en la faisant.

Comme c'est principalement cette attention à l'intérieur qui en relève la valeur, qui en rend la pratique méritoire, et qui en adoucit les difficultés; et que cela manquoit à la plupart des anciennes Instructions, c'est aussy ce qu'on a jugé plus nécessaire d'ajouter à celle-icy. Il serviroit peu d'avoir des Instructions par écrit, si on ne les lisoit pas assez souvent, pour les bien sçavoir. Ainsi l'ancien de chaque chambre les lira lui-même, et aura soin que tous ceux de sa chambre les lisent toutes, sans y manquer, au moins une fois le mois. Il aura soin d'avertir avec charité ceux qui manqueroient à en observer quelqu'une. Cela suppose qu'il les garde lui-même en perfection. Quant aux instructions propres et particulières, chacun les lira une fois la semaine aussi longtemps qu'il sera chargé de quelque petit employ particulier. Pour trouver plus aisément les instructions dont on aura besoin, [8] il y aura à la fin du livre une table de tout ce qui y est contenu, et de la page où se trouve chaque chose.

Those who have the misfortune in the course of their lives to leave the Society, either did not observe them at the Novitiate or else, viewing these regulations as practices for novices, they forgot them as soon as they had more liberty. However, these Instructions are only given to us here so that most of them will serve to direct us later, and that applies to all the articles that do not specifically concern the place where we live today. There is almost no action that, if well done, should not be done in the Colleges and in the Houses, as at the Novitiate. This is a reason for becoming accustomed early to doing these actions as our Instructions order. We work for our entire life, and once we have acquired good habits, nothing will be an effort.

We are not talking about those who, not content with scorning or neglecting the Instructions, by their discourse and their tepid principles cause others to neglect them or scorn them. Beyond the fact that [6] they would make themselves guilty before *God* for a great number of sins, and perhaps for the very soul of their Brethren whom they may have diverted from their duty and hardened in imperfection, and for several souls that their Brethren, being holy, would have won for *God* in the future, they ought to expect nothing from the Superior but the most rigorous chastisements. One can favor for awhile a limb that is merely useless to the body, but it is misplaced compassion to want to preserve a gangrened limb: it might corrupt the others; it must be cut off without pity, and as quickly as possible.

At the Novitiate there are instructions that are common to all, and there are special ones for those who have been assigned certain little tasks. One will find the former in this book, and the others should be asked about every time one is assigned these little tasks, either from those whose week is drawing to a close, or from our Brother Admonitor. In addition, each instruction, be it general or specific, will distinguish between two things: that which, so to speak, forms its body, and that which forms its soul. [7]

The body of the instruction is what is ordered concerning the time and the manner of doing each action. The soul is the inner spirit with which everything that is ordered must be done, the motives that should animate one's action, the pious and solid considerations with which one can busy oneself and sustain oneself while doing it.

Since it is principally this attention to the interior that enhances the value, that makes the practice meritorious, and that sweetens the difficulties, and since this was lacking in most of the old Instructions, it is also what was judged the most necessary to add to these Instructions. It would serve little to have written Instructions if they were not read often enough to know them well. Thus the senior of each bedchamber will read them himself and will take care that everyone in his chamber reads them in full, without fail, at least once a month. He will take care to give a charitable admonition to those who fail to observe any of them. This supposes that he will observe them himself to perfection. As for the instructions that are individual and special, everyone will read them once a week during the entire time he is assigned some specific little task. To make it easier to find the necessary instructions, [8] at the end of the book there is a full table of contents, with the page where each thing is to be found.

Il ne reste qu'à finir par où l'on a commencé: *Custodite et facite ea quæ præcepit Dominus Deus vobis: non declinabitis neque ad dextram, neque ad sinistram.*[2] C'est le Seigneur vostre *Dieu* qui parle, il veut être obéi et il le mérite. Ne vous écartez donc point du chemin qu'il vous marque, ni à droite, ni à gauche, ne fût-ce que d'un seul pas. [9]

Inctructions pour le Noviciat

Les Instructions communes à tous

Instruction première
De l'ordre du jour

Règlement extérieur

Les jours ordinaires, les jours de fête, les jours de jeûne, les jours de récréation, et les jours qu'on repose, l'ordre du jour n'est pas le même.

Ordre pour les jours ordinaires

À 4 heures, le lever, on couvre son lit, on visite le Saint Sacrement et la Sainte Vierge, et on repasse sa Méditation s'il reste du temps. [10]

À 4 heures 1/2, l'Oraison d'une heure.

À 5 heures 1/2, l'Examen de l'Oraison, ensuite on se peigne, on fait son lit, et on approprie toutes choses en sa place.

Au petit coup [de la cloche] devant 6 heures on va à la Messe, et après la Messe on se rend vite à la chambre. Les jours d'Exhortation, on répète, depuis 5 heures jusqu'au petit coup devant 7 heures, ce qui s'est dit à l'Exhortation.

---

[2] Deuteronomy 5:32, *Custodite igitur et facite quæ præcepit Dominus Deus vobis: non declinabitis neque ad dextram, neque ad sinistram.*

This brings us back to where we began: "Keep therefore and do the things which the Lord God hath commanded you: you shall not go aside neither to the right hand, nor to the left." It is the Lord your *God* who is speaking, he wants to be obeyed and he deserves to be. Therefore, do not stray from the path he marks for you, neither to the right nor to the left, not even a single step. [9]

Inctructions [7]
for
the Novitiate

Common Instructions for everyone

First Instruction
For the order of the day

Outer regulation

On ordinary days, feast days, fasting days, recreation days, and days of rest, the order of the day is not the same.

The order for ordinary days

At 4 o'clock, wake up: one pulls up the covers of one's bed, one visits the Blessed Sacrament and the Blessed Virgin, and one reviews one's Meditation if time remains. [10]

At 4:30, Prayer [8] for an hour.

At 5:30, the Examen of Prayer, then one combs one's hair, makes one's bed, and puts everything in its proper place.

At the little ring [of the bell] before 6 o'clock, one goes to Mass, and after Mass one quickly returns to the bedchamber. On Exhortation days, one reviews, from 5 o'clock until the little ring before 7, what has been said at the Exhortation.

---

[7] *Errare humanum est.* One can imagine the copyist, so intent on his calligraphy that he failed to notice he had misspelled a key word in the title! This oh-so-human error has been preserved in the frontispiece and in the French and English texts.

[8] That is, the *Oraison*, done twice daily: for one hour upon rising and for a half hour at 5 o'clock in the afternoon. (Contemporary English-speaking Jesuits call this the "meditation.") See the Introduction, n. 58.

À 7 heures, l'Exhortation ou la Répetition. Quand il y a Exhortation, après qu'elle est finie on la répète pour la première fois jusqu'aux 3/4.

À 7 heures 3/4, on va déjeuner, à moins qu'il ne soit jour de jeûne, ou d'abstinence.

À 8 heures, l'exercice corporel.

À 9 heures, la lecture spirituelle.

Au petit coup devant 10 heures, on se rend au jardin, ou dans les salles pour apprendre par cœur.

À 10 heures 1/4, on va saluer le Saint Sacrement, ou chez le révérend père Recteur pour les Fautes: ce qui peut rester de temps est indifférent.

À 10 heures 1/2, l'Examen général de Conscience.

À 10 heures 3/4, le dîner.

Après le dîner on fait la récréation au jardin, ou dans les salles, après avoir été aux offices si on y est marqué.

Au petit coup pour 12 heures 1/2 on se rend à la salle pour les Litanies des saints.

Après les Litanies on va visiter le Saint Sacrement et la salle de Notre Dame. [11]

À 1 heure on apprend l'orthographe [*sic*].

À 1 heure 1/4, l'Examen particulier.

À 1 heure 1/2 on répète ce qu'on a appris par cœur, et un peu après on vient à la salle de Notre Seigneur pour le réciter à ceux qui sont marqués pour cela.

Au petit coup devant 2 heures on s'assemble à la salle de Notre Dame pour le Catéchisme le lundy et le mercredy; le vendredy au réfectoire pour les Tons; le samedy, le mardy et le jeudy quand on ne sort point, et toutes les veilles de Communion à la salle de Notre Seigneur pour recevoir de petits exercices.

À 2 heures 1/2, l'exercice corporel.

À 3 heures 1/2 on apprendra à écrire, à moins qu'on écrive déjà assez bien pour décrire quelque chose avec la permission du révérend père Recteur.

Au petit coup devant 4 heures on descend à l'église pour les Litanies de la Sainte Vierge, et de là on vient à la salle de Notre Dame pour les Litanies du Saint Nom de Jesus.

À 4 heures 1/4, la lecture spirituelle.

Au petit coup devant 5 heures on repasse le sujet de la seconde Méditation.

À 5 heures, la seconde Oraison d'une demie-heure.

À 5 heures 3/4 on va dire le Chapelet dans le jardin ou dans [les salles], [12] selon le temps qu'il fait.

À 6 heures, on prépare la Méditation du lendemain dans Avancin.

À 6 heures 1/4, le temps est indifférend: on peut aller chez le révérend père Recteur pour les Fautes.

At 7 o'clock, Exhortation or Repetition.[9] When there is Exhortation, after it is over, one reviews it for the first time until 7:45.

At 7:45, one goes to breakfast, unless it is a day of fasting or abstinence.

At 8 o'clock, bodily exercises.[10]

At 9 o'clock, spiritual reading.

At the little ring before 10 o'clock, one goes to the garden or to the community rooms, for memorization.

At 10:15, one goes to visit the Blessed Sacrament, or to Reverend Father Rector's quarters for Faults.[11] Whatever time remains is unassigned.

At 10:30, the general Examen of Conscience.[12]

At 10:45, the noonday meal.

After the noonday meal, one takes recreation in the garden or in the community rooms, after one has finished one's task in the service rooms [chiefly the kitchen and the refectory], if one is so assigned.

At the little ring for 12:30, one goes to the community room for the Litanies of the saints.

After the Litanies one goes to visit the Blessed Sacrament and the Hall of Our Lady. [11]

At 1 o'clock, one learns spelling.

At 1:15, the particular Examen.[13]

At 1:30, one repeats what one has learned by heart, and a bit after that one goes to the Hall of Our Lord to recite it to those who have been so designated.

At the little ring before 2 o'clock, one assembles in the Hall of Our Lady for Catechism on Monday and Wednesday; on Friday, to the refectory for the Tones; on Saturday, Tuesday, and Thursday, if one does not go outside, and on all Communion eves, to the Hall of Our Lord to be given brief exercises.

At 2:30, bodily exercises.

At 3:30, one learns writing, unless one already writes well enough to describe something, with the permission of Reverend Father Rector.

At the little ring before 4 o'clock, one goes down to the church for the Litanies of the Blessed Virgin, and from there one goes to the Hall of Our Lady for the Litanies of the Holy Name of Jesus.

At 4:15, spiritual reading.

At the little ring before 5 o'clock, one reviews the subject of the second Meditation.

At 5 o'clock, the second Prayer for a half hour.

At 5:45, one goes to say the Rosary in the garden or in [*lacuna*: the community rooms], [12] according to the weather.

At 6 o'clock one prepares the Meditation for the next day from Avancini.[14]

At 6:15, the time is unassigned: one can go to Reverend Father Rector's quarters for Faults.

---

[9] One or both of these activities are closely related to the "Conferences" (*Conférences*), [47], [48], and [50].

[10] Novices spent two hours daily doing the cleaning and maintenance chores known as the "bodily exercises," *exercices corporels*. See the Introduction, n. 61. For brevity, *exercice corporel* has sometimes been translated as "task."

[11] Novices privately requested permission from Father Rector to "declare one's Faults" (Instruction 25, [160]).

[12] That is, a general examination of one's overall conduct or state of soul.

[13] One examines one's failure or success in practicing a particular virtue or avoiding a particular sin.

[14] Nicola Avancini, S.J. (1612–1686). In 1672, a little in–12° French version of his "life and maxims" of Jesus, "reduced to meditations for each day of the year," was published in Paris. The *Instructions* presented here presumably post-date the publication of this pocket-sized book.

À 6 heures 1/2, le souper; les jours d'abstinence, après avoir dit le Chapelet et préparé la Méditation, le temps est indifférend jusqu'à 7 heures. Au 1/4 de devant, on va chez le révérend père Recteur si l'on y a affaire.

À 7 heures ou 7 heures 1/4, les jours d'abstinence, la récréation. On garde le silence jusqu'à ce que l'on ait sa bande: le frère Admoniteur nomme à mesure qu'on arrive.

Au 1/4 devant la fin de la récréation, on répète la Méditation d'Avancin.

Au petit coup devant 8 heures, on vient à la salle pour les Litanies de Notre Dame. Le dernier jour de chaque mois, on s'y rend dès le petit coup pour les 3/4, pour les Sentences.

Après les Litanies on visite le Saint Sacrement, la salle de Notre Dame, et l'on repasse la Méditation du lendemain.

À 8 heures 1/2, l'Examen général.

À 8 heures 3/4 on se couche: il faut être couché à 9 heures, et que la chandelle soit éteinte. [13]

Les jours de fête et de Communion

On fait toutes choses à l'ordinaire jusqu'au petit coup devant 6 heures, qu'on va au jardin ou dans les salles, selon la saison, pour réciter l'Office de Notre Dame.

À 6 heures 1/2 on va se laver les mains. Ceux qui craignent d'avaller de l'eau ne doivent pas se laver la bouche, mais simplement se la frotter avec le mouchoir.

À 6 heures 3/4 on se rend à la salle de Notre Dame pour entendre la lecture de l'*Imitation*, ou la petite Méditation.

Les jours de fête que l'on ne communie point, le temps est indifférend jusqu'au petit coup devant 7 heures, qu'on descend pour la Messe.

À 7 heures, la Messe. Les jours de Communion on fait son action de grâces jusqu'au *Sanctus* de la Messe suivante; après quoy on va visiter la salle de Notre Dame et celle de Saint Joseph. Les visites faites, on se rend à sa chambre. Les dimanches on fait la Récollection de la semaine, puis la lecture ou dans un livre qui traitte du Saint Sacrement, ou dans le livre ordinaire du matin, et non dans un autre sans permission particulière.

Les jours qu'on ne communie point, depuis 8 heures jusqu'à 9 heures on fait sa lecture dans le livre ordinaire du matin.

Vers 9 heures, quand la cloche sonne, on va au jubé entendre [14] une seconde Messe.

Après la seconde Messe, s'il fait beau on descend au jardin pour lire ou du Nouveau Testament dont on peut apprendre quelque chose par cœur, ou de quelqu'autre livre avec permission particulière.

À 10 heures 1/4 le temps est libre. S'il n'est pas jour de Communion, quoiqu'il soit fête, on peut aller chez le révérend père Recteur pour les Fautes.

At 6:30, supper: on days of abstinence, after having said the Rosary and prepared the Meditation, the time is unassigned until 7 o'clock. A quarter hour before that, one goes to Reverend Father Rector's quarters if one has business there.

At 7 o'clock, or 7:15 on days of abstinence, there is recreation. One remains silent until one's band has been formed: Brother Admonitor assigns people as they arrive.

A quarter hour before the end of recreation, one reviews the Meditation from Avancini.

At the little ring before 8 o'clock, one comes to the community room for the Litanies of Our Lady. The final day of each month, as soon as one hears the little ring a quarter before the hour, one goes there for the *Sententiæ*.[15]

After the Litanies one visits the Blessed Sacrament, the Hall of Our Lady, and one reviews the Meditation for the next day.

At 8:30, the general Examen.

At 8:45, one goes to bed: it is necessary to be in bed by 9 o'clock, and the candle must be extinguished. [13]

Feast days and Communion days

One does everything as usual until the little ring before 6 o'clock, when one goes to the garden or to the community rooms, according to the season, to recite the Office of Our Lady.

At 6:30, one goes to wash one's hands. Those who are afraid to swallow water should not rinse their mouths, but simply rub them with their handkerchiefs.

At 6:45, one goes to the Hall of Our Lady to listen to the reading of the *Imitation* or the little Meditation.

On feast days when one does not take Communion, the time is unassigned until the little ring before 7 o'clock, when one goes downstairs for Mass.

At 7 o'clock, Mass. On Communion days one offers thanksgiving until the *Sanctus* of the next Mass, after which one goes to visit the Hall of Our Lady and the Hall of Saint Joseph. These visits over, one goes to one's bedchamber. On Sundays one does the weekly Recollection,[16] then reads either a book about the Blessed Sacrament, or the ordinary book for the morning, and no other book without specific permission.

On days when one does not take Communion, from 8 o'clock to 9 one reads in the ordinary book for the morning.

Toward 9 o'clock, when the bell rings, one goes to the loft to hear [14] a second Mass.

After the second Mass, if the weather is fair one goes down to the garden to read either the New Testament, from which one can learn something by heart, or some other book with specific permission.

At 10:15, the time is free. If it is not a Communion day, even though it is a feast day, one can go to Reverend Father Rector's quarters for Faults.

---

[15] The French word is *Sentences*, from the Latin *sententiæ*, that is to say, the pithy maxims, figures of speech, and commonplaces that students memorized. See the Introduction, n. 54.

[16] Immediately after morning Mass on Sundays, novices returned to their bedchambers and did a "Recollection," a review of the week's Prayers. In addition, on fasting or free days, morning Prayer was followed by a meditative Recollection of the content of those prayers.

L'Examen, le dîner, la récréation et le reste se fait à l'ordinaire, jusqu'à 1 heure.

À 1 heure, l'Examen particulier, les jours qu'il y a sermon.

À 1 heure 1/4, on vient à la Modestie dans la salle de Notre Dame.

À 1 heure 3/4, le temps est libre.

À 2 heures le Colloque, jusque vers le petit coup pour les vêpres. Après le Salut on se rend à la salle de Notre Dame, pour y dire les Litanies de la Sainte Vierge et du Saint Nom de Jésus.

Les jours qu'il n'y a point de sermon, à 1 heure 1/4 le temps est libre, à 1 heure 1/2, la Modestie jusqu'à 2 heures 1/2.

À 2 heures 1/2, le temps est libre.

À 2 heures 3/4, le Colloque dans le jardin ou dans les salles, [15] selon le temps qu'il fait.

Au petit coup devant 4 heures, on se rend à l'église pour les Litanies. Le reste du jour se passe comme à l'ordinaire.

Les jours de jeûne

Tout se fait à l'ordinaire jusqu'à 10 heures 1/4.

À 10 heures 1/4 on apprend l'ortographe.

À 10 heures 1/2 on fait de petits exercices.

À 11 heures 1/4, la visite du Saint Sacrement, ou les Fautes.

À 11 heures 1/2, l'Examen général de Conscience.

La récréation ne finit qu'à 1 heure 3/4.

Le reste du jour tout est retardé d'une demie-heure, hormis le Cathéchisme. On descend pour collationner à 7 heures.

Les jours de récréation

À 5 heures, le lever.

À 5 h 1/2, l'Oraison.

À 6 heures 1/2, la Récollection; faire son lit.

À 7 heures la Messe, puis le déjeuner. Le temps est libre ensuite jusqu'à 8 heures.

À 8 heures on fait la récréation au jardin ou aux salles, selon le temps. [16]

À 9 heures on interrompt la récréation pour aller visiter le Saint Sacrement et la salle de Notre Dame.

À 9 heures 1/4 on retourne en récréation.

À 10 heures on fait la lecture dans sa chambre.

À 10 heures 1/4 le temps est libre.

À 10 heures 1/2, l'Examen, et le reste de l'ordinaire jusqu'à 1 heure.

The Examen, the noonday meal, recreation, and the rest takes place as usual, until 1 o'clock.

At 1 o'clock, the particular Examen, on days when there is a sermon.

At 1:15, one goes to Modesty[17] in the Hall of Our Lady.

At 1:45, the time is free.

At 2 o'clock, the Colloquy[18] until the little ring for vespers. After the Benediction of the Blessed Sacrament, one goes to the Hall of Our Lady to say the Litanies of the Blessed Virgin and those of the Holy Name of Jesus.

On days where there is no sermon, at 1:15 the time is free, and Modesty is from 1:30 to 2:30.

At 2:30, the time is free.

At 2:45, the Colloquy in the garden or in the community rooms, [15] according to the weather.

At the little ring before 4 o'clock, one goes to the church for the Litanies. The rest of the day is spent as usual.

Days of fasting

Everything is done as usual until 10:15.

At 10:15, one learns spelling.

At 10:30, one does little [devotional] exercises.

At 11:15, the visit to the Blessed Sacrament, or Faults.

At 11:30, the general Examen of Conscience.

Recreation does not finish until 1:45.

For the rest of the day, everything is delayed a half hour, except for Catechism. One goes downstairs to snack at 7 o'clock.

Recreation days

At 5 o'clock, wake up.

At 5:30, Prayer.

At 6:30, Recollection; make one's bed.

At 7 o'clock, Mass, then breakfast. The time is free after that until 8 o'clock.

At 8 o'clock, one goes to recreation in the garden or in the community rooms, according to the weather. [16]

At 9 o'clock, one interrupts recreation to go visit the Blessed Sacrament and the Hall of Our Lady.

At 9:15, one returns to recreation.

At 10 o'clock, one reads in one's bedchamber.

At 10:15, the time is free.

At 10:30, Examen, and the rest as usual until 1 o'clock.

---

[17] The assembly known as Modesty was held on feast days prior to the sermon. Transgressions against "modesty," that is, decorum, were pointed out publicly. For some of these transgressions, see [149], below.

[18] On the afternoon of a feast or communion day, novices gathered in the garden (or, if the weather was bad, in a community room or around the stove) to discuss among themselves the content of the most recent Exhortation or Exhortations. This is not the colloquy that typically concludes each meditation period (Prayer, *Oraison*), one in the morning (1 hour) and one in the afternoon (1/2 hour).

À 1 heure on sort s'il fait beau; s'il ne fait pas beau, à 1 heure on apprend l'ortographe.

À 1 heure 1/4 on fait l'Examen particulier: puis le temps est libre jusqu'à 2 heures.

À 2 heures on va en récréation.

À 3 heures on va saluer le Saint Sacrement et Notre Dame.

À 3 heures 1/4 on retourne en récréation.

À 4 heures les Litanies; et le reste du temps comme les autres jours. L'hyver, quand l'on sort et qu'on revient de bonne heure, on reprend au retour jusqu'au souper le même ordre d'exercices que s'il l'on [read: que si l'on] n'étoit pas sorty.

Les jours qu'on repose

À 5 heures, le lever.

À 5 h 1/2, l'Oraison.

À 6 heures 1/2, la Récollection. [17]

À 7 heures, la Messe, puis le déjeuner, et le reste à l'ordinaire. On ne changera quoy que ce soit dans l'ordre du jour, à moins qu'il n'arrive quelque chose d'extraordinaire, et que l'on n'en soit averty.

Direction intérieure

La fin extérieure de l'ordre du jour est que toutes choses se fassent avec règle et d'une manière uniforme. Cette suite d'actions coupées et variées sert beaucoup à empêcher l'ennuy. Mais la fin principale est qu'on apprenne à rompre sa propre volonté, et que l'on s'accoutume de bonne heure à faire ce que l'on doit, et non pas ce que l'on veut. On peut se promettre que ceux qui y seront fidels, le seront de même dans la suite, à faire exactement tout ce qui sera de leur obligation, et à ne pas perdre un seul moment de temps. Les autres étudieront quand il faudra prier, veilleront quand il faudra dormir, liront toute sorte de livres sans se fixer à rien, seront à la porte quand il faudra garder leur chambre, et leur classe sera aussi dérangée que leurs études et leurs dévotions; ils ne sçauront rien et ils enseigneront mal. [18]

Devant *Dieu* il y a une différence infinie, pour le mérite, entre ce qui se fait par caprice, et ce qui se fait par règle. Les moindres bagatelles sont d'une valeur infinie, quand on s'y applique par devoir. Il importe donc autant de se bien régler, qu'il importe de plaire à *Dieu*, de se rendre maître de ses passions, et de réprimer un certain libertinage si naturel à la plupart des hommes, et qui est la source de tout le mal qu'ils font. Enfin, ceux qui sont naturellement les plus vifs et les moins arrangés doivent se persuader que l'ordre du jour et des actions leur est plus nécessaire qu'à qui que ce soit; ne fût-il que pour une seule personne, il seroit pour eux.

At 1 o'clock, one goes outside if the weather is good; if it is not good, at 1 o'clock one learns spelling.

At 1:15, one does the particular Examen, then the time is free until 2 o'clock.

At 2 o'clock, one goes to recreation.

At 3 o'clock, one goes to visit the Blessed Sacrament and to greet Our Lady.

At 3:15, one returns to recreation.

At 4 o'clock, the Litanies; and the rest of the time is like other days. In winter, when one goes out and returns early, upon returning one resumes, until supper, the same order of exercises as if one had not gone out.

The days when one rests

At 5 o'clock, wake up.

At 5:30, Prayer.

At 6:30, Recollection. [17]

At 7 o'clock, Mass, then breakfast, and the rest as usual. One will change nothing whatsoever in the order of the day, unless something unusual happens and one is notified of it.

Inner guidance

The outer aim of the order of the day is that everything be done regularly and in a uniform manner. This sequence of separate and varied actions is very useful for preventing boredom. But the principal aim is to learn to break one's own will, and to become accustomed early to doing what one ought, and not what one wishes. One can anticipate that those who are faithful to these rules will be faithful to them in the future, will do with exactitude everything they are obliged to, and will not waste a single moment. The others will study when they are supposed to pray, will stay awake when they are supposed to sleep, will read all manner of books without concentrating on anything, will be at the door when they are supposed to remain in their bedchamber, and their class will be as disorganized as their studies and their devotions: they will know nothing, and they will teach badly. [18]

Before *God* there is an infinite difference, as to merit, between what is done out of caprice and what is done according to the rules. The least trifles are of infinite value when one applies oneself out of duty. It is therefore as important to be guided by the rules as it is to please *God*, to master one's passions, and to repress a certain dissoluteness that is so natural in most men, and that is the source of all the evil they do. Lastly, those who are naturally the most lively and the least ordered must become convinced that the order of the day, and of actions, is more necessary for them than for anyone else; and that if it should be necessary only for one single person, it would be for them.

Instruction seconde
Pour le lever et les actions qui précèdent
l'Oraison du matin

Règlement extérieur [19]

On doit se lever à l'instant même qu'on entend l'heure, ou si on ne l'entend pas, à l'instant qu'on entend quelqu'un de la chambre dire *Deo gratias*. On doit aussi répondre *Deo gratias*, pour faire sçavoir qu'on est éveillé.

D'abord on doit faire le signe de la croix † et élever son cœur à *Dieu*. C'est une louable coutume de baiser sa soutane avant que de la passer dans ses bras, pour remercier *Dieu* par ce signe de respect du bienfait de sa vocation. Il faut s'habiller promptement et d'une manière très modeste, comme étant sous les yeux de *Dieu* et des saints anges. Pour s'habiller plus vite, il faut en se couchant arranger tellement ses habits proche de soy, qu'on sçache où ils sont et qu'on puisse même les trouver de la main sans lumière.

Dès qu'on est proprement habillé, on peut se donner un coup de peigne, ensuite il faut couvrir son lit. Tout le temps que cela dure, on peut réciter le *Te Deum*, surtout sy l'on se sent trop assoupy encore pour s'entretenir avec *Dieu* sans parler.

En allant au Saint Sacrement, on peut repasser les points de sa Méditation, ou réciter quelques prières vocales. [20]

Au Saint Sacrement il faut faire le petit exercice du matin qu'on se sera prescrit, aussy bien qu'à la salle de Notre Dame. On ne doit point oublier, dans ses visites, de recommander à *Dieu* et à la Sainte Vierge le succès de son Examen particulier, comme saint Ignace l'ordonne au livre des *Exercices*.

Direction intérieure

La visite du Saint Sacrement est une action de justice. Un enfant bien né ne manque pas, le matin, de présenter les respects à son père. *Notre Seigneur* a prié pour nous toute la nuit, pendant que nous reposions. Ses prières nous ont préservé[s] de beaucoup d'accidents, et des illusions de l'Ennemy. Il étoit là pour nous servir de consolation et de viatique, si nous en avions besoin. Il faut l'en aller remercier. Tous les momens de notre vie lui appartiennent; il faut au moins lui en offrir les premiers. Sans son secours, nous ne ferions rien de bon toute la journée. Il faut lui aller demander sa grâce et sa bénédiction.

L'habitude d'aller visiter le Saint Sacrement tous les matins doit durer toute notre vie. Les supérieurs sont asseurés que nous sommes levés quand ils nous voient; et nous sommes comme asseurés nous-mêmes que nous ne manquerons jamais à faire l'Oraison dont [21] dépend notre sanctification et notre persévérence dans la Religion.

Second Instruction
For rising and the actions that precede morning Prayer

Outer regulation [19]

One should rise the very instant one hears the hour ring, and if one does not hear it, the instant one hears someone in the chamber say *Deo gratias*. One should also reply *Deo gratias*, to show that one is awake.

First one should make the sign of the cross † and raise one's heart to *God*. It is a praiseworthy custom to kiss one's soutane before picking it up, to thank *God*, by this sign of respect, for the blessing of one's vocation. It is necessary to dress promptly and in a very modest way, as being seen by *God* and the holy angels. To dress more quickly, when going to bed one should arrange one's clothes close at hand so that one knows where they are and can even find them by touch, without a light.

As soon as one is neatly dressed, one can run a comb through one's hair, then the bedcovers must be pulled up. All the while, one can recite the *Te Deum*, especially if one still feels too drowsy to communicate with *God* without speaking.

While going to the Blessed Sacrament, one can review the points in one's Meditation, or recite a few vocal prayers. [20]

At the Blessed Sacrament it is necessary to do the little exercise of the morning that one has chosen for oneself, and in the Hall of Our Lady as well. One should not forget, during these visits, to commend to *God* and to the Blessed Virgin the success of one's particular Examen, as Saint Ignatius orders in the book of *Exercises*.

Inner guidance

Visiting the Blessed Sacrament is an act of justice. A well-born child does not fail to pay his respects to his father each morning. *Our Lord* has prayed for us all night, while we were resting. His prayers have preserved us from many accidents, and from the Enemy's illusions. He was there to serve us as a consolation and a viaticum, if we needed them. It is necessary to go thank him. Every moment of our life belongs to him; he should at least be offered the first moments. Without his help, we would do nothing good all day long. It is necessary to go and ask him for his grace and his blessing.

The habit of going to visit the Blessed Sacrament every morning should continue for our whole life. The superiors are assured that we have risen when they see us; and we ourselves are, in a way, assured that we will never fail to do the Prayer upon which [21] our sanctification and our perseverance in Religion depends.

Pour la visite de Notre Dame, n'oublions pas qu'après *Dieu*, c'est d'elle et par elle que nous sont déjà venus, et nous viendront encore, toute sorte de biens.

Instruction troisième
Pour l'Oraison et la Récollection

Règlement extérieur

Sitôt que l'heure de l'Oraison sonne, on se découvre, on va prendre de l'eau bénite, on se place debout devant son oratoire, on fait le signe de la croix, et l'on se tient quelque temps en la présence de *Dieu*. Peu après, on se met à genoux, on baise humblement la terre pour adorer *Dieu*, puis on se relève, on s'agenouille sur le marchepied de son oratoire, et l'on commence sa Méditation. Cette même pratique doit s'observer au commencement de toutes ses Oraisons et de tous ses Examens.

On ne doit point s'appuyer sur son oratoire, ny s'asseoir pendant son Oraison, ny pendant les autres exercices de piété, à moins qu'on ne soit extraordinairement incommodé; et alors il en faudroit demander permission à l'ancien de sa chambre et lui dire pourquoy. Si l'on étoit trop fatigué de demeurer à genoux si [22] longtemps de suite, ou que l'on sentît fort assoupy, on pourroit se lever pendant quelques petits moments; mais cela doit être rare et ne peut guères se souffrir que dans ceux qui sont depuis peu au Noviciat.

Si l'on se trouvoit l'esprit distrait et hors de son sujet, on pourroit lire quelques lignes de son livre de Méditation; mais il ne faut pas trop s'y accoutumer, et cela ne sera pas fort nécessaire si l'on a bien préparé la Méditation après le Chapelet, le dernier 1/4 [d'heure] de la récréation, le soir après les Litanies, et le matin encor avant que de commencer.

On doit faire en sorte de ne jamais sortir de la chambre pendant les exercices de piété, surtout pendant l'Oraison et les Examens. Il faut prévenir les petits besoins naturelz, et si quelqu'un sortoit trop souvent pendant ces temps-là, l'ancien de la chambre doit en avertir le révérend père Recteur. L'Oraison finie, on dit pour conclusion un *Pater* et un *Ave*, on baise la terre une seconde fois, puis on s'asseoit pour faire l'Examen de l'Oraison pendant un petit quart d'heure le matin, et un peu moins après l'Oraison du soir.

Direction intérieure [23]

On trouvera ailleurs la manière de faire l'Oraison avec fruit, de bien choisir son sujet, de s'occuper dans ses distractions, et de faire la Récollection. Ce que l'on doit uniquement remarquer icy, c'est que de l'observation fidelle

As for greeting Our Lady, let us not forget that, after *God*, it is from her, and through her, that all sorts of good things have already come to us and will continue to do so.

Third Instruction
For Prayer and Recollection

Outer regulation

As soon as the hour for Prayer rings, one bares one's head, one goes to take holy water, one stands before one's prayer desk, one makes the sign of the cross, and one stays there for awhile in the presence of *God*. Shortly after that, one kneels, one humbly kisses the floor to adore *God*, then one rises, one kneels on the kneeler of one's prayer desk, and one begins one's Meditation. This same practice should be observed at the beginning of all one's Prayers and all one's Examens.

One should not lean on one's prayer desk, nor sit during Prayer or during the other exercises of piety, unless one feels unusually unwell; and then one must ask permission from the senior of one's chamber, and tell him why. If one was too weary to remain kneeling so [22] long, or if one should happen to feel very drowsy, one could rise for a few brief moments; but that should be infrequent and can scarcely be tolerated except among those who have recently come to the Novitiate.

If one were to find one's spirit distracted and not on the subject at hand, one could read a few lines of one's Meditation book; but it is necessary not to become too accustomed to this, and it will not be very necessary if one has carefully prepared the Meditation after the Rosary, during the final quarter hour of recreation, in the evening after the Litanies, and again in the morning before beginning.

One must take care never to leave the chamber during exercises of piety, especially during Prayer and Examens. One must foresee the need to relieve nature, and if someone were to go out too often at those times, the senior of the chamber should notify Reverend Father Rector about it. Prayer having ended, one concludes by saying a *Pater* and an *Ave*, one kisses the floor a second time, then one sits down to do the Prayer Examen for a bit less than a quarter hour in the morning, and a bit less after afternoon Prayer.

Inner guidance [23]

One will find elsewhere the way to do Prayer fruitfully, how to choose one's subject well, how to employ oneself when distracted, and how to do the Recollection. The unique thing to note here is that the success of Prayer depends,

de toutes les circonstances cy-dessus marquées, dépend plus qu'on ne pense le succès de l'Oraison. À ceux qui font ce qu'ils peuvent, *Dieu* donne des grâces pour faire ce qu'ils ne pourroient pas; le respect extérieur peut suppléer en partie au défaut de l'intérieur, surtout s'il est involontaire. On fait sa cour au prince en se tenant, en sa présence, dans une position composée, n'eût-on pas la liberté de lui parler, ny la consolation de l'entendre.

In[s]truction 4ᶜ
Pour faire son lit, etc.

Règlement extérieur

La Récollection finie, on se peigne. Ensuite on fait son lit, relevant le devant sur les pieds, et remuant un peu la paille avant que de le recouvrir. Il ne faut rien négliger [24] pour que tout soit proprement ajusté, et tous les lits doivent être faits de la même manière. On doit rapprocher ses rideaux de façon qu'en les relevant, on puisse les arrenger proprement sur le chevet, ou sur le pied du lit, selon qu'il se trouve disposé. On finit par se donner un coup de vergettes s'il est nécessaire, et relever les ordures de la main si on en a fait quelqu'une.

Direction intérieure

Notre Seigneur n'a point eu de valets pour le servir. Saint François Xavier, tout légat apostolique qu'il fût, disoit: 'Tandis que j'aurai ces deux bras, je ne donnerai de peine à personne.' Honorons les humiliations de notre Maître qui s'est fait esclave pour l'amour de nous, *formam servi accipiens,*[3] c'est l'esprit dans lequel tous les saints, et nos premiers Pères en particulier, bien loin d'avoir des serviteurs, se firent si souvent dans les hôpitaux les serviteurs des pauvres.

Instruction cinquième [25]
Pour assister à la Messe
Règlement extérieur

Dès qu'on entend le petit coup avant l'heure de la Messe, on doit descendre à l'église. On attend proche de la sacristie que tous à peu près soient assemblés, puis on avance à la file dans le milieu du sanctuaire. On fait la

---

[3] Philippians 2:7, *Sed semetipsum exinanivit formam servi accipiens, in simultudinem hominum factus, et habitu inventus ut homo.*

more than one might think, upon the faithful observation of all the above circumstances. To those who do what they can, *God* gives the grace to do what they could not do; being outwardly respectful can in part take the place of what is lacking inside, especially if it is involuntary. One pays court to the prince by keeping a composed demeanor in his presence, even if one might not have the freedom of speaking to him, or the consolation of hearing him.

Fourth Instruction
For making one's bed, etc.

Outer regulation

Recollection over, one combs one's hair. Then one makes one's bed, lifting the bedding down to the foot of the bed and stirring the straw a bit before covering it again. Nothing must be neglected [24] so that everything is neatly adjusted, and all the beds should be made in the same way. One should pull one's bed curtains together so that, by lifting them, one can arrange them neatly at the head of the bed, or at the foot of the bed, according to the way they are placed. One finishes by brushing one's clothes if necessary, and by picking up the trash if one has made any.

Inner guidance

Our Lord had no valets to serve him. Saint Francis Xavier,[19] even though he was a papal legate, used to say: 'As long as I have these two arms, I will make no one work.' Let us honor the humiliations of Our Master, who made himself a slave for love of us, "taking the form of a servant." That is the spirit in which all the saints, and our first Fathers in particular, far from having servants, so often made themselves the servants of the poor in hospitals.

Fifth Instruction
For attending Mass

[25]

Outer regulation

As soon as one hears the little ring before the hour for Mass, one should go down to the church. One waits near the sacristy until almost everyone has

---

[19] Francis Xavier (1506–1552) belonged to one of the groups of first companions who, under Ignatius of Loyola, founded the Society of Jesus. He subsequently spent ten years as a missionary in southern and eastern Asia. He was canonized in 1622 and became one of the most popular Saints of the time. The Parisian Novitiate was dedicated to him.

génuflexion profonde en passant devant le Saint Sacrement. Ceux qui vont les premiers doivent avancer plus ou moins loin, suivant qu'il y a plus ou moins de monde après eux. Pendant la Messe on ne doit lire dans aucun livre, non pas même dans les heures, si ce n'est quelqu'un nouvellement arrivé et qui n'est pas encore instruit de la manière de s'occuper durant le Saint Sacrifice.

On doit s'abstenir de souffler, de tousser, de cracher, de se moucher, autant qu'il se pourra; et si on veut cracher, qu'on le fasse proprement, et sans bruit, dans son mouchoir. On doit tenir sa birette à deux mains devant soy, ou le cacher sous sa robe; mais jamais ne la mettre par terre, ny derrière soy sur sa soutane. Cecy doit s'observer partout ailleurs où [26] on s'assemble pour prier *Dieu*.

À la fin de la Messe, quand quelqu'un veut communier, ceux derrière qui est la nappe de communion, doivent se lever et venir se mettre à genoux, vis-à-vis l'un de l'autre sur le passage du prêtre, en sorte que sans changer de place, ils puissent toujours suivre des yeux le Très Saint Sacrement.

Après la bénédiction du prêtre, ceux qui se sont déplacés doivent retourner à leur place. Enfin, on ne doit pas se lever pour sortir que le prêtre ne soit retourné à la sacristie.

Direction intérieure

Au temps que *Jésus Christ* s'offre à son père, on ne doit penser qu'à l'offrir, et à s'offrir avec luy. C'est l'esprit intérieur de cette grande action, sur laquelle il y a une instruction fort ample et fort utile.

Instruction sixième
Pour servir la Messe
Règlement extérieur [27]

On doit se rendre à la sacristie aussitôt qu'on entend la cloche pour la Messe qu'on doit servir. En attendant que le prêtre soit venu, on doit ou faire quelque prière, ou lire dans quelque livre de piété qu'on aura apporté, ou qui se trouvera dans la sacristie; mais jamais ne causer, ny avec le Sacristain ou avec les personnes du dehors qui peuvent se remontrer; ny s'asseoir indécemment; ny se courber le corps en lisant. On sonnera trois coups pour appeler ceux qui doivent servir les Messes au grand autel, deux coups pour les petits autels, et un seul pour la chapelle domestique.

Dès que le prêtre arrive, on tire son amict de la boëtte, on l'étend sur l'aube et puis on époussette son bonnet: on reçoit ensuite sa robe lorsqu'il la quitte, et on la place en quelque endroit propre où, après la Messe, on puisse la retrouver.

assembled, then one advances in single file to the middle of the sanctuary.[20] One genuflects deeply when passing before the Blessed Sacrament. Those who go first should advance more or less far, according to whether there are many or few people behind them. During Mass, one should not read any book, not even a book of hours, unless one is a recent arrival and has not yet been instructed about how to occupy oneself during the Holy Sacrifice.

One should abstain from whispering, coughing, spitting, blowing one's nose, as much as possible; and if one wishes to spit, then one should do it neatly and noiselessly, into one's handkerchief. One should hold one's birette in front of one with both hands, or hide it under one's robe, but never put it on the floor, or behind one, on one's soutane. This should be observed wherever [26] one assembles to pray to *God*.

At the end of Mass, when someone wants to take Communion, those who have their backs to the communion cloth should rise and go kneel opposite one another as the priest is about to pass, so that without changing their place, they can always keep their eyes on the Most Blessed Sacrament.

After the priest's benediction, those who moved should return to their place. Lastly, one should not rise to leave until the priest has returned to the sacristy.

Inner guidance

At the time when *Jesus Christ* is offering himself to his father, one should think only of offering him, and offering oneself with him. That is the inner spirit of this great action, about which there is a very ample and very useful instruction.

Sixth Instruction For serving Mass
Outer regulation [27]

One should go to the sacristy as soon as one hears the bell for the Mass that one is supposed to serve. While waiting for the priest to arrive, one should either say a prayer or read some devotional book that one has brought, or that is in the sacristy; but never chat, either with the Sacristan or with any outsiders who happen to make a remark; or sit down indecently, or bend forward while reading. One will ring three times to call those who are supposed to serve Masses at the high altar, twice for the small altars, and only once for the domestic chapel.[21]

---

[20] The sanctuary *(sanctuaire)* is the part of a church nearest to the high altar. It is usually surrounded by a balustrade. This balustrade is visible in fig. 4, left-hand plan.

[21] The "domestic chapel of St. Ignatius" was situated on the ground floor of the residential building (plan 1). The "small altars" were the side altars in the Novitiate church (fig. 4).

Lorsque le prêtre met l'amict, on le lève un peu sur ses épaules des deux côtés, à moins qu'il ne soit si petit qu'il ne puisse pas lui embarasser l'usage des bras.

On prend l'aube ensuite; et lorsqu'il présente la tête, on la lui passe, et non pas plutôt [read: plus tôt]; on l'étend ensuite sur ses habits de tous côtés, et on lève les manches, afin qu'il puisse voir où passer les bras. [28]

L'aube mise, on tient la ceinture étendue par-derrière, et on la met dans la main du prêtre, lorsqu'il la présente. La ceinture étant mise, on relève l'aube si elle est trop longue, la tirant au-dessus de la ceinture, jusqu'à ce qu'elle se trouve également à un doigt de terre tout autour.

On présente ensuite le manipule, l'approchant un peu de la bouche comme pour le baiser par honneur, et l'entr'ouvrant vers le côté qui n'est point cousu et par où le prêtre doit passer son bras.

On présente l'étole de la même manière, après l'avoir comme baisé, le petit bord du linge tourné vers soy, et les mains assés éloignées l'une de l'autre, pour que le prêtre prenant l'étole ne puisse point les toucher.

Le prêtre aiant mis l'étole, on prend garde que la croix du milieu réponde au milieu de son dos; et lorsqu'il la croise devant sa poitrine, on la retient derrière par les deux côtés pendant qu'il l'arrête avec les deux pendants de la ceinture.

On finit par lui présenter la chasuble, la tenant par le haut d'une main et l'ouvrant de l'autre, en sorte qu'il puisse commodément y passer la tête. Pendant qu'il attache la [29] chasuble, on la relève un peu par-derrière pour qu'il puisse agir des mains par-dessous, sans embarras.

Tout cela, aussi bien que beaucoup d'autres choses, s'apprennent mieux par la pratique encore que par la spéculation de la lecture.

Ainsi il faut que quand nos Frères nouveaux commencent à servir la Messe, ils aient toujours avec eux quelqu'ancien (pour l'ordinaire l'ancien de la chambre) qui leur montre et les avertisse de leurs fautes, jusqu'à ce qu'ils sçachent faire toutes choses avec la dernière exactitude et la plus grande propreté.

Le prêtre étant prêt d'aller à l'autel, le serveur doit prendre le livre entre ses bras, un peu panché vers le bras gauche, à moins qu'il ne soit déjà sur l'autel; puis faire l'inclination profonde au crucifix en même temps que le prêtre, et aller à l'autel lentement, deux pas devant luy.

Étant prêt [read: près] de l'autel, si le lieu d'où l'on vient est du côté de l'Évangile, le serveur passe devant le milieu de l'autel sans faire ny génuflexion ny inclination, et se va mettre à la droite du prêtre pour recevoir son bonnet. Si le lieu [30] d'où l'on vient est du côté de l'Épître, comme au Noviciat et à Saint-Louis, le serveur se recule de deux pas, étant proche du milieu de l'autel, et laisse passer le prêtre, après quoy il se rapproche et reçoit son bonnet. Le serveur ensuite fait la génuflexion, et monte à l'autel en même temps que le prêtre, mais toujours, par respect, un peu derrière luy. Il pose sur le coussin le missel fermé du côté du tabernacle, et va mettre le bonnet à

As soon as the priest arrives, one takes his amice from the box, one spreads it out on the alb, and then one dusts off his bonnet; then one takes his robe when he removes it, and one puts it in a clean place where one can find it after Mass.

While the priest is donning the amice, one lifts it a bit over both his shoulders, unless it is so small that it cannot restrict the use of his arms.

Next, one takes the alb; and when he puts his head forward, one passes it over his head, but not sooner; then one spreads it over his clothes on all sides, and one lifts the sleeves, so that he can see where to put through his arms. [28]

Once the alb is on, one stretches out the cincture behind, and one puts it in the priest's hand when he holds it out. Once the cincture is in place, one lifts the alb if it is too long, pulling it above the cincture until it is evenly one finger from the floor all around.

Then one presents the maniple, bringing it toward one's mouth a bit, as if to honor it with a kiss, and opening it on the side that is not sewn and through which the priest must pass his arm.

One presents the stole in the same manner, after having seemed to kiss it, with the little border of the linen turned toward one, and the hands separated enough so that the priest cannot touch them when taking the stole.

The priest having donned the stole, one checks that the cross in the middle corresponds to the middle of his back; and when he crosses it over his chest, one holds both sides in place behind, while he is attaching it to the two pendants of the cincture.

One finishes by presenting him with the chasuble, holding it at the top with one hand and opening it with the other, so that he can comfortably pass through his head. While he is attaching the [29] chasuble, one lifts it up a bit behind, so that he can move his hands under it without encumbrance.

All this, as well as many other things, are more easily learned by practice than by pondering over a text.

Therefore, when our new Brethren begin to serve at Mass, they must always have with them some senior (usually the senior of the bedchamber) who shows them and points out their mistakes, until they know how to do everything with total exactitude, and with the greatest neatness.

When the priest is ready to go to the altar, the server should take the book in both hands, tilted a bit toward his left arm, unless the book is already on the altar; then he should make a deep bow to the crucifix at the same time as the priest, and go to the altar slowly, two steps ahead of him.

Once near the altar, if the place from which one has come is on the Gospel side, the server passes in front of the middle of the altar without genuflecting or bowing, and goes to the right of the priest to take his bonnet. If the place [30] from which one has come is on the Epistle side, as at the Novitiate and at Saint-Louis, the server moves back two steps when he is near the middle of the altar and lets the priest pass, after which he approaches him and takes his bonnet. The server then genuflects and goes up the altar steps at the same time as the priest, but always, out of respect, a bit behind him. He puts the closed missal on

sa place. On doit voir en passant s'il y a du vin et de l'eau dans les burettes; et s'il n'y en a pas, y en mettre, tandis que le prêtre se prépare à commencer la Messe.

Le serveur se met ensuite à genoux du côté de l'Évangile, un peu derrière le prêtre, et à deux ou trois pas de luy, les mains jointes devant la poitrine; et il doit les avoir ainsi toute la Messe, si ce n'est qu'il fît beaucoup de froid, auquel cas il pourroit les cacher sous sa robbe ou dans les manches du surplis, surtout hors le temps qu'il répond au prêtre, mais jamais dans ses poches. Le prêtre étant [31] au bas de l'autel, le serveur fait une inclination de la tête, tandis que le prêtre fléchit le genouil; puis, en même temps que luy, fait le signe de la croix de la main droite, aiant la gauche étendue sur l'estomach, et répond à tout d'une voix distincte et au même ton que le prêtre, s'il est possible, sans luy couper la parole et sans manger aucune syllabe. Au *Gloria Patri, etc.*, il incline la tête, et à l'*Adjutorium* il fait un nouveau signe de la croix.

Pendant le *Confiteor* du prêtre, le serveur ne s'incline point et ne se frappe point la poitrine. Le prêtre aiant achevé son *Confiteor*, le serveur, le corps un peu incliné, dit *Misereatur* et *Confiteor*; et à *et tibi Pater*, et *et te Pater* il se tourne tant soit peu vers le prêtre. À *meâ culpâ*, il se frappe trois fois la poîtrine, les doigts serrés. Lorsque le prêtre a achevé le *Misereatur* et qu'il commence l'*Indulgentiam*, le serveur cesse de s'incliner.

Le prêtre montant à l'autel, le serveur s'agenouille sur le dernier degré, et il demeure là jusqu'à la fin de l'Épître. Toutes les fois que le prêtre, parlant haut, incline la tête, le serveur doit l'incliner aussi, comme quand il prononce [32] le nom de *Jésus*, de *Marie, etc.* À la fin de l'Épître, ayant répondu *Deo gratias*, le serveur vient à la droite du prêtre, un peu derrière et plus bas que luy, et attend qu'il faille tourner le livre. Si le prêtre fléchit le genouil, comme à *Veni Sancte* ou bien à *Adjuva nos Deus*, le serveur doit aussi le fléchir. Le graduel finy, le serveur porte le livre du côté de l'Évangile et le place sur le coussin, non pas vis-à-vis mais un peu de côté, vers la muraille. Le serveur demeure debout, un peu tourné vers le prêtre, jusqu'à ce qu'il ait commencé l'Évangile, et se signe du pouce droit comme luy, et en même temps que luy, le front, la bouche, et la poitrine; puis il repasse aussitôt en sa place du côté de l'Épître, où il entend l'Évangile debout et un peu tourné vers le prêtre.

L'Évangile finy, il s'agenouille jusqu'à ce que le prêtre ait dit *Dominus vobiscum*. Alors il répond et monte à l'autel, pour recevoir de luy le voile du calice et le placer sur le coussin vuide.

Pendant que le prêtre fait l'oblation de l'hostie, le serveur va prendre le bassin et les burettes, tenant le bassin d'une main et les burettes de l'autre, de crainte qu'elles [33] ne s'échappent. Il étend l'essuie-main sur le coin de l'autel, y met le bassin et la burette d'eau dessus, le bec tourné vis-à-vis les chandeliers, pendant que de la main droite il tient la burette de vin de la même manière, afin que le prêtre puisse les prendre par l'anse plus aisément, et il l'attend en cet état. Le prêtre arrivant à luy, il luy fait l'inclination de

the cushion [so that the opening is] toward the tabernacle, and goes to put the bonnet in its place. In the process, one should look to see whether there is wine and water in the cruets; and if there is none, fill them while the priest is preparing to begin Mass.

The server then kneels on the Gospel side, a bit behind the priest and two or three paces from him, hands clasped in front of his breast; and he should keep them that way throughout Mass, unless it is very cold, in which case he can hide them under his robe or inside the sleeves of his surplice, especially when he is not responding to the priest, but never in his pockets. The priest being [31] at the foot of the altar, the server inclines his head, while the priest genuflects; then, at the same time as the priest, he makes the sign of the cross with his right hand, his left hand spread over his heart, and he answers everything in a distinct voice, and on the same tone as the priest, if possible, without interrupting him and without muttering any of the syllables. At the *Gloria Patri, etc.*, he inclines his head, and at the *Adjutorium* he again makes the sign of the cross.

During the priest's *Confiteor*, the server does not bow and does not strike his breast. The priest having finished his *Confiteor*, the server, his body slightly inclined, says *Misereatur* and *Confiteor*; and at *et tibi Pater* and at *et te Pater*, he turns ever so little toward the priest. At *mea culpa* he strikes his breast three times, fingers clenched. When the priest has finished the *Misereatur* and has begun the *Indulgentiam*, the server stands up straight.

As the priest goes up the altar steps, the server kneels on the lowest step, and he remains there until the end of the Epistle [Reading]. Every time the priest, speaking aloud, bows his head, the server should bow his also, as when he pronounces [32] the names of *Jesus*, of *Mary*, etc. At the end of the Epistle, having replied *Deo gratias*, the server goes to the priest's right, a bit behind him and lower than he, and waits until it is time to move the book. If the priest genuflects, as at *Veni Sancte* or else at *Adjuva nos Deus*, the server must also genuflect. The gradual finished, the server carries the book to the Gospel side and places it on the cushion, not opposite, but a bit to the side, toward the wall. The server remains standing, turned slightly toward the priest, until he has begun the Gospel, and he makes the sign with the right thumb as the priest does, and at the same time as he does, forehead, mouth, breast; then he immediately goes back to his place on the Epistle side, where he listens to the Gospel, standing and turned slightly toward the priest.

The Gospel finished, he kneels until the priest has said *Dominum vobiscum*. Then he replies, and ascends to the altar, to take the veil of the chalice from him and place it on the empty cushion.

While the priest is doing the oblation of the host, the server goes to get the basin and the cruets, holding the basin in one hand and the cruets in the other, for fear they [33] will fall. He spreads out the hand towel on the corner of the altar, puts the basin there, with the cruet of water on top of it, the spout turned toward the candles, while in his right hand he holds the cruet of wine in the same manner, so that the priest can take them more easily by the handle, and he waits for him

tête, approche un peu de soy la burette, comme s'il vouloit la baiser, et la présente au prêtre; il la reprend en faisant un petit geste de la main, comme il avoit fait de la burette, et ne quitte point que le prêtre n'ait versé l'eau dans le calice et remis la burette sur le ba[s]sin. En quittant, il fait encore une inclination et va reporter la burette de vin où il l'avoit prise.

Aussitôt après, il remonte à l'autel, ôte la burette d'eau de dessus le bassin, la met sur le rebord de marbre et non pas sur la nappe, de peur de la gâter; prend le bassin de la main gauche, élève un peu l'essuie-main de la droite, en manière de piramide, et reprend la burette d'eau en attendant que le prêtre vienne laver. Après l'inclination [34] de tête, le serveur fait encore le petit geste de la burette, et luy verse de l'eau sur les doigtz doucement et sans remuer aucunement la main, jusqu'à ce qu'il fasse signe que c'est assés. Au signe, le serveur fait de nouveau l'inclination; et pendant que le prêtre s'essuie, il va remettre le bassin et la burette en leur place. De là il monte à l'autel, prend l'essuie-main, retourne à sa place, où il le plie, et attend que la Préface soit dite pour l'aller remettre sur les burettes: il doit être rendu à sa place pour répondre à l'*Orate fratres*; ou s'il n'étoit point encore rendu, il doit y répondre à genoux quelque part qu'il se trouve. On ne doit point répondre à l'*Orate fratres* que le prêtre n'ait achevé le tour tout entier. Au *Sanctus* le serveur doit sonner trois fois la clochette ou le tympan; les deux premières fois peu, à la troisième un peu plus longtemps, après quoy il reporte l'essuie-main, allume le cierge du côté de l'Épître les jours ordinaires, et des deux côtés les jours de fête, à moins qu'il n'y ait six cierges allumés sur l'autel. Lorsque le prêtre, prêt [*read*: près] de la consécration, étend les deux mains sur le calice, le serveur [35] vient au milieu de l'autel, fait la génuflexion, puis il se place à genoux sur le second degré, derrière le prêtre, un peu plus vers l'Épître, pour lever la chasuble plus commodément de la main gauche, et sonner de la droite. La chasuble ne doit se lever que quand le prêtre est prêt à faire la génuflexion, et on ne la doit lever qu'autant qu'il faut pour qu'elle ne l'incommode pas. Pendant qu'il lève le Corps et le Sang de *Notre Seigneur*, on sonne trois fois à la première élévation, l'une avant que le prêtre montre l'hostie, l'autre pendant qu'il la montre, et la troisième aussitôt qu'il a remis l'hostie sur l'autel, pour avertir les novices prosternés de se relever, et trois fois pareillement à la deuxième, la première avant qu'il lève le calice, l'autre pendant qu'il le lève, et la troisième après qu'il l'a remis sur l'autel, pendant qu'il fait la génuflexion. Ensuite le serveur fait la génuflexion; ensuite le serveur fait la génuflexion au bas des dégrés, dans le milieu, et vient reprendre sa place.

On ne doit sonner ny au *Nobis quoque peccatoribus*, ny au *Pater*, ny au *Domine non sum dignus*. Au *Nobis* [36] *quoque peccatoribus*, aux *Agnus Dei*, et au *Domine non sum dignus*, le serveur frappe sa poitrine, comme le prêtre.

Pendant que le prêtre, après s'être communié, achève de purifier la patenne sur le calice, et non plutôt [*read*: plus tôt], le serveur fait la génuflexion en sa place et va chercher les deux burettes, avec lesquelles il monte à l'autel et fait une seconde génuflexion en y arrivant. Il verse

in that position. The priest having come up to him, he inclines his head to him, moves the cruet a bit closer to himself, as if he wanted to kiss it, and presents it to the priest. He takes it back while making a little gesture with his hand, as he did for the cruet, and he does not move away until the priest has poured water into the chalice and put the cruet back on the basin. When leaving, he again bows and takes the cruet of wine back to where he got it.

Immediately afterward, he goes back up to the altar, removes the cruet of water from atop the basin, puts it on the marble border and not on the cloth, for fear of dirtying it; takes the basin in the left hand, lifts the hand towel a bit with the right hand into a pyramid, and takes back the cruet of water until the priest comes to wash. After bowing [34] his head, the server once again makes the little gesture with the cruet and pours a bit of water on the priest's fingers, gently and without moving his hand at all, until he signals that it is enough. At that signal the server again bows; and while the priest is drying himself, he goes to put the basin and cruet in their place. From there he goes up to the altar, takes the hand towel, returns to his place, where he folds it and waits until the Preface is said, in order to go and put it back on the cruets. He should be back in his place to reply to *Orate fratres*; or if he has not yet reached it, he should reply on his knees, wherever he happens to be. One should not reply to *Orate fratres* until the priest has finished turning around. At the *Sanctus* the server should ring the little bell or gong three times: the first two times very little, the third time a bit longer, after which he puts back the hand towel, lights the candle on the Epistle side on ordinary days, and on both sides on feast days, unless there are six candles lighted on the altar. When the priest, approaching the consecration, extends both hands over the chalice, the server [35] comes to the middle of the altar, genuflects, then kneels on the second step, behind the priest, a bit toward the Epistle [side], in order to lift the chasuble more conveniently with his left hand and ring the bell with the right one. The chasuble should only be lifted when the priest is ready to genuflect, and one should lift it only as much as needed so that it is not in the way. While he elevates the Body and Blood of *Our Lord*, one rings three times on the first elevation: once before the priest shows the host, the next while he is showing it, and the third as soon as he has put the host back on the altar, to warn the prostrate novices to rise; and likewise three times for the second elevation, the first before he raises the chalice, another while he is raising it, and the third after he has put it back on the altar, while he is genuflecting. Next, the server genuflects; then the server genuflects at the bottom of the steps, in the middle, and goes back to his place.

One should not ring either at the *Nobis quoque peccatoribus*, or at the *Pater*, or at the *Domine non sum dignus*. At the *Nobis* [36] *quoque peccatoribus*, at the *Agnus Dei*, and at the *Domine non sum dignus*, the server strikes his breast, like the priest.

While the priest, having taken Communion, finishes purifying the paten over the chalice, and no sooner, the server genuflects in place and goes to get the two cruets, with which he goes up to the altar and genuflects a second time upon

la première ablution de vin seulement debout à côté du prêtre, et la seconde d'eau et de vin un peu plus reculé et hors du marchepied. Avant que de verser, il fait toujours le geste de la burette et, après avoir versé, l'inclination.

Ayant remis les burettes en leur place, il va reprendre le livre où il est, pour le porter du côté de l'Épître. Avant que de quitter le côté de l'Évangile, il ajuste l'*In principio* sur le coussin placé un peu de côté, comme au premier Évangile. Il doit tâcher d'être revenu assés tôt du côté de l'Épître, pour donner le voile du calice au prêtre lorsqu'il en a besoin.

Après avoir placé le livre, il va éteindre le cierge qu'il avoit allumé après le *Sanctus*, et reprendre ensuite sa place du côté de l'Évangile. Les jours qu'on dit deux Évangiles [37] à la Messe, il reporte le livre du côté de l'Évangile après avoir répondu à l'*Ite missa est* ou au *Benedicamus te*. Il doit se mettre à genoux pendant la bénédiction, quelque part qu'il se trouve. L'Évangile commencé, après avoir fait les trois signes de croix sur soy, comme le prêtre, il repasse du côté de l'Épître et va remplir les burettes pour la Messe suivante, si elles ne le sont pas. Le frère Sacristain s'en charge pour l'ordinaire, et on peut s'en reposer sur luy. Il fléchit le genouil à *Et verbum caro*.

Après la Messe, si quelqu'un veut communier, il dit le *Confiteor* sans se précipiter, et s'agenouille sur le dernier degré de l'autel, le corps tourné de côté, en sorte que, sans remuer, il puisse toujours accompagner des yeux le Très Saint Sacrement. Si quelqu'un communie dans le balustre, il doit luy présenter une nappe de communion, ou l'essuie-main à son défaut.

Lorsque le Saint Sacrement est remis dans le tabernacle, et non plutôt [*read*: plus tôt], il va prendre le bonnet du prêtre, et attend au pied de l'autel qu'il en descende. Il doit être à genoux pendant qu'il donne la bénédiction d'après la Communion. Il donne le bonnet au prêtre quand il présente la main pour le recevoir, [38] fait la génuflexion avec luy et retourne à la sacristie, deux pas devant. Si la sacristie est du côté de l'Évangile, il passe par-derrière le prêtre, pour le devancer sans faire ny génuflexion nouvelle ny inclination.

Arrivé à la sacristie, il fait, un peu derrière le prêtre, l'inclination au crucifix en même temps que luy; et il se range à sa droite ou à sa gauche, selon la disposition du lieu, pour l'aider à se déshabiller. Il reçoit de sa main les ornemens, il étend la chasuble bien proprement sur la table, met l'étole et le manipule par-dessus, en sorte que les dentelles et les franges ne se touchent point ou très peu; la ceinture ensuite, qu'il doit prendre garde à ne point mêler, et l'aube par-dessus tout.

Il y a des manières plus ou moins propres de faire tout cela. Il faut apprendre la meilleure en voyant faire ceux qui en ont bien l'usage, et ensuite l'enseigner aux autres dans l'occasion.

Dès que le prêtre est déshabillé, après avoir reçu l'amict de ses mains,

arriving. He pours only the first ablution of wine while standing beside the priest, and the second ablution of water and wine a bit farther back, and away from the altar step. Before pouring it, he always makes the gesture with the cruet and, after having poured, the bow.

Having returned the cruets to their place, he goes to take the book from where it is and carries it over to the Epistle side. Before leaving the Gospel side, he adjusts the *In principio*[22] on the cushion, which is placed a bit to the side, as for the First Gospel. He should try to be back soon enough from the Epistle side, to give the veil for the chalice to the priest when he needs it.

After having put the book in position, he goes to extinguish the candle that he lighted after the *Sanctus* and then returns to his place on the Gospel side. On days when two Gospels are said [37] at Mass,[23] he carries the book to the Gospel side after having responded to the *Ite missa est* or to the *Benedicamus te*. He should kneel during the blessing, wherever he may be. The Gospel having begun, after having made the three signs of the cross on himself, like the priest, he returns to the Epistle side and fills the cruets for the next Mass, if they are not full. Brother Sacristan usually does this, and one can rely on him. He genuflects at *Et verbum caro*.

After the Mass, if someone wants to take Communion, he says the *Confiteor* without rushing and kneels on the lowest step of the altar, his body turned sideways, so that, without stirring, he can always keep his eyes on the Most Blessed Sacrament. If someone takes Communion at the rail, he must present him with a communion cloth, or a hand towel if no cloth is available.

When the Blessed Sacrament has been put back into the tabernacle, and no sooner, he goes to get the priest's bonnet and waits at the foot of the altar until he descends. He should be kneeling while he gives the blessing after Communion. He gives the priest his bonnet when he extends his hand to receive it, [38] genuflects with him, and returns to the sacristy, two steps ahead. If the sacristy is on the Gospel side, he passes behind the priest, in order to get ahead of him, without making either a new genuflexion or a bow.

Having reached the sacristy, a bit behind the priest he bows to the crucifix at the same time as the priest does; and he positions himself to his right or his left, according to the disposition of the locale, to help him disrobe. He receives the vestments from his hand, he spreads the chasuble out very neatly on the table, puts the stole and the maniple on top, so that the lace and fringes do not touch one another, or very little; next, the cincture, which he should be careful not to tangle, and the alb on top of everything.

There are more or less suitable ways of doing all this. It is necessary to learn the best way by watching those who are very experienced, and then teaching it to others when the occasion arises.

---

[22] In *principio*, "In the beginning," are the opening words of the Gospel of John, the Last Gospel (Second Gospel) recited at most Masses. To facilitate the celebrant's recitation, at the end of the Mass a plaque with this text from John, known as "the *In principio*," was placed on a cushion at the left (Gospel) side of the altar.

[23] That is, on days when both a ferial and a feast-day proper Gospel are said at Mass.

il faut luy présenter sa robbe, l'aider à la passer dans ses bras, et prendre bien garde de ne point luy donner celle d'un autre, ou de remettre son amict lorsqu'on l'a plié dans une autre boëte que la sienne. [39]

On ne met point icy les réponses de la Messe, parce que tous les sçavent assés et qu'elles se trouvent dans une infinité de livres où on pourra les apprendre; cependant voicy quelques petites remarques. Après le *Confiteor* du prêtre, on doit dire *Misereatur* tout d'abord, et non pas *Amen. Misereatur.* Dans le *Misereatur* on doit dire *et dimissis peccatis suis* et non point *et dimissis omnibus peccatis suis.* Au *Confiteor* on ne doit jamais dire *et omnes sanctis et tibi Pater* ou *et omnes sanctos et te Pater*; mais *omnibus sanctis, omnes sanctos* sans mettre *et.* À l'*Orate fratres* on ne doit point dire, *suscipiat Dominus hoc sacrificium,* mais *suscipiat Dominus sacrificium* sans ajouter *hoc.* Un peu avant le *Pater* on ne doit point dire *Ave salus, ave vita.* À la fin du dernier Évangile, on doit toujours répondre *Deo gratias,* soit que ce soit *In principio* ou quelqu'autre.

Tout ce que nous avons dit regarde les jours ordinaires, quand on sert la Messe au grand autel. Voicy quelque chose de particulier pour les petits autels, et pour de certains jours quand on sert la Messe au grand autel.

Avant que de partir de la sacristie, lorsqu'on va servir la Messe à un petit autel, il faut voir ou s'informer s'il y [40] a de l'eau et du vin, s'il y a au moins un coussin pour mettre le livre, et si les cierges sont allumés, ou si quelqu'un pense à les venir allumer. Cela se doit faire sans trop d'inquiétude ny trop de mouvement. On peut demander au frère Sacristain si tout est prêt.

On en [read: on ne] fait aucune génuflexion avant la consécration, mais des inclinations profondes toutes les fois qu'au grand autel on fait la génuflexion. Après la consécration on fait des génuflexions comme au grand autel. Pendant que le prêtre dit le dernier Évangile, on éteint le cierge du côté de l'Épître, on prend le livre et le bonnet de la main gauche, puis on passe du côté de l'Évangile pour éteindre le second cierge dès que le prêtre aura finy, si ce n'est qu'on doive dire une autre Messe après. Puis on revient au lieu d'où l'on doit rendre le bonnet au prêtre; et lorsqu'il l'a pris, on fait avec luy l'inclination profonde à l'autel, et on part. En allant à l'autel et en revenant, on fait une génuflexion toutes les fois que l'on passe par où repose le Très Saint Sacrement; et si, en passant, quelque prêtre en étoit à l'élévation à [41] quelqu'autel que ce fût, on fléchit les deux genoux, et l'on demeure en cette posture jusqu'à ce que le prêtre, ayant remis bas le calice, fasse la génuflexion. Enfin quelque part qu'on serve la Messe, aux petits autels ou au grand, on doit toujours prendre garde à ne tourner entièrement le dos ny au Saint Sacrement ny à l'autel.

Les jours qu'on sert la Messe en surplis, on doit prendre le surplis avant que le prêtre s'habille, et ne le quitter qu'après l'avoir aidé à se déshabiller.

Lorsqu'il y a deux serveurs, chacun garde pendant la Messe le côté où

As soon as the priest has disrobed, after having received the amice from his hands, he must present him with his robe, help him to get his arms into it, and be very careful not to give him someone else's robe or, having folded his amice, to put it away in a different box than his own. [39]

The responses for the Mass are not provided here, because everyone knows them well enough, and because they can be found in a infinite number of books where one can learn them; however, here are a few brief remarks. After the priest's *Confiteor*, one should say *Misereatur* first, and not *Amen. Misereatur*. In the *Misereatur* one should say *et dimissis peccatis suis*, and not *et dimissis omnibus peccatis suis*. At the *Confiteor* one should never say *et omnes sanctis et tibi Pater* or *et omnes sanctos et te Pater*, but *omnibus sanctis, omnes sanctos*, without an *et*. At the *Orate fratres* one should not say *suscipiat Dominus hoc sacrificium*, but *suscipiat Dominus sacrificium*, without adding *hoc*. A bit before the *Pater*, one should not say *Ave salus, ave vita*. At the end of the Last Gospel, one should always reply *Deo gratias*, whether it is *In principio*[24] or something else.

Everything that we have said applies to ordinary days, when one serves Mass at the high altar. Here is something particular about the small altars, and about certain days when one serves Mass at the high altar.

Before leaving the sacristy, when one is going to serve Mass at a small altar, one must see or inquire whether there is [40] water and wine, if there is at least a cushion on which to put the book, and if the candles are lighted, or if someone is planning to come and light them. That should be done without too much fretting and too much movement. One can ask Brother Sacristan if everything is ready.

One makes no genuflexion prior to the consecration, but bows deeply every time a genuflexion is made at the high altar. After the consecration, one does genuflections as at the high altar. While the priest is saying the Last Gospel, one extinguishes the candle on the Epistle side, one takes the book and the bonnet in one's left hand, then one passes to the Gospel side to extinguish the second candle as soon as the priest has finished, unless another Mass is supposed to be said afterward. Then one returns to the place where one is supposed to return his bonnet to the priest; and when he has taken it, one bows deeply to the altar with him, and one leaves. When going to the altar and returning, one genuflects every time one passes the place where the Most Blessed Sacrament reposes; and if, in passing, any priest happens to be at the elevation, at [41] any altar whatsoever, one bends both knees, and one remains in that posture until the priest, having lowered the chalice, genuflects. Lastly, wherever one serves Mass, be it at the small altars or the high altar, one should always take care not to turn one's back entirely to either the Blessed Sacrament or the altar.

On the days when one serves Mass in a surplice, one should don the surplice before the priest gets dressed, and not take it off until one has helped him disrobe.

---

[24] On feast days, the proper Gospel of that day was read at the end of Mass, as the Last (or Second) Gospel, in the place of the more usual reading from the Gospel of John, which begins: *In principio*. In short, irrespective of the text used for the Last Gospel, one replied *Deo gratias*.

il s'est placé d'abord. Le second ne fait que lever la chasuble de son côté pendant l'élévation, et porter le livre après la Communion et retourner aussitôt en sa place.

Lorsque le Saint Sacrement est exposé, arrivant à l'autel et en sortant, on fléchit les genoux avec le prêtre, et on fait la génuflexion devant le Saint Sacrement toutes les fois qu'on sort de sa place et qu'on y revient, et toutes les fois qu'on monte sur le marchepied de l'autel ou qu'on en descend. À l'Évangile, le livre ne se place point de côté sur le coussin, comme les autres fois, mais droit vis-à-vis [42] les chandeliers.

Pour donner à laver au prêtre, on descend au-dessous des degrés de l'autel, le visage tourné contre le mur, et assés éloigné du mur pour que le prêtre puisse tourner entre luy et le serveur. On soutient le bassin de la main gauche, aux doigts de laquelle pend l'essuie-main qu'on présente au prêtre, élevant un peu le bras après qu'il a lavé.

Lorsqu'il y a, à la Messe, plusieurs Épîtres, comme aux Quatre Temps, on ne doit quitter sa place pour aller tourner le livre qu'à la dernière; et quand on dit une Prose, comme aux fêtes de Pâques et de la Pentecôte, et surtout du Saint Sacrement [la Fête-Dieu] et des Morts, où les Proses sont plus longues, on ne part que sur la fin de la Prose.

Depuis Pâques jusqu'à l'Ascension, on allume le cierge pascal à l'Évangile de toutes les Messes du grand autel. Cela se fait pendant l'Épître, ou un peu auparavant, si on craint que le temps ne soit court. Ensuite on entend l'Évangile, proche du grand chandelier, pour éteindre le cierge aussitôt qu'il est achevé; puis on [43] repasse du côté de l'Épître.

L'hyver, quand le prêtre ne sçauroit lire qu'à la lumière, il y a un flambeau allumé proche le livre. On doit le moucher quand il y est nécessaire, et le transporter de tout côté avec le livre, à moins qu'il n'y en ait deux, comme il arrive les grands jours.

Avec le même flambeau on conduit le prêtre à donner la Communion lorsqu'il ne fait pas assés de jour. On le prend sur l'autel entre l'*Indulgentiam* et l'*Ecce Agnus Dei*. On se tient à genoux tout le temps que le prêtre est sur le marchepied; et lorsqu'il veut descendre, on luy éclaire sur les degrés et on le conduit aux personnes qui doivent communier, demeurant à la main gauche et le suivant d'assés près pour qu'il voie à prendre les hosties dans le ciboire et à les porter à la bouche de ceux qui communient. La Communion achevée, on reconduit le prêtre, l'éclairant toujours jusqu'à ce qu'il soit remonté à l'autel. On met ensuite le flambeau au lieu où il a été pris. On fait la génuflexion au Saint Sacrement, et puis on se retire. [44]

Pendant les plus grands froids, lorsqu'il y a un réchaud sur l'autel, le serveur doit prendre garde que rien ne brûle. Il ne doit jamais lui-même se chauffer à ce réchaud, mais il doit en approcher les burettes, s'il voit du danger que le vin et l'eau ne gelassent.

When there are two servers, during Mass each one stays on the side where he first stood. The second server merely raises the chasuble on his side during the elevation, and carries the book after Communion and immediately returns to his place.

When the Blessed Sacrament is exposed, one genuflects with the priest when arriving at the altar or leaving it, and one genuflects before the Blessed Sacrament every time one leaves one's place and returns to it, and every time one goes up the altar step or goes down. At the Gospel the book is not placed to the side on the cushion, as at other times, but straight and opposite [42] the candlesticks.

To give the priest the washing materials, one descends to below the altar steps, one's face turned to the wall, and far enough from the wall so that the priest can turn between it and the server. One supports the basin with the left hand, from the fingers of which hangs the hand towel that one is presenting to the priest, raising the arm a bit after he has finished washing.

When there are several Epistles [Readings][25] during Mass, as for the Ember Days, one should only leave one's place to go change the book at the last Epistle; and when one says a Sequence, as on the feasts of Easter and Pentecost, and especially for the Blessed Sacrament [Corpus Christi] and the Dead [the Faithful Departed], where the Sequences are longer, one does not leave until the end of the Sequence.

From Easter to Ascension, one lights the paschal candle at the Gospel of every Mass said at the high altar. This is done during the Epistle, or a bit before if one fears being short of time. Then one listens to the Gospel, near the great candlestick, to extinguish the candle as soon as it is finished; then one [43] goes back to the Epistle side.

In winter, when the priest cannot read without a light, there is a torch lighted near the book. One should trim it when necessary and carry it to one side or another with the book, unless there are two torches, as happens on special days.

With the same torch one conducts the priest to give Communion when there is not enough daylight. One takes it from the altar between the *Indulgentium* and the *Ecce Agnus Dei*. One remains kneeling all the time that the priest is on the altar platform; and when he wants to descend, one lights the steps for him and conducts him to the people who want to take Communion, remaining at his left and following him closely enough so that he can see to take the hosts from the ciborium and advance them to the mouths of the people taking Communion. Communion over, one conducts the priest back, lighting his way until he is back up at the altar. Then one puts the torch back where one found it. One genuflects to the Blessed Sacrament, and then one withdraws. [44]

During very cold weather, when there is a brasier on the altar, the server should be careful that nothing burns. He must never warm himself at this brasier, but he should bring the cruets near it, if he thinks there is danger that the wine and water will freeze.

---

[25] "Epistle," *Épître*, is properly used for one of the letters of the New Testament. It is employed loosely here, to denote the last of several readings at the Epistle or right-hand side of the altar, usually on the Ember Days. "Reading" (in square brackets) was inserted into p. [79], to call attention to what may be a similar loose usage.

Direction intérieure

Servir à la Messe, c'est un ministère si noble que les anges en seroient jaloux et qu'ils nous disputeroient volontiers. Appliquons-nous-y avec le même zele et la même ferveur qu'ils le feroint. Les saints, ne pouvant communier qu'une fois le jour, servoient autant de Messes qu'ils pouvoient, pour suppléer en quelque façon à des Communions multiples. Servir à la Messe, c'est faire par grâce ce que le diacre et le sou-diacre font d'office. Le serveur, après le prêtre, est celui qui participe le plus au Sacrifice. Il doit donc aussi servir à lui plus étroitement que personne: il ne fait et il ne doit faire qu'un avec lui. Le serveur ne parle guères en son [45] nom, mais au nom de toute l'Église. C'est une nouvelle manière de représenter, par la vivacité de sa foy, celle de tous les Catholiques répandue dans l'univers.

La raison pour laquelle, au défaut des ministres ordinés, on se sert communément d'enfants pour servir à l'autel, n'est pas seulement parce qu'ils s'y portent plus volontiers, et ne jugent point cela au-dessous d'eux, mais encor parce qu'on suppose avec raison qu'ils sont plus innocens que les personnes avancées.

La plupart des cérémonies que nous avons marquées pour le serveur son[t] tirées des rubriques romaines. C'est une raison de les garder plus diligemment encore que nos règles. Nous y sommes obligés, à peu près autant que le prêtre l'est, de garder les rubriques qui lui sont proposés.

Plus nous approchons au sacerdoce, plus nous devons nous tenir honorés de servir à l'autel; et c'est une honte bien mal entendue que de paroître en rougir. C'est à peu près comme si un ecclésiastique nommé à l'épiscopat ou déjà évêque rougissoit de dire la Messe en particulier. *Ubi ego sum, illic et minister meus erit*. Joannes, caput 12.[4] [46]

Instruction septième
Pour les Exhortations et les Répétitions
[Règlement extérieur]

Au retour de la Messe, les jours qu'il y a Répétitions d'Exhortation, on se rend promptement dans sa chambre, on s'approche les uns des autres sur sa chaise, et chacun répète ce qu'il a retenu, dans le même sens, s'il est possible, qu'il a été proposé.

Il faut prendre garde en répétant l'Exhortation à ne point parler trop haut, à ne point s'interrompre, à ne pas rire, ou dire une seule parole inutile et qui ne convienne pas au sujet, et à ne point faire paroître trop de

---

[4] John 12:26, *Si quis mihi ministrat, me sequatur: et ubi sum ego, illic et minister meus erit.*

Inner guidance

Serving Mass is a ministry so noble that the angels would be jealous and would willingly compete with us over it. Let us apply ourselves to it with the same zeal and the same fervor that they would. The saints, only able to take Communion once a day, served as many Masses as they could, to take the place, in some fashion, of multiple Communions. Serving Mass is doing, by grace, what the deacon and the subdeacon do by function. After the priest, the server is the person who participates most in the Sacrifice. And so, he should therefore serve it more strictly than anyone: he only acts, and should only act, as one with the priest. The server scarcely speaks in his own [45] name, but in the name of the entire Church. It is a new manner of representing, by the vivacity of one's faith, the faith of all the Catholics spread throughout the universe.

The reason why, for lack of ordained ministers, one commonly uses children to serve at the altar, is not only because they are more willing to do so, and do not judge it to be beneath them, but also because one rightly supposes that they are more innocent than older people.

Most of the ceremonies we have noted for the server are described in the Roman rubrics.[26] That is a reason to observe them even more diligently than our rules. We are obliged, almost as much as the priest is, to observe the rubrics that are proposed to him.

The closer we come to ordination, the more honored we should feel about serving at the altar; and appearing to blush over it is very inappropriate self-consciousness. It is a bit as if a churchman named to a bishopric, or already a bishop, blushed when saying Mass in private. "Where I am, there also shall my minister be," John, chapter 12. [46]

Seventh Instruction
For Exhortations and Repetitions
Outer regulation

Upon returning from Mass, on days when there are Repetitions of the Exhortation,[27] one promptly goes to one's bedchamber, everyone pulls their chairs together, and each one repeats what he has retained in the same sense that it was proposed, if possible.

---

[26] The rubrics are "the rules laid down for the recitation of the Divine Office, the celebration of the Mass, and the administration of the sacraments," and as "prescriptions for the good order of external worship in the Catholic Church" (*The Catholic Encyclopedia*, "Rubrics").

[27] The Exhortation was a sermon-like presentation urging the members of the Jesuit community to a more faithful living out of the Gospel, the practices of the Church, and the rules of the Society.

suffisance. On se tait au petit coup pour 7 heures, ou plutôt [*read*: plus tôt] si tout étoit répété auparavant, et on tâchera de se rendre les premiers dans la salle pour l'Exhortation.

En entrant dans la salle on fait à genoux une petite prière, et l'on s'asseoit dans le lieu marqué pour chaque chambre et non ailleurs. Le Père arrivant, on se met à genoux pour prier avec luy, et on ne se relève point qu'il ne soit relevé. On [47] ne s'asseoit point et on ne se couvre point qu'il n'ait dit le texte et qu'il ne se soit couvert.

Pendant l'Exhortation, aux noms de *Jésus* et de *Marie* on ne doit point se découvrir à moins que le Père ne se découvre, mais faire simplement une petite inclination de tête. Si quelqu'un s'endormoit, ses voisins tâcheront doucement de le réveiller. Après l'Exhortation, on se joint trois ou quatre ensemble, selon qu'on est averti, et on répète ce qui s'est dit jusqu'aux 3/4. Les jours de Répétition, celuy qui est averti répète ce qu'il a retenu, debout, la tête découverte, et d'une voix assés haute et assés distincte pour être entendu de tout le monde. Il se placera pour cela vers le milieu de la salle s'il s'en trouvoit trop éloigné. Après qu'il aura tout répété, il se mettra à genoux comme par manière de réparation de ce qu'il aura manqué de bien rapporter, et il ne se lèvera point que le Père ne luy fasse signe. Si, dans ce qui s'est dit, il se trouvoit quelque chose que quelqu'un n'eût pas assés bien compris, il pourra le proposer.

Il n'y a pas de temps où l'on doive être plus recueilly, ny plus modeste, qu'à celuy des Conférences. Le respect qu'on doit à la [48] parole de *Dieu*, et qu'on se doit les uns aux autres, le demande. Ainsi on n'égarera pas la vue, on ne mettra ny les genoux ny les pieds l'un sur l'autre, mais on cou[v]rira modestement ses pieds de sa soutane, on ne se tiendra pas dans une posture lâche, on ne se couchera point avec indécence; en un mot, on évitera tout ce qui pourroit causer de la distraction ou de la mauvaise édification.

À la fin de la Répétition, on avertit d'ordinaire des fautes qui se sont commises dans le Noviciat, et dont il faut se corriger. Ceux qui se sentent coupables doivent se mettre à genoux et entendre, dans cette posture humiliante, les avis qu'on a la charité de leur donner. À la fin de tout, avant que de se retirer, on salue la Sainte Vierge par une courte prière.

Direction intérieure

Comme il n'est point d'exercice au Noviciat qui puisse servir plus que les Exhortations et les Conférences à nous former et à nous instruire de nos devoirs, il n'en est point auquel nous devions assister avec plus d'envie d'en profiter. Il faudroit les venir entendre avec la même avidité qu'on [49] va au réfectoire lorsqu'on se sent un appétit extraordinaire; s'y rendre beaucoup plus attentif que ne sont aux explications de philosophie et de théologie ceux qui veulent devenir habiles dans ces sciences, car c'est là proprement notre classe et notre leçon.

Il faut nous imaginer que ce n'est point un homme, mais *Dieu* qui, par un homme, parle et parle à nous en particulier, car la chose est véritable;

One must be careful, in repeating the Exhortation, not to speak too loudly, not to interrupt one another, not to laugh or say a single idle word that is inappropriate to the subject, and not to appear too self-satisfied. One falls silent at the little ring at seven o'clock, or earlier if everything has already been repeated, and one will try to be among the first to enter the community room for the Exhortation.

Upon entering the community room, one says a brief prayer kneeling, and one sits in the place indicated for each bedchamber, and nowhere else. The Father having arrived, one kneels to pray with him, and one does not rise until he has risen. One [47] does not sit down, and one does not cover one's head until he has said the text and has covered his head.

During the Exhortation, at the names of *Jesus* and *Mary* one should not bare one's head unless the Father does so, but simply bow the head slightly. If someone should fall asleep, his neighbors will gently try to wake him. After the Exhortation, three or four join together, as notified, and one repeats what was said until 7:45. On Repetition days, the person who has been notified repeats what he remembers, standing, his head uncovered, and with a voice that is loud enough and distinct enough to be heard by everyone. For this, he will place himself near the middle of the community room, if he happened to be too far away. After he has repeated everything, he will kneel as a sort of reparation for what he failed to recall well, and he will not rise until the Father gives him a sign. If, in what was said, there was something that someone did not understand sufficiently, he can mention it.

There is no time when one should be more recollected or more modest than during the Conferences.[28] The respect one owes to the [48] word of *God*, and that one owes to one another, requires it. Thus one will not let one's eyes wander; one will not cross one's legs or feet, but will modestly cover one's feet with one's soutane; one will not slump into a relaxed posture; one will not recline immodestly. In a word, one will avoid everything that could be distracting or that is unedifying.

At the end of the Repetition, one usually points out faults committed at the Novitiate, and which must be corrected. Those who feel guilty should kneel and, in this humiliating posture, hear the opinions that are given to them out of charity. At the end of everything, before withdrawing, one greets the Blessed Virgin with a brief prayer.

Interior guidance

Since there is no exercise at the Novitiate that can serve better than the Exhortations and the Conferences to shape us and instruct us in our duties, there is none we should attend with a greater desire to profit from it. It is necessary to come and hear them with the same avidity with which one [49] goes to the refectory when one has an exceptional appetite; to be far more attentive there than people who want to become skilled in philosophy and theology are about explanations of those fields of knowledge, for strictly speaking that is our class and our lesson.

---

[28] These Conferences consisted of an academic or informational presentation on the origin, meaning, implementation of some point or points in Christian tradition and life, or on the way of life in the Society itself.

ainsi nous appliquer à nous-mêmes ce qui se dit et non point à d'autres. Il est certain que nous répondrons de tout ce que nous aurons ignoré et de tout ce qui nous aura peu touché, faute de nous appliquer là, comme il faut, à le bien comprendre et à le bien retenir. Les anciens Pères [du Désert] avoient un zèle inconcevable pour les conférences spirituelles, ils y passoient souvent les nuits, comme il se voit dans Cassien. Il arrivoit rarement qu'ils s'y assoupissent, cela étoit regardé comme une faute du premier ordre. L'un d'eux, pour s'être trouvé distrait pendant un de ces entretiens, à regarder des laboureurs qui travailloient à la campagne, se mit une chaîne au [50] col qui luy tenoit le corps courbé et le visage contre terre, sans qu'il pût porter les yeux vers aucun objet étranger; et il soutint pendant plusieurs années une si rigoureuse pénitence.

Pour profiter d'avantage des Exhortations, elles doivent faire le sujet ordinaire de nos entretiens dans les récréations et dans les Colloques. Les gens qui veulent devenir habiles dans certaines professions ne parlent presque jamais d'autres choses avec ceux du même métier. Il faut aussi souvent en tirer la matière de nos Oraisons et de nos Examens; autrement nous ne verrions nos défauts et nos besoins que comme cet homme dont parle saint Jacques,[5] qui voit sa difformité dans un miroir et qui demeure toujours difforme, parce qu'il ne se regarde pour ainsi dire qu'en volant. Enfin, comme c'est de *Dieu* et de sa grâce que viennent toutes sortes de bons sentimens, et de pieuses résolutions, nous devons faire les petites prières qui précèdent et qui suivent les Conférences avec un grand sentiment de notre ignorance et impuissance au bien, [51] et un grand désir d'être aidé de *Dieu*, à ne pas recevoir en vain sa sainte parole. Par la même raison il faut souvent, pendant les Conférences, élever notre cœur vers luy, pour demander l'esprit de sagesse et d'intelligence.

Instruction huitième
Pour le déjeuner
Règlement extérieur

Les jours qu'on a permission de déjeuner, on le fait d'ordinaire après la Conférence ou après la Messe. On lave ses mains avant que d'entrer au réfectoire, on fait une courte prière et un signe de croix, le dos tourné contre la table; puis le visage tourné vers la table, on mange le morceau de pain qu'on trouve vis-à-vis de soy ou l'on en prend soy-même, supposé qu'on n'en ait pas [52] coupé; et s'il n'y en avoit pas assés sur la table, on ne doit point en aller prendre dans le pannier, mais en demander au frère Crédencier. On ne doit boire qu'un coup, on va demander du vin, la tête découverte, au Frère qui le distribue, et on le mêle de beaucoup d'eau.

---

[5] James 1:23–26.

We must imagine to ourselves that it is not a man, but *God* who is speaking through a man, and who is speaking to us privately, for that is true; thus we apply what is said to ourselves, and not to others. It is certain that we will answer for everything we have overlooked, and for everything that has moved us little, for lack of applying ourselves, as we must, to understanding it fully and retaining it well. The ancient Fathers [of the Desert][29] had an inconceivable zeal for spiritual conferences, they often spent the night that way, as can be seen in Cassian. It rarely happened that they fell asleep, which was viewed as a first-class fault. One of them, because he had become distracted during one of these discussions by the sight of plowmen working in the fields, put a chain around his [50] neck to keep his body bent and his face toward the earth, so that he could not train his eyes on any foreign object; and he bore that very rigorous penance for several years.[30]

In order to profit more fully from the Exhortations, they should be the ordinary subject of our discussions during recreation and in the Colloquies. People who want to become skilled in certain professions almost never talk about other things with people of that same craft. It is also necessary to draw frequently from these discussions the subject matter of our Prayers and our Examens; otherwise we would only see our failings and our needs, as did the man about whom Saint James wrote, who saw his deformity in a mirror and who remained deformed because, so to speak, he only looked at himself in passing. Finally, since it is from *God* and his grace that all sorts of good sentiments and pious resolutions come, we should say the brief prayers that precede and follow the Conferences with a strong sentiment of our ignorance and our impotence for good, [51] and a great desire to be helped by *God*, not to receive his holy word in vain. For the same reason it is often necessary, during the Conferences, to raise our heart toward him, to request the spirit of wisdom and intelligence.

Eighth Instruction For breakfast
Outer regulation

The days when one is permitted to eat breakfast, one ordinarily does so after the Conference or after Mass. One washes one's hands before entering the refectory, one says a brief prayer and makes the sign of the cross, with one's back to the table; then, with one's face turned to the table, one eats the piece of bread

---

[29] The Fathers of the Desert, "*anciens pères*," were the hermits and cenobites of the Egyptian desert from about 250 a.d. to 500 a.d.

[30] The penance carried out by the monk Eusebius, as recounted by Theodoret of Cyr, appears to have been a favorite Jesuit example of "daily penance." The story was recounted by Giovanni Battista Scaramelli, S.J., *Direttorio ascetico* (Naples, 1752), translated into English under the title *Directorium asceticum* (Dublin, 1870), 1:351–52. Jesuit spiritual or ascetical writers of the time often drew on the *Apophthegmata Patrum, the Sayings of the Fathers*, for examples or stories of how to practice both penances and virtues.

On ne doit point s'essuier la bouche à la nappe avant que de boire, ou après avoir bu, mais faute de serviette on peut se servir de son mouchoir.

À la fin du déjeuner on ramasse les miettes comme aux autres repas; et l'on fait avant que de se retirer, pour actions de grâces, une courte prière comme on a fait en arrivant. Les jours qu'on va déjeuner seul par une permission particulière, on le doit faire avec les mêmes circonstances que quand tous y sont; c'est-à-dire avec la même modestie, le même silence, la même sobriété, et cela d'autant plus que l'on a [*read*: l'on n'a] que l'œil de *Dieu* pour témoin. [53]

Direction intérieure

On peut en déjeunant s'occuper de plusieurs saintes pensées: *Non in solo pane vivit homo sed in omni verbo quod procedit de ore Dei.*[6] *Cinerem tanquam panem manducabam et potum meum cum fletu miscebam.*[7] *Cibus meus est, ut faciam voluntatem ejus qui misit me.*[8] *Operamini non cibum qui perit, sed qui permanet in vitam æternam . . .*[9]

Combien de pauvres, et de pauvres qui ont été riches, et que [*read*: qui] par leur naissance doivent l'être, et qui ne sçavent où trouver un morceau de pain! Si ce qu'on nous présente est peu de chose, nous n'avons pas au moins d'inquiétude à le chercher. *Notre Seigneur* et ses apôtres n'avoient souvent que du pain d'orge. Quelques fois, allants par la campagne, ils tiroient les grains des épics de bled et les mangeoint tous cruds. Nos premiers Pères ne vivoient souvent que de pain mandié [*read*: mendié], et ramassé du reste des pauvres. [54]

Instruction neuvième
Pour les exercices corporels
Règlement extérieur

Aussitôt que le petit coup qui précède l'exercice corporel est sonné, il faut prendre sa nuptiale, son chapeau et ses souliers, aller ensuite voir au catalogue l'exercice auquel on est marqué. L'exercice corporel est d'ordinaire de balayer les chambres et la maison, cependant on sera prêt à en faire quelqu'autre que ce soit, comme de porter du bois, de travailler aux offices, de nétoyer le jardin, de transporter des pierres et des matériaux, *etc.* Ceux qui sont nommés pour balayer doivent aller prendre le balay qui est destiné pour

---

[6] Matthew 4:4, *Non in solo pane vivit homo, sed in omni verbo, quod precedit* [*sic*] *de ore Dei.*

[7] Psalm 101:10, *Quia cineram tamquam panem manducabam, et potum meum cum fletu miscebam.* The manuscript spells *cineram* and *tanquam* differently from the Lyons Bible published in 1676.

[8] John 4:34, *Dicit eis Jesus: Meus cibus est, ut faciam voluntatem ejus, qui misit me, ut perficiam opus ejus.*

[9] John 6:27, *Operamini non cibum qui perit, sed qui permanet in vitam æternam, quem filius hominis dabit vobis. Hunc enim Pater signavit Deus.*

one finds before one, or one cuts a piece oneself, in the event that none has been [52] cut; and if there was not enough bread on the table, one should not go get it from the basket, but ask Brother Pantryman for some. One should drink only one serving; one goes to ask for wine, bareheaded, from the Brother who is distributing it, and one mixes it with a lot of water. One should not wipe one's mouth on the tablecloth before drinking, or after having drunk; but for lack of a napkin one can use one's handkerchief.

At the end of breakfast one collects the crumbs, as at other meals; and before withdrawing, one says a brief prayer of thanksgiving, as one did upon arriving. On days when one goes to breakfast alone with special permission, one should do it under the same circumstances as when everyone is there: that is to say, with the same modesty, the same silence, the same sobriety, and all the more so because *God*'s eye is one's only witness. [53]

Inner guidance

While eating breakfast one can occupy oneself with several saintly thoughts: "Not in bread alone doth man live, but in every word that proceedeth from the mouth of God. For I did eat ashes like bread, and mingled my drink with weeping. My meat is to do the will of him that sent me. Labour not for the meat which perisheth, but for that which endureth unto life everlasting . . ."

How many poor people there are, and poor people who were once rich, and by their birth should be rich, and who do not know where to find a piece of bread! If what is given to us is not much, at least we do not have to worry about trying to find it. *Our Lord* and his apostles often had only barley bread. Sometimes, going through the countryside, they pulled grains from ears of wheat and ate them raw. Our first Fathers often lived only on bread they had begged or had gathered from the leftovers of the poor. [54]

Ninth Instruction
For bodily exercises
Outer regulation

As soon as the little ring that precedes bodily exercises has sounded, one must take one's duster, hat, and shoes, then go to consult the list to find the task to which one is assigned. Bodily exercises ordinarily consist of sweeping the bedchambers and the house. However, one will be ready to do anything else whatsoever, such as carry wood, work in the service rooms, clean the garden, carry stones and building materials, *etc*. Those who are named to sweep, should go get the broom intended for their task, for each task has its own broom, [55] and should use it as it is, without exchanging it for another one. If it is in such bad condition that it can no longer be used, one will notify our Brother Housekeeper.

leur exercice, car chaque exercice a le sien propre, et s'en [55] servir tel qu'il est, sans changer contre quelqu'autre. S'il étoit si mauvais qu'on ne pût plus s'en servir, on en avertira notre frère Propretaire.

Avant que de commencer, il faut ouvrir les fenêtres du lieu qu'on doit balayer, et les arrêter. On en ouvre plus ou moins selon la saison, et selon qu'on doit craindre de faire plus ou moins de poussière. Ensuite on jette de l'eau avec un arosoir: on doit en jetter aussi plus ou moins selon que le lieu ou la saison se trouvent secs ou humides. Dans le grand froid il n'en faut point jetter du tout, de peur qu'elle ne se glace; mais on peut mouiller un peu le balay, et cela se doit faire dans la barrique destinée à cet usage, et non dans une autre. Il ne faut plonger le balay dans l'eau que jusqu'aux liens; si l'eau est glacée, on peut répandre un peu de neige quand il y en a. [56]

C'est au grand puits du jardin, ou à l'auge de pierre du côté de la Retraitte, qu'il faut aller chercher de l'eau pour mettre dans les arrosoirs. Il est deffendu aux petits de se mêler d'en tirer du puits, les plus forts et les plus grands seront chargés de cette commission quand cela sera nécessaire, et ils auront la charité d'en distribuer aux autres. Il faut s'accoutumer en balayant à ne point trop lever son balay de terre: cela fait moins de poussière, et l'on n'est point exposé à éclabousser les murailles. On ne doit point ny ôter les liens qui se trouvent aux balays de jonc lorsqu'ils sont neufs ou presque neufs, ny s'approcher trop près du nœud du balay pour balayer plus vite: c'est flatter sa paresse et faire contre la pauvreté. Rien n'use plus vite les balays.

On ne doit point faire de difficulté d'employer l'heure [57] entière à son exercice si cela est nécessaire pour le bien faire; mais quelque petit qu'il soit, on doit du moins y employer une demie-heure pleine et entière, fallût-il recommencer deux ou trois fois. Si on ne cherche pas à finir vite, on trouvera aisément de quoy y employer toute la demie-heure, et il n'arrivera guères qu'on s'échauffe de manière à s'incommoder.

Après avoir balayé, il faut reporter le balay, l'arrosoir, le porte-ordure dans le lieu même où on les a pris. Ensuite on vient fermer les fenêtres, si ce n'est que, selon la saison, il vaille mieux les laisser ouvertes.

S'il arrive que pendant qu'on fait son exercice corporel on soit appellé ailleurs, on ira où il faut, mais on reviendra ensuite achever son exercice, ou pour le moins amasser les ordures et remettre chaque chose en bon état, si l'heure de l'exercice étoit finy. [58]

Ceux qui balayent les chambres ou les salles doivent, avant que de refermer les fenêtres, épousseter les meubles, les oratoires, les tables, les bancs, et générallement tout ce qui a pu prendre de la poussière. En faisant son exercice on ne doit pas s'amuser à regarder par les fenêtres ou ailleurs, quelque lieu que ce soit: c'est se divertir au lieu de travailler; mais si on trompe les hommes, on ne trompera pas *Dieu*. Enfin, l'exercice achevé, on quitte son chapeau, ses souliers, et sa nuptiale; et si l'on s'est échauffé, on prend sa robe pendant quelque temps.

Le lendemain qu'on est allé en ville ou en promenade, si on a ses souliers ou son manteau crotté, on doit les nétoyer pendant la seconde demie-heure

Before beginning, one must open the windows of the place to be swept, and block them. One opens them more or less, according to the weather, and according to whether one might fear making more or less dust. Then one sprinkles water with a watering-can: one should sprinkle more or less of it according to whether the place or season is dry or humid. When it is very cold, none should be sprinkled at all, for fear it freeze; but one can moisten the broom a bit, and that should be done in the barrel destined for that purpose, and in no other. The broom should only be plunged into the water as far as the ties. If the water is frozen, one can sprinkle a little snow, when there is some. [56]

It is from the large well in the garden, or from the stone trough over near the Retreat, that one must get the water to fill the watering-cans. It is forbidden for small-sized novices to be involved in drawing water from the well: the strongest and the tallest will be entrusted with that mission when necessary, and they will be so charitable as to distribute some water to the others. When sweeping, one must become accustomed not to lift the broom too far from the floor: that stirs up less dust, and one does not risk spattering the walls. One should neither remove the ties on the reed brooms when they are new or almost new, nor hold the broom too close to the knot in order to sweep faster: doing so would be humoring one's laziness and acting in a way that is contrary to poverty. Nothing wears out brooms faster.

One should not object to using the entire [57] hour for one's task, if that is necessary to do a good job; but however small the task might be, one should spend at least a full and entire half hour at it, even if one has to repeat it two or three times. If one does not try to finish quickly, one will easily find enough to do for the whole half hour, and it will rarely happen that one gets so hot as to feel unwell.

Having finished sweeping, the broom, the watering-can, the trash container must be returned to the same place where one found them. Then one goes to close the windows, unless, depending on the season, it is better to leave them open.

If it should happen that one is called elsewhere while doing one's bodily exercise, one will go where needed; but one will then return to complete one's task, or at least to collect the trash and put everything back in good order, if the exercise period has ended. [58]

Those who sweep the bedchambers or the community rooms should, before closing the windows, dust the furniture, prayer desks, tables, benches, and generally everything that may have gotten dusty. While carrying out one's task, one should not amuse oneself by looking out the windows or elsewhere, wherever one is: that is having fun instead of working, but if one fools men, one does not fool *God*. Lastly, having completed the task, one removes one's hat, shoes, and duster; and if one is overheated, one dons one's robe for awhile.

The day after one has gone about the city or on a walk, if one's shoes or mantle are covered with mud, one should clean them during the second half hour of the [bodily] exercise, unless they are not yet dry enough. The place to clean

de l'exercice, si ce n'est qu'ils ne fussent pas encore assés secs. Le lieu pour les nétoyer est la Propreté. On prend garde d'y bien garder le silence, de n'y pas rire, ny de faire aucune autre enfance, si on s'y trouve plusieurs ensemble. Quand on ne fait point d'exercice corporel, soit qu'on en ait été dispensé [59] par le révérend père Recteur, soit pour quelqu'autre raison, on ne doit pas manquer d'en avertir à temps notre frère Propretaire.

Direction intérieure

La fin naturelle des exercices corporels est de mettre un peu de variété dans les actions de la journée, et de donner au corps quelque mouvement, ce qui sert beaucoup à la santé, et comme dit la règle, d'empêcher que l'esprit ne soit longtemps de suite appliqué et bandé à des exercices sérieux; mais la fin surnaturelle est bien plus noble et plus sublime, et c'est celle que nous devons principalement nous proposer.

Les exercices corporels doivent se faire pour exécuter contre nous-mêmes la sentence où *Dieu* a condamné l'homme pécheur au travail: *In sudore vultûs tui vesceris pane.*[10] Saint Paul, tout l'apôtre qu'il étoit, [60] faisoit le métier de tapissier, et il en trouvoit bien le temps. Les anciens habitans du désert ne vivoient que du travail de leurs mains, et il leur restoit encore de ce qu'ils gagnoient de quoy faire de grandes aumônes. Nos premiers Pères demeuroient presque toujours à l'hôpital; et avant que d'aller à leurs fonctions apostoliques, ils faisoient les lits et balayoient les salles des pauvres. Ceux qui assistèrent au Concile de Trente ne s'en crurent point dispensés.

Un autre motif plus parfait encore est d'honorer et d'imiter les exercices de la vie caché de *Notre Seigneur Jésus Christ* pendant les trente ans qu'il demeura à Nazareth. Les anges le regardoient avec extase et son Père le voyoit du Ciel avec complaisance, occupé qu'il étoit des plus menus soins d'un pauvre ménage. Par là il opéroit notre salut, et glorifioit son Père ny plus ny moins que quand il préchoit ou qu'il mouroit [61] en croix. L'esprit et le cœur remplis de ces grandes vues, le tems ne nous paroîtra jamais trop long; nous y trouverons de la grandeur et de la consolation; nous la ferons d'une manière digne de *Dieu* et de *Jésus Christ,* à qui nous les rapporterons. Qu'on nous voye ou qu'on ne nous voie pas, ce sera toujours la même application. Sans ces vues surnaturelles, nous n'aurions aucun mérite d'une action si basse et pénible d'elle-même; et n'agissant que par nécessité, nous nous confondrions avec les esclaves et les plus viles mercénaires. Seroit-il rien de plus digne de compassion? Quand nous avons quelque grâce à obtenir de *Dieu* pour nous ou pour d'autres, nous pouvons nous offrir le travail de nos exercices à cette intention, *Vide humilitatem meam et laborem meum et dimitte universa delicta mea. Respice in me et miserere mei quia egenus, et pauper sum ego.*[11] [62]

---

[10] Genesis 3:19, *In sudore vultus tui vesceris pane, donec revertaris in terram de qua sumptus es: quia pulvis es, et in pulverem reverteris.*

[11] Psalm 24:18–19, *Vide humilitatem meam, et laborem meum: et dimitte universa dilecta mea.* Psalm 85:16, *Respice in me, et miserere mei, da imperium tuum puero tuo: et salvum fac filium ancillæ tuæ. Psalm 108:22, Quia egenus et pauper ego sum: et cor meum, conturbatum est intra me.*

them is the Cleanliness Room. One is careful to remain silent there, not to laugh there or do any childish thing, if one finds several people together there. When one does not participate in bodily exercise, having been dispensed from it [59] by Reverend Father Rector, or for any other reason, one should not fail to notify our Brother Housekeeper in time.

Inner guidance

The natural goal of bodily exercises is to give a bit of variety to the day's activities, and to give the body a chance to move, which is very good for one's health, and as the rule says, to prevent the spirit from being diligent and straining over a succession of serious exercises for too long; but the supernatural goal is far more noble and more sublime, and that is what we should principally set before ourselves.

Bodily exercises should be done to carry out, against ourselves, the sentence by which *God* condemned sinful man to labor: "In the sweat of thy face shalt thou eat bread." Although he was an apostle, Saint Paul [60] was a tent-maker, and he found sufficient time for it. The ancient inhabitants of the desert lived only from the labor of their hands, and enough of their earnings remained for them to give large alms. Our first Fathers spent most of their time at the hospital, and before going about their apostolic functions, they made the beds and swept the wards of the poor. Those who attended the Council of Trent did not think they were dispensed from these tasks.

Another motive, more perfect yet, is to honor and imitate the [bodily] exercises of the hidden life of *Our Lord Jesus Christ* during the thirty years he lived in Nazareth. The angels watched him in ecstasy, and his Father watched him from Heaven with pleasure, occupied as he was with the most menial tasks of a poor household. By doing this, he brought about our salvation and glorified his Father neither more nor less than when he was preaching or when he was dying [61] on the cross. If our spirit and heart are filled with these grand outlooks, the time will never seem too long to us: we will find grandeur and consolation, we will do it in a manner worthy of *God* and of *Jesus Christ*, to whom we will offer them. Whether we are watched or whether we are not watched, our application will always be the same. Without these supernatural outlooks, we would gain no merit from an action that is so base and laborious in itself; and acting only from necessity, we would resemble slaves and the vilest mercenaries. Would there be anything more worthy of compassion? When we have some grace to obtain from *God* for ourselves or for others, we can offer ourselves the labor of our [bodily] exercises to this end: "See my abjection and my labour; and forgive me all my sins. O look upon me, and have mercy on me, for I am poor and needy." [62]

Instruction dixième
Pour les lectures spirituelles
Règlement extérieur

Les lectures spirituelles se doivent faire assis sur sa chaise, vis-à-vis son oratoire, si ce n'est que le défaut de lumière obligeât quelqu'un à s'approcher de la fenêtre. L'hyver quand le jour manque, on les fait assis autour du chandelier au milieu de la chambre, et c'est alors qu'il faut s'observer plus que jamais, pour ne point rire ny faire rien qui puisse distraire ou mal édifier les autres. La lecture du matin se fait toujours dans Rodrigués ou dans quelqu'autre livre aussi propre à se bien instruire des devoirs de la vie religieuse qu'aura marqué le révérend père Recteur. La lecture [63] du soir se fait ordinairement dans un livre d'histoire tels que sont les vies de nos Pères ou des relations édifiantes. Dans les temps indifférents on peut lire ou quelqu'un des livres de la chambre, ou quelqu'autre que le révérend père Recteur aura donné ou permis.

On ne doit jamais lire, le matin, le livre du soir, ny celuy des temps indifférens; et quelque lecture que l'on fasse, il faut tâcher de ne point s'endormir. On peut lire quelque temps debout pour combattre l'assoupissement et le sommeil.

Il faut faire ses lectures spirituelles avec la même attention qu'on liroit des livres de philosophie ou de théologie, car il s'agit d'étudier et de bien retenir ce qui doit servir à nous conduire, et à bien conduire les autres dans les voyes du salut tout le temps de notre vie.

Il ne faut point avoir d'empressement pour lire beaucoup à la fois. On lit toujours assés quand on s'imprime dans l'esprit ce qu'on lit, de manière à ne l'oublier jamais. [64]

Il ne serait pas même hors de propos de relire plus d'une fois les endroits dont on se sent le plus édifié et le plus touché; mais il n'est pas permis de faire aucune collection par écrit sur ses lectures sans une permission particulière. On doit mortifier la curiosité qui porte à lire dans un livre certain endroits avant les autres: il faut attendre que chaque chose se présente à son rang.

Si on trouvoit dans un livre quelque endroit dont l'imagination fût blessée, il faut avoir la fidélité ou de le passer ou, si l'on a été surpris, de ne le pas lire une seconde fois. Une faute du premier ordre au Noviciat seroit de lire aucun livre, quel qu'il fût, sans permission, soit qu'on l'eût trouvé ou qu'on l'eût reçu de quelqu'autre du dedans ou du dehors. Plusieurs ont mérité par là qu'on les renvoyât. Il est vray qu'une pareille liberté conduit presque toujours à d'autres plus grands désordres.

Tenth Instruction
For spiritual reading
Outer regulation

Spiritual reading should be done sitting in one's chair, opposite one's prayer desk, unless the lack of light obliges someone to approach the window. In winter, when daylight is lacking, one does the readings around the candlestick in the middle of the bedchamber, and it is then that it is necessary to watch oneself more than ever, in order not to laugh or do anything that might distract or be unedifying to the others. The morning reading is always in Rodríguez[31] or in some other book equally suitable for learning the duties of the religious life that Reverend Father Rector may have indicated. The afternoon reading [63] is ordinarily in a history book such as the lives of our Fathers or edifying narratives. During times when there is no assignment, one can either read one of the books in the bedchamber, or some other book that Reverend Father Rector has given or permitted.

One should never read, in the morning, the book for the afternoon or the book for unassigned times; and whatever one reads, it is necessary to try not to fall asleep. One can read awhile standing, to combat drowsiness and sleep.

It is necessary to do one's spiritual reading with the same attention one would give to books on philosophy or theology, for it is a question of studying and adequately retaining what should serve to guide us, and to help us guide others well, in the ways of salvation throughout our lives.

There must be no eagerness to read a lot at a time. One is always reading enough when one impresses on one's spirit what one is reading, so as never to forget it. [64]

It would not even be inappropriate to reread more than once the passages where one feels the most edified and the most touched; but it is not permitted to make a written collection of what one has read, without specific permission. One should mortify the curiosity that prompts reading certain parts of a book before the others: it is necessary to wait until each thing is presented in its place.

If one has found in a book some passage that wounded the imagination, it is necessary to have the trustworthiness either to skip over it or, if one has been caught unawares, not to read it a second time. At the Novitiate a very serious fault would be to read any book whatsoever without permission, irrespective of whether one found it or whether one received it from someone else, inside or outside. This has earned dismissal for several novices. It is true that such liberty almost always leads to other greater disorders.

---

[31] Alphonsus Rodríguez, a Spanish-born Jesuit (1538–1616), was the author of *Exercicio de Perfeción y virtudes Christianas*, published in 1609. This very popular book of practical instructions about the virtues that make up Christian life was translated from the Spanish into more than 20 languages and was in widespread use in religious communities all the way up to Vatican II. It was put into English several times under the title *Practice of Perfection and Christian Virtues*; and it was translated into French by Paul Duez, in 1621, the first of a succession of translations into French.

Quand nous prions, nous parlons à *Dieu*; quand nous lisons, c'est *Dieu* qui nous parle. On ne peut guères dire lequel mérite un plus grand respect.

Le fruit de nos lectures dépend principalement de les faire dans cet esprit, d'y écouter *Dieu* et de n'y écouter que *Dieu*. Alors, quel que soit le livre, françois ou latin, en beau ou en vieux langage; et quand même par-cy, par-là, il s'y trouveroit quelque simplicité, nous en retirerons toujours du profit et de l'édification. C'est une délicatesse tout à fait préjudiciable de rejetter un livre, ou de ne le parcourir qu'avec nonchalance, parce qu'on s'y trouve arrêté quelque part. Un portrait ne laisse pas d'être un beau portrait, quoy qu'il soit habillé à l'antique; et un arbre produit souvent d'excellent fruits, quoy qu'il soit vieux, et que l'écorce en soit grossière et raboteuse. Il seroit à souhaiter peut-être qu'on voulût retoucher de certains livres et les renouveller un peu; mais ce seroit une grande perte [66] de ne les point lire d'icy là, et peut-être seroit-il à craindre que dans des éditions plus polies, ils ne perdissent beaucoup de leur onction et de leur noble simplicité. Il vaut donc mieux changer de goût: le bon fera oublier le mauvais. Une des choses à quoy l'on connoît le mieux, dans un novice, le progès ou qu'il a fait ou qu'il veut faire, c'est quand il devient indifférent au regard de toute sorte de livres.

Par cette application à toute sorte de lecture, on juge encore, par la suite de la vie, qu'on s'accoutumera à ne lire que ce qu'il faut, et non pas ce qui feroit le plus de plaisir. Quiconque aujourd'huy quitte Rodrigués pour lire une relation curieuse, quittera un jour son grec et son latin, sa théologie peut-être, et ses cas de conscience, pour étudier du françois et des romans.

Les livres d'instructions et d'histoire peuvent se lire plus vite, mais toujours pourtant avec réflexion. [67] Les livres dont le stile est plus serré et plus sententieux doivent se lire pendant un demi d'heure; leur lecture est une manière de petite Méditation.

Ce qu'il faut retenir dans les histoires, sont des traits de vertus héroïques, de certaines paroles qui renferment un grand sens, des préceptes qui, comme dans un seul principe, contiennent une grande multitude de conclusions pratiques; et enfin, comme c'est de la grâce que vient principalement le fruit que nous attendons de nos lectures, il les faut interrompre par de courtes mais ferventes élévations vers *Dieu*. *Loquere Domine quia audit servus tuus. Tu intus es Doctor et illuminator cordium.*[12] [68]

Instruction onzième
Pour apprendre par cœur

---

[12] The first part of the quotation is 1 Samuel (1 Kings) 3:9, *Vade, et dormi: et si deinceps vocaverit te, dices: Loquere Domine, quia audit servus tuus.* A specific source for the remainder of the Latin text was not located

When we pray, we speak to *God*; when we read, it is *God* who speaks to us. One can scarcely say which deserves a greater respect.

The fruit of our reading depends principally upon doing it in that spirit, listening to *God* and listening only to *God*. Then, whatever the book, French or Latin, in a fine style or in outdated parlance, and even if there should happen to be some simple-mindedness here and there, we will always find something profitable and edifying. It is a totally prejudicial delicacy to reject a book, or to go through it nonchalantly, because one has encountered an obstacle somewhere in it. A portrait is still a good portrait, even if the person is dressed in old-fashioned clothes; and a tree often produces excellent fruit, even if it is old and its bark is coarse and rough. It would perhaps be desirable to want to improve upon certain books and make them a bit more up-to-date; but it would be a great loss [66] not to read them until that has been done; and perhaps there is reason to fear that, in more polished editions, books lose a great deal of their unction and their noble simplicity. It is therefore better to change one's taste; the good shall cause the bad to be forgotten. One of the things by which one best recognizes, in a novice, the progress he has made or that he wants to make, is when he becomes indifferent to what all sorts of books look like.

By this application to all sorts of reading, one also judges how, in the course of one's life, one becomes accustomed to reading only what is necessary, not to what would give the most pleasure. Whoever, today, puts down Rodríguez in order to read an intriguing narrative, will one day abandon his Greek and his Latin, his theology perhaps, and his cases of conscience, in order to study French and novels.

Books of instructions and history books can be read more quickly, but nonetheless always reflectively. [67] Books whose style is more dense and more sententious should be read for a half hour; reading them is a sort of little Meditation.

What must be retained from history books are the passages about heroic virtues; certain words that convey a great meaning; precepts that, as in a single principle, contain a great multitude of practical conclusions; and finally, since the fruit we expect of our reading chiefly comes from grace, it is necessary to interrupt our reading by brief but fervent elevations toward GOD. "Speak, Lord, for thy servant heareth. Thou art inside, the teacher and illuminator of the hearts." [68]

Eleventh Instruction
For learning by heart

Règlement extérieur

Pour pouvoir employer le quart [d']heure tout entier à apprendre, on se rend aux salles ou jardin, selon le temps qu'il fait, aussitôt qu'on entend sonner le petit coup devant l'heure.

On apprend par cœur en se promenant lentement. On ne doit pas être ensemble plus de deux ou trois dans les grandes allées du jardin, ny plus d'un dans les contre-allées. On ne doit point s'asseoir ny se retirer à Saint Ignace ou à Saint Xavier, ou sous le berceau ou sous la galerie d'ardoise, sans permission et à moins qu'on ne soit incommodé. [69]

Si l'on arrive tard au jardin ou dans la salle où l'on va apprendre, on ne doit pas manquer de s'excuser au frère Admoniteur, ou en son absence à l'ancien du Bienheureux Goto, et cela se doit pratiquer généralement toutes les fois qu'on se rend tard à quelque exercice où se trouvent tous les novices; et personne n'en doit sortir qu'il n'en demande de la permission au frère Admoniteur ou à l'ancien du Bienheureux Goto, et qu'il ne lui dise pourquoy il sort.

On apprend par cœur du livre qui aura été marqué par le révérend père Recteur. On sera obligé d'apprendre la valeur de huit ou dix vers [h]examètres; mais cette obligation ne dispense nullement ceux qui ont plus de mémoire, après avoir appris ce qui est ordonné, d'apprendre encore quelque chose, et c'est l'intention des supérieurs.

À 1 heure 1/2 la cloche sonne, pour repasser ce que l'on a appris à 10 heures, et un *Miserere*; après, on teinte [*read*: tinte] pour aller réciter dans la salle de Notre Seigneur. On le récite à celuy qui est marqué. La conscience est chargée d'avertir le [70] révérend père Recteur si quelqu'un venoit à négliger cet exercice si utile et si recommandé. On conseille à tous de repasser le samedy, dans quelqu'un des tems indifférens, ce qu'ils ont apris pendant toute la semaine, pour s'affermir de plus en plus la mémoire.

Direction intérieure

Une des fins de la Compagnie étant de se rendre utile au prochain par l'étude des sciences, et l'étude des sciences dépendant infiniement de la mémoire, on n'a guères de zèle pour le prochain si l'on ne s'affectionne à la cultiver de tout son pouvoir. *Tantùm scimus, quantùm memoriâ retinemus.*[13] C'est pour cela que la Compagnie, qui nous interdit au Noviciat toute sorte d'études particulières, a toujours excepté le temps qui seroit nécessaire à apprendre quelque chose par cœur. Comme la mémoire se fortifie autant à apprendre des [71] choses saintes que des choses profanes, on a préféré avec raison celles-là à celles-cy dans le lieu où nous sommes. Ainsy il n'y a point à craindre de perdre le recueillement ny

---

[13] This maxim is an abbreviated version of Cicero, *Academica*, 2, 22, [*Memoria*] *non modo philosophiam, sed omnem vitæ usum omnesque artes una maxime continet,* that is: Memory contains not only philosophy, but in and by itself the whole experience of life and all the arts.

Outer regulation

In order to employ the entire quarter hour for learning, one goes to the community rooms or to the garden, according to the weather, as soon as one hears the little ring before the hour.

One learns by heart while walking slowly. No more than two or three should be together in the principal paths of the garden, and no more than one in the side paths. One should not sit down or withdraw to Saint Ignatius or Saint Xavier,[32] nor under the arbor or the slated gallery, without permission and unless one is not well. [69]

If one arrives late in the garden or in the community room where one is going to learn, one should not fail to apologize to Brother Admonitor or, in his absence, to the senior of Blessed Goto,[33] and in general this should be done whenever one is late for an exercise where all the novices are present; and no one should leave without begging permission of Brother Admonitor or the senior of Blessed Goto, and without telling him why one is leaving.

One learns by heart from the book selected by Reverend Father Rector. One is obliged to learn what amounts to eight or ten hexameter lines; but this obligation does not dispense those who memorize more easily from learning something more, after they have learned the assignment, and that is the superiors' intention.

At 1:30 the bell rings for the review of what one learned at ten o'clock, and for a *Miserere*. After that, the bell is rung, to go recite in the Hall of Our Lord. One recites it to the person who has been designated. One's conscience bears the burden of notifying [70] Reverend Father Rector if someone has neglected this exercise that is so useful and so recommended. Everyone is advised to review on Saturday, during one of the times with no specific assignment, what they have learned during the week, in order to strengthen the memory more and more.

Inner guidance

Since one of the goals of the Society is to make oneself useful to one's neighbor by studying the scholarly disciplines; and since studying these disciplines depends infinitely on memory, one scarcely shows zeal for one's neighbor if one does not become fond of cultivating one's memory with all one's might. "We know as much as we retain in our memory." This is why the Society, which at the Novitiate forbids us every sort of private study, has always made an exception for the time needed to learn something by heart. Since the memory is strengthened as much by learning [71] sacred things as profane things, the former have rightly been preferred over the latter in the place where we are. Thus there is no reason to fear

---

[32] These seem to be the names given to the two arcaded buildings of the Retreat.

[33] A bedchamber named for John Soan de Goto, who was crucified with twenty-five other Catholics during the persecution of Christians. Like the other "martyrs of Japan," Goto was beatified in 1627 and canonized in 1862.

l'esprit de dévotion. Il sert même pour l'Oraison et pour s'occuper de *Dieu* pendant le jour, d'avoir dans la tête les plus beaux endroits de l'Écriture, surtout du Nouveau Testament. Ce sont d'assés grandes raisons pour se bien appliquer à cet exercice, et le faisant par ces vues saintes et religieuses de le rendre grandement méritoire.

Instruction douzième
Pour les visites du Saint Sacrement
Règlement extérieur

Outre les deux fois qu'on descend chaque jour à [72] l'église pour entendre la Messe et pour reciter, à 4 heures d'après-midi, les Litanies de la Sainte Vierge, on va encore au jubé visiter le Saint Sacrement régulièrement, cinq fois le jour: le matin après qu'on est levé, à 10 heures 1/4 après qu'on a appris par cœur, sur le midy après les Litanies des saints, après l'Oraison du soir, avant le Chapelet, et à la fin de la journée après les Litanies de la Sainte Vierge que recite toute la Communauté. On doit faire ces visites aussi longues que le peut permettre l'exercice qui doit suivre immédiatement.

On ne doit point se mettre à genoux sur les marchepieds, d'où l'on puisse voir ce qui se passe dans l'église, mais à terre. Outre que cette posture est plus respectueuse en la présence de *Dieu* si humilié dans son Sacrement, on n'est point exposé à avoir beaucoup de distractions causées par ce qui est et se passe en bas. Le même respect demande aussi qu'on ne s'appuie [73] pas. En allant au Saint Sacrement et en revenant, on doit garder un profond silence et une parfaite modestie.

Direction intérieure

Quel honneur et quelle grâce d'avoir ainsi *Jésus Christ* dans nos Maisons, et de pouvoir aller lui rendre visite dans une espèce de déshabillé! À quel prix devions-nous l'acheter, cette grâce, si nous ne l'avions pas; et si quelque pape, quelque prélat vouloit nous la disputer, que ne donnerions-nous pas, et combien de visites à l'église promettrions-nous chaque jour, pour nous la conserver?

Dans les païs hérétiques on va chercher l'église à plusieurs lieues de chés soy. Les personnes dévotes quittent leurs maisons pour venir icy faire leurs prières. Avec tant de commodités qu'ils n'ont pas, pourrions-nous ne pas remplir un devoir si juste, ou ne nous en acquiterions-nous [74] qu'avec nonchalance? Les saints sçavoient bien mieux estimer ce bienfait. Saint François de Borgia passoit tous les tems libres devant le Saint Sacrement. C'est luy qui ordonna que dans toutes nos Maisons il y eût des tribunes où l'on pût commodément l'adorer. Saint François Xavier restoit ordinairement la nuit dans l'église, et le peu de repos qu'il étoit obligé de prendre après ses longues oraisons, c'étoit

the loss of recollection or of the spirit of devotion. It even serves for Prayer and for busying oneself with *God* during the day, to have in one's head the most beautiful passages of the Scriptures, especially the New Testament. These are sufficiently great reasons for carefully applying oneself to this exercise and, by doing it from these holy and religious viewpoints, make it greatly meritorious.

Twelfth Instruction
For visiting the Blessed Sacrament
Outer regulation

In addition to the two times when one goes down to the church each day, [72] to hear Mass and to recite the Litanies of the Blessed Virgin at four o'clock in the afternoon, one also goes to the loft to visit the Blessed Sacrament regularly, five times a day: in the morning after rising, at 10:15 after memorization, at noon after the Litanies of the saints, after afternoon Prayer, before the Rosary, and at the end of the day after the Litanies of the Blessed Virgin that are recited by the entire Community. These visits should be as long as permitted by the exercise that is supposed to follow immediately.

One should not kneel on the kneelers, from where one can see what is going on in the church, but on the floor. Beside the fact that this posture is more respectful in the presence of *God*, so humiliated in his Sacrifice, one is not exposed to a lot of distractions caused by what is below, and what is going on below. The same respect also demands that one not lean. [73] While going to the Blessed Sacrament and returning, one should observe a profound silence and perfect modesty.

Inner guidance

What an honor, and what a grace, to have *Jesus Christ* in our Houses in this way, and to be able to pay him a visit in, so to speak, our house clothes! For what sum would we purchase this grace, if we did not have it? And if some pope, some prelate wanted to contend with us for it, what would we not give, and how many visits would we promise to pay to the church each day, in order to keep it?

In heretic countries, people go to churches that are several leagues from home. Devout people leave their houses to come here to pray. With so many conveniences that they do not have, could we not fulfill a duty so just, or would we only acquit ourselves of that duty [74] nonchalantly? The saints knew far better how to esteem this boon. Saint Francis Borgia[34] passed all his free time before

---

[34] Spanish-born Francis Borgia (1510–1572), Duke of Gandia, became a Jesuit (secretly) in 1546 and was elected third superior general in 1565. He was canonized in 1671. The *Instructions* were therefore written after that date.

sur le marchepied même de l'autel qu'il le prenoit. Nos premiers Pères étoient indifférens dans le choix de leurs chambres: cependant un dessous degré était brigué, pourvu qu'il fût plus dans le voisinage de l'église.

Le Père Dupont [de La Puente] demeura, jusqu'à l'extrême vieillesse, dans une infirmerie très haute. Il compta pour rien la peine d'en descendre et d'y monter, par la seule raison qu'entre ce lieu et l'église où reposoit *Notre Seigneur*, il n'y avoit qu'un petit mur de séparation.

Pour faire utilement les visites du Saint Sacrement, il [75] faut se recueillir d'abord le plus qu'il se peut, entrer en esprit dans le tabernacle, et s'y enfermer avec *Jésus Christ*; et là, seul avec luy, après l'avoir adoré, y traiter des importantes affaires qui nous amènent. Si c'est à *Jésus Christ* même que nous parlons, le supplier par l'état où il se trouve là de nous accorder nos requêtes: si c'est à *Dieu* que nous nous adressons, prier *Jésus Christ* de parler avec nous, ou plutôt de parler en notre place, et que nous souscrirons à tout ce qu'il dira, à tout ce qu'il demandera, et à tout ce qu'il promettra; qu'il dise, et que nous n'aions qu'à répondre: *Amen, finit.*

Nos visites doivent être proportionnées à l'heure du jour, au temps de l'année, et à la situation présente où nous nous trouvons.

À l'heure du jour: le matin, remercier *Notre Seigneur* de nous avoir conservé[s] la nuit, et lui demander la grâce d'employer saintement la journée. À 10 heures 1/4, offrir les résolutions qu'on a faites dans ses lectures, et en former pour le repos et la récréation qui approchent. [76] Après la récréation, se mettre en ferveur: si on se sent un peu dérangé, demander la victoire de la pesanteur et de la paresse dont on se trouve saisi en ce temps-là: *Incursu, et dæmonio meridiano.*[14] Après l'Oraison du soir, renouveller les bons sentimens qu'on y a eus, et s'y fortifier auprès de *Notre Seigneur*. Après 8 heures, demander une sainte nuit et une mort heureuse: *finem perfectum.*

On doit encore proportionner ses visites au temps de l'année. Pendant l'Avent, par exemple, adorer le Verbe incarné, et renouvellement [*read*: renouveller] dans l'Eucharistie les humiliations de sa demeure obscure dans le sein de la glorieuse Vierge. Après Noël, comme les roys et les pasteurs, le visiter. De là jusqu'au Carême, honorer les états obscurs, les travaux de sa Sainte Enfance. Pendant le Carême, luy tenir compagnie au désert. Vers la Passion, parcourir les endroits où il souffroit tant d'approches et de tourmans: l'Eucharistie est une représentation de sa mort. *Recolitur memoria passionis ejus.*[15] Après Pâques, aller visiter [77] son sépulchre comme l'image de cette solitude intérieure et extérieure de ce tombeau dont nous sortirons un jour glorieux avec luy. *Mortui estis, et vita vestra abscondita est cum Christo in Deo. Cum Christus apparuerit, vita vestra; tunc et vos similes ei eritis in gloria.*[16] Le reste de l'année,

---

[14] Psalm 90:6, *A sagitta volante in die, à negotio perambulante in tenebris: ab incursu, et dæmonio meridiano.*

[15] This is a line from *O Sacrum convivium.*

[16] Colossians 3:3–4, *Mortui enim estis, et vita vestra est abscondita cum Christo in Deo. Cum Christus apparuerit, vita vestra; tunc et vos apparebitis cum ipso in gloria.* A brief modification inserted into the second verse, makes a considerable difference: the Biblical text, which means "You too will appear with him in glory, becomes "You too will be like him in glory."

the Blessed Sacrament. It is he who ordered that, in all our Houses, there should be elevated galleries from which one can conveniently adore it. Saint Francis Xavier usually remained in the church at night, and the scant rest he was obliged to take after his long prayers took place on the very step of the altar. Our first Fathers were indifferent about choosing their chambers: nonetheless there would be maneuvering for one of low prestige, as long as it was near the church.

Until an advanced age Father de La Puente[35] dwelled in an infirmary on an upper floor. He counted for nothing the pain of going up and down stairs, for the sole reason that there was only a little separation wall between that spot and the church where *Our Lord* reposed.

To pay visits to the Blessed Sacrament usefully, it [75] is first necessary to be as recollected as possible, to enter the tabernacle in spirit, and to shut oneself up there with *Jesus Christ*; and there, alone with him, after having adored him, to handle the important affairs that bring us there. If it is to *Jesus Christ* himself that we are talking, to beg him, by the state in which he finds himself there, to grant our requests; if it is *God* whom we are addressing, to beg *Jesus Christ* to speak with us, or rather to speak in our place, and that we will subscribe to everything he says, to everything he asks, and to everything he promises; let him speak, and we have only to answer: "Amen, he is dead."[36]

Our visits should be in accord with the time of day, the season of the year, and the current situation in which we find ourselves.

As for the time of day: in the morning, thank *Our Lord* for having preserved us during the night, and ask him for the grace to employ the day in a saintly way. At 10:15, offer the resolutions one has made while reading, and make some for the rest and recreation that approach. [76] After recreation, become fervent: if one feels a little unsettled, request victory over the heaviness and sloth in whose grip one is at this time: "Invasion, and the noonday devil." After afternoon Prayer, renew the good feelings one has had, and strengthen oneself while close to *Our Lord*. After eight o'clock, ask for a blessed night and a happy death: "a perfect ending."

One should also regulate one's visits according to the season of the year. During Advent, for example, adore the Incarnate Word, and in the Eucharist renew the humiliations of his dark residence in the womb of the Glorious Virgin. After Christmas, visit him, like the kings and the shepherds. From then until Lent, honor the lowly conditions, the labors of his Holy Infancy. During Lent, keep him company in the desert. As the Passion approaches, run through the places where he suffered so many aggressions and torments: the Eucharist is a representation of his death, "The memorial of his passion is renewed." After Easter, go visit [77] his tomb, as the image of the inner and outer solitude of

---

[35] The Venerable Luis de La Puente (1554–1622), also known as "Dupont" or "De Ponte," was the author of a highly esteemed book of meditations. He also wrote a "spiritual guide" about the active and contemplative lives and their various practices.

[36] The Latin in the manuscript, *Amen, finit*, must be translated literally as "he is dead." In short, the novice who once lived in the world is now dead to that world.

quand il n'y a point de mystère particulier, le regarder au Saint Sacrement comme il est au Ciel, priant sans cesse son Père; et, comme dit saint Paul, l'interrompre sans cesse sur nos divers besoins: *Semper vivens ad interpellandum pro nobis*[17]; ou bien comme Verbe incarné environné des milices célestes qui se couvrent de leurs ailes par respect, et qui chantent: 'Saint, Saint, Saint, *Cum quibus et nostras voces, ut admitti jubeas deprecamur, etc.*'[18] Enfin, notre situation présente nous apprendra comme nos visites doivent se faire.

Tantôt, comme Magdelaine, nous irons pleurer [78] nos péchés dont nous aurons été frappés et effrayés, et nous tâcherons d'aimer assés pour entendre: *Remittuntur tibi peccata, vade in pace.*[19] Tantôt comme le lépreux, le paralitique, l'aveugle de l'Évangile, fatigués de nos maux divers, nous en irons demander la guérison. *Domine ut videam [sic], si vis potes me mundare. Jesu fili David misere mei. Anima mea valde vexatur à dæmonio, descende priùs quam moriatur.*[20] Un jour nous irons luy demander conseil dans nos doubtes. *Quid faciendo vitam æternam possidebo? Quod est magnum mandatum in Lege? Magister verax es, et viam Dei in veritate doces, dic nobis licet hoc facere, an non?*[21] Une autre fois nous viendrons nous consoler dans nos ennuis et dans nos tentations: *Si fieri potest transeat à me calix iste. Deficit in dolore vita mea. Infixus sum in limo profundi, et non est substantia.*[22] Il envoiera l'ange consolateur, ou bien nous l'entendrons [79] nous dire lui-même: *Noli flere: Ego sum, noli timere. Confide, ego vici mundum.*[23] Enfin, en quelqu'état que nous nous trouvions, ne le point quitter que nous ne soyons remplis du désir d'être à luy, et de confiance en sa bonté: *Inveniet enim [sic] nec dimittam te donec benedixeris mihi.*[24]

---

[17] Hebrews 7:25, *Unde et salvare in perpetuum potest accedentes per semetipsum ad Deum: semper vivens ad interpellandum pro nobis.*

[18] From the Ambrosian mass: *Cum quibus et nostras voces, ut admitti jubeas deprecamur.*

[19] Luke 7:48 and 50, *Remittuntur tibi peccata.... Fides tua te salvum fecit: Vade in pace.*

[20] Luke 18:41, *Dicem: Quid tibi vis faciam? At ille dixit: Domine ut videaum.* Luke 5:12, *Domine, si vis poter me mundare.* Luke 18:38, *Jesu fili David misere mei.* Psalm 6:4, *Et anima mea turbata est valde.* Matthew 15:22, *Miserere mei Domine fili David filia mea male à dæmonio vexatur.* John 4:49, *Descende prius quam moriatur filius meus.* This pieced-together quotation, like the quotations in the next few notes, demonstrates how the author of the *Instructions* fuses scriptural passages into a sentence that reinforces the point he is making.

[21] Luke 10:25, *Magister, quid faciendo vitam æternam possidebo?* Matthew 22:36, *Magister, quod est mandatum magnum in Lege?* Matthew 22:16–17, *Magister, scimus quia verax es, et viam Dei in veritate doces, et non est tibi cura de aliquo: non enim respicis personam hominum: Dic ergo nobis quid tibi videtur, licet censum dare Cæsari, an non?*

[22] Matthew 26:39, *Pater mi, si possibile est, transeat à me calix iste.* Psalm 30:11, *Quoniam deficit in dolore vita mea.* Psalm 68:3, *Infixus sum in limo profundi: et non est substantia.*

[23] Tobias 5:26, *Dixitque ei Tobias noli flere salvus perveniet filius noster et salvus revertetur ad nos et oculi tui videbunt eum.* Isaiah 43:5, *Noli timere quoniam tecum ego sum ab oriente adducam semen tuum et ab occidente congregabo te.* John 16:33, *In mundo, pressuram habebitis: sed confidite, ego vici mundum.*

[24] The author appears to have borrowed some words from Genesis 32:26, *Dixitque ad eum: Dimitte me, jam enim ascendit aurora. Respondit: Non dimittam te, nisi benedixeris mihi.* The results do not, however, make a coherent sentence. Something seems to be missing between *enim* and *nec*, something along the lines of the italicized words in this tentative reconstruction: "For he will find you, *and you will say to him,* I will not let thee go, except thou bless me."

this tomb from which we will one day emerge glorious with him. "For you are dead: and your life is hid with Christ in God. When Christ shall appear, who is your life, then you, too, will be like him in glory." The rest of the year, when there is no special mystery, see him in the Blessed Sacrament as he is in Heaven, ceaselessly praying to his Father; and, as Saint Paul said, interrupt him ceaselessly about our various needs: "Always living to make intercession for us"; or else, as the Incarnate Word surrounded by the heavenly hosts that cover themselves with their wings out of respect, and that sing, 'Holy, Holy, Holy, "We entreat thee, do thou command our voices to be heard with theirs, singing with lowly praise," *etc.*' Lastly, our present situation will teach us how our visits should be conducted.

Sometimes, like Mary Magdalene, we will go and weep over [78] our sins that have smitten and startled us, and we will try to love enough to hear: "Thy sins are forgiven thee. Go in peace." Sometimes, like the leper, the paralytic, the blindman in the Gospel, wearied by our divers ills we will go request healing: "Lord, that I may see. If thou wilt, thou canst make me clean. Jesus, Son of David, have mercy on me. My soul is troubled exceedingly, troubled by a devil. Come down before I die." One day we will go ask him advice about our doubts: "What must I do to possess eternal life? Which is the great commandment in the law? Master, we know that thou art a true speaker and teachest the way of God in truth. Tell us therefore what is lawful, or not?" Another time we will come there to console ourselves about our worries and our temptations: "If it be possible, let this chalice pass from me. For my life is wasted with grief, I stick fast in the mire of the deep and there is no sure standing." He will send the consoling angel, or else we will hear him [79] say to us himself: "Weep not: I am here, fear not. But have confidence. I have overcome the world." Finally, in whatever state we may find ourselves, we will not leave him until we are filled with the desire to belong to him, and with confidence in his goodness: "For he will find you [*lacuna*: and you will say to him] I will not let thee go, except thou bless me."

Instruction treizième
Pour les Examens de Conscience

On commence tous les Examens comme l'Oraison, par prendre de l'eau bénite, se mettre en la présence de *Dieu*, et l'adorer en baisant la terre, ensuite de quoy on demeure tout le temps respectueusement à genoux sur son marchepied.

Le mercredy et le vendredy, à la fin de l'Examen [80] particulier, l'ancien va trouver en leurs places tous ceux de sa chambre, tour à tour. Il leur demande les fautes qu'ils ont remarquées en luy, contre les Instructions et contre les règles depuis la dernière fois. Ensuite il les avertit réciproquement, chacun en particulier, des fautes qu'il a remarquées en eux.

Cecy doit se faire avec beaucoup de sérieux, de simplicité, et de cordialité; et l'on doit prendre garde ou que la crainte d'être averty n'empêche qu'on avertisse, ou qu'on ne parle moins par désir d'aider son Frère à se corriger et par charité, que par une petite pointe d'aigreur, de ressentiment, et de vengeance. Si quelqu'un s'échappoit de son devoir à cet égard, celuy qui se sentira offensé aura d'autant plus d'attention à ne rien dire qui puisse avoir lieu de réplique et de représaille. C'est la meilleure [81] manière de faire rentrer en lui-même celui qui auroit comme attaqué.

On ne met rien icy d'avantage d'un pareil Examen. On trouvera ailleurs des méthodes fort exactes, et où les choses, comme pour l'Oraison, sont traitées à fond.

Instruction quatorzième
Pour les repas
Règlement extérieur

Dès que la cloche aura sonné pour le repas, si c'est le matin, après avoir dit *Pater* et *Ave* et baisé la terre pour conclure l'Examen, ou si c'est le soir, après avoir dit dévotement l'*Angelus*, on descendra modestement et en silence au réfectoire. On doit toujours, avant le repas, se bien laver les mains et les essuier, en quelque saison que ce soit. Ensuite on prendra sa serviette [82] dans sa boëtte, si ce n'étoit qu'il y eût du linge blanc, et on se place au réfectoir comme on se trouve, tantôt à droite tantôt à gauche. Pendant que l'on s'assemble et qu'on dit le *Benedicite*, on demeure debout, les yeux baissés, la birette devant la poitrine, et le dos tourné vers la table, contre laquelle il ne faut point s'appuyer. On doit répondre au *Benedicite* d'une voix haute et distincte, faire l'inclination de tête au *Gloria Patri*, et le signe de la croix pendant le *Benedic Domine* et un *Pater* avec un signe de croix.

S'il arrivoit qu'aucun prêtre ne se trouvât au commencement de la table

Thirteenth Instruction
For Examens of Conscience

One begins all Examens as one begins Prayer, by taking holy water, putting oneself in the presence of *God*, and adoring him by kissing the floor, after which one remains the entire time respectfully kneeling on one's kneeler.

On Wednesdays and Fridays, at the end of the particular Examen, [80] the senior goes to each member of his bedchamber in turn. He asks what faults they have observed in him since the last time, contrary to the Instructions and the rules. Then he points out to them reciprocally, each one privately, the faults he has remarked in them.

This should be done with great seriousness, simplicity, and cordiality; and one should take care that the fear of being admonished does not prevent one from admonishing, or that one does not speak less from a desire to help one's Brother correct himself, and out of charity, than from a little jab of bitterness, resentment, and vengeance. If someone strayed from his duty in this regard, the one who feels offended will be all the more careful to say nothing that can give rise to a rejoinder or to retaliation. This is the best [81] manner to make the person who has, so to speak, attacked, examine his conscience.

Nothing more will be said here about this type of Examen. Very exact methods are to be found elsewhere, where things are discussed in depth, as for Prayer.

Fourteenth Instruction
For meals

Outer regulation

As soon as the bell has rung for the meal, if it is before noon, after having said *Pater* and *Ave* and kissed the floor to conclude the Examen, or if it is after noon, after having devoutly said the *Angelus*, one will go down modestly and silently to the refectory. Before a meal one should always wash one's hands well and dry them, whatever the season. Then one takes one's napkin [82] from its box, unless there is clean linen, and one takes a place in the refectory, wherever one happens to be, sometimes to the right and sometimes to the left. While assembling and saying the *Benedicite*, one remains standing, eyes lowered, birette over one's breast, and one's back turned to the table, against which one must not lean. One should reply to the *Benedicite* in a loud and distinct voice, bow one's head at the *Gloria Patri*, and make the sign of the cross during the *Benedic Domine*, and a *Pater* with a sign of the cross.

If it should happen that no priest is present at the start of the sitting, to say

pour donner la bénédiction, chacun dira le *Benedicite* tout bas et en particulier, comme le soir des jours de jeûne, et on se placera à l'ordinaire. [83] On diroit de même les Grâces au cas qu'il ne se trouvât pas de prêtre, le lecteur ayant finy.

Le *Benedicite* achevé, on se met à table; on se recueille quelque temps avant que de déplier sa serviette, pour offir à *Dieu* le repas qu'on va prendre, et demander la grâce de faire saintement cette action toute animale. Ensuite on déplie sa serviette dont une partie, sur laquelle on pose l'assiette, doit couvrir la nappe et l'autre partie la poitrine, de crainte qu'en mangeant on ne gâte ses habits. Pendant le repas on doit prendre garde à bien garder la modestie, la propreté, et la tempérance. Voicy la pratique de chacun de ces points en particulier:

Pour la modestie

Les yeux ne doivent point s'égarer légèrement deçà ny delà, pour voir ce que font les voisins, ou ce qui se passe d'un autre côté dans le réfectoire. On ne doit pas non [84] plus les avoir trop près ny trop fixément attachés sur son plat. Il faut qu'ils soient modestement entr'ouverts vis-à-vis de soy, à une distance raisonnable. Cependant on doit prendre garde à ce qu'on fait, et on peut de temps en temps les détourner pour voir s'il ne manque rien à ceux qui sont à ses côtés, et les élever quelquefois vers le lecteur si l'on est placé de sorte qu'on le puisse voir. Il faut avoir les yeux absolument baissés dans son verre pendant qu'on boit. Les mains doivent être posées sur la serviette, lorsqu'elles ne sont pas en action; et l'on ne doit point les avancer de telle sorte que la soutanne, les bras, et moins encore les coudes se trouvent sur la table.

On ne doit point tenir le couteau ou la fourchette à la main, ou en l'air, le poing appuié sur la table lorsqu'on ne s'en sert point. On ne doit ~~point~~ jamais se servir de [85] la main gauche pour couper, ny pour rien porter de la fourchette à la bouche, mais de la main droite seulement. On tient la fourchette de la main gauche pendant qu'on coupe les viandes de la droite. Mais pour manger, on repasse ensuite la fourchette de la gauche à la droite. Le pain et le fruit se portent de la main à la bouche; le reste s'y porte avec la fourchette, si ce n'est quelque chose de fort sec et qui ne puisse point salir les doigts.

Les pieds doivent être un peu écartés et couverts de la soutanne ou de la robbe, et l'on ne doit point les croiser l'un sur l'autre, non plus que les genoux. Le corps ne doit être ni lâchement appuyé contre la muraille, ny trop panché sur la table. Il faut seulement l'avancer un peu lorsqu'on mange, surtout quelque chose de liquide, pour ne se pas gâter.

Pour la propreté

On doit prendre garde à ne rien gâter, à ne rien toucher [86] de ce qui se sert, soit pain, soit viande, soit fruit, afin que si on laisse quelque chose, il puisse être dans le besoin présenté une seconde fois à d'autres, sans leur causer du dégoust. Le pain doit se couper également, c'est-à-dire la mie avec la croûte; et avant que d'y toucher, on doit essuyer son couteau et ses doigts

the blessing, each one will softly and privately say the *Benedicite*, as on the evening of fast days, and one will take a place as usual. [83] One would say Grace in the same way if no priest should happen to be present, the reader having finished.

When the *Benedicite* is over, one sits down at the table; one remains recollected for awhile before unfolding one's napkin, to offer *God* the meal one is about to eat, and to ask for grace to perform this totally animal act in a saintly way. Next, one unfolds one's napkin so that part of it, on which one puts the plate, covers the tablecloth and the other part covers the chest, for fear of soiling one's clothes while eating. During the meal one should take great care to observe modesty, cleanliness, and temperance. Here is the procedure for each of these points in turn:

For modesty

The eyes should not dart lightly here and there, to see what one's neighbors are doing, or what is happening on the other side of the refectory. Nor should one [84] keep them too downcast, or trained too fixedly on one's plate. They must be modestly half open and looking straight ahead, at a reasonable distance. However, one should be careful about what one is doing, and from time to time one can turn them to the side, to see if anything is lacking for one's immediate neighbors, and one can sometimes raise them toward the reader, if he is in a place where one can see him. It is necessary to have one's eyes absolutely lowered to one's glass while drinking. One's hands should be placed on the napkin, when they are not moving; and one should not extend them in such a way that the soutane, the arms, and still less the elbows are on the table.

One should not hold one's knife or one's fork in one's hand or in the air, with the fist resting on the table, when one is not using them. One should never use [85] the left hand to cut, or to carry anything from the fork to the mouth, but only the right hand. One holds the fork in the left hand while cutting food with the right hand; but when eating, one shifts the fork from the left hand to the right one. The hand carries bread and fruit to the mouth; the rest is carried by the fork, unless it is something very dry that cannot dirty the fingers.

The feet should be slightly separated and covered by the soutane or the robe, and one should not cross them, one over the other, nor cross the knees. The body should neither lean loosely against the wall, nor be bent too far over the table. It must simply be advanced a bit while eating, especially something liquid, in order not to get dirty.

For cleanliness

One should be careful not to dirty anything; not to touch anything [86] that is being served, be it bread, meat, or fruit, so that if one leaves something, it can, if need be, be presented a second time to others, without disgusting them. The bread should be cut equally, that is to say, some softer bread and some crust; and before touching it, one should wipe one's knife and fingers, if they are dirty. One can wipe one's fingers and one's knife on a little piece of bread that one

s'ils sont sales. On peut essuyer ses doigts et son couteau à un petit morceau de pain que l'on mange ensuite, mais jamais à la nappe ny au morceau de pain entier. On ne doit couper de son pain qu'une tranche à la fois; cette tranche doit se mettre non pas en petits morceaux, mais la couper de sorte que tous les morceaux tiennent encore ensemble, et qu'avec la main on puisse aisément les détacher à mesure qu'on en aura besoin. On ne doit pas mettre à la bouche les morceaux si gros que les joues ne soient enflées, ni qu'on ne puisse pas dire une parole s'il étoit nécessaire. Quand on doit manger des [87] œufs à la coque, on peut auparavant préparer quelques mouillettes; et pour achever de les vuider, on se sert de sa cueillère ou du couteau. On ne doit point toucher aux pots sans s'être essuié les mains à la serviette, ni boire qu'on ne se soit essuyé les mains et la bouche et qu'on n'ait la bouche bien vuide. On ne doit point tellement remplir son verre qu'en versant ou en buvant on répande rien sur la serviette ou sur la nappe. En se servant à boire, il ne faut point verser de haut le vin ny l'eau, ny tenir à la main son verre ou son gobelet. En buvant on doit prendre son verre ou son gobelet par le corps et non point par le pied, de crainte qu'il n'échappe. On doit boire lentement, mais non pas à reprise. Il ne faut ny boire avant que d'avoir mangé, ny tremper jamais son pain dans le vin. Enfin, après avoir bu on doit encore essuyer sa bouche avant que de se remettre à manger. Il n'est [88] peut-être pas trop civil de ne boire qu'à demy ce qu'on a versé dans son verre, mais l'usage a prévalu parmy nous, pour éviter l'incommodité de se verser à boire si souvent. À la fin du repas on ne doit pas rincer sa bouche en faisant du bruit, rien de plus dégoûtant pour ceux qui l'entendroient.

On ne doit tirer de son plat que ce qu'on a besoin de manger, et à mesure qu'on la veut manger, afin que ce qui restera n'ait point été gaspillé. Ce qu'on aura tiré de son plat, on le coupera en petits morceaux sur son assiette; et l'on ne mettra dans le plat ny les arrêtes ny les os, surtout s'il y a de la saulce que cela pourroit gâter: ils demeureront sur un des bords de l'assiette. On ne doit rien tremper dans la saulce avec les doigts, mais avec la fourchette. On peut, avec la fourchette, aussy y mettre un peu de pain; mais c'est une grande malpropreté de sembler vouloir nettoyer les plats et faire qu'il n'y reste rien du tout, ni de [89] reporter au plat un morceau de pain qu'on auroit déjà porté à la bouche. Le poisson sec peut, étant sur l'assiette, se manger avec les doigts, pourvu qu'il n'y ait pas de danger de les trop gâter. On ne doit guères sucer ses doigts, ni les os pour en tirer ce qui est dedans.

On peut humer le bouillon dans l'écuelle, la tenant par les deux oreilles lorsqu'il n'y a plus de pain; mais on ne doit mettre le nés dans aucun autre plat, non pas même dans les petites jattes à lait.

Si l'on met du pain dans le potage ou dans le lait, il ne faut pas en mettre tant que rien puisse se répandre: qu'on y revienne plutôt à diverses reprises.

C'est une grande incivilité de prendre le sel dans la salière avec les doigts, ou de l'y remettre quand on en a pris un peu trop, ou de saler son pain ou sa viande dans la salière même. Il faut prendre peu de sel à la fois, de peur qu'il n'en reste, et le prendre du bout du couteau bien essuyé. [90]

then eats, but never wipe them on the tablecloth or on the loaf of bread. One should cut one's bread only a slice at a time; this slice should not break into little bits, but should be cut so that all the pieces still hold together, and so that one can easily break them off by hand, as needed. One should not put into one's mouth pieces so large that one's cheeks puff out, or so that one cannot speak if necessary. When eating [87] soft-boiled eggs, one can prepare in advance a few strips of bread to dip into them; and to completely empty the eggshells, one uses one's spoon or knife. One should not touch the pitchers without having wiped one's hands on the napkin, nor drink unless one has wiped one's hands and mouth, and unless one's mouth is quite empty. One should not fill one's glass so full that, when pouring or drinking, one will spill something on the napkin or tablecloth. When pouring oneself a drink, neither wine nor water should be poured from high up, nor should one hold one's glass or goblet in one's hand. While drinking, one should take one's glass or goblet by the globe, not the foot, for fear it drop. One should drink slowly, but not repeatedly. Before having eaten, nothing should be drunk, nor should bread ever be dipped into the wine. Finally, after having drunk, one should wipe one's mouth again before resuming eating. It is [88] perhaps not too civil to drink only a little at a time of what one has poured into one's glass, but the custom has prevailed among us, in order to avoid the inconvenience of pouring drinks so often. At the end of the meal, one should not rinse one's mouth noisily: nothing is more disgusting to those who might hear it.

One should take from the serving dish only the amount one needs to eat, and as much as one wishes to eat, so that what remains will not be wasted. On one's plate one cuts into small pieces what one has taken from the serving dish; and one does not place in the serving dish either fish bones or meat bones, especially if there is a sauce that could be spoiled: they are to remain on one part of the plate rim. One should not use one's fingers to dip anything into the sauce, one uses one's fork. One can, with the fork, also dip a bit of bread into the sauce; but it is a very unsavory thing to appear to be wanting to clean the serving plates and to be making sure that nothing at all remains, or to [89] put back on the serving dish a piece of bread that one has already raised to one's mouth. Once it is on the plate, dried fish can be eaten with one's fingers, as long as there is no danger of getting them too dirty. One should only rarely suck one's fingers, or suck meat bones in order to get out what is inside.

When there is no more bread in one's porringer, one can sip the bouillon, holding it by the two handles; but one should not stick one's nose into any other plate, not even into the little milk bowls.

If one puts bread into the soup or into the milk, one must not put so much that it cannot expand: rather, do it several times.

It is a great incivility to take the salt from the saltcellar with one's fingers, or to put salt back if one has taken a bit too much, or to dip one's bread or meat into the saltcellar itself. A small amount of salt should be taken at a time, for fear that some be left over, and it should be taken with the tip of a knife that has been carefully wiped. [90]

Si l'on a besoin de se moucher pendant la table, on doit le faire le visage caché de sa serviette. Quelques-uns se couvrent du bonnet ou de la birette, mais cela n'est pas si bien, et parce qu'il peut tomber des cheveux, et parce qu'il y faut porter les mains en danger de les engraisser. S'il faut cracher, on le doit faire dans son mouchoir, à moins qu'on ne soit au bout d'une table, et alors il faut promptement mettre le pied sur ce qui est sorty. Si on avoit porté quelque chose à la bouche dont on fut dégoûté, il faut, sans qu'on s'en apperçoive, le recevoir dans la main et le faire tomber sous la table. Ce seroit une insigne malpropreté, de remettre dans le plat ou sur l'assiette ce qu'on auroit déjà porté à la bouche, ou à demi mâché.

Quand on mange des raisins ou des cerises, la peau et les noyaux doivent de même se recevoir de la bouche dans la main, d'où on les met dans le petit plat, et non pas les [91] jeter de la bouche même dans le plat.

À table on ne doit porter ny les mains à la tête, ny les doigts aux oreilles. On ne doit pas même trop s'y nettoyer les dents, si ce n'est dans un grand besoin, et caché derrière sa serviette, en sorte que personne ne puisse s'en appercevoir.

S'il vient à tomber quelque chose par terre, comme du pain, un couteau, une fourchette, à moins qu'on ne puisse le relever sans incommoder personne, il faut prier le serveur de le ramasser.

À mesure qu'on ne mange plus d'une chose, on doit avancer le plat sur le bord de la table pour la commodité du serveur. La portion doit se mettre sur l'assiette, de sorte toujours que si on laisse quelque chose, il ne soit mêlé de rien de mauvais ou de malpropre.

Pour la tempérance

La tempérance est quelque chose de moins que la mortification. Les religieux doivent donc s'étudier à la [92] plus grande tempérance, et leur tempérance doit même être mêlée d'un peu de mortification. Ainsi on ne doit ny choisir sa portion sur la planche, ny regarder à côté de soy si ses voisins sont mieux ou plus mal partagés, ni faire changer sa portion lorsqu'on n'a pas si bien rencontré, ni regarder de près, ni flairer ce qui se présente, ni rien prendre pour soy de ce que les autres ne mangent pas, ni se faire rapporter une seconde fois de ce qui se sera servy, pour changer contre quelqu'autre mets moins agréable au goût, ni rien recevoir des malades à qui on donne quelque chose d'extraordinaire, non plus que de religion, de pénitence, et d'humilité.

Quand on trouve sur l'assiette ou sur la table un reste de pain, ou du pain rassis, on doit toujours le manger avant que de passer au pain entier ou au pain tendre. [93] C'est une grande immatification de chappeler son pain, à moins qu'il ne fût tout brûlé, ou de l'écroûter tout autour et de laisser la mie. Pour qui seront les restes?

Il faut s'accoutumer autant qu'il est possible à manger de tout. S'il y a quelque chose dont on ne puisse pas manger, se garder bien de paroître le mépriser, et vouloir en dégoûter les autres. Ceux qui ne mangent point de

If one needs to blow one's nose while at table, one should do it while hiding one's face in one's napkin. Some people cover their faces with their bonnet or their birette, but that is not as good, both because hair might fall, and because putting the hands there risks getting the head-cover greasy. If it is necessary to spit, one must do it into one's handkerchief, unless one is at the end of the table, and then one must promptly put one's foot on what came out. If one has brought something disgusting up to one's mouth, without permitting anyone to notice, it must be placed in the hand and dropped under the table. It would be a conspicuous filthiness to put back onto the serving dish, or onto one's own plate, something that one has already lifted to one's mouth or has partially chewed.

When eating grapes or cherries, the skin and the pits can, in like manner, be received from the mouth into the hand, from whence one puts them on the little serving dish, and [91] does not spit them directly from one's mouth into the serving dish.

At table, one should not bring one's hands up to one's head, nor one's fingers to one's ears. One should not work too hard at cleaning one's teeth, unless there is a great need, and hidden behind one's napkin, so that no one can notice.

If something happens to fall on the floor, for example bread, a knife, or a fork, unless one can pick it up without inconveniencing anyone, the server must be asked to pick it up.

When something is no longer being eaten, one should advance the serving dish to the edge of the table for the convenience of the server. One's portion should be put on one's plate, so that if something is left over, it will not be mixed with anything nasty or dirty.

For temperance

Temperance is something less than mortification. Religious must therefore strive for the [92] greatest temperance, and their temperance should even be mingled with a bit of mortification. Thus one should not choose one's portion from the cutting board, nor look to the side to see if one's neighbors are better or worse served, nor have one's portion changed when one has not been as fortunate as they, nor look closely at it, nor sniff what is presented, nor take for oneself anything that the others are not eating, nor have the serving dish brought back a second time in order to exchange it for some food less agreeable to the taste, nor accept anything from the sick who have been given something special, not for religion, nor penance, nor humility.

When one finds on one's plate or on the table some leftover bread or some stale bread, one should always eat it before moving on to a new loaf or soft bread. [93] It is excessive daintiness to scrape the crust off one's bread, unless it is totally burned, or to remove all the crust and keep only the soft part. Who will eat the leftovers?

It is necessary to become accustomed, as much as possible, to eating everything. If there is something one cannot eat, it is necessary to be careful not to appear to scorn it and to want to make the others hold it in disgust. Those

certaines choses, de beurre, par exemple, avec le poisson, au lieu de se faire servir du poisson où il n'y en ait pas, doivent plutôt le retirer proprement de la saulce et le manger; ni, à moins qu'on ne soit tout à fait dégoûté, se faire des ragoûts particuliers, surtout avec des assaisonnemens qu'on auroit apporté du dehors. En un mot, il faut de soi-même apprendre à se contenter de ce qui se présente à la Communauté, ou à s'en passer, si ce n'est que les supérieurs y pourvoient d'une autre manière. On ne doit man[ger] [94] ni trop de sel, ni trop de vinaigre: cela nuit à la santé.

On ne doit apporter quoi que ce soit pour manger à table, ni en rien emporter pour manger chés soi en particulier.

Comme on ne nous sert guères que ce qu'il faut, surtout les jours ordinaires, notre tempérance, régulièrement parlant, consiste moins à nous régler sur la quantité qu'à nous modérer dans la manière de manger. Ainsi on doit toujours le faire sans qu'il paroisse d'avidité, ni de trop grand épanchement, et du reste user avec beaucoup de simplicité, et sans se chicanner de ce qu'on nous présente. Cela n'empêche pas qu'on ne doive prendre garde à ne pas manger jusqu'à se faire mal, et qu'on ne puisse par mortification s'abstenir toujours à table de quelque petite chose qui fasse plaisir. Dans le doute, il faut demander conseil. [95] Pour le vin, on ne doit jamais le boire pur, et il faut tellement le mêler, surtout jusqu'à un certain âge, que ce ne soit guères que de l'eau rougie. Enfin, on se souviendra que la première règle de la tempérance est de ne point manger des choses qui nuisent à la santé. Cela ne regarde pas les mets dont on ne sçauroit se passer, il y faut moins de scrupule, mais ceux qui ne sont qu'accessoires, comme de la salade et certains fruits.

Quand on voit approcher la fin du repas, il faut un peu se presser plutôt que de faire attendre la Communauté après soy. Si on a un peu moins mangé à un repas, on se dédommagera dans l'autre.

Direction intérieure

On doit être modestes par respect pour la présence de *Dieu*: *Exultent justi et epulentur in conspectu Dominum, Non quæ sua sunt singuli considerantes, sed quæ aliorum; et semper*[25]; [96] par esprit de mortification et de pénitence: *Cinerem tanquam panem manducabam, et potum meum cum fletu mascebam.*[26] On ne doit user de la nourriture que comme d'un remède, et d'un remède humiliant et dangereux. Saint Bernard versoit des larmes, et saint Augustin trembloit lorsqu'il falloit aller à table, de crainte d'y faire des fautes de sensualité. Plusieurs autres mêloient de la cendre et de l'absynthe à ce qu'ils mangeoient, pour avoir un contre-poison aux recherches de l'amour-propre. Pour nous, il suffira que nous gardions bien les règles qu'on vient de nous prescrire, à moins que nous n'eussions permission de faire quelque chose de plus. La lecture servira beaucoup, si l'on s'y applique doucement, à faire diversion de

---

[25] Psalm 67:4, *Et justi epulentur, et exultent in conspectu Dei: et delectentur in lætitia*. Philippians 2:4, *Non quae sua sunt singuli considerantes sed et ea quæ aliorum.*

[26] Psalm 101:10, *Quia cinerem tanquam panem manducabam, et potum meum cum fletu miscebam.*

who do not eat certain things, for example butter with fish, instead of asking for a serving of fish that has none, must instead take the fish neatly from the sauce and eat it; nor, unless one simply cannot stomach something, must one prepare special stews, especially with seasonings brought from outside. In a word, it is necessary to learn, on one's own, either to be content with what is presented to the Community, or to do without, unless the superiors provide in another way. One should not eat [94] too much salt or too much vinegar: it is bad for the health.

One should not bring to the table anything whatsoever to eat, nor take anything away to eat privately in one's quarters.

Since we are rarely served anything beyond what is necessary, especially on ordinary days, our temperance, regularly speaking, consists less of being guided by the quantity than of moderating our way of eating. Thus one should always eat without any appearance of greed or excessive effusiveness, and in addition should behave with a great deal of simplicity and without quibbling about what is presented to us. That does not prevent one from having to be careful not to eat until one gets sick and, out of mortification, from always abstaining, while at table, from eating some little thing that gives pleasure. When in doubt, it is necessary to seek advice. [95] As for wine, one should never drink it pure, and it must be diluted to such a degree, especially up to a certain age, that it is scarcely anything but reddened water. Lastly, one will remember that the first rule for temperance is not to eat things that are bad for the health. That does not apply to dishes one cannot do without, there are less scruples about them, but to dishes that are only accessories, such as salad and certain fruits.

When one sees that the end of the meal is approaching, it is necessary to hurry a bit, rather than make the Community wait for one. If one eats a bit less at one meal, one will make up for it at the next.

Inner guidance

One should be modest out of respect for the presence of *God*: "And let the just feast and rejoice before God. Each one not considering the things that are his own, but those that are other men's, and always," [96] from a spirit of mortification and penance: "For I did eat ashes like bread, and mingled my drink with weeping." One should treat food only as one would treat a remedy, a humiliating and dangerous remedy. Saint Bernard wept, and Saint Augustine trembled when it was time to eat, for fear they would commit faults involving sensuality. Several others mingled ashes and absinth with what they ate, as an antidote to the pursuits of self-love. For us, it will suffice to observe carefully the rules that have just been laid down for us, unless we have permission to do something more. If one calmly pays attention to it, the mealtime reading goes a long way toward diverting the excessive attention one might pay to eating and drinking. In addition to the fact that one can learn a great deal in one year if one strives to listen to a history or a devotional book every day for an hour, it is also necessary to reflect on the mistakes about which one informs the reader, in order not to make them when one's own turn comes to read. [97] When the reader has

l'attention trop grande qu'on auroit au boire et au manger. Outre qu'on peut apprendre beaucoup en une année, quand on tâche de suivre une histoire ou un livre de dévotion chaque jour pendant une heure, il faut aussi faire réflexion aux fautes dont on avertit le lecteur, afin de n'y pas tomber quant [*read*: quand] on lira à son [97] tour. Quand le lecteur a cessé, et qu'on a encore besoin de temps pour finir, comme à la seconde table, on peut penser au fiel et au vinaigre qu'a bu *Notre Seigneur*, ou à tant de mauvais repas qu'il fit pendant trente ans à Nazareth, et ensuite dans ses courses apostoliques.

Enfin, devant et après le repas, on ne doit jamais parler de la table, ni s'il est possible y penser. Jamais non plus se plaindre ny murmurer de ce qu'on n'est pas assés à son gré. Beaucoup de pauvres, s'ils étoient comme nous, se trouveroient trop bien. L'appétit est le plus grand de tous les assaisonnemens et supplée à tout le reste, pourvu qu'on ait de bon pain. Or, c'est ce qui ne nous manque presque jamais.

Le repas finy, on reprend sa place pour dire Grâces comme le *Benedicite* [*read*: on reprend, pour dire Grâces, sa position comme pour le *Benedicite*]. On doit répondre à tout, et se souvenir de faire l'inclination de tête au *Gloria Patri* et au *Sit nomen Domini benedictum*. Les jours d'abstinence et de jeûne, et lorsqu'on mange en seconde, on ne dit pour Grâces qu'*Agimus tibi gratias, retribuere dignare, fidelium animæ*,[27] et un *Pater*. Il est de la propreté de laver ses [98] mains au sortir de la table. On peut aussi rincer sa bouche au lave-main; mais il **ne** faut pas l'appliquer au robinet. On met de l'eau dans sa main et on la porte à la bouche. Ensuite on s'essuye le visage à l'essuie-main[s] destiné à cet usage, où l'on ne doit point se frotter les dents, ny laisser aucune marque de sang, et puis les mains aux essuie-mains ordinaires.

Instruction quinzième
Pour quand on est aux offices
Règlement extérieur

Être aux offices, c'est servir au réfectoire, soit à la première, soit à la seconde table, ou laver la vaisselle, ou aider à la crédence. On traitera ces quatre choses successivement.

Pour servir à la première table

On est toujours deux à servir en première, si ce n'est qu'il y eût peu de monde et qu'un seul suffise, comme pendant les vacances et les pèlerinages. Quelques fois aussi on est jusqu'à trois, comme en Carême et certains grands jours de [99] l'année.

D'abord, les deux ou trois serveurs portent de tous côtés le potage ou le premier mets. Le plus ancien ordinairement doit servir à la table des Pères, et il est du respect qu'on n'en serve point d'autres avant celle-cy. Aussi faut-

---

[27] These are phrases from the postprandial prayer.

stopped, and when one still needs time to finish, as at second table, one can think about the gall and vinegar that *Our Lord* drank, or about the many wretched meals he ate during his thirty years in Nazareth, and then during his apostolic wanderings.

Finally, before and after the meal, one should never talk about food nor, if possible, think about it. Never, in addition, complain or mutter about things not being sufficiently to one's liking. Many paupers, if they were in our place, would be very pleased. Appetite is the greatest of all seasonings and compensates for everything else, provided one has good bread. Now, bread is something we almost never lack.

When the meal has ended, one assumes, for saying Grace, one's position for the *Benedicite*. One should reply to everything and bow one's head at the *Gloria Patri* and at the *Sit nomen Domini benedictum*. On days of abstinence and fasting, and when one eats at second table, for Grace, one says only: "We give Thee thanks. Vouchsafe to reward the souls of the faithful," and a *Pater*. Cleanliness means washing one's [98] hands after leaving the table. One can also rinse one's mouth at the hand basin; but one should not touch it to the faucet. One fills one's hand with water and brings it to the mouth. Then one wipes one's face on the hand towel destined for that purpose, on which one should not rub one's teeth or leave any blood spot, and then one wipes one's hands on the ordinary hand towels.

Fifteenth Instruction
For when one works in the service rooms
Outer regulation

Working in the service rooms means serving in the refectory, at either first or second table, or washing dishes, or helping in the pantry. These four things will be discussed in turn.

For serving first table

Two novices always serve first table, unless there are few people and one server suffices, as during vacation or pilgrimages. And sometimes there can be as many as three, as during Lent and on certain very special days of [99] the year.

First, the two or three servers bring the soup or the first dish to all the tables. The most senior server ordinarily should serve the Fathers' table; and from respect, the other tables are not served before that one. Thus it is necessary to leave a little time. Whatever one serves in turn, be it first courses, portions, or desserts, one should observe the same rule.

As soon as everyone has something in front of him, the first server will continue alone to bring in either the first courses or the portions, unless everything has already been prepared in the kitchen, in which case the second server, after

il laisser un peu d'avance: quelque chose qu'on serve dans la suite, entrées, portions, ou desserts, on doit garder la même règle.

Dès que tout le monde aura quelque chose devant soy, le premier serveur continuera seul à porter ou les entrées ou les portions, si ce n'est que tout fût déjà préparé à la cuisine, auquel cas le second serveur, après avoir fait deux ou trois tours par le réfectoir pour voir s'il ne manque rien à personne, pourroit aider au premier.

S'il y a de la chandelle au réfectoir, un des premiers soins du second serveur sera de la moucher si elle en a besoin, et il ne craindra pas de le faire deux fois pendant le repas. Ces petits soins ne doivent point l'empêcher de prendre garde à ceux qui viennent tard, pour qu'ils soient servis aussitôt. Si le premier serveur suffit à porter le reste, [100] le second, après avoir fait ce qu'on vient de dire, pourra commencer à desservir; sinon il aidera le premier. Vers le milieu du repas, le second portera l'eau et le pain où il en pourroit manquer.

Quand une fois les premières planches ont été portées, les serveurs doivent être attentifs à n'être jamais hors du réfectoire tous les deux à la fois. Ils n'en doivent jamais sortir, qu'ils n'aient jetté un coup d'œil pour voir si personne n'a besoin de leur ministère; et s'il tombe quelque chose par terre, ils iront promptement le ramasser.

En desservant, on ne portera jamais plus de douze ou quinze écuelles à la fois, et on prendra garde de n'en point mettre par-dessus celles où il seroit resté quelque chose. On peut les vuider toutes dans une ou deux, mais cela se doit faire proprement. On emportera les écuelles à l'avant-cuisine et les cueillères à la crédence, si ce n'est qu'il y ait à servir quelque chose à quoy elles soient nécessaires; et dans ce cas, on les remettra vis-à-vis de ceux qui auroient oubliés [sic] de les retenir. [101]

On doit prendre garde à ne desservir quoi que ce soit dont quelqu'un puisse vouloir encore manger. On peut desservir à la fois vingt plats d'entrées, prenant garde toujours de ne point mettre de plats sur ceux où il reste quelque chose, et de ne point mêler ce qui est propre avec ce qui est gâté.

Pour les portions, on n'en desservira jamais plus de six ou huit à la fois avec les assiettes, ayant toujours également soin de la propreté et de la pauvreté.

Les serveurs ne doivent point s'amuser à causer ou à se chauffer à la cuisine. Ils ne doivent point quitter le réfectoir pendant le repas, s'ils ne sont absolument nécessaires ailleurs. Si le Cuisinier leur ordonne quelque chose qui soit de leur ministère, ils luy doivent obéir.

En desservant les desserts, on gardera la même règle qu'aux entrées, si c'est quelque chose de liquide. Si c'est du fruit crud que l'on dessert, il ne faut pas le mêler avec les pelures. Il faut tâcher d'avoir, pour le mettre, un [102] petit panier sur le rondeau. Lorsqu'on est vers la fin du repas, l'ancien doit servir partout des plats de miettes, et se souvenir de saluer le Supérieur avant que de présenter le plat, et après l'avoir présenté.

On salue le Supérieur la première fois qu'on passe devant luy sans être chargé, quand on mouche la chandelle à sa table, quand on luy présente le plat des miettes, et qu'on vient le reprendre.

having gone around the refectory two or three times, to see that no one is lacking anything, can help the first server.

If there are candles in the refectory, one of the second server's principal concerns will be to trim them if necessary, and he will not hesitate to do so twice during the meal. These little concerns should not prevent him from keeping watch for latecomers, so that they will be served immediately. If the first server can bring in the rest all alone, [100] the second server, after having done what was just said, can begin to clear the table; if not, he will help the first server. Toward the middle of the meal, the second server will bring bread and water to wherever it might be lacking.

Once the first cutting boards have been brought out, the servers should take care never to be out of the refectory at the same time. They should never leave it until they have looked around to see if anyone needs their ministry; and if something falls on the floor, they will promptly go and pick it up.

When clearing the table, one never carries more than twelve or fifteen porringers at once, and one will be careful not to put them on top of porringers in which something remains. One can empty all of them into one or two porringers, but it should be done neatly. The porringers are carried to the fore-kitchen and the spoons to the pantry, unless something requiring them is going to be served; and in that case, one puts them back in front of those people who neglected to keep them. [101]

One should take care not to clear from the table anything that someone might still want to eat. One can clear twenty serving dishes for first courses at a time, always being careful not to put the serving dishes on serving dishes that still contain food, and not to mix what is clean with what is spoilt.

As for the portions, one will never clear away more than six or eight at a time, with the plates, always being equally careful about cleanliness and poverty.

The servers should not amuse themselves by chatting or warming themselves in the kitchen. They should not leave the refectory during the meal, unless they are absolutely needed elsewhere. If the Cook orders them to do something that is part of their ministry, they should obey him.

When removing desserts, one will observe the same rule as for first courses, unless the dessert is liquid. If one is removing fresh fruit, it must not be mixed with the peelings. One must try to put a little basket on the round board, [102] in which to put the fruit. When the end of the meal approaches, the senior server should distribute dishes for crumbs to every table, and should remember to greet the Superior before presenting the dish, and after having presented it.

One greets the Superior the first time one passes in front of him without carrying anything, when one trims the candle on his table, when one presents him with the dish for crumbs, and when one comes to take it back.

If time remains, one can set the places for second table; but there has to be enough time, and one must pay attention not to encumber the table to such a degree that those who are still there are inconvenienced. It would be preferable to put what will be served during second table on an empty table nearby. On the

S'il reste du temps, on peut préparer les places de la seconde table; mais il faut qu'il reste du temps, et qu'on fasse attention à ne point tellement embarasser la table que ceux qui y sont s'en trouvent incommodés. Il vaudroit mieux mettre sur quelque table vuide du voisinage ce qu'on doit servir à la seconde. On doit servir, sur les assiettes de la seconde, des restes de pain de la première; mais on prendra garde de ne pas mettre de trop petits morceaux de pain, ou du pain gâté [103] et mal conditionné. On prendra garde enfin, pendant la table, de ne desservir ny le pain ny le vin ni l'eau de devant ceux qui pourroient en avoir encore besoin.

L'hyver, lorsqu'on fait du feu pour nos Frères, sur la fin du repas le second serveur ira l'allumer; c'est-à-dire, le matin quand on lira le Martyrologe, et le soir un *Miserere* avant qu'on finisse. Il prendra garde, en portant du feu, qu'il n'en tombe nulle part, et si par malheur il en tombe, il l'éteindra du pied aussitôt. Dès que le feu sera allumé, il tournera le sable. C'est aussi luy qui doit allumer la chandelle de la grande salle lorsqu'il fait nuit, soit qu'on allume du feu ou non; mais s'il n'y a point de feu, il suffira d'allumer la chandelle pendant les Grâces. Si on se chauffe à un poêle, le soin du poêle regarde l'ancien du Bienheureux Goto, ou en son absence, le frère Admoniteur. Personne ne doit y toucher que l'un ou l'autre d'eux, ou tous les deux si cela est nécessaire. [104]

Tout à la fin de la table, les serveurs, avant que de se retirer, doivent saluer la Communauté; mais avant que de le faire, ils prendront bien garde si tout le monde a achevé, et si le lecteur n'a pas quelque papier à lire. On ne sçauroit désapprouver la coutume qu'ont nos Frères qui ont servy en première, d'aller à la crédence pendant les Grâces, commencer à nétoyer ce qui a servy au réfectoir; mais il vaudoit mieux qu'ils ne le fissent pas du tout que de le faire imparfaitement et légèrement, comme il arrive d'ordinaire. En voulant faire une espèce de charité pour quelqu'un de leur[s] Frères, c'est manquer d'égard et de charité pour toute la Communauté.

Pour servir à la seconde table

Celui qui sert en seconde, dès que les Grâces sont [105] finies, aiant pris le sablier, commencera par voir s'il ne manque rien aux places de ceux qui y doivent manger; et s'il y manque quelque chose, il y mettra et arrangera tout sur les tables, avec beaucoup de propreté.

Sitôt que quelqu'un arrivera, il ira chercher le potage ou les entrées à la cuisine, et les servira. Entre l'entrée et la portion, la portion et le dessert, il mettra le temps convenable pour que tout ce qui est chaud soit servy chaudement. Il prendra garde de ne point faire attendre ceux qui viennent plus tard que les autres. Il se mettra bien dans l'esprit que son devoir essentiel est de servir. Cependant, après avoir servy et examiné s'il ne manque rien à personne, il pourra aider le Crédencier à frotter les garde-nappes [106] et à essuier les pots à l'eau.

Il ne laissera au réfectoir, pendant la seconde, aucune chandelle allumée que celles qui sont absolument nécessaires pour voir à ce que l'on fait. Il desservira comme ceux qui servent en premier, mouchera les chandelles dans

plates for second table one should serve the remnants of the bread from first table; but one will be careful not to use too small pieces of bread, or bread that has been spoilt [103] and is in poor condition. Lastly, one will be careful, while people are at table, not to remove the bread, the wine, or the water from in front of anyone who might still need them.

In winter, when a fire is lighted for our Brethren, at the end of the meal the second server will go and light it: that is to say, in the morning while the Martyrology is being read, and in the evening before the end of the *Miserere*. He will be careful, when carrying the fire, that nothing drops anywhere; and if some unfortunately falls, he will immediately extinguish it with his foot. As soon as the fire is lighted, he will turn the hourglass. It is also he who should light the candle in the great hall when night has fallen, whether a fire is lighted or not; but if there is no fire, it will suffice to light the candle during Grace. If one is warming oneself before a stove, the care of the stove falls to the senior of Blessed Goto or, in his absence, to Brother Admonitor. No one but the one or the other, or both of them if necessary, should touch it. [104]

At the very end of the meal, before withdrawing, the servers should greet the Community; but before doing this, they will make very sure that everyone has finished, and that the reader does not have some paper to read aloud. One cannot disapprove of the custom of our Brethren who have served first table, of going to the pantry during Grace, to begin to clean up what was served in the refectory; but it would be better for them not to do it at all, than to do it imperfectly and carelessly, as usually happens. By wanting to do a sort of charity for one of their Brothers, they lack respect and charity for the entire Community.

For serving second table

As soon as Grace has been said, the person who is serving second table, [105], having taken the hourglass, will begin by seeing that nothing is missing at the places of those who will be eating; and if something is missing, he will put it there and will arrange everything on the tables, very neatly.

As soon as someone arrives, he will go get the soup or the first course in the kitchen and will serve them. Between the first course and the portion, the portion and the dessert, he will spend the appropriate amount of time so that every hot dish is hot when served. He will be careful to see that those who come later than the others do not have to wait. He will keep clearly in mind that his essential duty is to serve. However, after having served and checked that no one is lacking anything, he can help the Pantryman scrub the protective mats under the serving dishes [106] and wipe the water pitchers.

During second table, he will not leave any lighted candles in the refectory, beyond what is absolutely necessary to see what one is doing. He will clear the table as the servers did during first table, will trim the candles if necessary, and will not leave on the tables any serving dishes or plates that might cause inconvenience.

le besoin, et ne laissera point sur les tables de plats ou d'assiettes qui puissent incommoder.

S'il n'y a point de prêtre au réfectoir, il fera, en se découvrant, signe au lecteur de cesser. S'il y a des prêtres, il leur en demandera la permission. Si le révérend père Recteur ou le père Ministre y sont, c'est à eux à faire cesser le lecteur quand ils voudront. Le temps de faire cesser la lecture, c'est quand quelqu'un de la seconde est sur le point de finir, si ce n'est qu'on vît, dans quelqu'un de nos Frères, quelque sorte de précipitation; car il n'est pas juste, pour l'empressement d'un ou deux, de priver tous les autres du plaisir de [107] la lecture. Personne ne doit se lever de table en seconde avant que le lecteur ait finy, ou sans avertir le plus honorable du réfectoir, ou le lecteur, du besoin qu'on a de sortir plutôt [*read*: plus tôt].

Celuy qui sert en seconde ne doit point quitter le réfectoir le matin avant les 3/4, ni le soir avant la 1/2, les jours ordinaires, eût-il avoir finy tout ce qui est de son office. Les jours de dimanche et de fêtes, il ne doit point quitter avant midy, à moins que le Crédencier de son propre mouvement ne le renvoyât plutôt [*read*: plus tôt], ce qu'il ne doit jamais demander lui-même.

Pour ceux qui sont à la vaisselle

La vaisselle au Noviciat se lave dans l'avant-cuisine. On est ordinairement quatre ou cinq à la vaisselle; mais quand on est peu de monde à la Maison, on n'y [108] est que trois au plus. Chacun doit relever sa soutane par-devant, et trousser un peu ses manches de peur de les engraisser. On prend ensuite le tablier.

Le plus ancien de noviciat doit mettre la vaisselle dans le premier bassin, et la servir à celuy qui lave. Le second doit la laver et la mettre, à mesure qu'il la frotte, dans le troisième bassin. Le troisième doit la retirer du troisième bassin, l'étendre sur la claye, et la porter sur la table à ceux qui essuient. Il est aussi chargé de fournir de l'eau au premier et au second bassin, à moins qu'il n'ay[t] pas assés de force pour cela, et alors il doit prier quelqu'autre de le faire pour luy, si ceux qui lavent n'aiment mieux le faire eux-mêmes. Les deux ou trois derniers doivent essuier, et le dernier de tous essuyer les planches sur la fin, ou les apporter pour qu'on [109] les lave, et les reporter en leur place.

Cet ordre n'empêche point qu'on ne soit prêt à se soulager les uns les autres, et c'est une ridicule vanité de vouloir s'obstiner à laver lorsqu'on est ancien, si on n'a pas ou assés de force ou assés d'adresse pour le bien faire. Il faut plutôt en prier quelqu'autre; mais personne ne s'en mêlera qu'il ne soit prié.

Il n'y a point de règle déterminée pour changer l'eau. On en doit changer au moins deux fois; mais ce ne sera point trop de trois, lorsqu'il y aura beaucoup de vaisselle, ou que l'eau ne sera point assés chaude. Celui qui sert l'eau ne doit remplir le sceau [*read:* seau] qu'à une hauteur proportionnée à ses forces, de peur de se blesser par quelqu'effort indiscret. Cette circonstance est importante, et il y faut faire attention.

Celui qui lave ne doit point se presser, de sorte qu'il ne fasse, pour ainsi dire, que caresser la vaisselle [110] au lieu de la bien laver. C'est une sotte gloire de vouloir paroître prompt quand on fait mal.

If there is no priest in the refectory, after removing his head covering, he will signal the reader to stop. If there are priests, he will beg their permission. If Reverend Father Rector or Father Minister are present, it is up to them to make the reader stop when they wish. The time comes to stop the reading when someone at second table is on the point of finishing, even if one happens to see some sort of precipitation in one of our Brethren; for it is unjust to deprive all the others of the pleasure of the reading, because one or two are in a hurry. [107] No one should rise from the table during second table before the reader has finished, or without notifying the most honorable person in the refectory, or the reader, that one must leave early.

The person serving second table should not leave the refectory in the morning before a quarter to the hour or, for meals later in the day, before the half hour, even if he has completed his duties. On Sundays and feast days, he should not leave before noon, unless the Pantryman, of his own volition, dismisses him early; but he himself should never ask.

For those who are washing dishes

At the Novitiate the dishes are washed in the fore-kitchen. Ordinarily four or five novices wash the dishes; but when few people are in the House, there are only [108] three at most. Each one should tuck up the front of his soutane and push up his sleeves a bit, for fear they will get greasy. Then one dons the apron.

The most senior novice should put the dishes into the first basin and present it to the person who is washing. The second should wash the dishes, and as he scrubs them, put them into the third basin. The third should take the dishes out of the third basin, spread them on the rack, and carry them to the table where the drying is being done. He is also entrusted with supplying water for the first and second basin, unless he is not strong enough to do it, and then he must ask someone else to do it for him, if those who are washing do not prefer to do it themselves. The final two or three should dry, and the last of them dries the cutting boards at the end, or brings them to [109] be washed and puts them back in place.

This order does not prevent one from being ready to help one another, and it is ridiculous vanity to insist obstinately on washing, when one is senior, if one lacks either sufficient strength or sufficient dexterity to do it well. Rather, someone else should be asked; but no one shall become involved unless asked.

There is no precise rule about changing the water. It should be changed at least twice; but three times is not too often when there are a lot of dishes, or when the water is not hot enough. The person bringing the water should only fill the pail to a level proportionate to his strength, for fear of injuring himself by some imprudent effort. This circumstance is important, and attention must be paid to it.

The person who is washing should not hurry, so that he merely caresses the dishes, so to speak, [110] instead of washing them thoroughly. It is foolish glory to want to appear speedy when one is doing poor work.

Les plats où il y a eu de l'huile doivent toujours se laver les derniers, parce qu'ils engraissent beaucoup l'eau. Il faut ordinairement les laver avec l'eau la plus chaude qu'il se peut. Avant que de finir, il faut regarder derrière soy s'il n'y a point de vaisselle de la seconde table à laver.

Ceux qui essuient ne doivent pas appuyer la vaisselle contre leur poitrine, mais l'essuyer en l'air, et ne pas se charger de plus d'une assiette ou de deux ou trois petits plats à la fois. Il faut serrer les mains en frottant, pour ne laisser à la vaisselle rien de gras ny de sale, et tellement manier son torchon qu'il serve par tous les endroits tour à tour.

Ceux qui achèvent les premiers, doivent venir au secours des autres, jusqu'à ce que tout soit finy. [111]

Avant que de jetter la dernière eau du bassin, on doit le bien frotter avec la lavette pour qu'il n'y reste que le moins qui se pourra de graisse. On le frotte ensuite avec un vieux torchon, surtout le matin, de crainte de trop salir ceux qui doivent encore servir le soir.

Tout étant achevé, on essuie les claies, on lave la pierre avec le balay, en versant à plusieurs reprises l'eau du second bassin. On remet le second bassin bien essuié dans sa place.

Nos Frères coadjuteurs ont soin de remasser les torchons dont on s'est servy, et de les étendre sur les barres de la cheminée, afin qu'ils puissent sécher. On lave ses mains avec un peu d'eau et de son, s'il y en a; puis on se retire. Si quelqu'un oublioit quelque chose de son devoir, celui qui s'en sera apperçu doit le faire dans sa place.

Pour ceux qui aident à la crédence [112]

On en marquera un ou deux tous les jours pour ce dernier office. S'ils sont deux, le dernier va d'abord chercher de l'eau dans un sceau [*read*: seau] à l'avant-cuisine. De ce sceau il verse l'eau dans les deux vases où l'on doit mettre les couteaux et les fourchettes, et dans le bassin où sont les cueillières et où l'on doit laver les plats de dessert s'ils en ont besoin.

En essuiant les fourchettes et les couteaux, il faut bien prendre garde qu'il n'y reste point d'eau, de peur qu'ils ne se rouillent. On doit mettre à part bien proprement tout ce qui se trouve dans les plats de dessert qui peut encor servir, comme fruits, fromages, reste de biscuit ou de gâteau. On ne quitte point que tout ne soit achevé, et qu'on ait nétoyé la table sur laquelle on a travaillé. En sortant, il faut bien se laver les mains et remettre son tablier où on l'a pris. [113]

Direction intérieure

C'est une nécessité de nous servir nous-mêmes, puisque nous ne sommes pas assés riches pour avoir tant de valets, et que nos Frères [coadjuteurs] en ce tems-là sont pour la plupart occupés ailleurs. Mais nous serions bien à plaindre si, de cette nécessité, nous ne sçavions point nous faire un mérite, et que nous n'allassions aux offices qu'en esprit d'esclaves et malgré nous. De plus, c'est une

The serving plates that had oil in them should always be washed last, because they make the water very greasy. Ordinarily they should be washed in the hottest water possible. Before finishing, one must turn around to see whether there are dishes from second table to wash.

Those who are drying should not lean the dishes against their chest, but dry them in the air, and not hold more than one plate, or two or three little serving dishes, at a time. The hands must press hard while rubbing, so that nothing greasy or dirty is left on the dishes, and one should manipulate the towel so that all parts are used in turn.

Those who finish first should go help the others, until everything is finished. [111]

Before emptying the final water from the basin, one should scrub it well with the scrubber so that the minimum of grease remains. One then rubs it with an old towel, especially in the morning, for fear of dirtying too much the towels that are supposed to be used again in the evening.

When everything is finished, one dries the racks, one washes the stone floor with the broom, sprinkling it several times with the water from the second basin. One puts the second basin, carefully wiped, back in its place.

Our coadjutor Brothers are entrusted with collecting the towels that were used and spreading them on the bars in the fireplace, so they can dry. One washes one's hands with a bit of water and bran, if there is any, then one leaves. If someone has forgotten to do one of his duties, the person who noticed it should do it in his stead.

For those who are helping in the pantry [112]

One or two will be chosen every day for this last duty. If two are chosen, the second goes first to the fore-kitchen to get a pail of water. From this pail he pours water into the two vessels where the knives and forks should be put, and into the basin where the spoons are and where the dessert dishes should be washed, if they need it.

While wiping the forks and knives, care should be taken that no water remains, for fear they rust. From the dishes used for dessert, one should neatly set aside everything that is still usable, such as fruit, cheeses, remainders of biscuits or cakes. One does not leave until everything is finished, and until one has cleaned the table on which one has worked. When leaving, it is necessary to wash one's hands thoroughly and put one's apron back where one found it. [113]

Inner guidance

It is a necessity for us to serve ourselves, since we are not rich enough to have so many servants, and since most of our [coadjutor] Brothers are busy elsewhere at that time. But we would be greatly to be pitied if we did not know how to turn this necessity into a merit, and if we only went to the service rooms feeling like slaves, and despite ourselves. Moreover, it is just that we render to all our Brethren

justice que nous rendions à tous nos Frères le même service qu'ils nous rendent à leur tour. Au Noviciat, le service qui se fait aux offices est une de nos six épreuves principales. Nous lisons, dans la vie de tous les saints, qu'ils vécurent en communauté, qu'ils [114] eurent beaucoup de zèle et d'affection pour ces emplois humilians et rabaissans. Ceux qui vécurent dans le siècle, firent pour les pauvres ce que nous faisons les uns pour les autres. C'est icy encore un devoir de pénitence que nous pouvons offrir en expiation de nos péchés et de ceux des personnes dont nous voulons recommander à *Dieu* le salut.

La règle qui nous porte à regarder *Jésus Christ* même, en personne, dans chacun de nos Frères, nous inspirera l'esprit avec lequel nous devons les servir. Nous laverons la vaisselle, comme si *Jésus Christ* devoit y manger; nous nous presserons de les servir comme si *Jésus Christ* attendoit.

C'est encore icy une manière d'honorer les états humilians du Sauveur dans sa Sainte Enfance, [115] comme on l'a dit dans l'instruction des exercices corporels. Nous ne sçaurions douter douter [*sic*] que le fils de *Dieu* n'ait été comme le valet de Joseph et de *Marie*. Il est très louable, et plusieurs de nos Pères le font partout, de ne pas commencer le travail des offices qu'on ait fait le signe de la croix, et offert son action à *Dieu*. On peut dire tout bas l'oraison *Actiones nostras*.

Une bonne marque que ces actions se font en esprit intérieur et avec mérite, c'est quand on ne manque rien, qu'on garde un silence exact, qu'on s'abstient de rire et de toute autre enfance, et qu'on ne quitte point que tout ne soit fait et bien fait. Un signe encore qu'elles se font [116] par religion, c'est quand, outre les offices pour lesquels on se trouve marqué, on est toujours prêt à suppléer pour ceux qui manquent, et que de tems en tems on demande permission d'aller aider à la crédence, ou d'aller faire la grosse vaisselle à la cuisine. Cette permission doit se demander au révérend père Recteur au sortir de la table, en fléchissant le genouil.

Instruction seisième
Pour la récréation
Règlement extérieur

Au sortir du réfectoir, à moins qu'on ne soit aux offices, on se rend aux salles ou au jardin, selon la saison. [117] Si on va au jardin, on va d'abord à la chambre pour prendre son chapeau, pour de là descendre au jardin.

Il faut, en allant, mortifier l'empressement qu'on a naturellement pour le délassement et pour le plaisir: ne point courir dans les galeries ny sur les montées; dire avec dévotion un *Ave Maria* dans sa chambre avant que de prendre son chapeau, et un autre après l'avoir pris, demandant à *Dieu* par la Sainte Vierge la grâce de faire une récréation toute religieuse; descendre par la montée qui est marquée pour chaque chambre, sçavoir la petite du jardin pour les curitoires

the same service they render us in turn. At the Novitiate, the service done in the service rooms is one of our six principal testing experiences.[37] In the lives of all the saints, we read that they lived in a community, that they [114] felt a great deal of zeal and affection for these humiliating and belittling occupations. Those who lived in the world did for the poor what we do for one another. Here is yet another duty of penance that we can offer in expiation for our sins, and for the sins of the persons whose salvation we wish to recommend to *God*.

The rule that leads us to see *Jesus Christ* himself, in person, in each of our Brethren, will inspire in us the spirit with which we should serve them. We will wash the dishes as if *Jesus Christ* were going to eat from them; we will urge ourselves to serve our Brethren as if *Jesus Christ* were waiting.

This is yet another way of honoring the humiliating states of the Savior in his Holy Childhood, [115] as was said in the instruction about the bodily exercises. We cannot doubt that the son of *God* was a sort of valet to Joseph and *Mary*. It is very praiseworthy, and several of our Fathers do it everywhere, not to begin work in the service rooms without making the sign of the cross and offering one's action to *God*. One can very softly say the prayer, *Actiones nostras*.

A good indication that these actions are being done from an inner spirit, and with merit, is when one does not fail to do something, one strictly observes silence, one abstains from laughing and any other infantilism, and one does not leave until everything is done and done well. Yet another sign that these actions are being done [116] from religion is that, in addition to the chores in the service rooms to which one has been assigned, one is always ready to step in for those who fail to do something, and that one begs permission from time to time to go help in the pantry or to go do the heavy dishwashing in the kitchen. This permission should be asked of Reverend Father Rector on bended knee, as one gets up from table.

Sixteenth Instruction
For recreation
Outer regulation

Upon leaving the refectory, unless one is working in the service rooms, one goes to the community rooms or the garden, according to the season. [117] If one goes to the garden, one first goes up to one's bedchamber to get one's hat, and goes down to the garden from there.

While going, it is necessary to mortify the haste one naturally feels about relaxation and pleasure: do not run in the hallways or on the stairs; devoutly

---

[37] More specifically, this paragraph is referring to the fourth of the six experiences a novice was required to complete. These *experimenta* are enumerated in the *Constitutions* of the Society: 1) make the Spiritual Exercises for one month; 2) serve for a month in a hospital; 3) spend a month on a pilgrimage, begging from door to door; 4) carry out various lowly tasks within the house, serving all the while as a good example; 5) explain Christian doctrine to boys and "other simple persons"; and 6) preach or hear confessions. *Constitutions*, 37–38 [64–70].

des Anges et des Martyrs, et la grande pour ceux du curitoire des Apôtres. Personne ne doit aller par celle de l'Horloge. Enfin, éviter toute sorte d'étude et d'affectation à se rendre précisément au tems qu'on prévoit qu'arriveroi[en]t certains de nos Frères avec qui l'on [118] aimeroit mieux se trouver.

Lorsque nos Pères font récréation dans la salle de Notre Seigneur, ceux de nos Frères qui demeurent dans le curitoire de nos Bienheureux Martyrs, lorsqu'ils ont affaire dans leur chambre, ils ne doivent pas passer pour s'y rendre par la salle de Notre Seigneur, mais par la salle de Notre Dame, d'où ils descendent à leurs chambres par la petite montée du jardin. Cela se doit garder tout le tems que nos Pères sont en récréation, et même après les Litanies les jours de fête, que quelques-uns qui sont venus tard du confessional n'ont pu se chauffer ou faire récréation avant les Litanies.

Lorsqu'on est arrivé au lieu de récréation, on ne doit pas parler que l'Admoniteur, ou l'ancien du Bienheureux Goto en son absence, n'ait assigné ceux qui doivent faire la récréation ensemble. Il doit toujours mettre avec [119] deux de la seconde année de noviciat quelqu'un de la première, de même qu'avec deux de la première année il doit toujours mettre quelqu'un de la seconde; et fussent-ils trois de la même année, ils ne doivent point parler qu'ils n'ayent un quatrième d'une année différente.

Quand on est quatre, et que deux viennent demander un troisième, c'est le dernier arrivé des quatre qui doit aller avec eux. Si les deux qui se présentent pour avoir un troisième étoient deux anciens, ils prendront celuy des nouveaux qui est arrivé le dernier, ou le moins ancien des nouveaux s'ils étoient arrivés tous ensemble. Si c'étoit deux nouveaux qui demandassent un troisième, et qu'il y eût plus d'un ancien dans la bande de quatre, ce sera le dernier arrivé des anciens qui se joindra à eux; ou s'ils étoient arrivés en même temps, ce sera le moins ancien de noviciat. Si c'étoit un ancien et un nouveau qui demandassent un troisième, ils prendront [120] le dernier venu, sans distinction d'ancien et de nouveau.

Il n'est jamais permis aux bandes de quatre de refuser le quatrième qui, selon la règle précédente, doit aller avec les deux qui arrivent nouvellement. Il est du devoir de ceux-cy d'aller à la bande de quatre, demander un troisième, afin que toutes les bandes soit de trois, autant qu'il se pourra. Ainsy il n'y aura jamais plus de deux bandes de quatre à la fois. Si quelqu'un en arrivant ne trouvoit pas de bandes de quatre pour faire la sienne, il doit se joindre à la première bande qu'il rencontrera, après avoir dit son *Ave*, et ne pas aller chercher celle qu'il aimeroit le mieux; et s'il paroissoit dans quelqu'un de l'affectation ou à rechercher de certaines bandes, ou à se joindre à certains de nos Frères, ou à en éviter quelqu'un, on sera obligé en conscience d'en avertir le révérend père Recteur.

Il n'est jamais permis de quitter sa bande pour se joindre à une autre que dans les cas susdits. Il ne [121] l'est pas même de parler d'une bande à l'autre ny, quand on est quatre, de s'entretenir deux à deux.

say an *Ave Maria* in one's chamber before taking up one's hat, and another after having picked it up, asking *God*, through the Blessed Virgin, for the grace to take part in a totally religious recreation; go down by the stairway that is assigned to each chamber, that is, the small garden stairway for the Curitories of the Angels and Martyrs, and the big stairway for the novices in the Curitory of the Apostles. No one should use the Clock Stairway. Lastly, avoid any sort of planning and foolish desire about arriving at exactly the same time as certain of our Brethren with whom one [118] would prefer to be.

When our Fathers are taking their recreation in the Hall of Our Lord, those of our Brethren who reside in the Curitory of our Blessed Martyrs, when they have something to do in their chamber, should not pass through the Hall of Our Lord to get there, but through the Hall of Our Lady, whence they will go down to their chambers by the little garden stairway. This should be observed all the while our Fathers are in recreation, and even after the Litanies on feast days, when some who came late from the confessional were unable to warm themselves or take recreation before the Litanies.

When one has reached the recreation place, one should not talk until the Admonitor, or in his absence the senior of Blessed Goto, has assigned those who should take their recreation together. He should always put someone from the first year with two second-year novices [119], just as he should always put a second-year novice with two first-year novices; and should there happen to be three from the same year, they should not talk until they have a fourth person from a different year.

When one is in a group of four, and two come to ask for a third person, the latest comer of the four should go with them. If the two who are lacking a third person happen to be two seniors, they will take the newcomer who arrived last, or the least senior of the newcomers if they all arrived together. If two newcomers should ask for a third person, and there is more than one senior in the band of four, the senior who arrived last will join them; or if they arrived at the same time, it will be the least senior novice. If a senior and a newcomer are asking for a third person, they will take [120] the last comer, without distinguishing between senior and new.

It is never permitted for bands of four to refuse the fourth person, who, according to the previous rule, should go with the two who have just arrived. It is the latters' duty to go to the band of four and ask for a third person, so that all the bands will have three people, to the extent possible. Thus there will never be more than two bands of four at once. If someone, upon arriving, should happen to find no bands of four to make his band, he should join the first band he meets, after having said his *Ave*, and should not go look for the one he would prefer; and if someone showed a foolish desire either to look for certain bands, or to join certain of our Brethren, or to avoid someone, one will by conscience be obliged to notify Reverend Father Rector.

It is never permitted to leave one's band to join another band, except in the above cases. It is not [121] even permitted to talk from one band to another, nor, when there are four, to converse two by two.

Lorsque nos Frères novices coadjuteurs viennent en récréation, on doit les recevoir avec beaucoup d'honnêteté et de charité, et leur témoigner qu'on les voit avec plaisir. Comme ils arrivent ordinairement assés tard, ils doivent s'arrêter à la première bande qu'ils rencontrent, fût-elle de quatre; ou s'ils étoient plusieurs, se partager et se joindre aux plus proches bandes, en sorte qu'il n'y en ait qu'un d'eux à chacune.

On doit prendre garde à ne pas parler trop haut, et à ne pas rire avec éclat en quelque lieu que l'on soit, mais surtout au jardin, pour l'édification qu'on doit aux personnes du voisinage. Pendant qu'il y a des séculiers en retraitte, on ne doit point faire la récréation dans l'allée qui est le long du jardin de la Retraite; et en quelqu'autre temps que ce soit, il n'est jamais permis de se retirer sous le berceau. [122]

On doit se traitter avec beaucoup de respect, de charité, d'honnêteté, et de simplicité: ne point interrompre ceux qui parlent; ne point les contredire durement; ne railler, ne contrefaire personne; ne point faire aussi de complimens séculiers ou affectés; ne point disputer avec opiniâtreté, crût-on avoir raison; ne point relever une simplicité, et beaucoup moins une parole à double sens qui auroit échappée, mais s'il y paroissoit quelqu'affectation, en avertir le révérend père Recteur; prendre garde aussi de ne rien dire de choquant, et si cela étoit arrivé, sur-le-champ même en faire excuse. Il ne faut toucher personne, ny par jeu ny d'aucune manière, quand ce seroit pour l'avertir de quelque chose, ou pour le rendre attentif à ce qui se dit. Il ne faut point chanter, ny badiner avec des baguettes, des pierres, des marons, ou faire aucune autre enfance. Enfin, il ne doit paroître aucun signe d'impatience, [123] de colère, de mépris, de dédain, ni d'aucune autre passion déréglée.

Pour la matière des entretiens, elle doit être toute de choses spirituelles, autant qu'il est possible; et jusqu'aux choses les plus indifférentes dont on parle quelquefois, il doit paroître dans l'air de celuy qui les dit, et dans l'expression, toujours quelque chose de modeste, de réservé, et de religieux. S'il arrive quelquefois qu'on parle de sciences, ce ne doit être que bien légèrement et en passant, sans qu'on semble trop les estimer, et montrer par avance qu'on aura [*read*: qu'on n'aura] guères que la vanité en tête. Il est recommandé, plus que tout le reste, qu'on ne parle n'y ny d'histoires, ni de tours d'écoliers, ny des Fautes qui sont dites au réfectoir, ny des pénitences qui se font en public ou en secret. Ceci est plus de conséquence [124] qu'on ne sçauroit se l'imaginer.

Le dernier quart d'heure de la récréation du soir, on répète la Méditation qu'on a préparé après le Chapelet, pour le lendemain. Chacun dit ce qu'il a retenu, commençant par les anciens. Il est fort recommandé que cela se fasse sérieusement, et avec assés d'attention pour se le rendre utiles [*sic*].

Le petit coup avant les Litanies venant à sonner, aussitôt on se tait et on se rend en silence au lieu où elles se doivent dire. Si l'on y arrive avant l'heure, on s'y asseoit de côté et d'autre sur les bancs.

En hyver, lorsqu'il n'y a point de poïle [*read*: poêle allumé] et qu'on allume du feu, il ne faut point y aller avec précipitation. On se partage en

When our coadjutor Brother Novices come to recreation, they should be received with a great deal of courtesy and charity, and they should be shown that one is pleased to see them. Since they usually arrive rather late, they should stop at the first band they encounter, even if there are four people; or if there are several coadjutors, they should split up and join the nearest bands, so that there is only one of them in each band.

One should take care not to talk too loudly, and not to burst out laughing wherever one is, but especially in the garden, for the edification one owes to the people in the neighborhood. When there are laymen in retreat, one should not take one's recreation in the path that runs along the garden of the Retreat; and whatever the weather, it is never permitted to withdraw under the arbor. [122]

One should treat one another with respect, charity, courtesy, and simplicity; not interrupt those who are speaking; not contradict them harshly; not mock or mimic anyone; likewise, not pay worldly or affected compliments; not argue obstinately, even if one believes one is right; not call attention to something simple-minded, and still less to a word with a double meaning that may have escaped, but if it appears to be intentional, notify Reverend Father Rector; also take care to say nothing shocking, and if it should happen, immediately excuse oneself. No one must touch anyone, either in play or in any manner, even to warn him about something or call his attention to what is being said. There must be no singing, nor playing with sticks, stones, chestnuts, nor any other sort of infantilism. Lastly, no sign of impatience, [123] anger, scorn, disdain, or any other uncontrolled passion should be visible.

As for the subject matter of conversations, as much as possible they should be entirely about spiritual things; and even for the most banal things that one sometimes says, something modest, reserved, and religious should always appear in the air and in the expression of the person speaking. If it should sometimes happen that one talks about scholarly subjects, this should only be very lightly, and in passing, without seeming to value them too highly and to demonstrate beforehand that one has scarcely anything but vanity in one's head. Above all else, it is recommended that one not talk about stories, or schoolboy tricks, or Faults declared in the refectory, or penance done in public or in secret. This is of greater consequence [124] than one can imagine.

During the final quarter hour of the evening recreation, one repeats the Meditation that one prepared after the Rosary for the next day. Each one says what one has retained, beginning with the seniors. It is strongly recommended that this be done seriously and with sufficient attention to make it useful to one.

The little ring before the Litanies having sounded, one immediately falls silent and goes in silence to the place where they are to be said. If one arrives ahead of time, one sits on the benches on one side or the other.

In winter, when there is no stove lighted, and a fire is lighted, it is necessary not to go there in haste. One splits up into three or four bands, according to the number of novices, so that everyone can warm himself a bit. [125]

trois ou quatre bandes, selon le nombre des novices qu'on est, pour que tout le monde puisse un peu se chauffer. [125]

C'est notre frère Admoniteur qui déterminera le nombre et le temps qu'on peut être au feu, ou en son absence l'ancien du Bienheureux Goto. Il faut que du nombre de huit ou neuf, il y ait toujours au feu trois ou quatre anciens qui soient entrelassés avec les nouveaux; et qu'on ne parle guères qu'à ceux qui sont autour de soi. Quand on sera averty du tems qu'il faut quitter le feu, ceux qui y seront se retireront de leur[s] places avant que les autres se lèvent pour venir les prendre. Hors du feu on gardera, pour s'unir, les mêmes règles qu'aux récréations ordinaires. En allant au feux, et tandis qu'on y est, on ne se sépare point de sa bande. S'il semble nécessaire de racommoder le feu, ce sera au plus ancien du Noviciat qui s'y trouvera à le faire. S'il est trop foible, ou qu'il n'en ait point le talent, il en donnera la commission à quelqu'autre, et [126] personne ne s'en mêlera que celui qu'il en aura averty. Personne aussi ne touchera au sable que lui seul, ou celui à qui il en donnera la charge.

Direction intérieure

Les récréations, surtout au sortir du repas, sont le temps de la journée le plus difficile à passer d'une manière ~~bien~~ religieuse. Manque d'y veiller sur soy-même, on y fait souvent plus de fautes, et des fautes plus considérables, qu'en tout le reste du jour. Pour en convenir, il ne faut que voir combien nos Examens et nos Confessions sont moins chargés pendant les jours de nos retraites que les jours de récréation. On ne doit donc rien négliger pour ne pas perdre, dans une ou deux heures, ce qu'on auroit bien eu de la peine [127] à acquérir pendant le reste du jour par tous les exercices de dévotion. Saint Ignace vouloit que les récréations se passassent si saintement qu'au sortir de là, on fût aussi présent à soi-même, aussi disposé à retourner à la prière et à d'autres exercices aussi sérieux. Celles de Berchmans étoient si réligieuses que non seulement il y prenoit une nouvelle ferveur, mais qu'il l'inspiroit à tous ceux qui avoient le bonheur de l'accompagner. Le père Vincent Caraffe, un jour qu'on demandoit en récréation ce que chacun voudroit faire s'il étoit averty de devoir mourir à une heure de là, répondit: 'Pour moi j'achèverois ma récréation.' Il falloit que cette récréation fût bien de celles que demande saint Ignace.

Plusieurs choses peuvent servir à rendre les [128] nôtres plus innocents et plus irréprochables de jour en jour:

1° Le soin de nous recueillir, ~~au sortir~~ depuis la sortie de la table jusqu'au temps que nous arrivons au lieu de la Communauté. Il faut remarquer alors les fautes où l'on a le plus coutume de retomber, renouveller les résolutions de s'en corriger, demander la grâce de n'y point retomber.

2° L'indifférence à se trouver avec ceux de nos Frères qu'ils [*read*: qui] se présenteront, sans chercher l'un plutôt que l'autre: car outre qu'on ne cherche guères naturellement que ceux avec qui l'on croit être plus en liberté, ce qui est déjà ouvrir la porte à bien de petits désordres, bien des médisances et

It is our Brother Admonitor who will determine the number who can be at the fire, and for how long, or in his absence the senior of Blessed Goto. Of the eight or nine novices, there must always be three or four seniors at the fire, intermingled with newcomers; and one rarely speaks, except to those around one. When one is notified that the time has come to leave the fire, those who are there will leave their places before the others rise to take them. Away from the fire, one will observe the same rules for assembling as for ordinary recreation. When going to the fire, and while there, one does not separate from one's band. If it seems necessary to tend to the fire, it is up to the most senior person at the Novitiate to do it. If he is too weak, or if he lacks the skill, he will pass the undertaking to someone else, and [126] no one will get involved other than the person he notifies. Also, no one but he, or the person to whom he gives the responsibility, will touch the hourglass.

Inner guidance

Recreation periods, especially after meals, are the most difficult times of the day to spend in a religious manner. If one neglects to keep an eye on oneself, one often commits more faults, and greater faults, then than during all the rest of the day. To be convinced, one need only note how our Examens and our Confessions are less burdened on our retreat days than on our recreation days. One should therefore neglect nothing in order to avoid losing, in one or two hours, what one may have painfully [127] acquired during the rest of the day through all the devotional exercises. Saint Ignatius wanted recreation to be conducted in such a saintly way that, at the end of it, one would be just as present to oneself, just as disposed to return to prayer and to other similarly serious exercises. Berchmans's recreations were so religious that he not only took from them a new fervor, he also inspired it in all those who had the good fortune to accompany him. One day when each person was asked, during recreation, what he would do if he was notified that he would die in an hour, Father Vincent Carafa replied: 'As for me, I would finish my recreation.'[38] This recreation certainly had to be the sort for which Saint Ignatius asks.

Several things can serve to make [128] our recreation more innocent and more irreproachable day by day:

1) Taking care to be recollected from the time we leave the table until the time we reach the community areas. At that time it is necessary to notice the faults into which one tends to fall, to renew one's resolutions to correct them, and to beg the grace not to fall into them again.

2) Indifference about finding oneself with those Brethren who happen to present themselves, without seeking out one rather than another: for in addition to the fact that naturally one scarcely seeks out any but those with whom one feels most free, this already opens the door to many little disorders, much backbiting

---

[38] Vincenzo Carafa, a noble Neapolitan, served as the seventh superior general of the Society, from January 1646 to June 1649.

des railleries du prochain, bien des murmures contre les supérieurs, bien des démonstrations de familiarité et d'amitié particulière, bien de [129] petites maximes de relâchement, bien des rapports indiscrets et des contestations. Outre cela, dis-je, vouloir converser avec qui l'on veut, n'est-ce pas toujours vouloir converser avec qui *Dieu* ne veut pas? Et peut-on compter d'avoir ce secours spécial et abondant, si nécessaire pour ne point faire de fautes en parlant? Nous avons grâce pour nous bien comporter avec ceux à qui *Dieu* et la règle nous adressent; il est au moins très douteux que nous l'aions avec les autres.

3° De petites élévations d'esprit et de cœur vers *Dieu*. L'horloge qui sonne sept ou huit fois en une heure, l'arrivée de quelqu'un de nos Frères, ou leur séparation d'avec nous, peuvent servir comme d'admoniteurs pour nous en faire ressouvenir.

4° L'usage que nous ferons de notre esprit et de notre mémoire, pour introduire et soutenir des discours de piété. Si chacun vouloit se faire part des [130] bons sentimens que Dieu lui a donné[s], ou qu'il a puisé[s] dans les lectures, en tout un jour il n'y auroit [*read*: il y auroit] une matière plus que suffisante à s'entretenir utilement durant deux récréations; mais plusieurs, au contraire, ne sont ingénieux qu'à détourner les discours édifians et sérieux. C'est un scandale et la marque d'un cœur bien vuide de *Dieu* et bien remply de bagatelles, s'il n'y a peut-être quelque chose de pis.

5° Rien ne contribue plus à rendre nos récréations honnêtes, utiles, agréables, et édifiantes tout à la fois que de les regarder comme une manière d'apprentissage et d'essai de nos conversations avec les personnes du dehors. Nous ne sçaurions croirions croire [*sic*] quel talent c'est pour bien gagner des âmes à *Dieu* que de sçavoir parler de luy à propos, et sans causer du dégoût et de l'ennuy. Cela ne vient pas [131] tout d'un coup; il faut s'y former de bonne heure. Faute de cela, ou bien nous traiterons avec les séculiers comme nous avons coutume de traitter ensemble, et ils n'auront point lieu d'être édifié, nous crierons, nous contesterons, nous interromperons, nous nierons une proposition, nous la distinguerons comme sur les bancs, nous dirons des puérilités, des simplicités; ou bien nous nous observerons alors pour ne pas tomber dans nos défautz ordinaires, et nous nous trouverons l'esprit glacé, nous ne sçaurons pas dire quatre paroles à propos, et l'on nous traittera d'ignorans et de stupides.

Instruction dix-septième
Pour les Litanies
Règlement extérieur

Tous les jours les Litanies des saints se disent après la récréation du matin, et celles de la Sainte Vierge après la récréation du soir, dans la salle d'en haut ou d'en bas, selon la saison. On se place trois à trois, le long des bancs, à la

and mocking of our neighbors, many mutterings against the superiors, many demonstrations of familiarity and particular friendship, many [129] little maxims of tepidity, many indiscreet connections and contestations. Besides that, I say, wanting to converse with whomever one wishes, is it not always wishing to converse with someone with whom *God* does not want us to talk? And can one count on having this special and abundant help that is so necessary to keep from committing faults while speaking? We have grace to behave well toward those to whom *God* and the rule recommend us; at least it is very dubious that we have it with the others.

3) Little elevations of the spirit and the heart towards *God*. The clock that rings seven or eight times each hour, the arrival of some of our Brethren, or their separating from us, can serve as admonitors to remind us of this.

4) The use we will make of our spirit and our memory, to introduce and sustain pious discourse. If each one were willing to take into consideration [130] the good feelings that *God* has given him, or that he has found in his reading, in an entire day he would have more than sufficient subject matter for conversing usefully during two recreation periods; but some, on the contrary, are only ingenious at deflecting discourse that is edifying and serious. It is a scandal, and the mark of a heart that is very empty of *God* and very full of trifles, if not, perhaps, of something worse.

5) Nothing contributes more to making our recreations upright, useful, agreeable, and edifying, all at the same time, than to view them as a sort of apprenticeship and practice for our conversations with people outside. We would never be able to believe the talent there is for winning souls to *God* by knowing how to speak about him appropriately, and without causing disgust or boredom. That does not come [131] all at once; it is necessary to begin training early. Without that, we will either behave with lay people as we are accustomed to behave with one another, and they will have no reason to be edified: we will shout, we will contest, we will interrupt, we will deny a proposition, we will draw distinctions as we do during our classes, we will say childish things, simple-minded things; or else we will be on our guard at such times, in order not to fall into our ordinary defects, and we will find our spirit frozen, we will be incapable of saying four appropriate words, and they will treat us as though we are ignorant and stupid.

Seventeenth Instruction
For the Litanies
Outer regulation

Every day the Litanies of the saints are said after morning recreation, and those for the Blessed Virgin after evening recreation, in the upper community room or in the lower one, according to the season. One sits three by three on the

droite et à la gauche du prêtre qui [132] les dit. Il faut tâcher que les rangs soient bien serrés et à distance égale. Ceux de nos Frères qui demeurent dans la galerie des Anges et dans la chambre de Saint Jacques se mettent à la gauche, et ceux de la galerie des Bienheureux Martyrs avec nos Frères coadjuteurs à la droite du prêtre. Quand les chambres de Saint Thomas et de Saint Mathieu sont habitées, une des chambres prend un côté et l'autre, l'autre. On ne doit pendant les Litanies ny s'ap[puyer] ny sur les chaises ni contre les bancs, et les premiers rangs doivent se tenir éloignés de la muraille de face au moins de cinq ou six pieds. Il faut répondre aux Litanies d'une voix haute et distincte, et ne point couper la parole à celui qui les dit. Outre les Litanies de la Sainte Vierge qui se disent le soir en communauté, on dit une autre fois les mêmes Litanies de la Sainte Vierge à l'église, dans le balustre, tous les jours à 4 heures aux tems ordinaires, et à 4 heures 1/2 les jours de jeûne, et en rentrant à la Maison lorsqu'on revient de la promenade. Celles-cy se doivent dire avec plus de lenteur encore, et à voix plus haute, à cause du respect qu'on doit au Saint Sacrement, et de l'édification qu'on doit [133] aux personnes du dehors qui s'y rencontrent. On prendra bien garde de ne jamais rire, quelque chose qu'y puisse arriver. On se place comme à la Messe, et tous nos Frères coadjuteurs novices qui seront à la Maison ne manqueront point de s'y trouver. Il faut tout quitter, pour s'y rendre, dès qu'on entend le petit coup devant l'heure. Quand elles sont finies, on monte à la salle de Notre Dame, où l'on dit ensemble les Litanies du Saint Nom de *Jésus* et d'autres prières, à l'ordinaire.

Direction intérieure

Les Litanies des saints sont la seule prière qui se fasse en commun, tous les jours, par toute la Compagnie. Il faut les dire avec d'autant plus de dévotion que nos Frères les récitent pour nous, et comme avec nous, par toute la terre, de même que nous les récitons avec eux et pour eux. Depuis, il n'y a point de prières dans l'Église où se trouvent, en moins de paroles, exprimés tout plus en détail, tous nos différens besoins, ni où interviennent plus d'intercesseurs capables de nous les obtenir, ni où on représente à *Dieu*, par *Jésus Christ*, plus de motifs capables de toucher sa miséricorde. Ce sont autant de nouvelles [134] raisons de faire alors un effort de ferveur.

Pour se fixer plus vite et se recueillir plus aisément, au sortir d'une récréation où l'on s'est souvent un peu dissipé, on peut se représenter qu'on est au lit d'agonie, prêt d'aller paroître devant *Dieu*, et qu'on appelle les saints à son secours dans ce passage redoutable. Il est certain que ce seront à peu près les mêmes invocations qui se feront alors pour nous; mais ou bien nous n'entendrons plus ce qu'on dira, ou, du moins en ce temps-là où l'on est si peu capable d'attention, il sera bien consolant de pouvoir dire en trois mots [*read*: en trois phrases]: 'Grands saints, n'oubliés pas maintenant les prières que je vous fis avec tant de confiance et de dévotion tous les jours de ma vie. Je ne puis plus rien dire, mais vous n'oubliérés pas ce que, tant de fois, je vous ai dis. Priés pour moi, fléchissés le Juge en ma faveur.'

benches, to the right and to the left of the priest who [132] is saying them. It is necessary to try to keep the rows close together and at an equal distance. Those of our Brethren who reside in the hallway of the Angels and in the bedchamber of Saint James sit to the left, and those from the hallway of the Blessed Martyrs sit with our coadjutor Brothers to the priest's right. When the chambers of Saint Thomas and Saint Matthew are occupied, one of these chambers goes to one side, and the other to the other. During the Litanies one should not lean on the chairs or against the benches, and the first rows should keep at least five or six feet away from the wall in front of them. It is necessary to reply to the Litanies in a loud and distinct voice, and not interrupt the person who is saying them. In addition to the Litanies of the Blessed Virgin that are said in common in the evening, one says the same Litanies of the Blessed Virgin another time in the church, inside the balustrade, every day, at four o'clock on ordinary days and at 4:30 on fasting days, and upon returning to the House after a walk. These Litanies should be said more slowly still than the others, and with a louder voice, because of the respect one owes to the Blessed Sacrament, and the edification one owes [133] to the people from outside who are present. One will be very careful never to laugh, no matter what happens. One positions oneself as for Mass, and all our coadjutor Brothers who are novices, and who are in the House, will not fail to be present. It is necessary to drop everything and go there as soon as one hears the little ring before the hour. When the Litanies are over, one goes up to the Hall of Our Lady, where one says together the Litanies of the Holy Name of *Jesus* and other prayers, as usual.

Inner guidance

The Litanies of the saints are the only prayer said in common, every day, by the entire Society. They must be said all the more devotedly because our Brethren recite them for us, and so to speak with us, throughout the world, just as we recite these Litanies with them and for them. Hence, there are no prayers in the Church in which one finds all our different needs expressed in fewer words yet in greater detail, nor in which more intercessors intervene who are capable of helping us obtain them, nor in which one presents to *God*, through *Jesus Christ*, more motives capable of moving his mercy. These are all so many new [134] reasons for making an effort at fervor at that time.

In order to settle down more quickly and be more easily recollected, upon leaving recreation, where one has often been a bit un-recollected, one can imagine oneself on one's deathbed, ready to go and appear before *God*, and that one is calling upon the saints to help in this awesome passage. It is certain that approximately the same invocations will be said for us at that time; but either we will no longer hear what is being said, or else, at a time when one is so incapable of paying attention, it will be very consoling to be able to say, in three sentences: 'Great saints, do not forget now the prayers I said to you with such confidence and devotion every day of my life. I can no longer speak, but you will not forget what I said to you so many times. Pray for me, move the Judge in my favor.'

Les Litanies de la Sainte Vierge ne se disent par toute la Compagnie que dans les besoins extraordinaires, mais la Communauté les dit tous les jours au Noviciat, parce que la bonne éducation des novices est un besoin qui, pour durer toujours, n'en est pas moins un besoin supérieur: la conservation de la Compagnie en dépend. Nous devons les réciter principalement à dessein [135] d'observer pour nous, pour tous nos chers Frères, la persévérance dans notre vocation, et l'esprit de notre vocation, sans quoi notre vocation même ne serviroit peut-être qu'à notre plus grande condamnation.

Pour les Litanies de 4 heures, elles ont été ordonnées à perpétuité dans cette Maison par le Révérend Père Mutio Viteleschi, sixième général de la Compagnie, vers l'an 1628, en mémoire et pour le repos de l'âme de Monsieur du Tillet, notre digne Fondateur, d'autant plus que pendant sa vie il se tint toujours caché, et n'en voulut jamais avoir ni le nom, ni les honneurs.

Instruction dix-huitième
Pour apprendre à écrire bien correctement
Règlement extérieur

Il y a, dans l'ordre du jour, une demie-heure marquée pour apprendre à bien écrire, et 1/4 [d']heure pour apprendre l'ortographe. Qui que ce soit n'y doit manquer sans une permission expresse du révérend père Recteur, qui jugera de ceux qu'on peut dispenser de l'un ou de l'autre, ou de tous les deux à la fois. Ceux qui en sont dispensés demanderont, pour ce temps-là, quelque chose à écrire qui puisse leur servir [136] dans la suite. On donne à ceux qui doivent apprendre à écrire, des exemples sur lesquels ils puissent ~~appren~~ former leur écriture. S'ils veulent avancer, il faut qu'ils passent leur demi-heure entière à n'écrire plutôt que quatre à cinq lignes, et les écrire tout de leur mieux.

Pour l'ortographe, on copie quelque chose d'un livre bien imprimé et en françois moderne; et on doit s'appliquer, en le copiant, à observer non seulement comme sont écrits tous les mots, mais encore tous les points et les virgules, comment ils sont placés, et où il faut employer les lettres majuscules et les petites lettres.

Direction intérieure

C'est une chose incommode aux autres de ne pas écrire au moins d'une manière lisible, et une chose honteuse à des gens de lettres d'écrire souvent aussi peu correctement que des femmes et des ignorants. La fin des supérieurs, en ordonnant qu'on apprît à écrire et l'ortographe, a été d'obvier à ces inconvéniens; mais la fin des particuliers doit être d'obéir aux supérieurs, sans trop examiner leurs raisons. Dans les anciens livres de la Maison, où les novices écrivent qu'ils ont suby l'Examen quatre fois en deux ans, on remarque deux

The Litanies of the Blessed Virgin are only said by the entire Society when there is extraordinary need; but the Community says them every day at the Novitiate, because the good education of novices is a need that, if the Society is to continue, is nothing short of an important need: the conservation of the Society depends on it. We should recite these Litanies chiefly for the purpose [135] of observing for ourselves, for all our dear Brethren, the perseverance in our vocation and the spirit of our vocation, without which our vocation itself would perhaps serve only for our greatest condemnation.

As for the four o'clock Litanies, they were ordered in perpetuity at this House by Reverend Father Muzio Vitelleschi, sixth General of the Society, circa 1628, in memory of, and for the repose of the soul of Monsieur du Tillet, our worthy Founder,[39] all the more so because during his life he continually concealed his actions and never wanted to be named or honored.

Eighteenth Instruction
For learning to write very correctly

Outer regulation

In the order of the day there is a half hour set aside for learning to write well, and a quarter hour for learning to spell. No one, whoever he may be, should miss these sessions without specific permission from Reverend Father Rector, who will decide who can be excused from the one or the other, or from both. During that time, those who are excused will ask for something to write that can serve them [136] in the future. Those who should be learning to write are given examples upon which they can model their writing. If they wish to make progress, they must spend the entire half hour writing only four or five lines, and writing them as best as they can.

As for spelling, one copies something from a nicely printed book in modern French; and while copying it, one should apply oneself to observing not only how all the words are written, but also all the periods and commas, how they are placed, and where one should use capital letters and lower-case letters.

Inner guidance

Others are inconvenienced when someone does not write at least legibly, and it is a shameful thing that lettered people often write as incorrectly as women and the uneducated. The superiors' goal in ordering that one learn to write and spell was to prevent these inconveniences; but the goal of individuals should be to obey the superiors, without scrutinizing their reasons too much. In the old record books

---

[39] For Hélie du Tillet, see the Introduction, p. 9.

choses: la première, qu'il [137] n'en est presque pas dont l'écriture ne fût méconnoissable au bout de six mois, tant ils s'étoient avancés dans l'écriture; la seconde, que ceux qui dans la suite de leur vie ont le plus travaillé à la gloire de *Dieu*, sont presque toujours aussi ceux dont l'écriture sembloit la plus changée. C'est que le même principe qui donne de la diligence pour ces menus devoirs, dès le commencement, fait aussi que, dans tout le reste de la vie, on s'applique à proportion à tout ce que demande le zèle et l'obéissance. Quand on fait écrire à nos Frères des suffrages, des catalogues, des lettres circulaires pour envoyer dans la Province, c'est alors plus que jamais que l'obéissance et la charité les obligent à écrire tout de leur mieux, et de ne faire aucune sorte de fautes s'il est possible.

Instruction dix-neuvième Pour le Chapelet
Règlement extérieur

Le Chapelet se dit tous les jours, ou dans les salles ou dans le jardin, selon le temps et la saison. Il commence un quart d'heure après l'Oraison du soir. On se rend pour le dire au petit coup devant les 3/4. [138]

Quoy qu'il n'y ait qu'un 1/4 [d']heure marqué pour dire le Chapelet, il faut pourtant trouver tout le temps nécessaire pour le bien dire. On peut commencer en allant au Saint Sacrement, et en revenant, et le continuer jusqu'à 6 heures. On prépare ensuite la Méditation.

On doit toujours dire le Chapelet en se promenant, à moins qu'on ne soit grandement incommodé; et alors on demande permission de s'asseoir à notre frère Admoniteur ou à l'ancien du Bienheureux Goto; mais on ne doit jamais s'asseoir assé[s] près de quelqu'autre, pour faire soupçonner que le silence ne se garde pas exactement.

Il y a chaque mois des Chapelets à dire par obligation, entre ceux qu'extraordinairement on intime au réfectoir, ou que le révérend père Recteur peut faire ordonner en particulier. Il y en a aussi pour chaque semaine et pour chaque année. Pour n'oublier d'en dire aucun, il faut se faire un petit catalogue sur lequel soient marqués, par autant de demi-croix, le nombre des Chapelets qu'on doit dire; et à mesure qu'on les acquitte, on achève d'un trait de plume la croix. Cette pratique a plusieurs bons effets: 1° on ne dit pas son Chapelet à l'avanture et sans avoir dirigé son intention vers ceux pour qui l'on prie; 2° on sçait toujours combien il reste de Chapelets dont on puisse disposer selon sa dévotion; [139] 3° on s'accoutume, pour quand on sera prêtre, à marquer de la même manière les Messes qu'on aura à dire par devoir et celles dont l'application demeure libre, et ceci est d'une grande importance. Il faut s'accoutumer à marquer, de la même

of the House, where the novices state in writing that they have been subjected to the Examen four times in two years,[40] two things can be observed: first, the [137] writing of almost all of them was unrecognizable after six months, because they made such progress in writing; second, those who, during the rest of their lives, worked hardest for the glory of *God*, also are almost always the ones whose writing seemed the most changed. Thus the same principle that, from the beginning, gives rise to diligence about small tasks, also makes one apply oneself proportionately, for the rest of one's life, to everything that zeal and obedience demand. When our Brethren are ordered to write *suffrages*,[41] catalogues, or circular letters to send into the Province, it is then, more than ever, that obedience and charity oblige them to write their very best, and to make no mistakes if possible.

Nineteenth Instruction
For the Rosary
Outer regulation

The Rosary is said daily, either in the community rooms or in the garden, according to the weather and the season. It begins a quarter hour after afternoon Prayer. One goes to recite it at the little ring just before the final quarter of the hour. [138]

Although only a quarter hour is assigned for saying the Rosary, it is nonetheless necessary to find all the time needed to say it well. One can begin while going to the Blessed Sacrament and returning, and continue it until six o'clock. After that one prepares the Meditation.

One should always say the Rosary while walking, unless one feels quite ill; and in that case, one begs our Brother Admonitor or the senior of Blessed Goto for permission to sit; but one should never sit close enough to someone else to raise suspicions that silence is not being strictly observed.

Every month there are Rosaries to say by obligation, among those announced in the refectory for special occasions, or that Reverend Father Rector may order said in private. There are also Rosaries for each week and each year. In order not to forget to recite any of them, one must make oneself a little catalogue on which are marked, by incomplete crosses, the number of Rosaries one is supposed to say; and as one says them, one completes the cross with a dash of the pen. This practice

---

[40] During their two years of probation, novices have the opportunity and the responsibility to review the General Examen that is antecedent to the *Constitutions* themselves (*Constitutions*, 23–53). The first review is offered as they enter the Society. Then, every six months they have the opportunity to review the text again, in order to renew their awareness of the life and mission of the Society (27 [18], 44–45 [98], and 73 [146]). In France, in the seventeenth century, on each of these occasions the novice wrote a statement to this effect in a register.

[41] This may refer to a notice of Masses and prayers to be offered by the Society for a deceased Jesuit, rather than to the more common seventeenth-century meaning: "a declaration one makes of one's opinion, one's will, and that one gives orally, or in writing, or in some other manner, when there is an election" (*Dictionnaire* of the French Academy, 1694).

manière, les *Pater* et les *Ave* que chaque semaine on est obligé de dire à certains intentions: autrement il arrive qu'on les oublie tout à fait, parce qu'ils n'ont pas un temps marqué, comme le Chapelet.

Direction intérieure

La dévotion à la Sainte Vierge étant si recommandée et ne pouvant trop l'être aux enfans de la Compagnie, n'eût-on pas de Chapelets à dire par obligation, on ne devroit passer aucun jour sans le dire par dévotion. Nous devons aujourd'huy d'autant plus nous affectionner à cet ancien usage de nos premiers Pères, que le culte de la Sainte Vierge est plus négligé de la plupart des fidelles, qu'il est plus attaqué des novateurs, et que par cet endroit nous devons en quelque manière la dédommager. Ne doutons point qu'elle ne rassemble sur nous cette multitude de grâces dont elle est la dispensatrice, et qu'elle auroit dû partager autrefois sur un plus grand nombre [140] de serviteurs.

Ce n'est point assé[s] d'avoir un chapelet sur soy, il faut le porter toute sa vie à sa ceinture, et que tout le monde puisse le voir. Les premiers Jésuites, en traversant l'Allemagne, le portoient au col. Rougirons-nous de passer pour dévots à la Sainte Vierge, et de paroître couvert de ses livrées? Ne craignons-nous point qu'elle rougisse de nous à son tour, en présence de son fils? Ceux qui disent que cela sent le moine sont bien ridiculement vains, et méritent aussi que la protection de *Marie* soit pour les moines et non pas pour eux.

Hors du Noviciat le tems ordinaire de dire le Chapelet est après les Litanies du soir; mais comme le temps alors est bien court pour le faire et préparer la Méditation du lendemain, les plus arrangés en disent une partie après la récréation du matin, et réserve[nt] l'autre pour après celles du soir. Quelques-uns en récitent une dizaine après chaque visite du Saint Sacrement, et le reste ou au commencement de la Messe, ou dans quelqu'autre visite qu'ils font à la Sainte Vierge pendant le jour. Chacun peut suivre sur cela sa dévotion, mais toujours qu'on ne manque jamais de dire le Chapelet.

On se doit faire un grand scrupule de ne pas acquitter exactement au moins les Chapelets qui sont ordonnés par [141] les supérieurs et par la règle. Car quoique nous ne nous engagions pas, par des contracts formels, à prier pour les morts et pour nos bienfaiteurs, il y a pourtant sur cela une obligation tacite d'honneur et de justice. Il ne faut pas que nous soyons moins fidelles à payer nos dettes parce qu'on s'en fie à notre parole. Ceux qui font si peu d'état de prier pour autrui, méritent qu'un jour, lorsqu'ils seront en Purgatoire, *Dieu* permette qu'on les oublie avec la même dureté. Ils crieront qu'on les secoure, et tout sera insensible.

Il y a diverses méthodes pour bien dire le Chapelet et pour se tenir l'esprit appliqué et recueilli en le disant. Celle que tout le monde sçait est de méditer, à chaque dizaine, quelqu'un des mystères de la vie de *Notre Seigneur* ou de la Sainte Vierge, les partageant en plusieurs classes, comme un jour les mystères joieux, l'autre les mistères douloureux, le troisième les

has several good effects: 1) one does not say one's Rosary at random and without having directed one's intentions toward the persons for whom one is praying; 2) one always knows how many Rosaries remain that can be distributed according to one's devotions; [139] 3) one becomes accustomed to marking in the same way, when one is a priest, the Masses one will have to say by duty and the ones whose pursuance remains free, and this is of great importance. It is necessary to become accustomed to marking, in the same manner, the *Pater*'s and the *Ave*'s that one is obliged to say each week for certain intentions: otherwise it can happen that one forgets them totally, because no time is marked for them, as for the Rosary.

Inner guidance

Since devotion to the Blessed Virgin is so strongly recommended, and cannot be too highly recommended for the children of the Society, even if one did not have Rosaries to say from obligation, one should not pass a single day without saying the Rosary from devotion. Today we should become all the more attached to this old usage of our first Fathers, because devotion to the Blessed Virgin is more neglected by the majority of the faithful, because it is under increased attack from innovators, and because under those circumstances we should in some way make amends for this. Let us not doubt that she gathers above us that multitude of graces of which she is the dispenser, and which she has distributed in the past to a greater number [140] of servants.

It is not enough to have a rosary on one's person. Throughout one's life it must be worn at the cincture, so that everyone can see it. While crossing Germany, the first Jesuits wore it around their necks. Should we blush at being taken for devotees of the Blessed Virgin, and at being seen wearing her livery? Do we not fear that she will in turn blush about us, in the presence of her son? Those who say that it smacks of the monk are indeed ridiculously vain, and they also deserve that *Mary* protect monks and not them.

Outside the Novitiate, the ordinary time to say the Rosary is after the evening Litanies; but since the time is very short then to say it and prepare the next day's Meditation, those who are most organized say part of the Rosary after morning recreation, and they reserve the rest for after the afternoon recreation. Some recite a decade after each visit to the Blessed Sacrament, and the remainder either at the beginning of Mass or during another visit they pay to the Blessed Virgin during the day. Each person can let his devotion be his guide, but still, let one never fail to say the Rosary.

One should have great qualms of conscience about not completing with exactitude at least the Rosaries ordered by [141] the superiors and by the rule. For although we are not committed, by formal contracts, to pray for the dead and for our benefactors, on that point there is nonetheless a tacit obligation to honor and justice. Because people trust our word, we must not be less faithful about paying our debts. Those who care so little about praying for others deserve that one day, when they are in Purgatory, *God* will permit us to forget them just as harshly. They will cry out for help, and everyone will be indifferent.

mistères glorieux. Quelques-uns en ont d'autres. Ceux-ci parcourent sur chaque dizaine, ou plutôt sur chaque *Ave Maria*, quelqu'une des qualités que l'Église donne à la Mère de *Dieu* ou à *Notre Seigneur* dans les Litanies du Saint Nom de *Jésus* ou de la Sainte Vierge. Ceux-là, en récitant l'*Ave Maria*, cherchent, au nom de *Jésus* ou à celui de la Sainte Vierge, quelqu'épithète qui leur convienne, et l'ajoutent en passant. [142] D'autres ont de petits vers artificiels où sont enchaînées toutes les actions de la Vierge; et sur chaque *Ave* ils appliquent un mot de ces petits vers. Tout cela est bien; mais avant que de commencer le Chapelet, il faut déterminer la manière à laquelle on veut s'en tenir, au moins ce jour-là.

Le quart d'heure après le Chapelet s'emploie au Noviciat à préparer la Méditation du lendemain dans Avancin. Quand le jour manque dans les salles, il faut mettre de la lumière en divers endroits, pour que tous puissent lire commodément. C'est à l'ancien de chaque salle d'y pourvoir. De même quand on récite l'Office de Notre Dame en hyver.

On n'est pas obligé absolument de faire la Méditation d'Avancin; mais ceux même qui auront la permission ou la dévotion d'en faire quelqu'autre, ne laisseront pas de préparer assés celle-ci pour pouvoir en rendre compte au dernier quart de la récréation. Ils prépareront ensuite, à 8 heures et 1/4 [du soir], celle qu'ils ont dessein de faire.

Instruction vingtième
Pour les tems libres et indifférens
Règlement extérieur [143]

On appelle libres ou indifférens les tems de la journée où les Instructions ne marquent rien à faire de particulier et de distinct, et ceux qui peuvent rester après avoir achevé ce qui est ordonné pour une certaine heure. Jamais alors même, il n'est permis de ne rien faire du tout, mais on peut faire ce que l'on veut, pourvu qu'il soit utile, honnête, et raisonnable. On peut donc lire ou écrire une lettre, tailler des plumes, aller faire coudre ou demander quelque chose à la couturerie ou à quelqu'autre office avec permission, parcourir quelque livre de la chambre, écrire quelque chose pour son utilité, *etc*.

Direction intérieure

Qui sçaura connoître le prix du temps ne consentira jamais à en perdre un seul instant. *Particula bonae diei non te prætereat.*[28] Si un damné ou une âme du

---

[28] Ecclesiasticus 14:14, *Non defrauderis a die bono, et particula boni doni non te prætereat.* The manuscript modifies the text slightly, merging the two halves of the verse into a statement that makes the author's point and reads: "Let not the part of a good *day* overpass thee."

There are diverse methods for saying the Rosary well, and for keeping one's spirit applied and recollected while saying it. Everyone knows the method according to which, for each decade of small beads, one meditates upon one of the mysteries of the life of *Our Lord* or that of the Blessed Virgin, subdividing them into several classes, such as the joyous mysteries one day, the sorrowful mysteries the next day, and the glorious mysteries the third day. Some people use other methods. For each decade, or rather for each *Ave Maria*, some go through one of the qualities that the Church gives to the Mother of *God* or to *Our Lord*, in the Litanies of the Holy Name of Jesus or those of the Blessed Virgin. Others, while reciting the *Ave Maria*, seek, at the name of *Jesus* or that of the Blessed Virgin, some epithet appropriate for them, and they add it in passing. [142] Others invent little poems where all the actions of the Virgin are linked together; and to each *Ave* they apply a word from these brief lines. All of that is fine, but before beginning the Rosary, it is necessary to determine the manner in which one wishes to do it, on that day at least.

At the Novitiate the quarter hour following the Rosary is used to prepare the next day's Meditation from Avancini. When there is not enough light in the community rooms, lights must be placed in various places, so that everyone can read conveniently. The senior of each community room sees to this, and likewise when one recites the Office of Our Lady in winter.

One is not absolutely obliged to do the Meditation from Avancini; but those who have the permission or the devotion to do a different one, will not shirk at preparing this Meditation sufficiently to be able to report on it during the final quarter hour of recreation. After that, they will prepare, at 8:15 in the evening, the one they intend to do.

Twentieth Instruction
For free time and unassigned time
Outer regulation [143]

Free or unassigned times of day are times when the Instructions show nothing specific and distinct to be done, and any time that might remain after having completed what is ordered for a certain hour. Even then it is never permitted to do nothing at all; but one may do what one wishes, provided it is useful, upright, and reasonable. One can therefore read or write a letter, cut pen tips, go to have something sewn or to request something at the sewing room, or with permission go to some other service room, look through some book from the bedchamber, write something that will be useful to one, *etc.*

Inner guidance

Anyone who knows how to judge the value of time will never consent to waste a single instant. "Let not the part of a good day overpass thee." If a damned

Purgatoire pouvoit l'avoir cet instant, il suffiroit à l'un pour se réconcilier avec *Dieu* et faire changer son arrêt, et à l'autre pour hâter beaucoup son entrée dans le Ciel. Les petits moments mis bout à bout ne laissent point à la fin de la vie de faire de longues heures.

Il y a des gens qui ne sçauroient rien faire, à moins qu'ils ne voient devant eux beaucoup de temps. Il faut s'habituer à une conduite toute contraire: n'écriroit-on [144] que deux lignes, ne liroit-on que quatre versets, c'est toujours autant de gagné. Ensuite, dans les Collèges pendant ces petits intervalles, on préparera une matière, on cherchera des mots qu'on a rencontrés et qu'on ne sçait pas. On lira quelques thèmes de places, on insc[r]ira des billets de confession, on ira chercher ou reporter un livre à la bibliothèque, on balaiera sa chambre ou bien on l'arrangera, et on épargnera des tems sérieux qu'il faudroit ensuite donner à ces sortes de bagatelles.

Instruction vingt-unième
Pour la manière de se comporter dans la chambre
Règlement extérieur

Dans la chambre on doit garder le silence exactement, ou si on a quelque chose de tout à fait nécessaire à dire à quelqu'un, s'approcher de luy, parler la tête découverte, et si bas qu'on ne puisse être entendu que de lui seul. Les nouveaux doivent demander ce qu'ils ont à faire à l'ancien et non point à d'autres, à moins qu'il ne fût absent et que la chose ne pressât.

On doit, dans la chambre, avoir tous les égards imaginables pour ses compagnons; ne point se montrer dans aucun état qui soit contre la bienséance; ne se licentier en rien d'incivil ou [145] de libre; ne faire pas plus de bruit, s'il est possible, que si on y [*read*: on n'y] étoit pas; ne point traîner les chaises ou les remuer, ou les autres meubles, assés fort pour incommoder ceux qui logent au-dessous ou à côté; ne point cracher trop souvent ou se moucher trop fort, surtout pendant les exercices de piété. On ne doit point regarder par les fenestres, ni se considérer dans les vitres.

On doit tenir toutes choses proprement en sa place, ayant ses livres, ses papiers, ses hardes bien pliées et serrées, sans qu'on laisse rien traîner sur le pulpitre, sur l'oratoire, sur le lit que doit être toujours très proprement fait.

La chaise sur laquelle on met sa birette quand on prend son chapeau, doit se ranger contre le pied du lit, et le petit tabouret sur lequel on met son pulpitre proche de l'oratoire. Quand on ne se sert pas de sa robbe, on doit la plier proprement, et la mettre dans l'armoire, et jamais sur le lit ou sur la chaise pendant le jour. Quand on a pris quelque livre à la petite bibliothèque de la chambre, on doit l'y remettre aussitôt qu'on s'en est servy, sans le garder

person or a soul in Purgatory could have that instant, for the former it would suffice to reconcile himself with *God* and cause his fate to be changed, and for the latter to hasten greatly his entrance into Heaven. By the end of one's life, little moments put end to end will unfailingly make long hours.

There are people who are incapable of doing anything unless they have a lot of time before them. It is necessary to become accustomed to a totally different conduct: if one were to write [144] only two lines, read only four verses of the Scriptures, it is always that much time gained. Afterwards, in the Colleges, during such brief intervals, one will prepare a subject, one will look up some words that one has encountered and that one does not know. One will read a few compositions for the placement competition,[42] one will fill out confession slips, one will go get a book from the library or return it, one will sweep one's bedchamber or else one will arrange it, and one will economize, for serious things, the time it would otherwise be necessary to spend on these sorts of trifles.

Twenty-first Instruction
For the way to behave in the bedchamber
Outer regulation

In the bedchamber one should scrupulously keep silence; or if one has something absolutely necessary to say to someone, approach him, speak with a bared head, and so softly that one can only be heard by him alone. Newcomers should ask the senior what they are supposed to do, and not ask others, unless he should be absent and the matter urgent.

In the chamber one should show all imaginable consideration for one's companions; not show oneself in a state that offends propriety; not give oneself over to anything uncivil or [145] unrestrained; not make any more noise, if possible, than if one were not there; not drag chairs or move them or the other furniture so loudly as to inconvenience those who lodge below or in the next room; not spit too often or blow one's nose too loudly, especially during exercises of piety. One should not look out the windows or peer at oneself in the windowpanes.

One should keep everything neatly in place, having one's books, one's papers, one's clothing carefully folded and put away, without letting anything lie about on the lectern, the prayer desk, or the bed, which should always be neatly made.

The chair on which one puts one's birette, when one picks up one's hat, should be placed at the foot of the bed, and the little stool on which one puts one's lectern should be near the prayer desk. When one is not using one's robe,

---

[42] In Jesuit colleges, a special "place," in the sense of classroom rank (and, perhaps, seating), was conferred upon the winners of the Latin composition contest.

sur soy ou dans son oratoire, de crainte que quelqu'autre n'en ait besoin dans l'intervalle. La même doit s'observer à l'égard des petits meubles communs qui sont dans les chambres, comme ciseaux, vergettes, *etc.*

Si on avoit fait ou qu'on trouvât dans la chambre quelqu'ordure, comme de la paille, des flouons de laine, [146] des rognures de papier, il faut les relever et les mettre en lieu d'où on puisse les jetter par les fenêtres quand on les ouvrira.

Entrant dans la chambre et en sortant, on doit dire *Ave Maria* à genoux devant son oratoire.

Quand on sort de la chambre, à moins que ce ne soit pour un exercice commun, ou que l'ancien ne le sçache déjà, on lui doit dire à l'oreille où l'on va. Si l'ancien est absent, on le dit au plus ancien après lui, et l'ancien le dit au second, ou s'il n'y est pas, à celui qui est après lui.

Il faut tout quitter au premier son de la cloche, pour aller où l'on est appellé, ayant soin cependant de tout serrer [*read*: de serrer tout] ce qu'on a actuellement entre les mains. Quand on sort de la chambre, on doit toujours ouvrir les fenêtres et la porte pour donner de l'air, et les bien arrêter. Le dernier qui sort est chargé de cette commission. Si tous sortent ensemble, les plus proches de la porte et des fenêtres doivent s'en donner la peine.

Direction intérieure

Nous devons regarder notre chambre comme le tombeau où nous nous sommes volontairement enfermés pour *Jésus Christ*. Si, dès le commencement, nous nous accoutumons à la bien garder et à y être toujours occupés, elle nous deviendra agréable. *Cella* [147] *continuata dulcescit et malè custodita tædium generat*, dit l'autheur de l'*Imitation*; *si in principio conversionis tua eam benè incolueris, et custodieris, erit tibi posteà dilecta, amica, et gratissimum solatium.* On ne sort guères de sa chambre par ennui qu'on n'aille faire quelque faute ailleurs. *In cellâ invenies quod de foris sæpiùs amittes.*[29] Ce jeune homme qui se plaignoit à un ancien solitaire que sa cellule lui étoit insupportable: 'Mon cher enfant, lui répondit-il, c'est que vous n'avés jamais bien médité et où vous courrés risque encore de tomber.' Quant aux attentions à n'incommoder personne, c'est la charité qui doit en être le motif; et l'habitude qu'il faut prendre pour quand on demeurera seul, d'être toujours sous les yeux de *Dieu* et des saints anges, et de ménager aussi ses voisins et ceux qui demeurent au-dessous.

---

[29] Thomas à Kempis, *De Imitatione Christi*, liber primus, cap. 20, 5: *In cella invenies, quod de foris saepius amittes. Cella continuata dulcescit et male custodita taedium generat. Si in principio conversationis tuae bene eam incolueris, et custodieris, erit postea tibi amica dilecta, et gratissimum solatium.* The anonymous Jesuit's spelling of *dulcescit* reproduces its pronunciation in France. His other modification is very significant. Thomas à Kempis's term was *conversationis*, a word that is used in a neutral context and primarily denotes familiarity, intimacy, conduct, behavior – either positive or negative, depending on the people with whom one associates. In the *Instructions* the word is changed to *conversionis*, which has a positive connotation and is used in a religious context: one changes one's former life and becomes a more spiritual person, and therefore a better person.

one should fold it neatly and put it in the wardrobe, and never on the bed or on the chair during the daytime. When one has taken some book from the little library in the bedchamber, one should put it back as soon as one has finished with it, without keeping it on one's person or in one's prayer desk, for fear someone else will need it in the interval. The same should be observed concerning the little communal items that are in the chambers, such as scissors, whisk brooms, *etc.*

If one has made a mess, or if one should find one in the chamber, such as straw, lint, [146] little bits of paper, they must be picked up and put where one can throw them out the window when it is open.

When entering and leaving the chamber, one should say *Ave Maria*, kneeling before one's prayer desk.

When one leaves the chamber, unless it is for a communal exercise or unless the senior is already informed, one should whisper one's destination in his ear. If the senior is absent, one says it to the next most senior person; and the senior says it to the second most senior person, or if he is not there, to the person after him.

Everything must be put down at the first sound of the bell, to go where one is called, taking care however to stow away everything currently in one's hands. When one leaves the chamber, one should always open the windows and door to provide air, and block them well. The last person who leaves is entrusted with this task. If everyone leaves together, those closest to the door and to the windows should take the trouble to do it.

Inner guidance

We should view our chamber as the tomb in which we have voluntarily shut ourselves up for *Jesus Christ*. If, from the very beginning, we become accustomed to caring for it well and always being busy in it, it will become agreeable to us. "Your cell [147] will become dear to you if you remain in it, but if you do not, it will become wearisome," says the author of the *Imitation*. "If at the beginning of your entering the religious life, you live within your cell and keep to it, it will soon become a special friend and a very great comfort." One rarely leaves one's bedchamber from boredom without going to commit some fault elsewhere. "In your chamber you will find what too often you lose abroad." That young man who complained to an aged hermit that his cell was unbearable to him, received as a reply: 'My dear child, that is because you have never really meditated, and you still risk a fall.' As for being careful not to inconvenience anyone, the motive should be charity; and it is a habit that must be acquired for when one lives alone, to always be under the eyes of *God* and the holy angels, and to spare one's neighbors and those who reside beneath.

Instruction vingt-deuxième
Pour le silence et la modestie
Règlement extérieur

Hors le temps et le lieu de récréation, on doit garder le silence comme dans la chambre, ne parlant jamais que du pur nécessaire, debout, tout bas, et la tête découverte. [148] Il y a de certains endroits où on doit être plus attentif à garder le silence, parce qu'on est plus exposé à l'y rompre. Ces endroits sont la couturerie, où l'on ne doit jamais aller sans permission et n'être précisement que le temps qu'il faut pour demander ses besoins, ou pour faire coudre quelque chose; la sacristie, lorsqu'on va pour servir la Messe; la chambre des garçons lorsqu'on est chargé de leur faire quelque lecture; les divers offices de la Maison, lorsqu'il est nécessaire de demander quelque chose aux officiers; les chambres de nos Frères, où l'on ne doit pas entrer, mais dire sur le pas de la porte ou demander simplement en trois mot[s] le nécessaire; et en général tous les endroits écartés où l'on peut se trouver seul à seul, ou plusieurs ensemble, à faire quelque chose qui aura été ordonnée.

Il y a une manière de rompre le silence absolument interdite au Noviciat, et dont on ne se rendroit pas coupable sans mériter une sévère correction. Ce seroit de s'entretenir de billets et de se les donner furtivement. Cette liberté est toujours comme le premier prélude d'une vocation chancelante, et l'on a divers exemples de plusieurs que cela a conduit aux dernières extrémités. Ceux qui recevroient de ces billets sans en avertir, seroient aussi coupables que ceux qui les auroient donnés. On met encore au même rang ceux qui s'entreprêteroient des papiers volans ou des livres qu'ils auroient trouvés ou par hasard ou les aiant [149] cherchés, surtout si c'étoient des livres profanes ou dangereux.

Pour la modestie: outre ce qui est marqué dans nos règles qu'il faut lire souvent et observer avec exactitude, voici quelques fautes où nos Frères novices sont plus sujets à tomber s'ils n'y prennent garde: badiner avec leur chapelet ou la courroye de leur passe-partout; courrir en descendant les degrés ou les monter deux à deux; regarder derrière eux ou par les fenêtres pour voir ce qui se passe; se précipiter pour aller au feu ou en récréation; rire sans raison ou par la seule raison qu'ils en voient d'autres rire; porter leurs mains dans leurs poches, ou une main dans la poche et une dans la fente de la soutane au-dessus de la ceinture; éclatter en riant, ou battre des pieds et des mains pour applaudir à ce qu'on leur fait; balancer le corps ou traîner les pieds en marchant; faire des grimaces; pancher la tête d'un côté, ou avancer le col en priant *Dieu*; tourner les yeux légèrement, ou les avoir fixés contre terre, au lieu de les placer à une juste distance; paroître décontenancés quand on leur parle; prendre leur birette par le côté gauche et lui faire faire un demi-tour en se découvrant; avoir les pieds en dedans; marcher pesamment, ou au contraire se quarrer avec quelque sorte d'affectation en marchant; [150] tirer sa soutane par-derrière pour qu'elle fasse des plis réguliers; porter souvent les doigts

Twenty-second Instruction
For silence and modesty
Outer regulation

With the exception of the time and place of recreation, one should keep silence, as in the bedchamber, never speaking except from pure necessity, and standing and speaking very softly, head bare. [148] There are certain places where one should be more attentive about keeping silence, because one is more exposed to breaking it there. These places are the sewing room, where one should never go without permission, and should only be there just long enough to state one's needs or to have something sewed; the sacristy, when one goes there to serve Mass; the boys' chamber, when one is assigned to read something to them; the different service rooms in the House, when it is necessary to ask a staff member something; the chambers of our Brethren, which one should not enter, but speak from the threshold or simply make the necessary request in a few words; and in general all the distant places where one might find oneself alone with someone, or with several together, to do something one has been ordered to do.

There is a way of breaking silence that is absolutely forbidden in the Novitiate, and which one cannot commit without deserving severe correction: communicating by notes and passing them back and forth furtively. This liberty is always a sort of first prelude to a shaky vocation, and there are diverse examples of several persons whom this has led to the last extremity. Those who might receive such notes without informing about it would be as guilty as those who sent them. In this same category are those who loan loose pages or books they either found by chance or [149] sought out, especially if they are secular or dangerous books.

As for modesty, in addition to what is marked in our rules, which should be read often and observed with exactitude, here are a few of the faults that our novice Brethren are most prone to commit if they are not careful: playing with their rosary or the strap of their go-everywhere; running down the stairs, or going up them two at a time; looking over their shoulder or out the windows to see what is going on; rushing to get to the fire or to recreation; laughing for no reason or simply because they see others laugh; putting their hands in their pockets, or one hand in the pocket and the other in the slit of the soutane above the waist; bursting out laughing, or beating their hands and feet to applaud something that one has done; swinging their body or dragging their feet while walking; grimacing; leaning their head to one side or sticking out their neck while praying to *God*; letting their eyes dart about lightly or fixing them on the floor, instead of positioning them at a suitable distance; appearing discountenanced when someone speaks to them; removing their birette by grabbing it at the left side and spinning it a half revolution; turning in their toes; walking heavily or, on the contrary, strutting with a sort of affectation while walking; [150] pulling on the back of their soutane so that it makes even pleats; frequently lifting their fingers to their head, ears, or nostrils;

à la tête, aux oreilles, ou aux narines; s'appuier nonchalament lorsqu'ils sont assis; souffler du nés d'une manière à se faire entendre et reconnoître d'assés loin; parler dans leurs dents ou en nazillant. C'est donc sur toutes ces choses qu'ils doivent faire en partie leur Examen particulier, les quinze premiers jours après qu'ils ont pris la soutanne, et les relire ensuite assés souvent pour ne les point oublier, et observer s'ils n'y font pas de faute. À l'assemblée qui se fait pour la Modestie les jours de fêtes avant le sermon, on doit être fort sérieux, dire avec simplicité toutes les fautes qu'on croit avoir remarquées lorsqu'on est averty de le faire; et quand on fait soi-même la Modestie, ne point se donner des airs de vieux novice et de bel esprit: rien n'est plus pauvre et plus indigne de la noble simplicité dont nous devons faire profession. C'est toujours une puérilité de rougir des devoirs de son âge et de son état.

Direction intérieure

Le silence empêche que nos bons sentimens ne nous échapent, et la modestie que les mauvaises impressions du dehors n'entrent par les sens dans notre cœur. Ces deux, [151] bien entendues, suffisent pour faire connoître l'importance de nous étudier soigneusement au silence et à la modestie.

Les anciens religieux n'appelloient garder exactement le silence que quand on ne disoit pas une seule parole inutile, ni deux sillabes où une suffisoit. Quelques-uns imaginèrent une manière de parler par signes, et sans aucun mouvement de la langue et des lèvres. Cela est encore en usage dans plusieurs monastères, surtout depuis la fin du jour jusqu'à Primes. Par là, personne n'est interrompu dans son profond recueillement, et par signes l'on ne peut guères être tenté ni capable d'exprimer que les choses nécessaires. Méditons souvent la sentence de *Notre Seigneur*, qu'une seule parole inutile sera une matière de compte à son jugement.[30] Il n'a pas dit 'trois, deux paroles.' Nous ne douterons point que, par la raison des contraires, une seule parole retenue par principe de régularité ne doive avoir aussi une grande récompense. Ce n'est pas un si grand mal peut-être de dire un petit mot en passant, mais c'est un grand bien de ne le pas dire par esprit de régularité. En faudroit-il davantage pour une âme généreuse et bien déterminée à faire, en tout, ce qui est du bon plaisir de *Dieu*? On a connu des novices qui, au bout de deux ans, ne pouvoient pas se reprocher d'avoir dit, en tems de silence, six paroles tout à fait inutiles en les joignant toutes bout-à-bout. Que cela est louable, et digne de notre imitation!

Nous ne disons rien à ceux qui sont prêts à rire et à parler toujours, qui en prennent toutes les occasions, qui les cherchent même, qui semblent oublier que *Dieu* les voit partout [152] où les hommes ne les voient pas, qui se donneroient des rendés-vous pour s'entretenir plus à leur aise. Jamais, sans silence, ils n'auront de recueillement, jamais sans recueillement d'esprit d'oraison, sans esprit d'oraison jamais de vertus solides, et peut-être bien des vices qui pourroient les conduire aux derniers excès. *Nota bene.*

---

[30] Matthew 12:36, *Dico autem vobis, quoniam omne verbum otiosum, quod locuti fuerint homines, reddent rationem de eo in die iudicii.*

leaning nonchalantly when seated; blowing out through their nose in a way that can be heard and identified from quite a distance; speaking through their teeth or their nose. All these things should therefore be made part of their particular Examen, during the first two weeks after they have taken the soutane, and should be reread often enough not to forget them and to note whether they are committing a fault. At the assembly held for Modesty on feast days prior to the sermon, one should be very serious, state with simplicity all the faults one thinks one has observed when one is notified to do so; and when doing Modesty oneself, not assume the airs of an old novice and a fine wit: nothing is more paltry and unworthy of the noble simplicity that we should profess. It is always childishness to blush about the duties of one's age and rank.

Inner guidance

Silence prevents our good feelings from bursting forth, and modesty prevents bad outer impressions from entering our heart through the senses. These two, [151] of course, suffice to make known the importance of carefully schooling ourselves in silence and modesty.

The religious of old defined keeping strict silence as not saying a single idle word, nor two syllables where one would suffice. Some of them devised a way of speaking in signs, with no movement of the tongue or lips. That is still used in some monasteries, especially from the end of the day until Prime. In that way, no one is interrupted in his profound recollection, and by signs one can scarcely be tempted or be capable of expressing anything but necessary things. Let us meditate often on *Our Lord*'s statement that a single idle word will be taken into account on Judgement Day.[43] He did not say 'three words, two words.' Conversely, we shall not doubt that a single word held back on the principle of regularity should likewise receive a great recompense. It is perhaps not such a great evil to say a brief word in passing, but it is a great good, from a spirit of regularity, not to say it. Does a generous and very determined soul need more, in order to do everything that is *God*'s good pleasure? One has known novices who, at the end of two years, could not reproach themselves for having said, during periods of silence, six totally idle words joined end to end. How praiseworthy that is, and how worthy of being imitated by us!

We do not talk to those who are always ready to laugh or talk, who seize every opportunity to do so, who even seek such opportunities, who seem to forget that *God* sees them everywhere [152] where men do not see them, who would make appointments to talk together more at their ease. Never, without silence, will they attain a state of recollection; never, without a state of recollection, will they attain a spirit of prayer; never, without a spirit of prayer, will they acquire solid virtues, and perhaps a lot of vices that could lead them to the greatest excesses. *Note carefully.*

---

[43] Matthew 12:36, "But I say unto you, that every idle word that men shall speak, they shall render an account for it in the day of judgment."

Pour la modestie: outre qu'elle est une garde des plus asseurées de l'innocence, elle convient singulièrement aux personnes dont un devoir essentiel est d'édifier le prochain. On ne voit pas ce que nous sommes, on voit ce que nous paroissons être; mais par ce que nous paroissons être, on croit être en droit de juger de ce que nous sommes. Nous devons nous présenter sans cesse la personne adorable de *Jésus Christ*, notre grand modèle. Il est dit de lui que sa seule rencontre inspiroit la vertu et le respect, et que de ses yeux il sortoit une douceur pleine de majesté qui gagnoit tous les cœurs, *In primo ad se venientes trahere poterat aspectu.*[31] Que jamais on ne le vit crier, contester, rire avec éclat, on ne lui vit ni le visage triste, ni un air évaporé, ni des manières turbulentes et précipitées. *Non clamabit, non contendet: neque audietur vox ejus in plateis; non erit turbulentus. Christus numquam legitur risisse.*[32] *Ridere numquam visus, lacrymari sæpiùs, et hoc quidem dum deflet peccata nostra, etc.*[33]

La modestie de nos premiers Pères attira à la Compagnie un grand nombre d'excellens sujets; les premiers Jésuites de Paris étoient si composés que leurs ennemis disoient d'eux: [153] 'Ces Hypocrites, voïés comme ils sçavent se contrefaire.' Prenons garde que nous ne laissions à d'autres ce qu'ils ont empruntés de la Compagnie, que les religieux réformés par nous, et les ecclésiastiques des séminaires formés sur nous, ne soient beaucoup plus modestes.

Nous pouvons bien, hors d'icy, perdre la modestie parfaite que nous y aurons acquise; mais si nous n'emportons d'icy une grande modestie, il est comme impossible que nous en acquérions jamais beaucoup quand nous serons ailleurs.

Instruction 23ᵉ
Pour la propreté sur soy et dans la maison
Règlement extérieur

La pauvreté dont nous faisons profession n'est point opposée à la propreté. Au contraire, c'est parce que nous sommes pauvres qu'il faut être plus attentifs

---

[31] Saint Jerome, *Commentary on Matthew* (Matthew 9:9): *ex primo ad se videntes trahere poterat aspectu.* The Jesuit's version contains two variants. He wrote *in primo* ("with the first") instead of the original *ex primo* ("from the first"). He also used a different verb: "came" (*ad se venientes*) in the place of "saw" (*ad se videntes*). Be this second change accidental or intentional, it corresponds to the message being conveyed by the Reverend Father: he was not talking about "seeing" Jesus. Indeed, his previous sentence talks about "meeting" Jesus. In short, the novices were being prepared to "come" to Jesus, that is, to answer his call, as Matthew did in that particular verse. If *ad se venientes* should happen to be the intended wording, the Jesuit was grammatically incorrect in retaining the *ad*: he should have written simply *In primo se venientes.*

[32] Matthew 12:19, *Non contendet, neque clamabit, neque audiet aliquis in plateis vocem ejus.* Isaiah 42:4, *Non erit tristis, neque turbulentus, donec ponat in terra judicium.* Saint Anthony of Padua, Sermon for the fourth Sunday after Easter: *Christus descendit gemere et plangere, qui numquam legitur risisse.*

[33] This popular, but apocryphal text was part of a letter purportedly written by Publius Lentulus, a fictitious person said to have been governor of Judea before Pontius Pilate. The author of the *Instructions* may have consulted an expanded version of this text, for most versions of the letter do not contain the closing phrase: *Et hoc quidem dum deflet peccata nostra.* For further details, see *The Catholic Encyclopedia*, "Publius Lentulus."

As for modesty: in addition to the fact that it is one of the most certain guards of innocence, it is especially suitable for people who have, as one of their essential duties, edifying their neighbor. One does not see what we are, one sees what we seem to be; but by what we seem to be, one believes one is entitled to judge what we are. We should ceaselessly keep present in our thoughts the adorable person of *Jesus Christ*, our great model. It is said of him that simply meeting him inspired virtue and respect, and that from his eyes came a sweetness full of majesty that won every heart, "With the first meeting, he was especially able to attract by his face those who came to him." That no one ever saw him cry, argue, burst out laughing; he was never seen with a sad face, or venting his spleen, or behaving in turbulent and precipitous ways. "He shall not cry out, nor contend, neither shall any man hear his voice in the streets. He shall not be troublesome. He was never known to laugh, but often to weep, especially when he cried over our sins," *etc.*

The modesty of our first Fathers attracted to the Society a great number of excellent individuals. The first Jesuit fathers in Paris had such a grave air about them that their enemies used to say of them: [153] 'Those hypocrites, see how they know how to dissimulate.' Let us take care lest we leave to others what they borrowed from the Society, lest all the religious reformed by us, and the ecclesiastics in the seminaries modeled after us, be much more modest.

Outside this House, we can very well lose the perfect modesty that we have acquired here; but if we do not leave here with a great modesty, it is almost impossible for us ever to acquire much of it when we are elsewhere.

Twenty-third Instruction
For cleanliness for oneself and in the house
Outer Regulation

The poverty that we profess is not contrary to cleanliness. To the contrary, it is because we are poor that it is necessary to be more attentive not to allow one's clothes, or one's furniture, or one's books, or anything in general that we use, to become spoilt. It is therefore necessary to be careful to brush one's clothes often; to let nothing lie about; to remove the dirt from one's mantle and shoes as soon as possible; to have a snag mended before the hole gets bigger; [154] never to wear linens longer than a week, to fold one's dirty linens very neatly every Sunday, and take them and put them in the wardrobes destined for that purpose; to adjust the collar of one's shirt carefully; to remove a spot as soon as we notice it; not to comb one's hair without putting a kerchief over one's collar. When one kneels, to be careful where one does it; not to drag one's slippers along

à ne point laisser gâter ses hardes, ni ses meubles, ni ses livres, ni rien en général de ce qui est à notre usage. Il faut donc avoir soin d'épousseter souvant ses habits, de ne rien laisser traîner, de décrotter son manteau et ses souliers au premier moment, de faire recoudre un acroc avant que le trou soit plus grand, [154] de ne porter jamais de linge plus d'une semaine, plier bien proprement le sale tous les dimanches, de le porter et de le jetter dans les armoires destinées à cet usage; de bien ajuster le collet de sa chemise; d'ôter une tâche dès que nous l'appercevons, de ne point se peigner sans jetter un mouchoir sur son col. Quand on s'agenouille, de prendre garde où on se place; de ne point traîner ses pantoufles contre le plancher; de ne rien déplacer dans la chambre ou dans son oratoire qu'on ne le remette dans son lieu et en son ordre aussitôt qu'il se pourra. La même propreté qu'on a sur soy et dans la chambre, il faut l'avoir pour tout ce qui appartient à la Communauté. Ainsi, sans trop se chicanner pourtant, si l'on trouve dans les galeries quelqu'ordure, il faut l'ôter; quelque chose de déplacé, une chaise, un balay, un arosoir, le reporter; un[e] armoire, une porte ouverte, la fermer; un banc couvert de poussière, l'épousseter; un lieu sale, le nettoyer, surtout si on l'a saly soi-même; une fenêtre que le vent pourroit battre, l'arrêter ou la fermer selon l'heure et le temps; quelque chose d'oublié par quelqu'un, le garder pour le lui rendre; une lampe ou une plaque allumée hors de temps, l'éteindre et le cacher aux yeux des passans; en un mot, une attention singulière à ce que tout soit dans l'ordre, et que les séculiers les plus délicats, s'ils [155] entroient chés nous, ne vissent rien qui pût les choquer.

Direction intérieure

Autant qu'on doit avoir d'horreur d'une propreté affectée, et certains airs poupins et damerets, se peigner plusieurs fois le jour, avoir une ceinture différente des autres, un passe-partout sans courroie, une belle médaille, un joly chapelet, des souliers luisans, un bas bien tiré, un chapeau évuidé et en forme de goutière, autant doit-on éviter la crasse et la malpropreté. L'un vient de beaucoup de vanité et d'amour propre, l'autre de beaucoup d'abstraction et de négligence. La charité peut faire penser que l'extérieur n'est négligé que parce qu'on n'est occupé que de son intérieur; mais la raison et l'expérience feront plutôt que l'on croira que le dedans est à peu près comme le dehors, et chacun sçait bien ce qui en est. Il est des personnes pour qui ce n'est pas une vertu d'être propres et arrangés, mais c'est un grand vice dans la plupart d'être malpropres; et pour ceux qui le sont naturellement, se changer à cet égard, ce seroit une grande vertu, ce seroit une abnégation presque continuelle. Saint Ignace dit que la propreté sert beaucoup à la santé et à l'édification. Fût-il permis d'oublier ce qu'on doit à [156] sa propre conservation, il n'est jamais permis d'oublier ce que l'on doit à l'édification des autres.

the floor; not to displace anything in the bedchamber or in one's prayer desk without putting it back in its place, and in order, as soon as one can. The same cleanliness that one observes for oneself and for the chamber must be observed for everything that belongs to the Community. Thus, but without splitting too many hairs over it, if one finds some trash in the hallways, remove it; something out of place, a chair, a broom, a watering-can, put it back; a wardrobe or a door open, close it; a bench covered with dust, dust it; a dirty place, clean it, especially if one dirtied it oneself; a window that the wind could cause to slam, block it or close it, according to the weather; something that someone has forgotten, keep it safe and return it to him; a lamp or a wall sconce that is lighted when it should not be, extinguish it and hide it from the eyes of passers-by; in a word, special attention so that everything is in order, and so that if the most refined lay persons should happen [155] to enter our residence, they will see nothing that could shock them.

Inner guidance

As much as one should be horrified by affected cleanliness, and by certain mincing and effeminate airs, combing one's hair several times a day, having a cincture that is different from the others, a go-everywhere without a strap, a lovely medal, a pretty rosary, shiny shoes, nicely pulled-up stockings, a hat with a concave brim like a roof gutter, so should one avoid filth and slovenliness. The former results from a great deal of vanity and self-love, the latter from a great deal of absentmindedness and negligence. Charity might lead one to think that the exterior is only neglected because one is solely concerned with one's interior; but reason and experience will, rather, make one believe that the inside is approximately like the outside, and everyone knows full well what that means. There are people for whom it is not a virtue to be clean and tidy, but in most people being slovenly is a great vice; and for those who are naturally slovenly, changing in that respect would be a great virtue, it would be an almost continual abnegation. Saint Ignatius says that cleanliness contributes greatly to health and edification. Even if it were permitted to forget what one owes to [156] one's own preservation, it is never permitted to forget what one owes to the edification of others.

Instruction 24ᵉ
Pour se chauffer pendant l'hyver
Règlement extérieur

On ne doit jamais aller se chauffer hors le tems de récréation sans permission. On doit prendre bien garde de ne brûler ni ses bas, ni ses habits. L'usage a authorisé parmy nous une chose qui seroit une incivilité monstrueuse partout ailleurs, c'est de pouvoir se chauffer les pieds hors des souliers ou de la pantoufle. On doit user sobrement de cette licence, et ne la prendre jamais devant des personnes à qui on doit du respect à moins qu'elles ne l'ordonnent. *Expressément.*

Ceux qui ont de certaines incommodités doivent être seuls pour se la donner.

On ne doit point toucher au feu ni y mettre du bois sans un grand besoin. Il y en a un qui est chargé d'office de cette commission. S'il y manque, au moins qu'on se souvienne toujours de la pauvreté. Auprès du feu, plus que nulle part ailleurs, on doit garder le plus parfait silence. On doit faire place le plutôt [*read*: plus tôt] qu'il est possible à ceux qui arrivent de nouveau et auprès du feu ne s'avancent point [157] plus que les autres. On ne doit pas tenir devant le feu des livres: cela les gâte. On peut cependant porter un livre pour s'entretenir doucement; mais qu'on ne lise que deux ou trois lignes, et qu'on le referme aussitôt. Il vaudroit cependant mieux s'exposer à gâter un peu le livre que de causer, faute d'avoir à quoy penser.

Direction intérieure

L'incommodité des saisons est une des pénitences ordonnés de *Dieu* pour le péché du premier homme. Nos péchés personnels la méritent bien encore davantage. Il faut la prendre dans cet esprit. Cette espèce de pénitence vaut beaucoup mieux que celles qui sont de notre choix. Il y a quelque sorte de bisarrerie à en demander d'autres, si l'on ne sçait pas profiter de celle-cy. Plus on se chauffe, plus on devient frilleux, et plus on veut se chauffer. On remarque dans nos Maisons que ce sont presque toujours les mêmes qu'on trouve au feu. Comment peuvent faire tant de religieux qui vont nuds-pieds et mal vêtus? Comment font nos missionnaires du Canada, parmy lesquels il y a tant de tempéramens très délicats, si ce n'est qu'on peut s'accoutumer insensiblement à tout?

Comme on se trouve au feu plusieurs ensemble, on ne [158] peut faire de faute qui ne soit publique, et par conséquent plus considérable par le scandale; et par la même raison, la régularité y aura aussi un double mérite, celui de la régularité même et celui de l'édification.

Les vertus qui courent icy plus de risque, sont l'ordre, le silence, la

Twenty-fourth Instruction
For warming oneself in winter
Outer regulation

One should never go to warm oneself, outside recreation time, without permission. One should be very careful not to burn one's stockings or one's clothes. Among us, usage has authorized something that would be a monstrous incivility elsewhere, which is to warm one's feet with one's shoes or slippers off. One should be sober about taking advantage of this liberty, and never take it in front of people to whom one owes respect, unless they order it. *Expressly.*[44]

Those with certain ailments should be alone in order to take this liberty.

One should not touch the fire or put wood on it unless there is a great need. There is one person who is entrusted with this task. If he fails to do it, at least let us always think of poverty. Near the fire, more than anywhere else, one should keep the most perfect silence. One should make room as quickly as possible for those who have just arrived and are not moving as close to the fire [157] as the others. One should not hold books up to the fire: it damages them. One can, however, bring a book to keep oneself tranquilly occupied; but one should only read two or three lines, then close it at once. It would nonetheless be better to risk damaging the book a little, than to talk because one has nothing to think about.

Inner guidance

The uncomfortableness of the seasons is one of the penances ordered by *God* for the first man's sins. Our personal sins merit it even more. It must be taken in that spirit. This sort of penance is worth more than penances we choose. It is a form of extravagance to request penance from others, if one does not know how to profit from this penance. The more one warms oneself, the more sensitive one becomes to the cold, and the more one wants to warm oneself. In our Houses it has been observed that the same people are almost always found near the fire. How do the many religious survive who go around barefoot and poorly dressed? How do our missionaries in Canada get along, among whom there are so many very delicate temperaments, if not because one can gradually become accustomed to everything?

Since one is at the fire with several other people, any [158] fault one commits will be public, and will consequently be a greater scandal; and for the same reason, following the rules there will have double merit, merit for following the rules, and merit for being edifying.

The virtues that run the most risk here are order, silence, modesty, and mortification. Let one therefore watch oneself on all these points more than ever. It will be a very good practice to think about this while going to the warming room.

---

[44] This word was stretched out to fill an entire line. It is not clear that the person who copied out the *Instructions* also wrote this word.

modestie, et la mortification. Qu'on s'observe donc sur tous ces articles plus que jamais. Ce sera une très bonne pratique d'y penser en allant au chauffoir.

On perd beaucoup de temps auprès du feu, et quelquefois on y perd tout ce qu'on avoit pu acquérir de vertu. C'est une occasion prochaine de faire de grandes fautes. C'est auprès du feu qu'en s'entretenant saint Pierre renia *Jésus Christ* jusqu'à trois fois. Plusieurs de nos Frères novices se relâchent en cette saison-là, et ils ont ensuite beaucoup de peine à en revenir. Les plus vertueux aiment mieux souffrir un peu que de s'exposer à de pareilles suites. Le Père Fumechon, prêt de mourir, pour appaiser les craintes dont il étoit agité, disoit à *Dieu*: 'Seigneur, n'oubliés point que j'ai si fidellement gardé le silence auprès du feu. Voudriés-vous me perdre?' Cela veut dire: Souvenés-vous que tant de fois je me suis mis au-dessus du respect humain, de la curiosité de sçavoir ce qui se passoit, de la démangeaison de dire mon sentiment: ce n'est pas un petit sacrifice.

La pensée de l'Enfer, du Purgatoire ne devroit guères nous [159] quitter quand nous sommes auprès du feu. L'un ou l'autre sera cependant notre partage si nous ne sommes pas réguliers et véritablement religieux.

Règlement pour quand il y a un poêle

On allume guères [*read*: On n'allume guères] le poêle que pour les récréations et les Colloques, à moins qu'il ne faisse un très grand froid. C'est à l'ancien du Bienheureux Goto, ou en son absence au second de la même chambre, à demander au révérend père Recteur quand il faut faire du feu, et s'il ne seroit pas à propos d'en faire dans d'autres tems qu'à celui de la récréation, et si alors il sera permis de se mettre au poêle, ou de s'en approcher simplement en dehors. On se partage pour aller au poêle de la même manière que pour aller au feu, en deux ou trois bandes selon qu'il y a plus ou moins de novices. On ne se sépare point de ceux avec qui l'on est nommé, et on ne doit guères causer qu'avec eux, ou tout au plus avec les plus voisins. On ne change point de bande en sortant du poêle. [160]

Instruction 25ᵉ
Pour dire ses Fautes et en demander pardon
Règlement extérieur

On dit ses Fautes [*culpæ*], et on en demande pardon en deux occasions: quand on est marqué pour le faire, et qu'on en a la dévotion. Quand on est marqué pour en demander pardon, il n'est pas nécessaire d'en avoir d'autre permission. Quand on n'est pas marqué et qu'on a la dévotion de le faire, on en vient demander la permission à genoux au révérend père Recteur. Mais pour dire sa Faute, il faut toujours en venir demander la permission, déclarer la faute ou les fautes qu'on veut dire, et sçavoir la pénitence qu'on en fera.

One wastes a great deal of time near the fire, and sometimes one loses there all the virtue one had been able to acquire. It is a potential occasion for committing serious faults. It was at the fire, while chatting, that Saint Peter denied *Jesus Christ* three times in succession. Several of our novice Brethren slacken off during that season, and they then find it very difficult to recover. The most virtuous prefer to suffer a bit, rather than expose themselves to similar consequences. To calm the fears that agitated him as he was dying, Father Fumechon[45] said to *God*: 'Lord, do not forget how faithfully I kept silence near the fire. Would you be willing to damn me?' Which means: Remember how many times I put myself above consideration for what others might think,[46] curiosity about what was going on, and the urge to express my feelings. That is no small sacrifice.

The thought of Hell, of Purgatory, should scarcely leave us [159] when we are near the fire. The one or the other will, moreover, be our lot if we are not observant of the rules and truly religious.

Regulation for when there is a stove

One rarely lights the stove for anything but recreation and Colloquies, unless the weather is very cold. It is up to the senior of Blessed Goto or, in his absence, the second of that chamber, to ask Reverend Father Rector when a fire should be lit, and whether it will be appropriate to light one at another time than recreation, and whether in that case it will be permitted to go near the stove, or to simply stay at a distance from it. One divides up, for going to the stove, in the same way one does for going to the fireplace, in two or three bands, according to the number of novices. One does not separate oneself from those to whom one is assigned, and one should scarcely speak to anyone but them, or at the very most to the people who are nearest. One does not change one's band upon leaving the stove. [160]

Twenty-fifth Instruction
For declaring one's Faults and begging pardon
Outer regulation

One declares one's Faults [*culpæ*] and begs pardon on two occasions: when one is assigned to do it, and when one is moved by devotion. When one is assigned to beg pardon, no other permission is needed. When one is not assigned, and devotion makes one want to do it, one goes to Reverend Father Rector to beg permission on one's knees. But in order to declare one's Faults, it is always

---

[45] This person, doubtlessly a Jesuit, has not been identified.

[46] This is how this edition translates the expression *le respect humain*, literally "human respect." For a discussion of this term, see below, "Appendix II, Orest Ranum," "Schooling and Courtesy," pp. 220–221.

Pour demander pardon de ses Fautes, on se rend au réfectoir en nuptiale, et l'on demeure debout, le long des tables du bas du réfectoir, jusqu'après le *Benedicite*. Après le *Benedicite* on se met à genoux proche de la plus petite table, et par ordre d'antiquité on prononce à voix haute et distincte la formule suivante, sans y changer un *jota*:

'Mes Révérends Pères et très chers Frères, de la part de la sainte obéissance je demande pardon des fautes que j'ai [161] commises en l'observation de règles, et de la mauvaise édification que j'ai donné dans ma conversation; et pour ce, la sainte obéissance m'a donné pour petite pénitence de baisser [*read*: baiser] les pieds et demander l'aumône.'

Les novices ne doivent prononcer la formule qu'après les Pères et nos Frères qui ont fait leurs vœux, s'il y en a. La formule étant achevé[e], on se lève, on met sa birette ou son bonnet quelque part: puis d'un air recueilly et humilié, on baise les pieds de toute la Communauté, commençant par les supérieurs et par les prêtres. Quand on a baisé les pieds de tous ceux qui sont à table, on va se laver les mains, et le visage si on en a besoin; puis on vient manger à genoux à la petite table, ou sur quelqu'autre bout de table s'il y avoit trop de monde à celle-là. On va chercher soi-même à la cuisine de quoy manger, et l'on se dessert aussi, à moins que les serveurs le fassent de leur bonne volonté.

On va demander aux tables, tantôt à l'une, tantôt à l'autre, du vin, de l'eau, et les autres petites choses dont on a besoin, comme du sel, du vinaigre, *etc*. Nos Pères demandent à la table des Pères et des Frères, mais les [162] novices ne vont point à la table des Pères, et rarement dans les Collèges à la table du Supérieur. Le repas finy on se retire, pendant les Grâces, où l'on étoit pendant le *Benedicite*.

Pour dire sa Faute ou ses Fautes, on se range pendant le *Benedicite* le long de la table la plus proche de la chaire du lecteur. *Benedicite* achevé, tout le monde étant à table, et après que ceux qui demandent pardon de leurs Fautes ont achevé, s'il y en a quelques-uns, on monte dans la chaire du lecteur, on fait le signe de la croix sans rien dire, puis d'une voix assés haute pour être entendu de tout le monde, on dit: 'Mes Révérends Pères et très chers Frères, de la part de la sainte obéissance je vous dis ma faute, d'avoir rompu le silence,' par exemple, ou bien, 'je vous dis deux de mes fautes, la première d'avoir cassé un verre, la seconde d'avoir parlé avec peu de charité à un de nos chers Frères,' après quoi l'on adjoute, 'et pour ce, la sainte obéissance m'a donné pour petite pénitence de . . .' On dit la pénitence, comme, 'de dire un *Pater* et un *Ave*,' ou bien 'de baiser les pieds à trois de nos chers Frères.'

Cecy étant finy, on descend de la chaire, et les autres y montent tour à tour, les prêtres les premiers [163], ensuite ceux qui ont fait leurs vœux, puis les novices, comme ils se rencontrent. Si le tems et le lieu de faire la pénitence n'étoit pas marqué par le révérend père Recteur, c'est toujours au milieu du réfectoir, à genoux le long des tables, de façon que les serveurs aient le passage libre, qu'on la fait, avant que de se mettre à table.

necessary to beg permission to declare the fault or the faults one wants to declare, and to know the penance one will do.

To beg pardon for one's Faults, one goes to the refectory in one's duster, and one remains standing along the tables in the back part of the refectory until after the *Benedicite*. After the *Benedicite* one kneels down close to the smallest table, and by order of seniority one utters, in a loud and clear voice, the following formula, without changing an iota:

'My Reverend Fathers and my beloved Brethren, on behalf of holy obedience, I beg pardon for the faults I have [161] committed in following the rules, and for the poor edification I gave in my conversation; and for this, holy obedience has given me, as a small penance, to kiss feet and beg for alms.'

Novices should only say this formula after the Fathers and our Brethren who have taken their vows, if there are any. Having finished the formula, one rises, puts aside one's birette or bonnet; then, with a recollected and humble air, one kisses the feet of the entire Community, beginning with the superiors and the priests. When one has kissed the feet of everyone seated at the table, one goes to wash one's hands, and one's face if necessary; then one goes to eat on one's knees at the little table, or at the end of some other table if there happen to be too many people at the little one. One goes oneself to the kitchen to get something to eat, and one also clears one's place, unless the servers are willing to do it.

One goes to the tables, sometimes to one, sometimes to the other, to ask for wine, water, and the other little things one needs, such as salt, vinegar, *etc*. Our Fathers make these requests at the table of the Fathers and Brethren, but [162] novices do not go to the Fathers' table, and rarely, in the Colleges, to the Superior's table. When the meal is over, during Grace one withdraws to where one was during the *Benedicite*.

To declare one's Fault or Faults, during the *Benedicite* one stations oneself along the table that is closest to the reader's pulpit. When the *Benedicite* is over, and while everyone is at table, and after those who are begging pardon for their Faults have finished, if there are any, one climbs up into the reader's pulpit, one makes the sign of the cross without saying a word; then, with a voice loud enough to be heard by everyone, one says: 'My Reverend Fathers and beloved Brethren, on behalf of holy obedience I declare to you my fault. I broke silence,' for example, or else, 'I declare to you two of my faults, the first having broken a glass, the second having spoken uncharitably to one of our dear Brethren,' after which one adds, 'and for this, holy obedience gave me, as a small penance, to . . .' One states the penance, such as 'to say a *Pater* and an *Ave*,' or else 'to kiss the feet of three of our dear Brethren.'

When this is done, one descends from the pulpit, and the others go up in turn, the priests first, [163] then those who have taken their vows, then the novices, in the order of their arrival. If the time and place for doing penance was not specified by Reverend Father Rector, it always takes place in the middle of the refectory, kneeling along the tables, so that the servers can pass freely, and so that one does it before going to the table.

Les fautes qu'on doit dire sont celles qui ont pu donner mauvaise édification, qui sont contre les règles et les Instructions, et surtout celles qui blessent tant soit peu la charité et la pauvreté. On peut dire aussi celles qui humilient d'avantage, pourvu cependant que le révérend père Recteur l'ait approuvé.

Ceux qui servent en première ne doivent pas dire leur Faute ce jour-là. Si le lecteur la disoit, il fera devant le Saint Sacrement la pénitence qu'on lui aura donné[e]. Dans les Collèges c'est au père Ministre qu'on demande permission, un genouil en terre, de dire la Faute, et toujours au Supérieur la permission d'en demander pardon. Le respect demande qu'on aille trouver celui-cy dans sa chambre, si cela se peut sans une grande incommodité. On y [*read*: On n'y] doit jamais manquer aux approches de toutes les bonnes fêtes. [164]

Direction intérieure

Dire ses Fautes et en demander pardon ne sont que de grandes grimaces si cela ne se fait par esprit intérieur. La règle dit que cela se doit faire en signe du désir qu'on a de son avancement spirituel; mais le désir de l'avancement spirituel demande plus que cela: il faut former devant *Dieu* la résolution de ne plus commettre la faute dont on s'accuse; il faut aussi, de toutes les fautes qu'on commet, s'accuser de celles qui nuisent davantage à l'avancement spirituel, comme sont celles d'orgueil ou de quelqu'autre passion déréglée; il faut n'être pas plus fâché d'entendre dire sa Faute par quelqu'autre que de la dire soi-même; jamais n'en parler ensuite pour s'excuser ou pour se plaindre, fût-elle donnée, comme dit la règle, pour un manquement supposé, ou auquel la mauvaise volonté n'auroit eu quelque part. Avec ces circonstances ce sera un acte véritable de religion et non pas une cérémonie toute pure. Ces sortes de corrections qu'on peut nous faire n'approcheront jamais de celles qui se font aux chapitres dans toutes les communautés où il y a de la règle et de l'ordre. L'usage des Fautes ou des Coulpes, comme on les appelle, est aussi ancien que l'état religieux même. Cassien rapporte que les premiers Cénobites faisoient en public jusqu'à des [165] espèces de confessions générales de leurs plus grands désordres dans le siècle, et que les supérieurs le permettoient quelquefois.

Aions du respect pour ce qui est d'usage parmy nous à cet égard, et n'en laissons nulle part abolir la louable et sainte coutume. Pour ce qui est de baiser les pieds, on le doit faire pour imiter, du moins en partie, l'exemple du *Sauveur* qui lava ceux de ces [*read*: ses] disciples. *Exemplum enim dedi vobis, ut quemadmodum ego feci a vobis, ita et vos faciatis.*[34] La différence qu'il y a, c'est que l'Innocence même se prosterna aux pieds de Judas, au lieu qu'aujourd'huy c'est peut-être Judas aux pieds de ceux qui représentent *Jésus Christ*. Il y en a toujours plusieurs à qui nous serions heureux de servir de marchepied en Paradis; craignons plutôt d'être aux pieds des démons et des réprouvés.

S'il est quelqu'un de nos Frères que nous aions offensés, c'est encore là l'endroit d'en faire le désaveu, en attendant l'occasion effective de lui donner des

---

[34] John 13:15, *Exemplum enim dedi vobis, ut quemadmodum ego feci vobis, ita et vos faciatis.*

The faults one should declare are those that may have been unedifying, that are contrary to the rules and the Instructions, and especially those that offend charity and poverty ever so little. One can also declare those that humiliate still more, provided however that Reverend Father Rector has approved.

Those who serve at the first sitting should not declare their Fault that day. If the reader happens to declare his Fault, he will do the penance that has been ordered for him before the Blessed Sacrament. In the Colleges, it is Father Minister from whom one begs permission, one knee on the floor, to declare the Fault, and one always asks the Superior for permission to beg pardon for it. Respect demands that one go find the latter in his chamber, if one can do so without great inconvenience. One should never fail to do it when all the special feast days are approaching. [164]

Inner guidance

Declaring one's Faults and begging pardon for them are only big grimaces if they are not done from an inner spirit. The rule says that this should be done as a sign of one's desire for spiritual advancement; but the desire for spiritual advancement demands more than that: it is necessary to form, before *God*, the resolution not to commit again the fault of which one is accusing oneself. Of all the faults one commits, it is also necessary to accuse onself of those that are the most harmful to spiritual advancement, such as pride or some other unbridled passion; it is necessary not to be more displeased about hearing someone else talk about one's fault than about declaring it oneself; never to speak of it again in order to excuse oneself or to pity oneself, even, as the rule says, if the penance was for a presumed failure, or for one in which ill will may have played a part. Under these circumstances it will be a veritable act of religion, and not a mere ceremony. These sorts of corrections that we may receive will never approach those that take place in the chapters of every community where there is a rule and order. The usage of declaring Faults, or *culpae* as they are called, is as old as religious orders or congregations themselves. Cassian tells how the first Cenobites used to go so far as to conduct, in public, [165] sorts of general confessions about the greatest disorders they had committed while in the world, and that their superiors sometimes permitted it.

Let us show respect for the usage among us in this regard, and let us nowhere abolish this praiseworthy and saintly custom. As for kissing feet, one should do it in order to imitate, at least in part, the example of the *Savior* who washed his disciples' feet: "For I have given you an example, that as I have done to you, so you do also." The difference is that Innocence itself prostrated himself at the feet of Judas, while today it is perhaps Judas at the feet of those who represent *Jesus Christ*. There are always several persons for whom we would be happy to serve as a step to stand on in Paradise: let us rather fear being at the feet of the demons and the damned.

If the person we offended is one of our Brethren, this is also the place to retract it and await a suitable occasion to show him signs of cordiality; if someone's

marques de cordialité. S'il en est dont la sainteté nous fasse envie, entrer dans notre néant à leur rencontre: *Qui post me venit, ante me factus est, cujus ego non sum dignus solvere corrigiam calceamenti.*[35] Enfin, s'il s'en trouvoit que notre humeur maligne et critique condemnât, jetter les [166] yeux sur nous-mêmes, et voir si nous n'avons pas les mêmes, ou de plus grands défauts qu'eux. Ainsi tout sera mis à profit; et cet exercice, outre le mérite, nous sera d'une grande utilité pour le présent.

Demander l'aumône est de toutes les pratiques d'humilité celle qui signifie le moins. Il faut remercier *Dieu* de ce que, comme tant d'autres, il ne nous a pas réduits à demander sans recevoir; nous souvenir, pour le moins, que nous ne recevons rien de sa main que par pure charité, et qu'il est bien bon de fournir un nécessaire si abondant à un serviteur inutile, et quelquefois ingrat et perfide.

Instruction 26ᵉ
Pour les Tons
Règlement extérieur

Les Tons sont un exercice aussi ancien que la Compagnie même. Dans les commencements, ce n'étoit pas une chose extraordinaire qu'étant à table, on avertit quelqu'un de quitter son repas et d'entretenir l'assemblée à la place du lecteur sur quelque matière de piété qu'on lui assignoit. [167]

Les Tons se font au Noviciat tous les vendredys à 2 ou 3 [heures], les jours ouvriers qui ne sont point de Confession. On en avertit deux, au sortir des Litanies, de préparer un petit discours sur le texte qu'on leur donne par écrit. Ils vont faire leur visite du Saint Sacrement, ensuite ils viennent à leurs chambres travailler et apprendre jusqu'à 2 heures. Ce jour-là ils sont dispensés de l'Examen particulier et de venir réciter avec les autres.

Aux Tons on se range comme on se trouve, sur les bancs des tables vis-à-vis la chaire. L'ouverture se fait par deux qu'on avertit de réciter la formule commune; suivent les deux petits discours; on finit par avertir de ses fautes celui qui lit actuellement en première. On doit s'étudier à bien dire la formule ordinaire, parce qu'il y a lieu de prendre en la disant tous les différents ports de voix qui sont d'usage dans la chaire; et c'est ce qui fait nommer cet exercice-cy 'les Tons.'

Le petit discours ne doit pas être plus long que la formule, et il peut l'être beaucoup moins. Il vaut mieux qu'il soit plus court et que la mémoire ne travaille pas; pour être bien fait, il devroit [168] contenir tous les divers mouvements qui sont contenus dans la formule: l'exposition, l'application

---

[35] John 1:30, *Post me venit vir, qui ante me factus est: quia prior me erat.* John 1:27, *Ipse est, qui post me venturus est, qui ante me factus est: cujus ego non sum dignus ut solvam ejus corrigiam calceamenti.*

saintliness makes us jealous, to enter into our nothingness when we encounter them: "After me there cometh a man, who is preferred before me, the latchet of whose shoe I am not worthy to loose." Finally, if there should be some whom our malignant and critical mood might condemn, to cast our eyes [166] upon ourselves and see whether we do not possess the same, or even greater faults than they. Thus everything will be turned to a profit; and this exercise, in addition to merit, will be of great use to us at present.

Of all the practices of humility, begging for alms is the one that signifies the least. It is necessary to thank *God* that he has not reduced us to asking without receiving, as he has so many others; remembering, at the very least, that we receive nothing from his hand other than by pure charity, and that it is very good to provide so abundant a necessity to a servant who is idle, and sometimes ungrateful and perfidious.

Twenty-sixth Instruction
For the Tones
Outer regulation

The Tones are an exercise as old as the Society itself. In the early days, it was not an unusual thing, while at table, for someone to be notified to leave his meal and, in the reader's stead, talk to the assembly about some pious subject he was assigned. [167]

The Tones are conducted at the Novitiate every Friday at two or three o'clock, on workdays when there is no Confession. As they leave the Litanies, two novices are notified to prepare a little speech on the written text they are given. They go pay their visit to the Blessed Sacrament, then they go to their bedchambers to work and learn until two o'clock. That day they are dispensed from the particular Examen and from coming to recite with the others.

For the Tones, one takes the closest place on the benches of the tables opposite the pulpit. The opening is done by two novices who are notified to recite the customary formula; the two little speeches follow. One finishes by notifying the person who is reading first about his mistakes. One should pay attention to say the ordinary formula well, because while saying it, there are opportunities to assume all the different tones of voice that are used in the pulpit; and that is why this exercise is called 'the Tones.'[47]

The little speech should not be longer than the formula, and it can be much shorter. It is better for it to be shorter, and for memorization to play no part. To be done well, it should [168] contain all the different parts of a discourse contained in the formula: the exposition, the application to ordinary conduct,

---

[47] See below, pp. 206–209, for contemporary Jesuit instructions on how to do the Tones.

aux mœurs, les apostrophes diverses, et la conclusion. Il n'est pas question de faire là une division marquée, ni d'apporter des preuves en forme, ni d'entrer dans un grand détail de morale. C'est plutôt comme la péroraison d'un grand discours: après avoir supposé, on ramasse les preuves en peu de mots, et l'on doit parler comme devant une assemblée de séculiers.

Ceux qui écoutent doivent être fort sérieux, ne point rire, ni dire leurs sentimens les uns aux autres. En la place de celui qui parle, ils seroient peut-être bien neufs et plus embarassés que luy.

Ceux qu'on interroge, après que chacun a parlé, doivent dire ce qu'ils croient avoir remarqué de défectueux d'une manière courte et précise, et avec beaucoup de simplicité et de charité; mais il faut en croire au sentiment du Père qui y préside.

Direction intérieure

On ne doit point avoir l'ambition de bien prêcher, mais il faut tâcher de se former à parler en public comme si l'on avoit toute l'ambition du monde: la Compagnie et le zèle des âmes le demandent.

En faisant les Tons, ou on réussit bien, ou on réussit [169] mal. Si on réussit mal, il faut en offrir à *Dieu* la petite mortification et ne point se décourager; c'est peut-être *Dieu* qui le permet pour punir l'envie déréglée de trop bien faire. Ceux qui cherchent de faux brillants mériteroient chaque fois une pareille confusion. Si on réussit bien, il ne faut pas s'en faire accroire, ni penser qu'on doive devenir un fameux prédicateur. On en a vu quantité au Noviciat qui passoient pour avoir de vrais talents, qu'on en flatta et qui s'en flattèrent, et tout cela s'est en allé depuis en fumée. La souveraine vanité seroit s'apporter des discours médités longtemps auparavant, de les faire venir à son texte, et de les donner pour des impromptus.

Instruction 27ᵉ
Pour les jours qu'on se confesse
Règlement extérieur

On se confesse toutes les veilles de Communion, a moins qu'il n'y ait plusieurs Communions de suite; auquel cas la Confession seroit libre le deuxième jour, et même le troisième s'il s'en trouvoit trois de suite.

L'heure de la Confession est depuis 4 heures 1/2 du soir jusqu'au souper; il n'y a guères que celui qui revient [170] de Saint-Louis, et ceux qui auroient été absents qui puissent se confesser le matin; et ils le doivent faire au sortir de l'Oraison sans attendre après l'Office de Notre Dame. Ce temps est destiné pour ceux à qui il seroit revenu quelque chose qui les peinât; mais il ne faut pas se peiner d'un rien, ni revenir plusieurs fois, ou si tard que cela retarda [*read*: retardât] la Messe de Communion.

various apostrophes, and the conclusion. It is not a question here of making a clear division of the whole into its [rhetorical] parts, or of bringing forth formal proofs, or of going into great detail on moral theology. Rather, it is like the peroration of a long speech: after having stated one's assumptions, one assembles one's proofs in a few words; and one should speak as one would before an assembly of lay people.

Those who are listening should be very serious, should not laugh or tell the others what they think. In the place of the person who is speaking, they would perhaps be very inexperienced and more embarrassed than he.

After each novice has spoken, those who are questioned should state in a brief and precise manner, and with great simplicity and charity, the defects they think they have noticed; but the opinion of the Father who is presiding must be accepted.

Inner guidance

One should not harbor the ambition to preach well, but one must try to train oneself to speak in public as if one had all the ambition in the world. The Society and zeal for souls require it.

While doing the Tones, one is either very successful or quite unsuccessful. [169] If one is unsuccessful, it is necessary to offer the little mortification to *God*, and not become discouraged: it may be that *God* is permitting it as punishment for the immoderate desire to do too well. Those who seek false brilliance would merit a similar embarrassment every time. If one is very successful, it is necessary not to be deluded by it, nor to think that one will become a famous preacher. At the Novitiate a quantity of novices have been seen who passed for having real talent, who were flattered and who flattered themselves about it, and subsequently it all went up in smoke. The crowning vanity would be to bring speeches worked out long in advance, to adjust them to one's text, and to present them as impromptu.

Twenty-seventh Instruction
For the days when one confesses
Outer regulation

One confesses every Communion eve, unless there are several consecutive Communion days; in which case Confession is a matter of choice on the second day, and even on the third day, if there are three in a row.

The hour for Confession is from 4:30 in the afternoon until supper. Only someone returning [170] from Saint-Louis, and those who may have been absent, can confess in the morning; and they should do so at the end of Prayer, without waiting until after the Office of Our Lady. This time is destined for those who have recalled something that troubles them; but it is necessary not to be troubled over trifles, or to return several times, or so late that it might delay the Communion Mass.

On commence la Confession par les chambres de Saint Matthieu, de Saint Thomas, et de Saint Jacques lorsqu'elles sont habitées, puis celles des Bienheureux Goto, Michi, Kisai, enfin celles des Saints Anges Raphaël, Gabriel, et Michel. Les derniers de chaque chambre se confessent les premiers, et toujours en remontant. La préparation à la Confession peut servir d'Oraison ces jours-là: et ceux qui n'ont pu l'achever devant la Confession l'achèvent après, ou devant le Saint Sacrement ou dans la chambre.

On doit dire son *Confiteor* avant que d'entrer, afin de ne pas faire attendre; on peut faire sa Confession par écrite, mais il faut qu'elle soit exacte et précise, et réduite à cinq ou six articles tout au plus.

On se confesse après avoir fait le signe de la croix. On commence par *Benedic mihi Pater quia peccavi*, et l'on finit par *de istis et omnibus ante actæ vitæ peccatis contra, etc., veniam à Deo peto et a te Pater absolutionem meâ culpâ, etc.* [171]

Pendant qu'on reçoit l'absolution, on ne doit penser qu'à faire l'acte de contrition. Aussitôt après la Confession on va dans la salle de Notre Dame ou devant le Saint Sacrement, faire une petite action de grâce, renouveller ses résolutions, et accomplir sa pénitence, s'il se peut, de crainte qu'en différant on ne l'oubliât.

Ceux qui n'ont pu faire leur lecture devant la Confession, la doivent faire après dans le livre ordinaire du soir jusqu'à 5 heures 3/4, qu'on va aux salles ou au jardin dire le Chapelet à l'ordinaire. Ceux qui se confessent des derniers peuvent faire leur lecture, leur Oraison, et dire même le Chapelet avant la Confession. En un mot, qu'on s'arrange de cette sorte que tout ~~soit prêt avant~~ se trouve fait devant le souper.

Direction intérieure

On n'a pas besoin de dire de quelle importance il est de ne rien négliger pour bien faire cette action; on en trouvera une pratique pleine et exacte dans un traité particulier.

Instruction 28ᵉ
Pour rendre compte de Conscience [172]
Règlement extérieur

On ne doit pas attendre qu'on soit appellé pour aller découvrir au révérend père Recteur ses peines et ses difficultés. On y est toujours bienvenu en tout temps; seulement, à moins d'un très grand besoin, il n'y faut point aller après huit heures du soir, ni le matin avant l'Exhortation. Voici à peu près les choses dont il faut rendre compte, soit qu'on soit interrogé ou non:

S'il y a quelques peines sur sa vocation, ou sur quelqu'une des règles ou des coutumes de la Compagnie. Comment on s'est servy des conseils qu'on a

Confession begins with the chambers of Saint Matthew, Saint Thomas, and Saint James, when they are occupied, then those of Blessed Goto, Blessed Miki,[48] Blessed Kisai,[49] and finally those of the Holy Angels Raphael, Gabriel, and Michael. The newest in each bedchamber confesses first, and on up, one by one, to the senior. The preparation for Confession can serve as Prayer on those days; and those who were not able to finish it before Confession, finish it afterwards, either in front of the Blessed Sacrament or in the bedchamber.

One should say one's *Confiteor* before entering, in order not to make people wait. One can prepare a written list for Confession, but it must be accurate and precise, and reduced to five or six items at the most.

One confesses after having made the sign of the cross. One begins with, 'Bless me Father, for I have sinned'; and one ends with, 'For these and all the sins of my past life' *etc*, 'I ask pardon of God and absolution from you, Father, *mea culpa*,' etc. [171]

While receiving absolution, one should think only of making the act of contrition. Immediately after Confession, one goes to the Hall of Our Lady or before the Blessed Sacrament, to say a brief thanksgiving, renew one's resolutions, and do one's penance if possible, for fear that by delaying, one might forget it.

Those who were unable to do their reading before Confession should do it after Confession, from the ordinary book for the afternoon, until 5:45, when one goes to the community rooms or to the garden to say the Rosary, as usual. Those who are among the last to confess can do their reading, their Prayer, and even their Rosary before Confession. In a word, let one arrange things so that everything is done before supper.

Inner guidance

There is no need to say how important it is to neglect nothing in order to do this action well. One will find complete and exact information about how it is practiced in a special treatise.

Twenty-eighth Instruction
For giving an account of Conscience [172]
Outer regulation

One should not wait until one is called, to go reveal to Reverend Father Rector one's troubles and one's difficulties. One is always welcome there at any time; only, unless there is very great need, one should not go there after eight in

---

[48] Paul Miki, a Japanese, was educated in the Jesuit college of Anziquiama and became a Jesuit in 1580. Like the other "martyrs of Japan," he was beatified in 1627 and canonized in 1862.

[49] Another one of the "martyrs of Japan," the Jesuit James Kisai (or Kizayemon), was a temporal coadjutor.

reçu[s], surtout depuis la dernière fois. Quelle a été la matière de l'Examen particulier, et comment on s'y est appliqué et quel progrès on y a fait. Si l'on a chaque jour de plus hautes idées de la perfection de son état, si on l'estime davantage, si l'on a plus ou moins de désir d'y arriver, si l'on cherche *Dieu* purement, si l'on n'est point dominé du respect humain. Si l'on a point [*read*: Si l'on n'a point] découvert dans soi-même quelque nouvelle passion qu'on n'ait pas connu auparavant, et quelles mesures on veut prendre pour la combattre. Si l'on avance dans la victoire de ses vivacités, de son naturel et de son humeur, s'il n'y a point quelque crainte ou quelque désir trop violent pour l'avenir ou pour le présent. Si le cœur est bien libre, s'il n'y a point quelqu'attache particulière ou quelque sorte d'aversion; si [173] l'on n'a point été tenté contre quelqu'un de ses devoirs, et quel fruit on a retiré de la tentation. Si l'on acquiert de la facilité aux exercices de la piété, l'Oraison, les Examens, la Confession, la Communion et qu'elle [*read*: quelle] méthode on y observe. Si l'on est exact à bien garder toutes les Instructions, soit pour le règlement extérieur, soit pour la direction intérieure, si on les lit avec application aux tems marqués, et plus souvent même. Si l'on ne se bande pas trop la tête, et si l'on agit moins de l'esprit que du cœur et de la volonté. Qu'elles [*read*: Quelles] mortifications extérieures l'on fait, et si l'on ne pourroit point y ajouter quelque chose de plus. Si l'on a la conscience bien formée. Si l'on ne se trouble point hors de propos, et comment on se comporte dans ses scrupules. Si l'on ne se sent pas quelque désir pour les missions et quelqu'envie de travailler et de souffrir beaucoup pour *Dieu*. Si l'on ne trouve pas au Noviciat quelque chose qui soit un obstacle à son avancement, soit chose, soit personne, et dont par charité pour les particuliers et par zèle pour le bien public, on croye selon la règle être obligé d'avertir le Supérieur.

Direction intérieure

La reddition du compte de Conscience est ce qu'il y a certainement de plus propre à nous rendre parfaits. Rien n'a été plus recommandé par les pères spirituels, et saint Ignace l'a regardé dans la Compagnie comme le préservatif et le cœur [174] de tout le mal qui pourroit arriver au corps et aux membres, et comme le grand instrument de notre conservation et de notre avancement. Les Congrégations Générales l'ont mises [*sic*] au rang des choses qui sont comme substantielles à notre institut, *Substantialia instituti*. *Dieu* donne une telle bénédiction à l'usage de ce moien qu'il n'est pas extraordinaire qu'on aille inquiet et peiné à son Supérieur, et qu'avant que d'avoir encore ouvert la porte, on se sente déjà éclairé et soulagé; c'est que *Dieu* se plaist à répandre sa grâce sur les humbles de cœur et sur ceux qui le cherchent avec droiture.

On ne doit pas craindre ou de fatiguer son Supérieur, ou de se perdre de réputation dans son esprit en lui découvrant ses misères et ses infirmités. Il n'est en place que pour nous aider, et il nous estimera toujours cent

the evening, nor in the morning before the Exhortation. Here is an approximate list of the things about which one should give an account, irrespective of whether one is questioned or not:

Whether there are some troubles about one's vocation, or about one of the rules or customs of the Society. The use one has made of advice received, especially since the last time. What was the topic of the particular Examen, and how one applied it, and the progress that has been made. Whether every day one has more elevated ideas about the perfection of one's state, whether one esteems it more, whether one has a greater or lesser desire to reach this perfection, whether one seeks *God* purely, whether one is not dominated by consideration for what others might think. Whether one has not discovered in oneself some new passion that one did not feel before, and what measures one plans to take to combat it. Whether one is advancing toward victory over one's hastiness, one's nature, and one's humor, whether there is not some fear or some desire that is too violent for the future or for the present. Whether the heart is truly free, whether there is not some personal attachment or some sort of aversion; whether [173] one has not been tempted not to do one's duties, and what profit one obtained from the temptation. Whether one has acquired ease in doing exercises of piety, Prayer, Examens, Confession, Communion, and what method one is using. Whether one carefully follows all the Instructions, both for outer regulation and inner guidance, whether one reads them assiduously at the specified times, and even more often. Whether one is straining too much, and whether one acts less from the spirit than from the heart and the will. What outward mortifications one is carrying out, and whether something more could not be added. Whether one's conscience is well formed. Whether one is not worrying inappropriately, and how one behaves about these scruples. Whether one feels some desire for the missions, and some urge to work and suffer a great deal for *God*. Whether one finds something at the Novitiate that is an obstacle to one's advancement, be it a thing or a person, and about which, through charity for the individuals and zeal for the public good, one believes obliged, by the rule, to notify the Superior.

Inner guidance

Giving an account of Conscience is certainly what is most appropriate for making us perfect. Nothing was more highly recommended by the spiritual fathers; and, within the Society, Saint Ignatius viewed it as the protector and the heart, [174] against all the evil that could befall the body and the limbs, and as the great instrument of our conservation and our advancement. The General Congregations have placed it among the things that are, so to speak, the substance that nourishes our institute, the Substantials of the Institute. *God* gives such a blessing for using this means, that it is not extraordinary for one to go worried and troubled to one's Superior, and before having even opened the door, one already feels enlightened and relieved. That is because *God* takes pleasure in showering his grace on the humble in heart, and on those who seek him with rectitude.

One should not fear either fatiguing one's Superior or diminishing one's reputation in his spirit by revealing to him one's misery and weakness. He only

fois plus pour notre sincérité, notre humilité, et notre confiance qu'il ne pourra nous mépriser pour nos foiblesses. Il sçait par lui-même quel est le néant et la corruption de l'homme, et avec cela combien il est orgueilleux et naturellement porté à se cacher.

Ce moien est encore plus nécessaire à ceux qui commencent qu'à qui [que] ce soit, parce qu'ils ont peu d'instruction et d'expérience. Ce seroit pour eux un orgueil insupportable de se croire maîtres avant que d'avoir été disciples. Ils ne croiroient pas pouvoir apprendre seuls quelqu'art ou quelque science que [175] ce fût. Comment se pardonneroient-ils de vouloir être leurs propres guides dans les routes les plus difficiles et les plus inconnues? Il est sûr que nos directeurs ne nous apprennent rien que de nouveau sur la matière de nos consultations; mais ne nous disent-ils que ce que nous avions déjà pensé, nous aurions une double raison de nous en tenir à nos pensées, et par là un dégré beaucoup plus grand d'asseurance et de tranquilité.

Si nous ne profitons pas de ce moien qu'on nous présente, viendra le tems que nous en aurons le dernier besoin, où nous le regretterons, où nous le désirerons, et où pour notre punition nous ne trouverons peut-être personne qui veuille, ou qui puisse nous diriger. Profitons du tems et du secours tandis qu'on nous l'offre, et qu'on nous presse de l'accepter. Un novice ne doit point sortir d'icy qu'il ne soit assés formé pour pouvoir se donner conseil à lui-même dans tous les événements, du moins ordinaires. Cela demande qu'on interroge souvent, et sur toutes les matières imaginables qui regarde[nt] nos devoirs et la manière de les bien remplir.

Instruction 29ᵉ
Pour quand on reçoit des lettres
et qu'on en écrit
Règlement extérieur [176]

On ne doit pas même se mettre à composer des lettres avant que d'en avoir obtenu la permission du révérend père Recteur, qui donnant la permission donne ordinairement du papier, ou permet d'en demander à notre frère Admoniteur, et désigne le tems qu'on y emploiera.

Peu après qu'on est arrivé, on doit écrire à messieurs ses parents, et à ceux de qui on a été aidé dans sa vocation, son arrivée, l'état de sa santé, et si on est bien content; mais ensuite on ne doit plus écrire que de très loin à loin. Il faut leur mander d'une manière honnête et polie que ce n'est point indifférence, et que tandis qu'ils n'auront point de nouvelles, c'est signe que tout va bien.

occupies that position in order to help us, and he will always value us a hundred times more for our sincerity, our humility, and our trust, than he can scorn us for our weaknesses. He knows for himself man's nothingness and corruption, and how proud he is, and how naturally prone to be secretive.

This means is all the more necessary to those who are beginning than to anyone else, because they have scant instruction and experience. It would be unbearable pride for them to believe themselves masters before having been disciples. They would not imagine that they could learn, all on their own, any art or science [175] whatsoever. How would they pardon themselves for wishing to guide themselves along the most difficult and unknown roads? It is sure that our directors bring us nothing but new things on the subjects about which we consult them; but even if they were to tell us what we have already thought, we would have a double reason to abide by our thoughts, and in so doing have a greater degree of assurance and tranquility.

If we do not profit from this means that is presented to us, the time will come when we will need it desperately, when we will regret it, when we will desire it, and when, as punishment, we will perhaps find no one who wants to, or who can direct us. Let us take advantage of the time and the help while it is being offered to us, and while we are being urged to accept it. A novice should not leave here unless he has been sufficiently formed to be able to give himself advice about everything that occurs, or at least about ordinary occurrences. That requires one to question oneself frequently, on all the imaginable matters that concern our duties and the manner of fulfilling them well.

Twenty-ninth Instruction
For when one receives letters
and writes them
Outer regulation [176]

One should not even begin to write letters before having obtained permission from Reverend Father Rector, who, when giving permission, usually supplies paper or permits one to ask our Brother Admonitor for some, and specifies the time to spend at it.

Shortly after arriving, one should write to one's male relatives, and to the people who helped with one's vocation, concerning one's arrival, one's state of health, and whether one is very satisfied; but after that, one should only write at very distant intervals. It is necessary to inform them, in a respectable and polite way, that this is not from indifference, and that as long as they receive no news, it is a sign that everything is going well.

If one is a bit trained in writing, time should not be wasted making two copies. If one is not, it is necessary to make a rough draft and then write.

Si l'on est un peu stilé à écrire, il ne faut point perdre de tems à faire deux copies; si on l'est pas [*read*: si on ne l'est pas], il faut faire un brouillon et puis d'écrire.

Nos lettres, pour être bien faites, doivent ne contenir rien d'inutile, rien d'obscur pour le sens ou pour les paroles, et avec cela être honnêtes, mais simples et toutes religieuses; point de nouvelles séculières, de mauvaises plaisanteries ou de basses familiarités, de complimens affectés, de vains offres de services, ni aucun récit touchant une tierce personne qu'en tout honneur et respect. On ne pourra pas envoier celles où il se trouvera quelque chose de pareil; il faut prendre garde de ne pas faire l'entendu, ni l'habile homme en voulant parler de *Dieu* et de choses spirituelles: cela ne convient ni à notre âge ni à notre rang. On peut dire, avec une manière de [177] défiance de soi-même, quelque bon mot appuié avec grâce sur une parole de *Notre Seigneur* ou de quelque saint. En disant ce que l'on sent, il est difficile qu'on ne le dise naturellement et bien; il faut tâcher qu'il n'y ait dans la lettre ni mots affectés, ni fautes pour l'ortographe, ni abbréviations, et qu'elle soit d'un caractère médiocre et bien lisible.

Il ne faut point faire faire de complimens à son inférieur par un supérieur [*read*: il ne faut point faire de complimens à son supérieur par un inférieur],[36] sans en paroître peiné et lui en demander la permission; il y a des personnes si supérieures à d'autres qu'on ne doit jamais en prendre la liberté.

Si l'on traitte de diverses choses en passant d'un article à un autre, il faut commencer une autre ligne. On doit toujours signer au bas: 'Votre très humble et très obéissant serviteur en *Notre Seigneur* et Novice de la Compagnie de Jésus.'

On apprendra de l'ancien de la chambre, si on ne le sçait pas, la manière d'arranger les pages selon nos usages, de placer la datte, le titre, et le P[etit] C[ompliment], de plier ensuite la lettre et de mettre le dessus selon nos manières, laissant la place pour le cachet; mais pour instruire les autres, il faut que l'ancien lui-même soit parfaitement instruit.

La lettre étant toute prête, il la faut porter au Supérieur; s'il a le loisir de la lire sur-le-champ, attendre ce qu'il en dira pour s'instruire; s'il ne l'a pas, la lui laisser et ne plus se mettre en peine s'il l'envoiera ou non, à moins qu'on eût quelqu'occasion [178] présente [*read*: pressante] pour l'envoier, ce qu'il faudroit lui dire. Il n'est pas permis d'inserrer dans une lettre déjà cachetée aucun billet sans une nouvelle permission, non plus que d'écrire ou lettre ou billet à qui que ce soit de la Maison ou de la ville, sans un congé exprès. Si les personnes qui visitent apportoient ou billet ou lettre de qui que ce fût, ou de quelqu'endroit qu'elle vînt, il est deffendu de la lire ou même de la décacheter avant que de la porter au Supérieur. S'ils attendoient réponse, il faut leur dire honnêtement, et sans aucun respect humain, qu'on va demander congé de lire la lettre et d'y répondre ou par écrit ou de paroles.

---

[36] *Supérieur* and *inférieur* appear to have been transposed in the first clause of this sentence. Indeed, the second clause shows unequivocally that the entire paragraph concerns compliments addressed to one's superiors.

To be correctly done, our letters should contain nothing idle, nothing whose meaning or wording is obscure, and at the same time very respectable, yet simple and very religious: no secular news, bad jokes or implied familiarities, no affected compliments, no vainglorious offers of service, nor any account about a third party that does not express honor and respect. One will not be able to send letters in which anything of the sort is to be found. When talking about *God* and spiritual things, it is necessary to be careful not to sound well-versed, or like a clever man: that is not suitable to our age and our rank. With a sort of [177] mistrust of oneself, one can gracefully say something witty based on some words of *Our Lord* or of some saint. When saying what one feels, it is difficult not to say it naturally and well. It is necessary to try to keep the letter free of affected words, spelling mistakes, and abbreviations, and it should be of a middling style and very legible.

An inferior should not pay compliments to his superior without appearing distressed about it and begging his permission[50]; there are people so superior to others that one should never take the liberty to do so.

If one discusses a variety of things, when passing from one subject to another it is necessary to begin a new line. One should always sign at the bottom: 'Your very humble and very obedient servant in *Our Lord* and Novice of the Society of Jesus.'

One will learn from the senior of the chamber, if one does not already know, how to arrange the pages according to our usages, to place the date, the person's title, and the Little Compliment,[51] and then to fold the letter and write on the outside according to our ways of doing it, leaving room for the seal; but in order to instruct others, the senior himself must be perfectly informed.

When the letter is all ready, it must be taken to the Superior. If he has the leisure to read it at once, wait for what he says about it, in order to learn; if he does not have time, leave it with him, and after that do not worry about whether he will send it or not, unless there was some urgent reason [178] for sending it, and then one should tell him. It is not permitted to insert any note into a letter that has already been sealed, without receiving permission anew, nor to write a letter or a note to anyone, whether in the House or in the city, without express permission. If visitors were to bring either a note or a letter from anyone or any place whatsoever, it is forbidden to read it or even unseal it, before taking it to the Superior. If they happen to be waiting for a reply, they must be told honestly,

---

[50] This sentence tacitly incorporates the reading proposed for the French text which, without its editorial modification, reads: "A superior should not cause compliments to be paid to his inferior, without appearing pained about it and begging his permission." As modified within square brackets, the French text reflects the precepts outlined in *Nouveau Traité de la civilité qui se pratique en France parmi les honnêtes gens* (Paris, 1750), based on Antoine Courtin's popular handbook first published in the 1670s. Especially useful are comments about a lowly person's exchanges with someone of higher rank: "With persons who are superior, shame and fear can make one modest" (294); or, "If a noble person asks us to sit down, one must obey with some little demonstration that this is doing violence to the respect we owe" (75).

[51] "The Little Compliment," *le Petit Compliment*, is the somewhat flowery opening sentence in which the correspondent alludes to previous favors and expresses his hopes that this attachment or benevolence will continue. The greater or lesser space separating the addressee's name from the beginning of the Compliment was proportionate to that person's greater or lesser rank.

Quand le Supérieur aura donné quelque lettre à quelqu'un, il faut mortifier l'empressement qu'on auroit à la lire promptement, et surtout ne jamais la lire aux approches des exercices de piété, qui demandent beaucoup plus de recueillement. Il ne faut jamais ni garder sans nécessité les lettres qu'on a reçues, ni les relire plusieurs fois pour les mieux goûter: nous avons assés de distractions naturellement sans en chercher de nouvelles. Il faut les reporter au Supérieur, ou les déchirer, ou les jeter. Il ne faut point garder les copies de ses lettres pour s'en servir plusieurs fois ou à plusieurs personnes: c'est une paresse ou une stérilité qu'il faut s'accoutumer à vaincre.

Si l'on étoit obligé d'écrire à quelque personne d'une grande distinction, on sçaura du Supérieur même comment il faut écrire le dedans et le dessus de la lettre.

Direction intérieure

Nous sommes icy dans un lieu où nous devons être bien aises d'oublier le monde et d'en être oubliés. C'est un motif pour n'écrire qu'avec une grande raison de justice, de charité, et de bienséance. On doit prendre beaucoup plus garde encore à ses lettres qu'à ses entretiens, [179] parce que les paroles passent et que l'écriture demeure. Avant que d'écrire, il faut demander à *Dieu* la grâce de le faire sagement et utilement.

Saint Antoine répondit à quelqu'un qui le félicitoit d'avoir reçu des lettres de l'empereur Constantin: 'Réjouissons-nous, mes frères, de ce que Dieu dans ses Écritures nous a envoié comme des lettres du Ciel, et des nouvelles de cet autre monde, et de ce que, sans l'embarras de l'écriture, nous pouvons à chaque moment y addresser nos vœux et des nouvelles de nos différends besoins.' On doit écrire comme on parle; pour bien écrire donc des choses de *Dieu*, il faut apprendre à en bien parler.

Instruction 30ᵉ
Pour parler aux personnes de dehors
Règlement extérieur

On ne doit parler à aucune personne du dehors sans une permission expresse du révérend père Recteur, ou en son absence du père Compagnon, ou s'il n'y étoit pas, du frère Admoniteur. Si donc on rencontroit à la porte ou ailleurs quelqu'un de connoissance, ne fût-ce qu'un domestique qui voulut parler, il faut lui dire honnêtement qu'on va revenir, et aller demander la permission. [180]

and with no consideration for what others might think, that one is going to beg permission to read the letter and reply to it in writing or verbally.

When the Superior has given someone a letter, it is necessary to mortify the haste one might feel about reading it promptly, and above all never to read it if exercises of piety are approaching, for they demand much more recollection. Letters one has received are never kept unnecessarily, nor are they read several times in order to savor them more; we have enough distractions naturally without seeking new ones. The letters must be returned to the Superior, or torn up, or thrown away. Copies of one's letters should not be kept, to be used several times or for several persons: that is a slothfulness and a sterility that one must become accustomed to overcoming.

If one should be obliged to write a person of great distinction, one will learn from the Superior himself what one must write in the letter, and on the outside of the letter.

Inner guidance

We are in a place, here, where we should be very comfortable to forget the world and to be forgotten by it. That is a motive for writing only with great consideration for justice, charity, and propriety. One should take even greater care in one's letters than in one's verbal exchanges, [179] because words are fleeting but writing remains. Before writing, it is necessary to ask *God* for the grace to do it wisely and usefully.

Saint Anthony [the Abbot] replied to someone who was congratulating him on having received letters from Emperor Constantine: 'Let us rejoice, my brethren, that God in his Scriptures sent us what amount to letters from Heaven, and news of that other world, and that, without having to pick up a pen, we can at every moment dispatch our wishes and our news about our different needs.'[52] One should write as one speaks: therefore, in order to write well about the things of *God*, it is necessary to learn to speak well about them.

Thirtieth Instruction
For speaking to outsiders
Outer regulation

One should not speak to any outsider without the express permission of Reverend Father Rector or, in his absence, of Father Socius, or if he happens not to be there, Brother Admonitor. If, therefore, one should meet an acquaintance at the door or elsewhere, even if it is only a domestic who wants to speak to one, it is necessary to tell him courteously that one will return, and go ask permission. [180]

---

[52] This is a paraphrase of Athanasius, *Vita S. Antoni*, 81.

On ne doit jamais aller parler seul, à moins que le Supérieur ne le dise. S'il ne dit rien, c'est signe qu'il veut qu'on se fasse accompagner. C'est ordinairement l'ancien de la chambre qui accompagne, ou en son absence le plus ancien de noviciat. L'ancien se fait accompagner lui-même par le plus ancien des deux, trois ou quatre autres. On ne doit pas plus se peiner d'avoir là quelqu'un qui accompagne, que lorsqu'on va faire des visites en ville. On parle seul à nos Pères, mais on ne doit pas être qu'un quart d'heure avec eux, non plus qu'avec les autres, à moins que ce ne soit l'heure du Colloque, ou qu'on n'en ait permission. Nos Pères seront très édifiés de voir qu'on soit exact à ses [*read*: ces] règles; et s'ils ne l'étoient pas, on ose dire qu'il conviendroit de ne les pas voir. Le quart d'heure doit se mesurer de bonne foy, mais aussi sans trop se chicanner. Ceux qui sont priés d'accompagner ne doivent pas se rendre difficiles. Crussent-ils faire là une assés triste figure, ils servent d'anges gardiens à celui qu'ils accompagnent, et si ce n'est pas pour le contenir dans le devoir, c'est pour empêcher ceux qui le visitent de s'échapper peut-être. Ceux qui accompagnent doivent garder, comme sur un secret de Confession, le silence sur tout ce qu'ils peuvent entendre, principalement si l'on parle de l'intérieur des familles. En y manquant, ils rendroient odieux un usage si saint et si nécessaire à notre conservation, et pourroient blesser grièvement la charité. Si les séculiers [181] sembloient se formaliser de voir un compagnon, il faut dire honnêtement: 'C'est un de mes amis, c'est icy notre usage.'

Le compagnon ne doit entrer dans l'entretien que lorsqu'il voit qu'il n'y est pas de trop. Si la personne qui visite vouloit dire quelque chose en particulier, celui qui est visité demandera permission à son compagnon de se retirer un peu, et le compagnon en avertira ensuite le Supérieur.

Si ce sont des dames qui demandent à parler à l'église, à moins que ce ne soit des plus proches parentes, on aura du moins un compagnon, et la chose paroît encore plus nécessaire qu'ailleurs. S'il arrive que nos Frères viennent dire les Litanies de 4 heures, on les entendra à genoux, après avoir prié les personnes de ne le pas trouver mauvais. On doit se placer en sorte qu'on ne les voie point en face, et il n'y a d'exception qu'à l'égard d'une mère tout au plus.

Quelque visite qu'on reçoive, on doit couper court dès que les tints sonnent pour l'Oraison. Si c'étoit une nécessité de continuer, on viendra demander une permission particulière.

La matière de l'entretien doit être, autant qu'il se peut, de choses bonnes et édifiantes; c'est là où il faut commencer de faire un petit essay du talent que nous avons acquis de parler bien et agréablement de *Dieu*, [182] nous faire honte si nous nous trouvons à sec pour si peu de temps, et prendre la résolution de rendre plus saints nos entretiens ordinaires. On ne doit point demander des nouvelles de guerre, ni de ville, et si on en apprend quelqu'une, de bien garder, comme dit la règle, de venir sans fruit la rapporter.

One should never go talk alone, unless the Superior tells one to. If he says nothing, it is the sign that he wants one to be accompanied. It usually is the senior of the chamber who does the accompanying, or in his absence, the one who has been a novice the longest. The senior himself is accompanied by the most senior of two, three, or four others. One should not be more concerned about having someone there, accompanying one, than when one is going about the city. One speaks alone to our Fathers, but one should spend only a quarter hour with them, or with the others, unless it is the hour for the Colloquy, or unless one has permission. Our Fathers will be very edified to note that one is exact about these rules; and if they were not edified, one dare say that it would be appropriate not to see them. The quarter hour should be timed in good faith, but also without too much hair-splitting. Those who are asked to accompany someone should not raise difficulties. Even if they think they look sadly out of place, they are serving as guardian angels to the person they accompany; and if they are not doing this to keep him dutiful, it is to prevent those who visit him from perhaps being too free. Those who accompany should keep silent about anything they hear, as they would for a secret of the confessional, principally if people are talking about things within the family. By failing to do this, they would render odious a usage that is so saintly and so necessary to our preservation, and that could grievously offend charity. If lay people [181] appear to take offense at seeing a companion, it is necessary to say politely: 'This is one of my friends, it is our custom here.'

The companion should not participate in the conversation unless he sees that they want to include him in it. If the person who is visiting wishes to say something in private, the novice being visited will ask his companion's permission to withdraw a bit, and the companion will then notify the Superior.

If ladies ask to talk with one in the church, unless they are very close relatives one will have at least one companion, and this is even more necessary than elsewhere. If it should happen that our Brethren come to say the four-o'clock Litanies, one will listen to them on one's knees, having first begged these people not to be offended. One should position oneself so that one does not look directly into their faces, and the only exception is, at the very most, one's mother.

Whatever the nature of the visit one is receiving, one should cut it short as soon as the ring sounds for Prayer. If it is necessary to continue, one will come and request special permission.

The subject of the verbal exchange should, as much as possible, be about good and edifying things. Here is where it is necessary to begin doing a little test of the talent we have acquired in speaking well and agreeably about *God*, [182] and to be ashamed if our thoughts run dry in so short a time, and to resolve to make our ordinary conversations more saintly. One should not ask news about war[53] or about the city; and if one learns something, be very careful, as the rule says, not to repeat it without profit.

---

[53] France waged the so-called "second war" against the Dutch from 1672–1678; 1683–1684 brought conflict along France's northern frontier with the Spanish Netherlands (Belgium); and 1688 marked the beginning of France's decade-long "third war" (the War of the League of Augsburg) with the German states along her eastern border. Every summer, for three decades, Parisians were therefore closely following the latest skirmishes and battles.

Direction intérieure

Il est visible, par toute cette instruction, qu'on a eu dessein d'ôter aux personnes du monde l'envie de venir trop souvent nous interrompre, et à nous le trop grand empressement où nous aurions pu nous livrer dans ces sortes d'entretiens. Assujettissons-nous-y dans ce double esprit. Nous ne sçaurions ignorer l'horreur qu'avoient les anciens religieux de voir même leurs plus proches. Cela alloit jusqu'à une espèce de cruauté; mais ils s'en faisoient gloire. Nous pouvons lire ce qu'en rapporte Rodrigués dans le traitté de l'affection déréglée envers les parents. On nous borne, nous autres, à quelque chose de bien plus modéré, mais ne passons point les bornes.

Plusieurs novices ont perdu jusqu'à leur vocation dans l'entretien avec les personnes du dehors. Ne tentons point *Dieu*; c'est le tenter de ne pas garder fidèlement nos Instructions. Elles ont été faites par des personnes bien sages, et qui avoient cent fois plus d'expérience et de connoissance du monde que nous. Si nous ne voions pas leurs raisons, soumettons notre jugement à leur autorité. [183]

Instruction 31ᵉ
Pour quand on sort de la Maison
Règlement extérieur

On ne sort ordinairement au Noviciat que pour aller à la promenade ou à Saint-Louis. On va à Saint-Louis avec un des nos Frères, et à la promenade tous en corps.

Dès qu'on entend sonner la cloche du réfectoir pour sortir, on doit aller, sans différer un moment, à sa chambre prendre son manteau, son chapeau, et ses souliers, pour de là se rendre à la salle où l'on doit donner les compagnons. Il vaut mieux attendre les autres un demi quart d'heure que de se faire attendre [le temps d']un *Pater*. La charité et la civilité le veulent ainsi. On fait des bandes de trois ou quatre, parmi lesquels doit être toujours quelqu'un de la deuxième année, et il n'est pas permis de changer de compagnons en allant ou en revenant.

Les compagnons étant assignés, on passe par le jubé, où l'on ne fait qu'une très courte prière. On se joint à la porte d'où tous partent ensemble. On [184] doit tâcher de bien serrer les rangs, et que les bandes soient à une égale distance les unes des autres.

En marchant dans les rues on ne regardera ni les passans, ni les équipages, ni les affiches; et s'il se trouve des gens sur la route qui aient envie de rire, ou qui disent des plaisanteries, on leur répondra par une plus grande modestie que jamais. On doit garder un grand silence jusqu'à ce qu'on soit hors de la barrière. Si c'est l'après-dîner, on fait l'Examen particulier jusques

Inner guidance

It can be seen, by the full contents of this Instruction, that the plan has been to discourage the worldly-minded from wanting to come and interrupt us too often, and to discourage us from being overly eager about participating in these sorts of conversations. Let us curb ourselves for both reasons. We cannot overlook the horror that the religious of old used to feel at seeing even their closest relatives. They carried it to the point of a sort of cruelty, but they gloried in it. We can read what Rodríguez says in his treatise on uncontrolled affection for one's relatives. We others are limited to something much more moderate, but let us not exceed the limits.

Several novices have gone so far as to lose their vocation as a result of talking with outsiders. Let us not tempt *God*. We tempt him when we do not faithfully observe our Instructions. They were drawn up by very wise persons who had a hundred times more experience and familiarity with fashionable society than we do. If we do not see their reasons, let us subject our judgement to their authority. [183]

Thirty-first Instruction
For when one leaves the House
Outer regulation

One ordinarily does not leave the Novitiate except to take a walk or go to Saint-Louis. One goes to Saint-Louis with one of our Brethren, and everyone goes for walks together.

As soon as one hears the refectory bell ring for going out, without delaying for a moment one should go to one's bedchamber to get one's mantle, one's hat, and one's shoes, and from there go to the community room where companions are to be assigned. It is better to wait for the others for half a quarter hour than to make people wait for one the length of a *Pater*. Charity and civility also require this. One forms bands of three or four, among whom there should always be someone from the second year, and it is not permitted to change companions when going or returning.

Companions having been assigned, one stops at the loft, where one merely says a very brief prayer. One joins the others at the door, from where everyone goes off together. One [184] should try to keep the rows very close together, and keep the bands at an equal distance from one another.

When walking through the streets one will look neither at passers-by, nor at vehicles, nor at placards; and if there should be people along the way who feel like laughing or who make humorous remarks, one will reply to them with greater modesty than ever. One should keep deep silence until one has passed the customs barrier. If it is afternoon, one does the particular Examen until then; if it

là; si c'est le matin et qu'on n'ait pas fait son Oraison, on le commence dès la Maison, et on ne la finit qu'auprès de Montrouge; mais quand l'Oraison seroit faite avant que de partir, on garde le même silence jusqu'à la barrière. On doit toujours relever son manteau au moins jusqu'à mi-jambes, de crainte d'incommoder les autres et de s'incommoder soi-même par la poussière. À la ville on le doit faire de crainte de se crotter. Les bras doivent toujours être enfermés sous le manteau; quand on en prend l'habitude, on ne marche jamais les bras pendants, ce qui est hors de contenance et fort immodeste quoiqu'aujourd'huy chose commune, surtout parmy les jeunes gens.

Quand on va à Montrouge et qu'on revient pour le souper, on fait sur le chemin, en revenant, l'Oraison du soir, et l'on dit le Chapelet, à moins qu'on ne doive [185] être de retour avant 5 heures. On cesse de parler au même endroit qu'on a commencé.

Le Chapelet, quand on revient en corps, se dit par les trois qui composent chaque bande. L'ancien commence le *Credo*, le deuxième dit le premier *Pater*, et le troisième le premier *Ave Maria*, et ainsi tout de suite jusqu'à la fin. On conclud selon l'ancien usage par le *Laudate Dominum omnes gentes, etc.*, et le *De profundis* et l'oraison *Fidelium*. Les bandes de quatre ne font que deux chœurs: deux commencent et les deux autres continuent tout de suite. On ne doit point à la campagne être moins modestes que partout ailleurs, se séparer, ni parler d'une bande à l'autre.

Au retour de la promenade on dit les Litanies de la Sainte Vierge à l'église; et l'on ne monte dans sa chambre qu'après avoir été à la salle de Notre Seigneur, où l'on dit ensemble les Litanies du Saint Nom de Jésus. Quand on doit aller à Saint-Louis, on en avertit le frère Couturier avant le dîner. On lui porte à garder le pacquet de ses hardes et papiers enfermés dans sa nuptiale avec son nom dessus, et on se rend à la porte pour l'heure qu'il a marquée. C'est ordinairement à 1 heure 1/2; on porte sa birette avec soy et l'instrument de pénitence. Dans le chemin on doit être très modeste et très recueilli, et ne point parler, comme dit la [186] règle, où il y a beaucoup de monde.

Direction intérieure

On trouve en sortant de la Maison mille dangers qu'on n'a pas chés soi, c'est pourquoi il faut se recommander à *Dieu* avant que de partir. Pendant qu'on est dehors, garder ses yeux, sa langue, et ses oreilles plus que jamais; et au retour remercier *Dieu* des grâces de préservation qu'on a reçues, ou lui demander pardon des fautes qu'on a pu commettre.

Les exercices de piété qui se font dehors courent grand risque d'être malfaits si on ne s'y applique d'une façon singulière; mais si on les fait bien aussi, c'est la marque d'une grande fidélité qui ne sçauroit manquer d'attirer une plus ample récompense.

On rencontre mille choses allant à la campagne et par la ville qui peuvent élever à *Dieu*. C'est en se promenant sur le bord de la mer que saint Augustin

is morning and one has not done one's Prayer, one begins it as soon as one leaves the House, and one does not finish it until one approaches Montrouge[54]; but when Prayer has been done before leaving, one keeps the same silence until reaching the barrier. One should always lift one's mantle at least to the knees, for fear of inconveniencing the others or becoming inconvenienced oneself by the dust. In the city one should do it for fear of getting spattered with mud. One's arms should always be covered by the mantle. Once one has become accustomed to this, one never walks with one's arms hanging down, which is unseemly and very immodest, although today it is a very common thing, especially among young people.

When one goes to Montrouge and returns for supper, on the road, on the way back, one says afternoon Prayer, and one says the Rosary unless one is going [185] to be back before five o'clock. One ceases speaking at the same place where one began speaking.[55]

When everyone returns together, the Rosary is said by the three who make up each band. The senior begins the *Credo*, the second says the first *Pater*, and the third the first *Ave Maria*, and so on until the end. One concludes, according to the old usage, with the *Laudate Dominum omnes gentes, etc.*, and the *De profundis* and the prayer *Fidelium*. Bands of four form only two choirs: two begin and the other two continue immediately. In the country, one should not be less modest than everywhere else, separate oneself from the band, or talk from one band to another.

On returning from the walk, one says the Litanies of the Blessed Virgin in the church; and one does not go up to one's bedchamber until one has been to the Hall of Our Lord, where one says together the Litanies of the Holy Name of *Jesus*. When one is supposed to go to Saint-Louis, one notifies Brother Sewer prior to the noon meal. One carries to him for safekeeping the package containing one's clothing and papers, wrapped up in one's duster with one's name on it, and one goes to the door at the appointed hour.[56] It is ordinarily at 1:30. One takes one's birette along, and the instrument of penance. Along the way one must be very modest and very recollected, and not speak, as the rule specifies, [186] where there are a lot of people.

Inner guidance

When leaving the House, one encounters a thousand dangers not found at home. That is why it is necessary to recommend oneself to *God* before leaving. While one is away, watch one's eyes, one's tongue, and one's ears more than

---

[54] The Society had a country house situated south of Paris near the village of Montrouge, a walk of slightly more than three kilometers, each way.

[55] In the margin: "R.N. des Cha." The rest was cut off by the binder. This almost certainly refers to the rue Notre-Dame-des-Champs, which the novices would have crossed roughly halfway to the customs barrier.

[56] This suggests that a novice might be sent to Saint-Louis for some weeks (or months?) as part of his probations, and that before leaving the Novitiate he observed a longstanding practice in the Society: "In accordance with our inviolable custom, when we leave a place, we leave behind everything we found when we entered that place, and we do not carry off anything but ourselves" (*Selon l'inviolable coustume que nous avons de laisser au lieu d'où nous sortons, tout ce que nous avons trouvé à l'entrée, et de n'en emporter autre chose que nous mesmes*), Daniello Bartoli, S.J. (1652), tr. by Thomas Le Blanc, S.J., as *La Vie du Cardinal Carafe* (Lyons, 1653), 142.

apprit combien le mistère de la Sainte Trinité est incompréhensible. À la vue de l'oiseau qui fondoit sur sa proie, saint François de Borgia se défioit des violences et des artifices du Démon. Un troupeau qui suit le berger, ou que le berger frappe de sa houlette, enseigne la dépendance où nos devons être de *Dieu* et comment nous devons recevoir ses châtimens; et ainsi de mille autres réflexions pieuses qui naissent de tout ce qui se trouve quand on est bien remply de *Dieu*. [187]

C'est ce que saint Ignace appelle 'voir *Dieu* dans ses créatures, et toutes les créatures en lui.'[37] Dans les rues, en voiant un train magnifique, Monsieur de Renty, devenu pauvre pour *Jésus Christ*, s'écrioit: 'Seigneur, que vous ai-je fais pour n'être pas demeuré toute ma vie du nombre de ces malheureux que vous avés comme maudit.' *Væ qui habetis omnem consolationem.*[38] L'ancien philosophe disoit: 'Que de choses dont je n'ai que faire!' Nous pouvons ajouter que, de toute cette foule de gens, il en est peu qui travaillent à sauver leurs âmes; et qui leur iroit demander à quoy ils pensent, que pourroient-ils répondre?

Instruction 32ᵉ Pour Montrouge
Règlement extérieur

On va à Montrouge ou pour y passer la journée toute entière, ou pour y dîner et revenir souper à la Maison, ou simplement pour y passer l'après-dîner. On n'y fait aucun repas depuis l'Avent jusqu'après Pâques; depuis Pâques jusqu'à l'Avent, de deux semaines [188] l'une on y va dîner un jour; on y dîne et on y soupe depuis environ la mie-may jusqu'auparavant la mie-aoust. Icy on marquera ce qu'il y a de commun, et ce qu'il y a de particulier pour ces jours-là.

Ce qu'il y a de commun

On n'entre jamais dans la maison, jamais on n'en sorte qu'on n'aille dire un *Ave Maria* à genoux dans la chapelle. On ne doit jamais laisser traîner son

---

[37] *Spiritual Exercises*, no. 235: "To look how God dwells in creatures . . . : and so in me, giving me being, animating me, giving me sensation and making me to understand."

[38] Luke 6:24, *Verumtamen væ vobis divitibus, quia habetis consolationem vestram.*

ever; and upon returning, thank *God* for the graces of preservation that one has received, or else beg his pardon for the faults one may have committed.

Exercises of piety done outside run a great risk of being badly done, if one does not apply oneself in a singular fashion; but if one does them well there, it is the mark of a great fidelity that cannot fail to attract a more ample reward.

One encounters a thousand things on the way to the country, and in the city, that can raise one to *God*. It was while walking on the seashore that Saint Augustine learned how incomprehensible is the mystery of the Blessed Trinity.[57] Seeing a bird swoop down on its prey, Saint Francis Borgia put himself on guard against the Demon's violences and artifices. A flock that follows the shepherd, or that the shepherd strikes with his crook, teaches the dependence in which we should be with *God*, and how we should receive his chastisements; and so forth, for a thousand other pious reflections that are stirred by everything one encounters when one is very full of *God*. [187]

This is what Saint Ignatius calls 'seeing *God* in his creatures, and all the creatures in him.' In the street, when he saw someone's magnificent trappings, Monsieur de Renty, who had become poor for *Jesus Christ*, would exclaim: 'Lord, what have I done to you by not remaining all my life among those wretches whom you appear to have cursed?' "Woe to those who have every consolation."[58] The ancient philosopher used to say: 'So many things that I can do without!'[59] We can add that, of this whole crowd of people, there are few who work at saving their souls; and if someone were to go ask them what they think, what could they reply?

Thirty-second Instruction
For Montrouge
Outer regulation

One goes to Montrouge either to spend the entire day there, or to eat the noon meal and return to the House for supper, or simply to spend the afternoon there. No meals are eaten there from Advent until after Easter; from Easter to Advent, every other week [188] one goes there one day for the noon meal; one eats both the

---

[57] This apparently refers to the apocryphal tale of how St. Augustine came to understand the mystery of the Trinity while talking with a little boy who was digging in the sand. The story can be found in Erasmus, *Opus Epistolarum Des. Erasmi Roterodami*, ed. P.S. Allen (Oxford, 1906–58), 2:270. Allen points out that the story is found in Peter de Natalibus's *Catalogus Sanctorum* (Vicenza, 1493).

[58] Jesuit-educated Gaston-Jean-Baptiste de Renty (1611–1649) withdrew from the royal court in 1638 and devoted his energy and his fortune to charitable activities. This is a paraphrase of a longer account in the biography by Renty's spiritual director, Jean-Baptiste de Saint-Jure, S.J., *La Vie de M. de Renty: ou, modèle du parfait chrétien* (Paris, 1651), 45–46 of the translation by E.S. Gent, *The Holy Life of Monsieur de Renty* (London, 1684).

[59] This may allude to Diogenes Laertius's account (*Lives and Opinions of Eminent Philosophers*, vi, 37) of how Diogenes of Sinope threw away his single possession, a wooden bowl, when he saw a child drinking water from his cupped hands; but if so, these specific words were not borrowed directly from Laertius.

manteau; il faut le garder sur soy, ou le mettre dans quelque lieu bien propre où l'on puisse le retrouver aisément, et prendre garde, si le tems menace de la pluie, qu'il en soit à couvert.

On ne doit être nulle part moins de trois ou quatre ensemble, et des trois ou quatre il doit toujours y avoir pour le moins un ancien.

On ne doit guères se retirer dans les bosquets, et ceux surtout que l'on soupçonne de se trouver plus volontiers ensemble doivent éviter de s'y rencontrer. On ne monte au billard qu'après que tout est préparé, et que la cloche en avertit. On ne doit point passer tout son tems à jouer. Il faut entrecouper le jeu d'entretiens, et de promenades pour prendre l'air. Deux ou trois parties de billard de suite, ce n'est que trop. Quand on perd, on dit à genoux un *Ave Maria* pour ceux qui ont gagné; et quand les parties sont finies, [189] on avertit ceux qui doivent jouer à leur tour. En jouant au billard on doit quitter son manteau, et retrousser sa soutane, pour ne faire que très peu de poussière. Si on joue aux échecs, il faut prendre garde à ne point trop se bander la tête, et à ne point se picquer. En jouant, on doit s'appliquer assés pour ne pas faire de peine à ses compagnons; on ne doit point se mocquer de ceux qui jouent mal, ni s'obstiner, ni s'entredire de paroles dures, ni parler sur le jeu d'autrui, à moins qu'on n'en soit prié, et que l'émule ne le trouve bon. Les jeux d'exercices, les quilles, la boule sont très louables et bons pour la santé. En y jouant, on doit prendre garde à ne rien faire d'indécent, et à ne point dire de mauvais quolibets.

Au réfectoir, mais surtout pendant le déjeuner et la collation, on doit prendre garde à ne faire aucune badinerie. Dès qu'on entend sonner la cloche pour quelqu'exercice, on doit tout quitter pour faire la chose dont on est averty. On fait ses lectures et ses autres exercices de piété dans les allées en se promenant, ou assis au pied d'un arbre s'il fait beau. S'il pleut, on les va faire dans la chapelle, et alors un seul lit pour tous, et s'il faut dire le Chapelet, on le dit assis à deux chœurs.

Quand on sort de la maison pour s'aller promener, on peut ne point porter son manteau. Dès qu'on se sent échauffé, soit à la maison, soit au terme de la promenade, il faut prendre un peu de repos, et s'il est nécessaire se couvrir de son manteau. On ne doit point boire sans [190] permission au moins du frère Admoniteur. Il ne la donnera pas à ceux qui seront trop échauffés. Quand il fait chaud, d'abord en arrivant il faut tirer de l'eau du puits, afin qu'on n'en boive point qu'elle n'ait été quelque temps à l'air à perdre sa plus grande fraîcheur.

On sonne deux fois la cloche pour le départ. À la première fois on prend son manteau et on s'assemble; à la seconde on dit l'*Ave Maria* dans la chapelle, on reprend ses compagnons, et l'on part.

noon meal and supper there from approximately mid-May until approximately mid-August. Here are indications of what is usual and what is special for those days:

What is usual

One never enters the house, one never leaves it without going to say an *Ave Maria*, kneeling, in the chapel. One should never allow one's mantle to lie about; it is necessary to keep it with one, or to put it in some very clean place where one can easily find it, and to be careful, if rain threatens, that it is protected.

Nowhere should one be fewer than three or four together; and of the three or four, there must always be at least one senior.

One should rarely withdraw into the groves; and above all, those who are suspected of preferring to be together should avoid meeting there. One only goes upstairs to the billiard table after everything is prepared, and the bell announces it. One should not spend all one's time playing there. It is necessary to alternate games with verbal exchanges and walks to get fresh air. Two or three games of billiards in a row are simply too many. When one loses, one says on one's knees an *Ave Maria* for those who have won; and when the matches are over, [189] one notifies those who should play next. While playing billiards, one should remove one's mantle and tuck up one's soutane, so as to make a bare minimum of dust. If one plays chess, it is necessary to be careful not to strain too much, and not to take offense. While playing, one should apply oneself enough so as not to pain one's companions; one should not make fun of those who play badly, or be obstinate, or exchange harsh words, or talk about someone else's playing, unless one is asked and one's opponent approves. Exercise games, quoits, bowling are very praiseworthy and good for the health. When playing them, one should be careful not to do anything indecent, and not to make nasty jeers.

In the refectory, but especially during breakfast and the snack, one should take care to avoid all banter. As soon as one hears the bell ring for some exercise, one should drop everything, to do the thing that has been announced. One does one's reading and other exercises of piety while walking in the paths, or while seated under a tree if the weather is fine. If it rains, one goes to do them in the chapel, and then one person reads for everyone; and if it is necessary to say the Rosary, one says it seated in two choirs.

When one leaves the house to go for a walk, one need not wear one's mantle. As soon as one feels overheated, either in the house or at the end of the walk, it is necessary to rest a bit and, if necessary, wrap oneself in one's mantle. One should not drink without [190] at least Brother Admonitor's permission. He will not give it to those who are too overheated. When the weather is hot, water must be taken from the well immediately upon arriving, so that one will not drink it until it has been in the air for awhile and has lost most of its coolness.

One rings the bell twice for the departure. The first time, one gets one's mantle and one assembles; at the second ring, one says the *Ave Maria* in the chapel, one rejoins one's companions, and one leaves.

Ce qu'il y a de particulier selon de différents jours
Les jours qu'on passe tout entiers à Montrouge [191]

On se lève ordinairement à quatre heures. On fait son lit, et on visite le Saint Sacrement en habit de ville. Au petit coup devant quatre heures et demie on va prendre ses compagnons dans la grande salle de récréation [la salle de Saint Joseph], et on se rend à la porte. En passant par la salle, on salue le crucifix qui est au-dessus de la cheminée. On fait son Oraison et sa Récollection depuis la Maison jusqu'à l'avenue de Montrouge.

Vers six heures qu'on arrive, on entend la Messe dans la chapelle, ensuite l'on déjeune, et l'on ne joue pas avant tout ce temps-là. Sur les neuf heures on sonne pour la lecture de l'*Imitation* d'un bon quart d'heure. Vers dix heures et demie on sonne pour l'Examen, ensuite l'on dîne. On lit à table pendant le repas en première et en seconde. Après dîner on fait la récréation comme à la Maison, pendant laquelle on ne joue pas sans une permission expresse du révérend père Recteur, ou du père Compagnon en son absence. La récréation fini, on dit les Litanies des saints et celles de la Sainte Vierge tout de suite, puis l'*Angelus*.

Après les Litanies, si le temps ne permet pas d'aller à la promenade, on fait l'heure de repos: on l'emploie à [192] l'Examen particulier, après lequel on peut lire, se promener, ou reposer. Le silence est très recommandé pendant cette heure-là. L'heure du repos étant finie, on se divertit à la maison comme le matin. Une heure avant le souper on sonne l'Oraison de demie heure. Ensuite on fait la Récollection et l'on dit le Chapelet, chacun en particulier. Si après que le frère Admoniteur a donné le signal de la fin du Chapelet, il reste encore du tems, on peut jouer. La seconde table étant finie, on sonne à l'ordinaire les deux coups pour le départ. Il faut si bien prendre ses mesures qu'on arrive à la Maison avant la nuit. Arrivant à la Maison, on va saluer le Saint Sacrement, faire l'Examen, et se coucher. On peut aller boire un coup au réfectoir si l'on en a un grand besoin, et qu'on ne soit pas trop échauffé. Le lendemain on repose; la Messe se dit à sept heures, au sortir de laquelle on déjeune, si ce n'est point jour de jeûne ou d'abstinence. L'Exhortation se fait à 7 heures 3/4 précisément; l'exercice corporel à 8 heures 1/2; la lecture à 9 heures 1/4; le reste à l'ordinaire.

Les jours qu'on dîne à Montrouge
sans y souper [193]

Le révérend père Recteur détermine, selon la saison, l'heure du lever, de l'Oraison, de la Messe, et le tems du départ. On fait à Montrouge le petit quart d'heure de lecture coupant en deux la matinée, et l'Examen avant le dîner. Après la récréation, on dit seulement les Litanies des saints et l'*Angelus* dans la chapelle. Un peu avant le départ, on sonne la collation; on revient à la Maison plûtôt [*read*: plus tôt] ou plûtard [*read*: plus tard] selon la saison, mais il faut toujours s'être rendu d'assés bonne heure pour dire les Litanies de la Vierge à l'église, et quitter ses habits de ville avant souper. En chemin on fait l'Oraison du soir et on dit le Chapelet.

What is special according to the different days [60]
The entire days one spends at Montrouge [191]

One usually rises at four o'clock. One makes one's bed, one visits the Blessed Sacrament in city clothes. At the little ring before 4:30, one goes to meet one's companions in the great recreation Hall [of Saint Joseph], and one goes to the door. When passing through the Hall one reverences the crucifix that is above the fireplace. One does one's Prayer and one's Recollection from the House until the avenue leading to Montrouge.

At about six o'clock one arrives, one hears Mass in the chapel, then one has breakfast, and one does not play for that entire time. At nine o'clock the bell rings for reading the *Imitation* for a good quarter hour. Towards 10:30, the bell rings for the Examen, then one eats the noon meal. One reads at the table during the meal, at both first and second table. After this noon meal one takes part in recreation, as at the House, during which one does not play without express permission from Reverend Father Rector, or in his absence, from Father Socius. When recreation is over, one says the Litanies of the saints and those of the Blessed Virgin immediately, then the *Angelus*.

After the Litanies, if the weather does not permit going for a walk, one rests for an hour, during which one does [192] the particular Examen, after which one can read, walk, or rest. Silence is highly recommended during this hour. When the hour of rest is over, one diverts oneself at the house, as in the morning. An hour before supper one rings for a half hour of Prayer. Then one does the Recollection, and each one says the Rosary in private. If time remains after Brother Admonitor has given the signal to end the Rosary, one can play. When second table has finished, the bell is rung twice, as usual, for the departure. It is necessary to be so attentive that one reaches the House before nightfall. Upon reaching the House, one goes to visit the Blessed Sacrament, does the Examen, and goes to bed. One can go get a drink in the refectory, if one feels a great need and one is not too overheated. The next day one rests; Mass is said at seven o'clock, and immediately afterwards one breakfasts, if it is not a day of fasting or abstinence. The Exhortation is done at 7:45 precisely, bodily exercises at 8:30, reading at 9:15, and the rest as usual.

The days one eats the noon meal at Montrouge but does not sup there [193]

Reverend Father Rector determines, according to the season, the hour for rising, for Prayer, for Mass, and for departing. At Montrouge there is a short quarter hour of reading that cuts the morning in half, and the Examen is before the noon meal. After recreation one says only the Litanies of the saints and the *Angelus* in the chapel. Shortly before leaving, the bell rings for the snack. One returns to the House earlier or later, according to the season; but it is always

---

[60] A large, black, triangular design fills the space between this title and the subtitle that follows, covering some of the flourishes that the copyist routinely added to titles. Was the copyist disguising an ink blot?

Les jours qu'on ne va que promener à Montrouge

On part après les Litanies du matin et la visite du Saint Sacrement, et l'on fait l'Examen particulier jusqu'à la barrière. On joue et on se promène à Montrouge comme quand on y dîne. Si les jours sont assés longs, on ne revient que pour le souper; s'ils sont courts, on est de retour avant la nuit, et on fait à la Maison l'Oraison du soir, et tout ce qui suit jusqu'au souper à l'ordinaire. [194]

Direction intérieure

Dieu et la Compagnie ont beaucoup d'indulgence pour nous de nous accorder tant de récréations: n'en abusons pas; et ce que nous perdons d'un côté, tâchons de le regagner sur l'autre, veillant sur notre intérieur ces jours-là plus que d'autres, en dressant souvant notre intention, ne nous permettant ni plus de divertissemens, ni d'autres divertissemens que ceux que la religion nous accorde et avec toutes les circonstances qu'elle nous les accorde.

Le Père Dupont [de La Puente], résolu de se faire religieux et délibérant sur l'institut qu'il embrasseroit, se détermina à la Compagnie, touché de la modestie et de la retenue singulière des jeunes Jésuites qu'il vit à leur maison de récréation d'un lieu où il s'étoit caché pour les épier. Il ne crut pas qu'un ordre où les divertissemens à cet âge même se passoient d'une manière si réligieuse pût être qu'un ordre très saint.

On a dans les divertissemens mille occasions de pratiquer la vertu, si l'on sçait en profiter: ne point tempêter au jeu, ni faire paroître aucune opiniâtreté ni mauvaise humeur, demeurer égal soit qu'on gagne ou qu'on perde, céder volontiers sa place à d'autres, se rappeler de tems en tems à *Dieu*, ne faire aucun excès de bouche quand on est plus dans l'abondance, s'édifier dans les entretiens. Ce sont là des pratiques de vertu qui ne laissent pas d'avoir leur prix: ne les laissons point échapper, et qu'il paroisse les jours suivans que nous ne nous relâchons que pour nous remettre mieux à nos devoirs. [195]

On ne doit point négliger d'apprendre les jeux qui sont d'usage, comme le billard et les échecs: cela sert chés nous à faire diversion à d'autres divertissemens plus dangereux. Dire à quelqu'un des Nôtres, dont l'entretien pourroit ne nous pas édifier, 'Je veux aller jouer,' c'est une excuse honnête pour le quitter et ne le pas joindre. Quelquefois aussi, chés les séculiers, lorsqu'il s'y trouve et qu'il y vient de certaines compagnies qui ne nous conviennent pas, on se retire sous prétexte d'aller ou achever une partie, ou reprendre sa revanche, comme si on avoit la chose fort à cœur. Outre que ces jeux honnêtes donnent droit de ne jamais jouer à d'autres jeux comme les cartes, *etc.*

necessary to be back early enough to say the Litanies of the Virgin in the church, and to remove one's city clothes before supper. Along the way one says afternoon Prayer, and one says the Rosary.

The days when one only takes a walk to Montrouge

One leaves after the morning Litanies and the visit to the Blessed Sacrament, and one does the particular Examen until the barrier. One plays and one walks at Montrouge, as one does when eating the noon meal there. If the days are long enough, one only returns for supper; if they are short, one is back before nightfall, and at the House one says afternoon Prayer and everything that follows until supper, as usual. [194]

Inner guidance

God and the Society are very indulgent in granting us so much recreation: let us not abuse it; and what we lose on the one hand, let us try to regain on the other, watching over our interior on those days more than on others, by frequently recalling our intention, by not permitting ourselves either additional amusements or amusements other than those that religion permits us, and under all the circumstances where it permits them.

Father de La Puente, who had resolved to become a religious and was debating about which institute he would embrace, decided on the Society because he was touched by the modesty and the unusual restraint of the young Jesuits he saw at their house of recreation, from a place where he had hidden to spy on them. He did not believe that an order where the amusements of people that age took place in such a religious way could be anything but a very holy order.

During one's amusements one has a thousand occasions to practice virtue, if one knows how to take advantage of it: not rage about a game or show any sign of stubbornness or ill humor, remain equable whether one wins or loses, willingly yield one's place to others, remember oneself to *God* from time to time, not overeat when one is surrounded by abundance, benefit morally and spiritually from conversations. These are virtuous practices that nonetheless have their price: let us not waste the opportunity, and on the following days, let it be seen that we only relax in order to do our duty better. [195]

One should not neglect learning games that are in general use, such as billiards and chess: among us they serve to divert us from other more dangerous amusements. Saying 'I want to go play,' to one of Ours whose conversation may not edify us, is a polite excuse for leaving him and not joining him. Sometimes also, when one is among lay persons, and certain parties who do not suit us are there, or arrive, one withdraws on the pretext of going to finish a game, or to get even with someone, as if one held it dear to one's heart. In addition, these honest games make it possible never to play other games such as cards, *etc.*

Instruction 33ᵉ
Pour quand on va aux Halles

Règlement extérieur

On va aux Halles depuis la Toussaint jusqu'à la mi-aoust tous les samedis, à moins qu'il ne soit fête ou jour de Communion, ou que ce ne soient les samedis entre Noël et la Purification, ou que le révérend père Recteur n'en dispense pour justes raisons.

On y va deux ensemble, et c'est ordinairement un ancien et un nouveau. Notre frère Manupducteur avertit, la veille, notre frère Admoniteur de l'heure qu'il [196] faut partir selon la saison, et l'Admoniteur avertit ceux qui y doivent aller le lendemain. Le samedy à l'heure marquée on descend en souliers, en chapeau, et en nuptiale au bas du grand escalier, et l'on y trouve le Jardinier avec qui l'on part.

Pendant tout le chemin on doit marcher d'un air modeste et composé, et garder un grand silence, tâchant de s'occuper de *Dieu*, à moins qu'il n'y eût quelque nécessité de se dire un petit mot l'un à l'autre.

Arrivé aux Halles, tandis qu'on est chés le marchand à se reposer un peu, et à attendre que le Frère ait acheté ce qu'il faut apporter, on doit faire quelque prière ou quelque petite lecture; après quoi, si cela duroit un peu trop longtems, on pourroit s'entretenir un peu de bonnes choses avec son compagnon, mais non pas avec les séculiers, si ce n'est pour leur dire un petit mot d'édification. Quant aux nouvelles qui pourroient se dire, bien loin de s'en informer, on ne doit pas même y prêter l'oreille. Dès qu'on a reçu sa charge on reprend en silence la route du Noviciat, sans qu'il puisse être permis de s'écarter du chemin le plus droit, ni d'entrer dans aucune maison, fût-ce chés les personnes de sa famille ou de sa connoissance.

Quand on est entré, on va prendre quelque chose au réfectoir, à moins qu'il ne fût jour de jeûne et qu'on eût l'âge de jeûner. Ensuite on entend la Messe, si ce n'est qu'on ne l'eût entendu avant que de partir; puis on reprend l'ordre des actions ordinaires de la matinée, on fait son lit si on est de retour assés tôt pour le faire [197] avec les autres. À cela près, on ne fait point d'exercice corporel ce jour-là.

Direction intérieure

On seroit bien à plaindre si une action aussi humiliante et aussi extraordinaire que celle-cy se faisoit sans esprit intérieur, et sans mérite. Cet exercice est aussi ancien que la Compagnie même. Il n'est pas d'usage seulement au premier noviciat, les Pères du troisième an, à plus de trente ans et étant déjà prêtres, le pratiquent aussi. Ce que nous faisons deux ou trois fois l'année, les premiers Jésuites le faisoient très souvent, et beaucoup d'autres choses ~~encore~~ plus mortifiantes encore par elles-mêmes et par leurs circonstances, comme de

Thirty-third Instruction
For when one goes to the Central Market

Outer regulation

Every Saturday, from All Saints Day to mid-August, one goes to the Central Market, unless it is a feast day or a Communion day, or unless it is one of the Saturdays between Christmas and Purification, or unless Reverend Father Rector dispenses one from going for just reasons.

Two novices go together, and it usually is a senior and a newcomer. The evening before, our Brother Manuductor notifies our Brother Admonitor of the hour when it [196] is necessary to leave, according to the season; and the Admonitor notifies those who should go the next day. On Saturday, at the specified time, one goes down to the bottom of the great staircase in shoes, hat, and duster, and there one finds the Gardener, with whom one leaves.

All along the way one should walk with a modest and composed air and keep a deep silence, trying to be occupied with *God*, unless there is some need to say a brief word to one another.

Upon reaching the Market, while one is at the shop, resting a bit and waiting until the Brother has bought what must be carried, one says a prayer or reads a brief text; after which, if it is taking a bit too long, one could talk a little with one's companion about good things, but not with lay persons, other than saying a brief word of edification to them. As for news that might be talked about, far from inquiring about it, one should not even lend an ear. As soon as one has received one's burden, one regains in silence the route to the Novitiate, without being permitted to diverge from the straightest path or enter any house, not even that of family members or friends.

When one is back inside the House, one goes to the refectory to eat something, unless it happens to be a fast day and one is old enough to fast. Next, one hears Mass, if one did not hear it before leaving; then one resumes the usual order of morning activities, one makes one's bed if one is back in time to do it [197] with the others. Except for that, one does not do bodily exercises that day.

Inner guidance

One would be greatly to be pitied if so humiliating and unusual an action as this one were done without inner spirit and without merit. This exercise is as old as the Society itself. It is not only carried out during the two years of a novitiate, the third-year [Tertianship] Fathers, who are over thirty years old and are already priests, do it too. What we do two or three times a year, the first Jesuits did very often, and many other things still more mortifying in themselves and in their circumstances, such as driving a manure cart or going to get provisions with a

conduire une charette de fumier, ou d'aller chercher les provisions avec une bête de somme. C'étoient les plus qualifiés, et ceux qui avant que d'entrer avoient le plus brillés par leur science et par leurs emplois, qui étoient les moins épargnés. Plusieurs eussent voulu qu'on leur eût permis outre cela de courir les rues dans cet équipage ridicule, et quelquefois on le leur permettoit. Saint Ignace avoit fait quelque chose de pareil dans une ville d'Italie. [198]

L'intention de toutes ces pratiques étoit qu'on foulât aux pieds les usages du siècle, et que sous ses propres yeux on triomphât de lui en quelque manière.

C'étoit une application de la règle qui nous ordonne de mépriser ce que le monde estime, et d'embrasser ce que *Jésus Christ* a aimé et estimé, et d'être bien aises de passer même pour des insensés, sans y donner occasion que par des actions vertueuses au jugement de tous les vrais sages.

S'il arrivoit donc que sur la route que nous trouvassions des gens qui insultassent ou de paroles ou de quelqu'autre façon, des gens qui traitassent ceci de puérilité, ou d'autres à qui nous parussions faire compassion, il ne faudoit répondre aux premiers que par un recueillement plus grand: *Spectaculum Deo Angelis et hominibus*[39]; aux autres que par plus de compassion de leur jugement dépravé: *Nolite flere super me, sed super vos. Nos stulti propter Christum, vos autem prudentes, vos nobiles, nos autem ignobiles, maledicimur, et benedicimus: blasphemamur, et obsecramus, tanquam purgamenta hujus mundi, omnium per ipsema [sic] usque adhuc.*[40]

L'exercice le plus utile en allant et en revenant doit être d'accompagner en esprit *Notre Seigneur* et de nous unir à lui lorsqu'au travers des rues et des places de Jerusalem, Hérode le renvoia à Pilate en habit de fol; ou lorsque Pilate lui-même le présenta au peuple, la couronne d'épines en tête, le manteau de pourpre déchiré sur ses épaules, le roseau à la main; ou enfin lorsque ce divin Sauveur des hommes allât [*read*: alla] au Calvaire chargé de sa croix. [199]

C'est encore icy un des tems de notre vie le plus propre à demander à *Dieu*, et à obtenir de lui la victoire de notre orgueil, et la grâce de ne faire jamais dans la Compagnie aucune de ces fautes par où tant d'esprits superbes se sont malheureusement perdus.

Enfin, on doit faire réflexion au ridicule qu'il y auroit d'aller aux Halles de tems en tems par mortification, et par mépris du monde, et d'affecter ensuite dans sa personne aucun de ces usages de vanité, et d'avoir honte ou de se fâcher de porter un habit et des souliers usés et rapiécés, d'être vu par des séculiers balayant une salle du dehors ou rendant quelques services aux offices. Pourroit-on donner une meilleure preuve qu'on ne fait le premier que malgré soi? Ne seroit-ce pas comme se dédire, et comme se repentir d'avoir eu pendant un tems trop de religion?

---

[39] 1 Corinthians 4:9, *Puto enim quod Deus nos Apostolos novissimos ostendit, tanquam morti destinatos: quia spectaculum facti sumus mundo, et Angelis, et hominibus.*

[40] Luke 23:28, *Filiæ Ierusalem, nolite flere super me, sed super vos ipsas flete, et super filios vestros.* 1 Corinthians 4:10, *Nos stulti propter Christum, vos autem prudentes in Christo: nos infirmi, vos autem fortes: vos nobiles, nos autem ignobiles.* 1 Corinthians 4:12–13, *Laboramus operantes manibus nostris: maledicimur, et benedicimus: persecutionem patimur, et sustinemus: Blasphemamur, et obsecramus: tanquam purgamenta hujus mundi facti sumus omnium perisema usque adhuc.*

beast of burden. It was the most qualified and those who, before entering, had shone the most by their knowledge and their occupations, who were spared the least. Several would have liked to be permitted, in addition, to go through the streets in that ridiculous state, and sometimes they were permitted to do so. Saint Ignatius did something similar in an Italian city. [198]

The intention of all these practices was to trample on the usages of the world and, before its very eyes, triumph over it in some manner.

It was an application of the rule that orders us to scorn what the world holds in esteem, and to embrace what *Jesus Christ* loved and esteemed, and even to be pleased to be accounted as fools, without causing all true sages to judge us for anything but our virtuous actions.

If it should happen, therefore, that along the road we encounter people who insult us verbally or in some other fashion, people who call this childishness, or others in whom we seem to be provoking compassion, the reply to the former would be merely greater recollection: "We are made a spectacle to the world and to angels and to men"; and to the others, more compassion for their depraved judgement: "Weep not over me; but weep for yourselves. We are fools for Christ's sake, but you are wise, you are honourable, but we without honour. We are reviled: and we bless. We are blasphemed: and we entreat. We are made as the refuse of this world, the offscouring of all, even until now."

The most useful exercise, while going and returning, should be to accompany *Our Lord* in Spirit and to unite ourselves with him when, through the streets and squares of Jerusalem, Herod sent him to Pilate in the garb of a fool; or when Pilate himself presented him to the people, the crown of thorns on his head, the torn purple mantle on his shoulders, the reed in his hand; or else when this divine Savior of men went to Calvary carrying his cross. [199]

This is also one of the most suitable times of our lives to request from *God*, and to obtain from him victory over our pride and the grace never again to commit, in the Society, any of those faults by which so many proud spirits have unfortunately been lost.

Lastly, one should reflect on how ridiculous it would be to go to the Market from time to time, from mortification and from scorn for the world, and then to adopt some of those vain usages in one's own person, and be ashamed or angry about wearing a worn and mended habit and shoes, about being seen from outside by lay people, sweeping a community room or rendering a few services in the service rooms. Could one offer better proof that one is only doing the first of these things [going to the Market] against one's will? Would it not amount to going back on one's word, and to repenting for having been too religious for awhile?

Instruction 34ᵉ
Pour quand on fait la Charité

Rendre au prochain quelque sorte de service que ce puisse être pour son bien et pour l'amour de *Dieu*, c'est lui faire la charité. Mais la Charité se prend icy pour une espèce particulière de bon office [200] qu'on rend à son Frère, et qui consiste à l'avertir des deffauts qu'on a apperçu en lui, et qu'il n'a peut-être pas apperçu lui-même, afin qu'il puisse les corriger. C'est donc une espèce de correction fraternelle, mais qui se fait en public, afin que non seulement le coupable, mais aussi tous les autres puissent profiter des avis qu'on lui donne, et dont quelquefois plusieurs n'ont pas quelquefois moins besoin que lui. Dans la plupart des ordres religieux on ne tient guères le chapitre qu'après que chacun s'est accusé de ses fautes et on ne fasse plusieurs Proclamations. La Proclamation consiste à avertir la communauté, avec la permission du supérieur, des fautes dont un ou plusieurs ont manqués [*sic*] de s'accuser. Ils prétendent que de là dépend toute la conservation du bon ordre et de la discipline. La Charité et les Fautes qui se donnent au réfectoir tiennent lieu au Noviciat de Proclamation.

Règlement extérieur

Les jours de Communion et de petites fêtes où il n'y a point de sermon et où on ne sort point, sont ordinairement les jours de Charité. Rien n'empêcheroit qu'on ne la pût faire quelqu'autre jour au lieu de la Modestie. Les jours qu'on est averty qu'il y aura Charité, l'Examen particulier étant finy, tous s'assembleront au tint de la cloche à la salle de Notre Dame. [201]

Ceux qui sont nommés recevoir la Charité se mettront à genoux et découverts au milieu de la salle, et écouteront avec toute sorte de sérieux et d'humilité les fautes dont on les avertira.

Il ne leur sera permis d'apporter la moindre excuse, ni de donner le moindre signe qu'ils soient peinés des deffauts qu'on leur reprochera, quand même il arriveroit qu'ils n'en fussent pas coupables, ou qu'on les exagerât, ou qu'il parût quelque passions dans ceux qui parleroient. On interroge tous ceux qui sont présens à leur tour, et l'accusé ne retourne point à sa place qu'il n'en soit averty par celui qui préside à l'assemblée, et qu'il n'ait baisé la terre.

Direction intérieure

L'esprit de Charité regarde et celui à qui on la fait, et ceux qui la font. Celui à qui on la fait doit se persuader qu'il en a grand besoin, et que quelqu'accomply qui [*read*: qu'il] soit à ses propres yeux, les autres sont en beaucoup de choses plus éclairés que luy. Il n'aura pas beaucoup de peine à en convenir, s'il fait attention à la multitude de défauts qu'il remarque lui-même dans ses Frères et sur lesquels, avec tant de bonne volonté, il est fort probable

Thirty-fourth Instruction
For when one does the Exercise of Charity

Rendering any sort of service whatsoever to one's neighbor that can be for his good and for the love of *God*, is being charitable to him. But, at the Novitiate, the Exercise of Charity refers to a special sort of good deed [200] that one does for one's Brother, and that consists of admonishing him for the defects one has observed in him, and that he himself may not have noticed, so that he can correct them. It is therefore a sort of brotherly correction, but which is carried out in public, so that not only the guilty party but all the others as well can profit from the opinions one gives him, and which several others sometimes need no less than he. In most religious orders, a chapter meeting is rarely held until each one has accused himself of his faults, and until several Proclamations have been made. A Proclamation consists of notifying the community, with the superior's permission, of the faults for which one or more religious have failed to accuse themselves. They claim that the entire conservation of good order and discipline depends on it. At the Novitiate, the Exercise of Charity and the Faults declared in the refectory take the place of the Proclamation.

Outer regulation

Communion days and lesser feast days when there is no sermon, and when one does not go out, are usually days for the Exercise of Charity. Nothing would prevent it from being done on another day, in place of Modesty. On days when one is notified that there will be Charity, after finishing the particular Examen, everyone will assemble in the Hall of Our Lady when the bell rings. [201]

Those who are named to receive Charity will drop to their knees in the middle of the Hall, bareheaded, and with all manner of seriousness and humility will hear the faults about which they are being admonished.

They will not be permitted to make the least excuse, or give the least sign that they are troubled by the defects for which they are being reproached, even if they should happen not to be guilty, or if there happens to be an exaggeration, or if the persons speaking were to let some passions show. All those present are questioned in turn, and the accused does not return to his place until he has been notified to do so by the person presiding over the assembly, and until he has kissed the floor.

Inner guidance

The spirit of Charity involves both the person to whom it is being done, and those who do it. The person to whom it is being done should be persuaded that he needs it greatly and that, no matter how accomplished he is in his own eyes, the others are more enlightened than he is about many things. He will not have much trouble agreeing, if he pays attention to the multitude of defects that he himself remarks in his Brethren and which, with so much good will, they would

qu'ils ne manquent à se réformer que parce qu'ils ne les connoissent pas, ou qu'ils [202] ne s'avisent pas de croire que les autres en puissent être offensés ou mal édifiés. Nous avons d'autant plus besoin qu'au Noviciat on nous fasse connoître nos défauts que, dans le reste de la vie, il se trouvera moins de personnes ou qui veuillent nous en avertir, ou de qui peut-être nous soions disposés à prendre les avis en bonne part.

C'est une raison non seulement d'être bien aises qu'aujourd'huy on nous parle en toute liberté, mais encore une raison de n'oublier jamais ce qu'on aura eu la bonté de nous dire. La Charité oblige encore ceux à qui on la fait de ne pas soupçonner aisément qu'en parlant on eût dessein de les peiner et de les choquer. Mais si leur mauvaise disposition ou quelque preuve certaine en apparence le leur suggère, ils se garderont bien d'en conserver aucun ressentiment, ou de s'en plaindre, ou de chercher l'occasion de rendre la pareille. La Charité oblige à pardonner bien d'autres injures plus considérables, et à prier même pour ceux de qui nous les aurions reçus.

Quant à ceux qu'on interroge, à moins qu'ils ne gardent avec attention toutes les règles qu'on va leur donner, ce ne sera pas une charité qu'ils feront, mais une passion qu'ils contenteront sous le voile sacré de l'amour fraternel. Ils doivent donc dire simplement ce qu'ils pensent, et ce qu'ils ont remarqués, n'emploiant aucun terme choquant ou injurieux. Ils ne doivent parler que des deffauts extérieurs et [203] habituels, extérieurs, dis-je, sans jamais pénétrer dans l'intention; habituels, car les fautes dont on s'est corrigé, ou qui ne sont arrivé[e]s qu'une fois, ne doivent plus être rapportées. S'ils doutent du motif qui les fait parler, peut-être vaudroit-il mieux qui [*read*: qu'ils] se tussent. Si le deffaut est fréquent et considérable, il n'aura pas échappé à tout le monde, et d'autres en avertiront; au moins qu'on ne parle jamais qu'on ne se soit recommandé à *Dieu*, et qu'on n'ait bien purifié son intention et bien pesé ce qu'on va dire, et la manière dont on le va dire. Hors du cas de la passion, il ne faut pas que le respect humain ou la crainte de faire de la peine ferme la bouche: ce seroit être cruel envers un malade que de lui déguiser son mal et son danger. Il faut présumer plutôt que ne lui parlant que par zèle et sans aucune aigreur, il en aura de la reconnoissance. Il sera aisé de garder le juste milieu si nous nous imaginons que *Dieu* nous appelle lui-même en témoignage, les uns contre les autres, car étant le *Dieu* de la vérité et de la charité, [204] il n'est permis en sa présence, ni de blesser l'une ni de dissimuler l'autre.

Enfin, pour parler avec plus d'assurance, voici en détail les principaux points dont il faut s'entr'avertir:

Non seulement les fautes contre les règles, et contre les Instructions, mais beaucoup plus le mépris qu'on paroîtroit en faire, ou par paroles ou par certains signes.

Le deffaut de propreté à table, et de tempérance, surtout à l'égard du vin. Tout ce qui étant contre la civilité, et un certain sçavoir-vivre, nous rendroit méprisables à des personnes polies et bien-élevées.

very likely fail to correct only because they are unaware of them, or because it [202] does not enter their heads to believe that others might find them offensive or unedifying. At the Novitiate we especially need to be informed of our faults because, for the rest of our lives, there will be fewer people who want to inform us, or whose opinion we might perhaps be disposed to view favorably.

Not only is their speaking to us today, in complete liberty, a reason to be very pleased, it is also a reason never to forget what they have been kind enough to tell us. Those who are given Charity are also obliged not to be easily suspicious that someone planned to pain or shock them, by speaking out. But if their bad disposition or some certain proof appears to suggest it to them, they will be careful not to hold any grudge, or complain, or seek an occasion to retaliate. Charity obliges us to pardon many other more consequential wrongs, and even to pray for those from whom we receive them.

As for those who are questioned, unless they follow attentively all the rules given below, they will not be doing a charity, they will be satisfying a passion under the sacred veil of fraternal love. They should therefore say what they think simply, and what they have observed, employing no shocking or injurious term. They should speak only about external and habitual defects [203]: external, I say, without ever delving into the intention; habitual, because faults that one has corrected oneself, or that took place only once, should no longer be reported. If they have doubts about the motive that makes them speak, perhaps it would be better for them to remain silent. If the defect is frequent and considerable, no one will have failed to notice it, and others will give notice of it. At least, let one never speak without having recommended oneself to *God*, and without having thoroughly purified one's intention and carefully weighed what one is going to say, and the manner in which one is going to say it. Except when passion is involved, consideration for what others might think, or the fear of causing pain, should not seal one's lips: it would be cruel to hide his illness and his danger from a sick person. Rather, it is necessary to presume that if one talks to him solely from zeal and without any bitterness, he will be grateful. It will be easy to keep to the golden mean, if we imagine that *God* himself is calling us to witness against one another: for since he is the *God* of truth and of charity, [204] in his presence it is not permitted either to do injury to the latter or to conceal the former.

Lastly, in order to speak with greater assurance, here in detail are the principal points about which we must admonish one another:

Not only faults against the rules and against the Instructions, but, even more, scorn for them that one would appear to show either by words or by certain signs.

Defects involving cleanliness at table and temperance, especially concerning wine. Everything that is against civility and a certain knowing how to live well, would make us contemptible to people who are polite and well brought-up.

Lack of respect and concern for one another in our conversations, shouting, contesting, being obstinate, saying harsh and shocking things.

Le manque de respect et d'égard les uns pour les autres dans les conversations, criant, contestant, s'obstinant, disant des paroles dures et choquantes.

La liberté trop grande à parler désavantageusement du prochain, ne fût-ce que d'histoires connues et de défauts naturels.

Les badineries, et tout ce qui sent l'écolier et le pensionnaire; une certaine nonchalance à s'acquitter de ses devoirs et surtout de ceux [205] de piété et de dévotion.

Tout ce qui ressent la vanité, la passion pour les sciences, l'intrigue, ou l'envie de briller et de se faire un nom à l'avenir.

Les petits airs délicats et proprets, et généralement tout ce qui paroît affecté dans la figure, dans la démarche, dans les manières d'agir et de parler.

La recherche de ses aises et de ses commodités, qui consiste principalement à choisir pour soy ce qu'il y a dans chaque chose de plus propre et de meilleur, détourner adroitement tout ce qui peine et ce qui contraint.

Les amitiés particulières, et tous les petits artifices pour se joindre aux uns et éviter les autres.

L'habitude de parler de soi avantageusement, de son païs, de ses parens, de sa noblesse, de ses connoissances, de mépriser et de rendre ridicule ce qui appartient aux autres.

Les inégalités d'humeur, les saillies d'un naturel [206] dur et farouche, se fâcher, s'emporter; ou bien être tantôt guay, tantôt mélancholique, aujourd'huy prêt à rire, et demain inabordable, disposé à se picquer de rien. Le matin léger jusqu'à une espèce de licence, le soir grossier, rustique, rebutant.

Les simplicités, les bévues qui échappent quand on veut faire l'entendu et l'habile homme, et qu'on parle de ce qu'on ne sçait pas et de ce qu'on ne doit pas sçavoir. En un mot tout ce qui seroit capable ou d'offenser d'honnêtes gens, ou de mal édifier des personnes de piété.

Ces fautes-là donc, et toutes les autres de même nature, doivent servir de matière et à la Charité qui se fait en public, et à celle qui se fait le mercredy et le vendredy dans la chambre après l'Examen particulier, et à ce qui se lit [*read*: dit] le samedy matin au réfectoir.

Custodite et facite quæ præcepit Dominus Deus vobis: non declinabitis neque ad dexteram, neque ad sinistram. Deuteronomie, chapitre 5, verset 32.[41] [207]

Hic liber mandatorum Dei, et lex, quæ est in æternum: omnes qui tenent eam, pervenient ad vitam; qui autem derelinquerint eam, in mortem.[42]

---

[41] Deuteronomy 5:32, *Custodite igitur et facite quæ præcepit Dominus Deus vobis: non declinabitis neque ad dexteram, neque ad sinistram.*

[42] Baruch 4:1, *Hic liber mandatorum Dei, et lex, quæ est in æternum: omnes qui tenent eam, pervenient ad vitam; qui autem dereliquerunt eam, in mortem.*

Excessive liberty in speaking disadvantageously about our neighbor, even if these are familiar stories and natural defects.

Bantering and everything that smacks of the schoolboy and the day-boarder; a certain nonchalance about completing one's duties, especially those [205] involving piety and devotion.

Everything that smacks of vanity, a passion for reasoned learning, intrigue, or a desire to shine and make a name for oneself in the future.

Little delicate and fastidious airs, and generally everything that appears affected in one's face, one's movements, and one's way of acting and speaking.

Seeking one's ease and convenience, which consists principally of always choosing for oneself what is cleanest and best, and adroitly pushing aside everything that causes pain and that constrains.

Particular friendships, and all the little artifices aimed at linking oneself to some people and avoiding others.

The habit of speaking advantageously about oneself, one's region, one's parents, one's nobility, one's acquaintances, and scorning or ridiculing what belongs to others.

Disparities in one's humor, outbursts stemming from a harsh and ferocious penchant, [206] becoming angry, losing one's temper; or else being sometimes gay and sometimes melancholy, ready to laugh today and unapproachable tomorrow, disposed to become irritated about nothing; light-hearted in the morning to the point of excess, and in the evening coarse, rustic, tiresome.

Artlessness, blunders one makes when trying to be the well-versed and able man, and when one is speaking about something one does not know about and should not know about. In a word, everything that might be capable of either offending respectable people or failing to edify pious people.

Those faults, then, and all others of a similar nature, should serve as subject matter for both the Exercise of Charity that is conducted publicly and the one that is done on Wednesdays and Fridays in the bedchamber after the particular Examen, and for what is said on Saturday morning in the refectory [the Faults].

"Keep therefore and do the things which the Lord God hath commanded you: you shall not go aside neither to the right hand, nor to the left."
Deuteronomy 5:32. [207]

"This is the book of the commandments of God, and the law, that is for ever: all they that keep it, shall come to life: but they that have forsaken it, to death."

This is the book of God's commandments, and the law that should last forever: those who keep it will end up living, but those who have abandoned it have fallen into the abyss of death, Baruch, chapter 4.

In a singular way, one can apply to us the words a prophet spoke to God's people: You are happy, Israel, and happy in everything that can make a nation

C'est icy le livre des ordonnances de Dieu, et la loy qui doit toujours durer: ceux qui la gardent arriveront à la vie; mais ceux qui l'ont abandonné sont tombés dans l'abîme de la mort. Baruch, chapitre 7 [*read*: 4].

On peut nous appliquer singulièrement à nous ces paroles d'un prophète au peuple de Dieu: Vous êtes heureux, Israël, et heureux par tout ce qui peut rendre une nation célèbre et florissante; mais ne vous y trompez pas, ce qui fait le comble de votre bonheur et de votre gloire, c'est que Dieu ait voulu manifester d'une manière si claire et si distincte tout ce qu'il souhaite que vous fassiés pour le servir selon ses inclinations.[43]

Beati sumus, Israël, quia quæ placita sunt [*sic*] *Deo,*
manifesta sunt nobis.[44]

fin

Dixi, nunc œpi. Psaume 76[45]
Custodiam legem tuam. Psaume 118[46] [208]

In his mandatis universa lex pendet, et prophetæ.
Matthieu 22, verset 40[47]

Hoc fac et vivez.[48]
Luc 10, verset 28 [209]

---

[43] Although inspired by Baruch 4:4, this is not a direct quotation.

[44] Baruch 4:4, *Beati sumus Israel: quia quæ Deo placent, manifesta sunt nobis.*

[45] Psalm 76:11, *Et dixi: Nunc cæpi: hæc mutatio dexteræ excelsi.*

[46] Psalm 118:60–61, *Paratus sum, et non sum turbatus: ut custodiam mandata tua, Funes peccatorum circumplexi sunt me: et legem tuam non sum oblitus.*

[47] Matthew 22:40, *In his duobus mandatis universa lex pendet, et prophetae.*

[48] Luke 10:28, *Dixitque illi: Recte respondisti; hoc fac et vives.*

famous and flourishing; but do not deceive yourselves. What constitutes the pinnacle of your happiness and your glory is the fact that God wanted to make manifest, in so clear and so distinct a way, everything he wishes you to do in order to serve him according to his inclinations.

"We are happy, O Israel: because the things that are pleasing
to God, are made known to us."

the end

"And I said, Now have I begun." Psalm 76
"That I may keep thy commandments." Psalm 118 [208]

"On these two commandments dependeth the whole law and the prophets."
Matthew 22:40

"This do: and thou shalt live."
Luke 10:28 [209]

Table [des Instructions]

[Avertissement].. 44
[Instructions communes à tous].. 50
   Ordre du jour 50
   Pour le lever 60
   Pour l'Oraison et la Récollection 62
   Pour faire son lit 64
   Pour assister à la Messe 64
   Pour servir la Messe... 66
   Pour les Exhortations.. 80
   Pour le déjeuner 84
   Pour les exercices corporels 86
   Pour les lectures.. 92
   Pour apprendre par cœur.. 94
   Pour les visites.. 98
   Pour les Examens 104
   Pour les repas 104
   Pour la modestie   ⎫ dans... 106
   Pour la propreté   ⎬ le... 106
   Pour la tempérance ⎭ repas.. 110
   Pour les offices 114
   Pour servir en première 114
   Pour servir en seconde 118
   Pour la vaisselle 120
   Pour la crédence 122
   Pour les récréations.. 124
   Pour les Litanies... 132
   Pour l'écriture... 136
   Pour le Chapelet 138
   Pour les tems libres 142
   Pour la chambre.. 144
   Pour le silence et la modestie 148
   Pour la propreté 152
   Pour le chauffoir 156
   Pour dire et demander pardon de ses Fautes 158
   Pour les Tons.. 164
   Pour les jours qu'on se confesse 166
   Pour rendre compte de Conscience...................................... 168
   Pour écrire des lettres 172
   Pour la porte 176
   Pour quand on sort de la Maison 180
   Pour Montrouge.. 184
   Pour quand on passe le jour entier à Montrouge................ 188
   Pour les jours qu'on y dîne seulement................................. 188
   Pour quand on va aux Halles 192
   Pour la Charité.. 196

Si diligamus invicem, Deus nobis manet et charitas ejus in nobis perfecta est.
1 Johannis, caput 4, versus 12[50]

[49] Here, and in the translation, the original page numbers have been replaced by the page numbers in this edition.

[50] 1 John 4:12, *Si diligamus invicem, Deus in nobis manet, et charitas ejus in nobis perfecta est.*

Table of Instructions[61]

Notice .... Page 45
Instructions that are common to all 51
  1 The order of the day 51
  2 For rising 61
  3 For Prayer and Recollection 63
  4 For making one's bed 65
  5 For attending Mass 65
  6 For serving Mass 67
  7 For Exhortations [and Repetitions] 81
  8 For breakfast 85
  9 For bodily exercises 87
10 For [spiritual] reading 93
11 For learning by heart 95
12 For visits [to the Blessed Sacrament] 99
13 For Examens [of Conscience] 105
14 For meals 105
      For modesty   ⎫ at 107
      For cleanliness ⎬ meals 107
      For temperance ⎭ 111
15 For the service rooms 115
      For serving first table 115
      For serving second table 119
      For washing dishes 121
      For the pantry 123
16 For recreation 125
17 For the Litanies 133
18 For [learning good] writing 137
19 For the Rosary 139
20 For free time 143
21 For the bedchamber 145
22 For silence and modesty 149
23 For cleanliness 153
24 For the warming room 157
25 For declaring one's Faults and begging pardon 159
26 For the Tones 165
27 For the days when one confesses 167
28 For giving an account of Conscience 169
29 For [receiving and] writing letters 173
30 For the door [speaking to outsiders] 177
31 For when one leaves the House 181
32 For Montrouge 185
      For when one spends the entire day at Montrouge 189
      For the days one only eats the noon meal there [or only takes a walk] ... 189
33 For when one goes to the Central Market 193
34 For the Exercise of Charity 197

"If we love one another, God abideth in us: and his charity is perfected in us."
I John 4:12

---

[61] Not all entries in this table of contents correspond exactly with the titles of the different instructions. Key divergences have been added within square brackets. In addition, to make this table of contents more useful, the number of each Instruction has been inserted before the title.

Appendix I

Les Tons[1]

Vous debvés sçavoir qu'estant homme par sa faute tombé en la disgrace du Créateur, et en la tyrannie de Satan, il s'est trouvé en grande misère et confusion; et que par le Sang de l'Agneau immaculé, il a esté affranchi de ce pesant joug et remis en l'amitié de son Dieu.

Et par tant il nous faut bien (mes très chers Frères) considérer attentifvement l'infinie bonté et démesurée bénignité de nostre Sauveur et Rédempteur, qui estant Dieu s'est fait homme, anéanissant [*read*: anéantissant] sa grandeur par notre petitesse, qui a voulu, pour toy, O ingratte créature, descendre des cieux et sortir du sein de son Père éternel, où comblé de joye, et d'honneur, il estoit assisté, servi et adoré des espri[t]s bienheureux, des Anges, des Archanges, des Principautés, et généralment de toute la cour céleste. O Chrestien, regarde ton Seigneur, comme pour toy il s'est fait serviteur! O bonté infinie, O très doux Agneau, qui vous a contraint à porter nos iniquités et endurer la mort pour donner la vie à nous, chétifs, ingrats et misérables pécheurs?

O endormis, et ensevelis au sommeil du péché, jusques à quant [read: quand] serés-vous insensés, jusques à quant [read: quand] aurés-vous les yeux et les oreilles fermés, et les sens assoupis? Oyés la voix du prophète Joël, *Canite tuba in Sion, sanctificate jejunum, congregate cœtum, vocate populem, sanctificate ecclesiam, coadunate senes, congregate parvulos et sugentes ubera.*[2] 'Chantés,' dit ce divin trompette, 'Chantés en Sion, sanctifiés le jeusne, assemblés le peuple, sanctifiés l'Eglise, assemblés les vieux, assemblés les petits, et suçans la mamelle.'

Ne voyés-vous point, ne voyés-vous point combien il y en a qui périssent? Pleurés donc, pleurés vos péchés, et ceux du peuple; et ce faisant, Dieu vous donnera sa grâce en se [*read*: ce] monde, et sa gloire en l'austre, à laquelle nous conduise, *etc.*

Observation sur les Tons

En premier lieu, il faut faire le signe de la croix et se couvrir, et puis poser les mains sur la chaire; et aiant un peu demeuré, faut commencer avec une voix modérée, la conduisant jusqu'en ce lieu: "Et par tant . . ."

---

[1] Bibliothèque nationale de France, ms. lat. 18209, fols. 40–42. The opening page of this manuscript volume bears the owner's name, "G. Dubois," and the date: "1623 24 may." The final sentences of the little speech appear to have been omitted: the manuscript ends with "et cetera." The three dots at the beginning or end of some sentences do not indicate excisions: they are original.

[2] Joel 2:15–16, *Canite tuba in Sion, sanctificate jejunium, vocate cœtum. Congregate populum, sancificate ecclesiam, coadunate senes, congregate parvulos, et sugentes ubera.* In this manuscript, *jejunium* and *populum* are misspelled, and the order of the verbs *vocate* and *congregate* is inverted. In addition, "call a solemn assembly" was omitted from the French paraphrase.

Appendix I

The Tones

You should know that, man having fallen, by his fault, into disgrace with the Creator, and into Satan's tyranny, he found himself in great misery and confusion; and that, by the blood of the immaculate Lamb, he was freed from this heavy yoke and restored to friendship with his God.

And consequently it is very necessary (my very dear Brethren)[1] for us to consider attentively the infinite goodness and unmeasured benignity of our Savior and Redeemer, who, being God, made himself man, annihilating his grandeur by our pettiness, who was willing for thee, Oh ungrateful creature, to descend from heaven and leave the bosom of his eternal Father, where, overwhelmed with joy and honor, he was assisted, served, and adored by the blessed spirits, the Angels, the Archangels, the Principalities[2] and generally by all the celestial court. Oh Christian, look at thy Lord and how he became a servant for thee! Oh infinite good, Oh very gentle Lamb, who forced you to bear our iniquities and endure death in order to give life to us, scrawny, ungrateful, and wretched sinners?

Oh sleepers, Oh persons buried in the sleep of sin, how long will you be senseless? How long will you keep your eyes and ears shut, and your senses deadened? Hear the voice of the prophet Joel: *Canite tuba in Sion, sanctificate jejunium, congregate cœtum, vocate populem, sanctificate ecclesiam, coadunate senes, congregate parvulos et sugentes ubera.* 'Sing,' says this divine trumpeter, 'Sing in Zion, sanctify fasting, assemble the people, sanctify the Church, assemble the old, assemble the little ones, and those who suck at the breast.'[3]

Do you not see, do you not see how many are perishing? Weep, then. Weep for your sins and for those of the people; and by doing this, God will give you his grace in this world and his glory in the other, to which we are led, *etc.*

Observation about the Tones

First of all, it is necessary to make the sign of the cross and cover one's head, and then put one's hands on the pulpit; and, having remained in that posture for a bit, it is necessary to begin with a moderated voice, continuing it until one reaches "And consequently . . ."

---

[1] The parentheses tell the orator to say these words as an aside, on a lower pitch and therefore with a different "tone" of voice. For the rhetorical figure known as "Parenthesis," see Patricia M. Ranum, *The Harmonic Orator* (Hillsdale, NY: Pendragon Press, 2001), 286–88.

[2] The Angels, the Archangels, and the Principalities are heavenly messengers. They constitute the third sphere or choir of angels.

[3] The misspelled Latin has been corrected here. Compare the inexact paraphrase (shown within single quotes) with the full Douai translation of Joel 2:15–16: "Blow the trumpet in Sion, sanctify a fast, call a solemn assembly, gather together the people, sanctify the church, assemble the ancients, gather together the little ones, and them that suck at the breasts."

Estant icy parvenu, faut s'arrester, puis commenser [*read*: commencer] et changer la voix, la poussant un peu, disant, "Pour toy, O ingratte créature." Il faut, avec dextérité, tourner la main droitte, la fléchissant un peu bas.

". . . Sortir du sein," il faut eslever les mains en haut, regardant avec modestie les auditeurs.

"Des Anges," il faut eslever la main droite et la bais[s]er. "Des Archanges," faire la maime [*read*: même] de la main gauche.

"Et généralement," des deux mains.

"O Chrestien," faut un peu eslever la voix, regardant les auditeurs, addressant vers eux la main droicte. "Regarde ton Seigneur," se tourner d'un costé, comme s'il y avoit quelque crucifix, le monstrant aux assistans: puis, se reposant un peu, avec une petite exclamation.

"O bonté infinie," *etc.*, faut séparer les deux mains, les fléchissant un peu, et croiser les deux bras en baissant un peu la teste et prononçant dévotement les paroles. "Pour donner la vie à nous," faut mettre la main à la poitrine, et commencer avec plus de véhémence. "O endormis," *etc.*, frapper de la main sur la chaire avec discretion.

"Oyés la voix," faut fléchir la main droicte. Le reste, la plupart avec la dextre, quelquefois avec la gauche, et quelquefois toutes deux.

"Ne voyés-vous point," faut monstrer avec la main droicte aux auditeurs, fléchissant deux fois, et la conduisant toujours plus bas, jusques à la fin.

Having reached this point, it is necessary to pause,[4] then resume speaking and change one's tone of voice, pushing it a bit when one says, "For thee, Oh ungrateful creature."[5] It is necessary to turn the right hand with dexterity, and bend it a bit downwards.[6]

". . . Leave the bosom," it is necessary to raise one's hands, looking modestly at those who are listening.

"The Angels," it is necessary to raise the right hand and lower it. "The Archangels," make the same gesture with the left hand.

"And generally," use both hands.

"Oh Christian," it is necessary to raise one's voice a bit,[7] looking at the listeners and stretching one's right hand toward them. "Look at thy Lord," turn to one side, as if there were a crucifix and you were showing it to the listeners: then, pausing a bit, with a little exclamation.

"Oh infinite good," *etc.*, it is necessary to separate both hands, flexing them a little, and to cross both arms while lowering the head a bit and saying the words devoutly. "To give life to us," it is necessary to put one's hand on one's breast, and with more vehemence, begin: "Oh sleepers," *etc.*, discreetly strike the pulpit with one's hand.

"Hear the voice," it is necessary to flex the right hand; and for the rest, usually use the right hand and sometimes the left one, and occasionally both.

"Do you not see,"[8] it is necessary to extend one's right hand toward the listeners, flexing it twice and carrying it progressively lower, until the end.

---

[4] This first paragraph forms the exordium or opening statement of the brief oration. The exordium states the central argument of the speech. It should be delivered with a calm and balanced tone of voice and restrained gestures. In the exordium the orator generally addresses the audience by name, in this case, "you, my very dear Brethren." For the exordium, see P. Ranum, *Harmonic Orator*, 87–91.

[5] The speaker pauses, to signal that he has reached the second section of his oration, the narration. He adopts an assertive yet pleasing tone, as he provides the background information that serves as the underpinning for his arguments. For the narration, see P. Ranum, *Harmonic Orator*, 91–93.

[6] This gesture imitates the concept "descend," *descendre*. For an overview of the link between voice, gesture, and concept in Jesuit education, see Sophie Conte, "Louis de Cressolles: le savoir au service de l'action oratoire," *XVIIe Siècle*, 59 (2007): 653–67.

[7] If the orator's tone of voice is supposed to be "raised" here, it is because he is beginning the third part of his speech, the confirmation. Here he tends to express his ideas by hyperbole and exclamations, which he accompanies with increasingly dramatic gestures such as raised arms and pounding hands. See P. Ranum, *Harmonic Orator*, 93–95.

[8] These words begin the peroration or conclusion of the oration. The peroration states, in a slightly different way, the point made in the exordium. In short, the orator returns to the point of departure: in this case, the image of the disgraced sinner is mirrored by the person weeping over his sins, and the person freed of his heavy yoke of sin is mirrored by the grace given by God to those who repent. As the orator begins his peroration, the emphatic tone of voice that characterized the third part of the speech gradually yields to this calm yet triumphant final statement. The speaker's calmer, "lower" gestures mirror this progressive return to calm. See P. Ranum, *Harmonic Orator*, 95–97.

Appendix II

Schooling and Courtesy

Orest Ranum

"One should treat one another with respect, charity, courtesy, and simplicity. . . . It is better to wait for the others for half a quarter hour than to make people wait for one the length of a *Pater*. Charity and civility also require this." (*Instructions*, [122], [183])

"Being outwardly respectful can, in part, take the place of what is lacking inside, especially if it is involuntary. One pays court to the prince by keeping a composed demeanor in his presence, even if one might not have the freedom of speaking to him, or the consolation of hearing him." (*Instructions*, [23])

Civility, respect, charity, courtesy, and simplicity are repeatedly invoked in the manuscript edited here, the *Instructions for the Novitiate* compiled by the Parisian Jesuits in the 1680s. Indeed, they are presented as the underpinnings of a code of conduct without which the Novitiate could not function.[1]

In 1980 I published an article[2] that proposed three themes: 1) courtesy might be a highly coercive political instrument to enforce, upon others, either individual or collective wills; 2) courtesies prevailing in the church, especially around the "courts" of high-ranking prelates, could humiliate, or shame, or ingratiate the individuals who performed them[3]; and 3) in the early-modern centuries, 1500–1789, there was an etiquette or civility that, with nuances for social rank, generally prevailed throughout society, and this civility and the absolutist courtesies established at the French court were not the same thing.

In that article, I cited Edmund Jephcott's translation of Norbert Elias, *The Civilizing Process: The History of Manners* (Oxford: Blackwell, 1978), a work I began to teach in graduate seminar soon after it became available. I also cited Erving Goffman's "The Nature of Deference and Demeanor,"[4] and Michel Foucault's *Naissance de la clinique* (Paris: P.U.F., 1963) and his *Surveiller et punir: Naissance de la prison* (Paris: Gallimard, 1975).

---

[1] For readers in need of a general introduction to the Society of Jesus, see Thomas Worcester, ed., *The Cambridge Companion to the Jesuits* (Cambridge: Cambridge University Press, 2008).

[2] "Courtesy, Absolutism, and the Rise of the French State, 1630–1660," *Journal of Modern History*, 52 (1980): 426–57.

[3] As monarchies adopted more and more antique ceremonial practices, there would be possibilities for transferring these practices to the Church: the manuscript contains a fine statement about how the marks of respect shown to a prince are appropriate for showing respect for God ([23]).

[4] *American Anthropologist*, 58 (1956): 473–502.

Back in 1980, I offered a few illustrative examples of the courteous power exerted by the high clergy, to suggest that the rules enforced in and by Versailles were ecclesiastical in inspiration. My aim here is to suggest how, when teaching courtesy, a major corporate "society" or "company" reached far beyond court culture and, indeed, even beyond elite social ranks. The French word *société* meant, and still means, a separate corps whose members are bound together by regulations common to all. The corporate "society" to which I am referring is, of course, *la Compagnie de Jésus*, the Society of Jesus. Put bluntly, the *collèges* run by the Jesuits, that is, their secondary schools, refined and extended the early sixteenth-century Humanist pedagogical movement, turning it into a civilizing process that touched more lives, more quickly and more deeply, than did the court. But before going further, let us glance at some studies that have kept coercive power in the equation.

It would be an enormous task to research all the works inspired by Elias, Goffman, and Foucault, but I do not think all that much has yet been done on the transfer of the "courtly" culture of prelates to that of the French Monarchy in the sixteenth and seventeenth centuries.

Research on *civilités* and *honnêtetés*, as we shall note further on, has deepened our understanding of these behaviors, often, though not always, under the rubric of sociability; but the characterization of power and its uses does not always seem to have been kept in mind. I must confess that I am a historian whose primary interest is the study of power, its expression and its use, in words and in action. For this reason I found (and find) Elias's work so interesting and important. In *Norbert Elias par lui-même*, Elias says: "I tried to develop a sociological theory of power." Having quoted these words in a very thoughtful biographical essay about Elias, Alain Garrigou and Bernard Lacroix remark: "Being precise is, however, not completely superfluous because this project has not always been understood, doubtlessly because it did not fit into the classifications accepted in universities."[5]

I reviewed Elias's *The Court Society* (New York: Pantheon, 1983) soon after it came out in America. I shall quote a few words from that review: "There is the inseparability between ranks, no matter how absurdly it seems to be defined, and power."

The volume edited by Garrigou and Lacroix goes a long way toward restoring the question of power in the social, as I think Elias would have wished. And Roger Chartier's introductions to the paperback editions of Elias's major works (translated into French) have historicized the imbalances by informing everyone of Elias's own critique of historical scholarship as it was practiced in Germany in the 1930s, and elsewhere decades later.

André Burguière's chapter in the Garrigou-Lacroix volume merits attention here, because it revisits the old question of whether or not, in the Ancien Régime, there were social and cultural presences, other than the court, that contributed to the

---

[5] "Préciser n'est pourtant pas complètement superflu puisque ce projet n'a pas toujours été compris, sans doute parce qu'il s'alignait mal sur les classifications admises dans les facultés," *Norbert Elias, la politique et l'histoire* (Paris: La Découverte, 1997), 25. Elias's comment reads: "J'ai essayé de développer une théorie sociologique du pouvoir."

structuring and even the construction of manners. He cites Françoise Autrand's work on the rise of the legal profession in the late Middle Ages (Paris: Sorbonne, 1981), and George Huppert's on the *bourgeois gentilhommes* (Chicago: University of Chicago Press, 1977), as describing distinct *auto-contraintes* or self-disciplines whose strengths in the society at large made their manners influential, through their articulation of the law and its enforcement, and through their quite wealthy town-country ability to command deference.

Robert Muchembled's *La Société policée* (Paris: Seuil, 1998) situates what Jean-Marie Constant and Arlette Jouanna have understood as political in the behavior of the nobility during the sixteenth and seventeenth centuries. This is essentially interpreted as increasing the king's control over the nobility through the court (and the state). In short, their work centers on the manners-power nexus: a suggestive and valuable *mise au point*, and a strong one, owing to the eclecticism of the sources.

Numerous other works could be mentioned, but these suffice to indicate that, while perhaps not the central focus in studies inspired by Elias, studies centered on the relation between the social and power, including both self-disciplinary and coercive power, have come along at a regular pace.

On what may be called the prescriptive aspect, Jacques Revel's chapter, "The Uses of Civility," in the Ariès-Duby *History of Private Life*, III (Cambridge: Belknap, 1989; French edition, 1986), sets Erasmian, Castiglionian, Della-Casian, and other works on courtesy in a context of Humanist culture. Revel presents a complex, multi-directional (if not contradictory in its presuppositions) study of what Elias understood to be quite linear. I cite two important points from Revel: "Books of manners were intended to create conditions under which social intercourse would be easier and more in conformity with the heightened requirements of religion" (182). Later, facing the issue of finding authority to uphold courtesy codes, he remarks: "In the French of the Age of Louis XIV civility became more or less synonymous with politeness" (202). For Revel, the success of the civility movement left it vulnerable to becoming routine or not-quite-conscious social interaction. In a sense, the court had required all that could be required of "correct" behavior. Revel is facing and answering very difficult questions here. On the one hand, there would seem to be a kind of secularization in favor of the *religion royale*, while the latter becomes weaker as it is diffused. In France there would be no Balinese ceremonial society (Clifford Geertz). From Erasmus to Antoine de Courtin, the *regard*, the gaze, turns away from the altar and focuses on the Hall of Mirrors; but as the Hall became so influential, there was little authority, other than one's fellow courtiers, to enforce the rules. Courtin is categorical about how individuals in the salon of a great noble ought never sit with their backs to the portrait of a high-ranking individual. Thus, in one little phrase, he suggests that while high-ranking nobles may have objected to menial tasks at court (it is questionable that they did object), from entire ranks of both court and society, they enjoyed marks of respect, formally coded and very, very prestigious. The vast literature on the *honnête homme*, the upright or moral man, especially by Domna Stanton and Emmanuel Bury, might be explored here; but it would not advance my theme, except in so far as the reality of it, in society, was like

the Robe or legal profession, and like Huppert's *bourgeois gentilhommes*. That is to say, there were distinct self-disciplined roles that intersected with, but that were not dependent upon, the codes of court society.

In 1995 Peter Burke published *The Fortunes of the Courtier* (Cambridge U.K.: Blackwell), a brilliantly learned study of the writing, publication, diffusion, reception, translation, adaptation, and influence of Baldassare Castiglione's *The Book of the Courtier*. Erasmus wrote about manners from the viewpoint of a learned Christian humanist, but Castiglione wrote as an experienced diplomat, courtier, and aristocrat who understood social relations as an art. His ideal man possessed not only noble birth, he was also endowed with "grace," a divine gift that, in the form of *sprezzatura*, enabled him to do and say the right thing in every social surrounding.[6] In its almost innumerable editions and translations, *The Courtier* offered far more than rules of conduct: its vision of society carried the stimulus for reflection, critical distance, and a celebration of what Western societies have come to define by the powerful slang term "cool." Like the other major works of Humanists, *The Courtier* is an ingenious assemblage of commonplaces drawn from ancient authors, notably Xenophon, Aristotle, Cicero, and Quintilian, and held together in a vivid and mordant literary evocation of historical people and places, particularly the small, highly cultured Italian courts of the early sixteenth century.

Burke notes in passing that some Jesuits participated in the movement to criticize and expurgate from *The Courtier* anything that could potentially be interpreted as immoral or critical of the Church. Other Jesuits were inspired by *The Courtier*, notably Baltasar Gracián, S.J., who in 1647 produced *The Oracle*, a brilliant, elliptic, and epigrammatic Spanish "translation" of Castiligione. *The Oracle* would set off another round of Europe-wide reading, translation, and adaptation of *The Courtier*. The reception of *The Courtier* by the Jesuits is a subject that awaits its historians, but in the main the *disciplinæ* of monastic communities, not *The Courtier*, would inspire the *Instructions for the Novitiate* edited here. Although not secular (readers of the time could not conceive of a non-religious society), what Castiglione called "grace" is somewhat cut loose from Christian moorings by the mere fact that the religious resonances of "grace" are not made explicit.

Marc Fumaroli's chapter on conversation, in Pierre Nora's *Lieux de Mémoire* (Paris: Gallimard, 1997), and his Introduction to a translation of Lord Chesterfield's *Letters to His Son* (Paris: Rivages, 1993), merit special mention here, because they suggest how ethical, indeed philosophical questions central to Humanist culture were made manifest in and through civil exchange. Appropriateness, *decorum*, infused and rationalized rules of conduct, to constitute a veritable way of life. Together, the studies by Revel, Huppert, Burguière, Fumaroli, and Burke build a solid and subtle understanding of the history of manners that, although respectful of Elias's work, offer alternative and corrective studies of it. True, these works rely on the prescriptive

---

[6] Although there has been much recent work on the subject, none surpasses the learned *sprezzatura* of Edouardo Saccone's "*Gracia, Sprezzatura* and *Affettazione* in Castiglione's *Book of the Courtier*," *Glyph*, 5 (1979): 34–54.

for their strong points, but they are full of telling examples and references to the social history researched by others.

For the later seventeenth and eighteenth centuries, Daniel Gordon's *Citizens without Sovereignty* (Princeton: Princeton University Press, 1994) merits particular attention, because it confirms and extends the current of what really is Humanist civil and moral thought. Gordon begins where Revel leaves the argument about the move from civility to politeness; but an egalitarian impulse, refracted in a congenial sociability and critical thought in conversation, becomes an elite cultural presence without consideration for profession or rank, an extension and sophistication of the *salon* in all its anti-courtly aspects. The Enlightenment is thus to be understood as a movement of ideas that had, as a foundation, the old Humanism: humanity remains a clarion call. Both possessed authority to speak and write derived from ideas about what is natural and communitarian. In Voltaire's *Dictionnaire*, manners become liberating in their variety, and in their independence from religion and the state.

I have come all the way to the eighteenth century before drawing the obvious conclusions: writings about manners, civility, and politeness are scarcely part of the preserve of the historian or the sociologist, except as sources. They are the stuff of moral philosophy. Out of the sixteenth-century frames of religion and Humanism that supported behavioral codes, there developed, without totally abandoning Humanism, a French royalist legitimation that would not so much disappear as it would simply weaken in favor of sociability.

To confirm this point about the courtesy book as moral philosophy, take the 1750 edition of Courtin's *Nouveau Traité de la civilité*. One of the overarching principles in the *Instructions for the Novitiate* is the demarcation between the *intérieur*, that is, the inner self, and the *extérieur*, that is, the self in relation to others. It would be incorrect to infer that this is derived directly from religious thought, where it is, of course, pervasive. But here is what Courtin says in that 1750 edition: "Nor is it simply this outer charm that we must strive for, as the principle of true politeness: we must simply aspire to something more solid that shows the good inner disposition."[7] The interior-exterior mode of analysis is present in Stoic thought, particularly in Seneca. It is not for us to untangle the strands here: suffice it to infer something of the philosophical seriousness of courtesy literature in the early-modern centuries.

And not only the moral foundations, but the religious ones as well. Indeed, they shape Courtin's presentation of *le respect commun*, "common respect": "Common respect is feeling modest about ourselves compared with those whom we deem worthy of our submissiveness and our love. This sentiment is natural within us: and God sows its seeds in our soul."[8]

---

[7] "Ce n'est pas non plus ce charme extérieur que nous devons seulement rechercher, comme le principe de la véritable politesse: nous devons seulement aspirer à quelque chose de plus solide, qui marque la bonne disposition du dedans," the successors of Antoine Courtin, *Nouveau Traité de la civilité qui se pratique en France parmi les honnêtes gens* (Paris, 1750), 16.

[8] "Le respect commun est un sentiment modeste de nous-mêmes à l'égard de ceux que nous croyons dignes de notre soumission et de notre amour. Ce sentiment est naturel en nous: et Dieu nous jette les semences dans l'âme," Courtin, *Nouveau Traité*, 34.

When the *Instructions* for the Novitiate refer to *le respect humain*, they are not far from this thought. Revel recognized the existence of the moral-philosophic and religious frames in courtesy literature. Tearing the prescriptive from these frames, as Elias did at least in part, may yield interesting social theory. It is doubtful whether Max Weber would have done so; but as is so often the case in German history, and in the social sciences in general, the state is privileged as the motor of change. Only through hierarchies of offices was the state separate from the court at Versailles. The ordering power was the same.

These moral-philosophic frames merit more study than we can give them here. They all have rationalist arguments and ethical goals. We shall learn that the religious frame was vigorous in the discipline of the Society of Jesus during the late seventeenth century. Let me mention two anecdotes about what took place at the Wissenschaftskolleg in Berlin in 1983, during an effort, directed by Elias and Ariès, to delineate what came to be called the "history of private life." The scholars from Germany (not Elias) argued for working out concepts before anything else could be done. The French (it was Maurice Aymard who made the point) argued that discussions could proceed and research be conducted, from which it eventually would be possible to work out a conceptual framework.

The other anecdote involves Elias himself. He used a personal story to raise the bar against any and all inferences based solely on philology and language. He mentioned that he knew about the existence of the "spare room" in English houses, and that from this he had tentatively inferred that the English were not only hospitable but fairly relaxed in their social relations with guests. He eventually was invited to stay in England, in someone's spare room; and upon coming down for breakfast, he was greeted with a "Good morning," after which his host returned to reading the morning paper. All that Elias saw of him were his hands, holding up the paper! Gesture trumped language. The import of this anecdote weighed very heavily on me, and it still does whenever I think about it. The slow reconstruction of the social act into something that can be understood and communicated, requires constant attention to every gesture, every convention, every phrase. Here was almost a manifesto for what Giovanni Levi, Michel de Certeau, and Luce Giard would be working out as micro-history and the study of the *quotidien* (daily life).

◆ ◆ ◆

George Huppert's *Public Schools in Renaissance France* (Chicago: University of Illinois Press, 1984) is of particular importance for understanding behaviors that are not centered on the court. The Humanist resonances from the sources are remarkably strong throughout the book, beginning with the phrase "public school." In charters of foundation, financing, teacher selection, and curricula, and above all in purpose, these schools were based on humanist principles, an urban setting, and civic ethos. (Paul Grendler and Arie Zamora have discovered a lot of evidence about humanist education in Italy in the fifteenth and sixteenth centuries.)

With university-trained teachers who may well have been hostile to the university for humanist-intellectual reasons, the schools that Huppert describes

taught a "classical morality" (chapter 6) grounded in Latin sources from antiquity that most certainly refracted an ethos of uprightness or *honestas,* and the pursuit of virtue through reading, acting, and *bildung*-formation. Erasmian learning came to be transformed into an ideal of life that doubtlessly posed difficulties for boys drawn from virtually all social backgrounds and possessing only rudimentary skills in reading when they began their studies.[9] What comes to be known as "civility" lay at the heart of these schools, however, and harsh discipline was discouraged. On page 81, Huppert relates a dialogue between a pupil and a master: it is a model of correct conduct in school, with deference and respect at its heart, framed by confidence and affection.

Given the number of these schools situated in towns and cities all across France, Huppert is tentative about the reasons for their decline and eventual near-disappearance. It is evident that church officials opposed these schools, in the belief that education was a part of *their* work and mission. The Catholic Reformation intensified this opposition. These urban schools were not hostile to religion or to the Church, but it seems that the principles on which they were founded did not put them under the jurisdiction of the Church. Owing to the fact that there was little formal training for teachers, cities had difficulty finding and keeping teachers who were successful in the classroom. The contracts between city fathers and teachers are very revealing about all the problems facing these schools. Royal officials would view struggling schools with contempt, particularly as cities verged on bankruptcy and teachers probably went unpaid. Certainly the climate of sectarian strife and violence, starting circa 1560, made matters worse.[10]

As an alternative to these city-administered public schools, another type of school appeared on the scene and soon gained a reputation for administrative orderliness and coherent, rational pedagogy. The schools of the Society of Jesus simply did not fold. From a doctrinal perspective, Catholics were assured of uniformity and obedience. Clashes between Jesuits and the Gallican legal profession were inevitable, but though the Society was expelled from France briefly, it returned in 1603.

The history of courtesy cannot, of course, be separated from the history of education. Major works on the latter, dating from the late nineteenth century, notably Jules-Gabriel Compayré's *Histoire critique des doctrines de l'éducation en France*

---

[9] One still finds studies that do not recognize the heritage or origins of courtesy books in the mirrors-of-princes genre. For the Middle Ages, two general studies shed light on these origins: Reto R. Bezzola, *Les origines et la formation de la littérature courtoise en occident (500–1200)* (Paris: Champion, 1944–63), 5 vols.; and Paul Saenger, "The Education of Burgundian Princes, 1435–1490," Ph.D dissertation, University of Chicago, 1972.

[10] Like George Huppert, Charlotte Wells, in *Law and Citizenship in Early Modern France* (Baltimore: The Johns Hopkins Press, 1995), does not take up the relations between civilities and the laws regarding citizenship. Torn as they were by religious and civil strife, sixteenth-century thinkers apparently did not conceive of a stable, peaceful society grounded solely on the all-pervading "good manners" (sociability) in favor of which Lord Shaftesbury would argue. Yet Wells observes that: "The metaphor of the state as city thus gave rise to a vision of the moral community of all citizens. It also produced a second set of powerful images, associated with the duty of the citizen to the state. . . . Their vision can be labeled a sort of French civic Humanism" (60). The jurist Bacquet called naturalization certificates *"lettres d'adoption"* as well as *"lettres de civilité."*

depuis le XVIe siècle (Paris: Hachette, 1879), 2 vols., and Paul Lallemand's *Histoire de l'éducation dans l'ancien Oratoire de France* (Paris: E. Thorin, 1889), contain much anecdotal information on manners and discipline. They are particularly strong on what I have called, in this essay, the "frames," that is, the religious-pedagogical principles that inspired early-modern education, and what Elias called the "civilizing process." Roughly a century passed before the appearance on the scene of new and pioneering works on education, the outlines of which appeared in the brilliant textbook by Roger Chartier, M.-M. Compère, and Dominique Julia, *L'Éducation en France du XVIe au XVIIIe siècle* (Paris: SEDES, 1976). In it, the implications of Elias's work for the history of education are explored (136–73). Tempting as it is to trace the history of civility in books about education down to the present,[11] I shall limit myself to one not very recent work that has not received the attention it deserves. Mark Motley confronts Elias's work in *Becoming a French Aristocrat; the Education of the Court Nobility, 1580–1715* (Princeton: Princeton University Press, 1990), and he concludes by saying:

> Finally, the growing formality of most public behavior of the aristocracy in the seventeenth century should not cause us to dismiss the equally important elements of informality, festivity, and disorder that continued to nourish relationships of household familiarity, worldly friendship, or corporate solidarity. Absolutism never completely eliminated such aspects of elite culture. (210)

The courtly society may have grown in exemplary strength under Louis XIV, but it did not entirely pervade or submerge aristocratic codes of courtesy.

I shall leave it to specialists in the field of education to work out the general differences between the curricula in the public schools and the *ratio studiorum* of the Jesuits and of the other teaching orders. Some of the evidence can certainly be deduced from the *Instructions* published here, to show that *civilités,* a code of manners, pervaded French urban society in the seventeenth century. And in contrast to the public schools, whose teachers were not trained to teach, the Jesuits extended uniformities and rationalities in just about every aspect of their relations with non-Jesuits, and primarily with their pupils. Is it possible to infer that, through its *collèges* and novitiates, the Society of Jesus had a far greater opportunity to teach and enforce manners than the court? For a century and a half, having attended a Jesuit *collège* became a hallmark throughout élite French society.

◆ ◆ ◆

A close reading of the *Instructions pour le Noviciat*, a hitherto little-known source on the life and training of the French Jesuits, provides evidence for the existence

---

[11] Indispensable for our purposes here is François de Dainville, S.J., *L'Éducation des jésuites* (Paris: Minuit, 1978). A fairly complete perspective on recent work in history may be found in G. Bartholeyns, "Sociologies de la contrainte en Histoire," *Revue historique*, no. 642 (April 2007): 285–323, which contains a critique of Hans Peter Duerr's *Der mythos vom Zivilisationsprozess* (Frankfurt: Suhrkamp, 1988–2002), 5 vols. See also Antoine Lilti, *Le Monde des salons, sociabilité et mondanité à Paris au XVIIIe siècle* (Paris: Fayard, 2005), an up-to-date presentation of the problems of sociabilité.

of *civilités* among the reverend fathers.[12] The manuscript lays out the initiation and discipline of what was, at the time, the most important teaching staff in Paris, Europe, and for that matter, the world.

If the courtesy books have the prince and the court as the beholder, the Jesuits have God and each other. The *Instructions* are as much a work of devotional practice as a "how to behave" book. Courtesy and worship are inseparable: both are dialogues with God and with one's fellow Jesuits. The author constructs his highly disciplined community on top of, or in addition to what he refers to as *"civilité,"* civility, that is, ways of behaving that are general and appropriate, and not particularly Jesuit. Let us look carefully at how the word *civilité* is used in this text. We shall begin by describing what the author characterizes as *incivil*, uncivil. May we infer that no matter how strong the corporate identity, there are secular and general rules for conduct that must be obeyed?

- Having described how to cut and eat bread, the author turns to drinking and remarks: "It is perhaps not too civil to drink only a little at a time of what one has poured into one's glass, but the custom has prevailed among us, in order to avoid the inconvenience of pouring drinks so often" ([87–88]).
- "It is a great incivility to take the salt from the saltcellar with one's fingers" ([89]).
- "And one should not work too hard at cleaning one's teeth, unless there is a great need, and unless one hides behind one's napkin, so that no one can notice" ([91]). In this instance the word *civilité* is not used, but the focus is on the beholder.
- "In the chamber one should show all imaginable consideration for one's companions; not show oneself in a state that offends propriety; not give oneself over to anything uncivil or unrestrained; not make any more noise . . . than if one were not there" ([144–45]).
- Concerning warming oneself before the fire: "Among us, usage has authorized something that would be a monstrous incivility elsewhere, which is to warm one's feet with one's shoes or slippers off" ([156]).
- Among a list of do's and don't's one finds: "defects involving cleanliness at table and temperance, especially concerning wine. Everything that is against civility and a certain knowing how to live well [*savoir-vivre*] would make us contemptible to people who are polite and well brought-up" ([204]).

---

[12] The history of the various constituent parts of the *Instructions* cannot be taken up here, but for pedagogical aspects, see Gabriel Codina Mir, S.J., *Aux Sources de la pédagogie des Jésuites: le "Modus parisiensis"* (Rome: Institutum Historicum Societatis Iesu, 1968). Michel Foucault offers a superficial "genealogy" of discipline, from the ancient Roman army and on to the Benedictines, the Brethren of Common Life, and the Jesuits, *Discipline and Punish*, trans. Alan Sheridan (New York: Vintage, 1979), 315. I owe this reference to Dr. Jotham Parsons. Foucault either was not familiar with, or chose not to engage with Elias's works. Superficial though it may be, Foucault's genealogy emphasizes institutions that developed particular disciplines, while Elias relies largely on prescriptive literature and memoirs.

These examples, which suggest a demarcation between general civil behavior and Jesuit discipline, might tempt one to explore the venerable stereotype of the very fat, dirty, disheveled monk whose utterances are coarse! That would lead us away from our subject.

Instead, let us pull together the words used in the sentences just quoted, to describe behavior. In addition to *civilité* in its various forms, including *incivilité*, we find *bienséance*, *savoir-vivre*, *personnes polies*, and *bien élevées*, that is, civility, incivility, decorum, *savoir-vivre*, and polite and well-brought-up persons. Together, these words provide the profile of civil or urban manners.

There is one expression that is more difficult to characterize, and it is used several times: *respect humain*, literally, "human respect." The two words are defined in Randle Cotgrave's French-English *Dictionarie* (London, 1611): *respect* means "respect, regard, account"; and *humain* means "gentle, courteous, friendlie, civile, mild, affable, tractable." The term is certainly ethical in implication, and social as well. In the *Instructions*, the context is complex. Whenever *le respect humain* is used, there is a hint that it includes a sensitivity to the opinion that another human, or other humans might have of one; and that this sensitivity might cause one to shirk one's duty, perhaps in order not to hurt someone's feelings, or perhaps in order not to incur disdain or lose one's standing in the opinion of others. Patricia Ranum has translated *le respect humain* as "consideration for what others might think."

Seen in this broad perspective, let us read closely the following examples of the context in which *le respect humain* is used:

- After expounding on the dangers to one's soul from chatting as one warms oneself by the fire, the author tells of Father Fumechon's deathbed plea to God: "Lord, do not forget how faithfully I kept silence near the fire. Would you be willing to damn me?" The author then explains what this means: "Remember how many times I put myself above consideration for what others might think [*le respect humain*], curiosity about what was going on, and the urge to express my feelings" ([158]). In other words, Father Fumechon refrained from chatting, even though it might have given pleasure to his neighbors.

- Or again: "Whether one seeks God purely, or whether one is dominated by consideration for what others might think [*le respect humain*]" ([172]). Here, what others might think can cause one to go astray.

- A novice who receives a letter must not open it until he is in the presence of Reverend Father Rector. "If [visitors] are waiting for a reply, they must be told honestly, and with no consideration for what others might think [*le respect humain*], that one is going to beg permission to read the letter and reply to it in writing or verbally" ([178]). In this instance, the novice must ignore the surprise he is sure to see on the visitors' faces.

• In the final example, our author provides a most welcome paraphrase! "Except when passion is involved, consideration for what others might think [*le respect humain*], or the fear of causing pain, should not seal one's lips: it would be cruel to hide his illness and his danger from a sick person" ([203]). In short, *le respect humain* is synonymous with "the fear of causing pain."

Consideration for, or respect for another human's reactions or thoughts? It is tempting to propose that *le respect humain* refers to the behaviors of every Frenchman, and that these behaviors are therefore accepted by the Jesuits, as already inculcated. Indeed, there is an entire layer of manners below the ones set forth in the *Instructions*. For the novice, one may be led astray by too much consideration for what others think, albeit correct and ethical. Or one's attention may be diverted. One's own trajectory, through conforming to the rules of the Society, must always prevail. *Le respect humain* is central to a more secular civility.

There are pyrrhonists in the social sciences. No matter how precise and rationally articulated, the prescriptive source is not about actual behavior. The usual strategy is to supply historical anecdotes to illustrate the prescriptive. The incredible obsession with evaluation in the Society of Jesus, in the late seventeenth century, permits a different approach. Like some other religious communities, the Jesuits obliged the errant or the non-conformist to confess his faults, and novices expected their fellow novices to report whatever was non-conforming in the behavior of any member of the group. An annual report of each Jesuit's physical, moral, and spiritual *état* was sent to Rome. These individual annual reports (beginning with inventories of clothing worn as young men donned their soutane for the first time) are still on the shelves of the principal Jesuit archive in Rome, the Archivum Romanum Societatis Iesu. For example, Francia 15 (1675) tells us this about Father Falluère, a native of Tours who had served as secretary to the General in Rome: "Ingenuity: good; judgement: good; prudence: great; experience of things: magisterial; perfected in letters: good; natural complexion: temperate; talented in: governing and confessions." Pyrrhonists must be acknowledged and thanked: they pose questions that prompt new research.

Selected Bibliography

Manuscript Sources

Archives nationales, Paris.
> MM 649. "Serments à la Vierge," 1631–1676.
> Minutier central. XXIII, 399. Testament of Étiennette Charpentier, deposited
> on March 22, 1709.
> Minutier central. XXIII, 399. Inventory of Étiennette Charpentier, April 5, 1709.

Archivum Romanum Societatis Iesu, Rome.
> Francia 15. Triennial catalogue for 1675.

Bibliothèque de l'Arsenal, Paris.
> Ms. 2042. "Cérémonial pour l'usage de la Congrégation érigée en la Maison professe
> des R.R.P.P. Jésuites rue St Antoine," 1733.

Bibliothèque Mazarine, Paris.
> Ms. 1793. "Instructions pour le Novitiat."
> Ms. 3335. "Hommes illustres de la Congrégation de la Vierge, maison professe des
> pères de la Compagnie de Jésus, à Paris."

Bibliothèque Nationale de France, Paris.
> Estampes. Hd 4b. Drawings and plans for the Paris Novitiate by Étienne Martellange, S.J.
> Manuscripts. Ms. latin 18209. "Livre d'oraison à l'usage du noviciat des Jésuites"
> of G. Dubois.

Published Sources

*Abrégé des faveurs illustres de la Mère de Dieu et des actions héroiques et charitables de ses grands
et dévots serviteurs, Congrégés aux Collèges et Maisons de la Compagnie de Jésus.* Lille:
I. and N. de Rache, 1656.

*Biblia Sacra, Vulgatæ editionis, Sixti V. Pont. Max. Iussu recognita, et Clementis VIII.
auctoritate edita.* Lyons: P. and B. Bailly, 1676.

Blondel, François, and Bullet, Pierre. *Plan de Paris.* Paris, 1676.

Cotgrave, Randle. *Dictionarie of the French and English Tongues.* London: Islip, 1611.

Courtin, Antoine. *Nouveau Traité de la civilité qui se pratique en France parmi les honnêtes gens.*
Paris: Durand, 1750.

Crasset, Jean. S.J. *Cantiques spirituels pour toutes les grandes festes de l'Année.* Paris: Coustelier,
1689.

——. *Des Congrégations de Notre Dame érigées dans les Maisons des Pères de la Compagnie de
Jésus.* Paris: Coustelier, 1694.

Gomboust, Jacques. *Plan monumental de Paris.* 1652.

Grimarest, Jean-Léonor Le Gallois de. *Traité sur la manière d'écrire des lettres.* Paris: Étienne,
1709.

Pommereu, Marie-Augustine de. *Les chroniques de l'ordre des Ursulines recueillies pour l'usage
des Religieuses du mesme Ordre.* Paris: Hénault, 1673.

Turgot, Michel-Étienne, and Bretez, Louis. *Plan de Paris, commencé l'annee 1734, levé et
dessiné par Louis Bretez, gravé par Claude Lucas, et écrit par Aubin.* Paris, 1739.

Secondary Materials

Ariès, Philippe; Duby, Georges; and Chartier, Roger, gen. eds. *A History of Private Life*. Vol. 3. Translated by Arthur Goldhammer. Cambridge: Belknap, 1989. (French edition: *Histoire de la vie privée*. Paris: Seuil, 1986.)

Autrand, Françoise. *Naissance d'un grand corps de l'état: Les gens du Parlement de Paris, 1345–1454*. Paris: Université de Paris-1, 1981.

Babelon, Jean-Pierre. *Demeures parisiennes sous Henri IV et Louis XIII*. Paris: Le Temps, 1965.

Barbiche, Bernard, and Chatenet, Monique, eds. *L'Édition des textes anciens, XVIe–XVIIIe siècle*. Paris: Inventaire général des monuments et des richesses artistiques de la France, 1990.

Bergin, Joseph. *Church, Society and Religious Change in France*, 1580–1730. New Haven: Yale University Press, 2009.

Bezzola, Reto R. *Les origines et la formation de la littérature courtoise en occident (500–1200)*. 5 vols. Paris: Champion, 1944–1963.

Bible. Douai-Reims translation. Online version, www.newadvent.org.

Brown, Elizabeth A.R. *Jean du Tillet and the French Wars of Religion*. Binghampton: Medieval and Renaissance Texts and Studies, 1994.

Burke, Peter. *The Fortunes of the Courtier*. Cambridge, U.K.: Blackwell, 1995.

Carayon, Auguste, S.J., ed. *Histoire abrégée des congrégations de la très-sainte Vierge par le P. J. Crasset*. Paris: Ruffet, 1863.

Chartier, Roger; Compère, M.-M.; and Julia, Dominique. *L'Éducation en France du XVIe au XVIIIe siècle*. Paris: SEDES, 1976.

Charvet, Léon. *Étienne Martellange, 1561–1641*. Lyon: Glairon-Mondet, 1874.

Chatenet, Monique. "Un lieu pour se promener qu'en France on appelle galerie." *Bulletin monumental of the Société française de l'archéologie* 166 (2008): 5–13. Special issue entitled "La galerie à Paris, XIVe–XVIIe siècle."

Ciprut, Édouard-Jacques. "Les Modèles de Martellange pour son Église du Noviciat de Paris." *XVIIe Siècle* 23 (1954): 583–93.

Codina Mir, Gabriel, S.J. *Aux Sources de la pédagogie des Jésuites: le "Modus parisiensis."* Rome: Institutum Historicum Societatis Iesu, 1968.

Compayré, Jules-Gabriel. *Histoire critique des doctrines de l'éducation en France depuis le XVIe siècle*. 2 vols. Paris: Hachette, 1879.

Conte, Sophie. "Louis de Cressolles: le savoir au service de l'action oratoire." *XVIIe Siècle* 59 (2007): 653–67.

Dainville, Francois de. *L Éducation des jésuites*. Paris: Minuit, 1978.

Delattre, Pierre, S.J., ed. *Les Établissements des jésuites en France depuis quatre siècles*. 5 vols. Enghien: Institut supérieur de théologie, 1940.

Descimon, Robert. "The 'Bourgeoisie seconde'; Social differentiation in the Parisian Municipal Oligarchy in the Sixteenth Century, 1500–1610." *French History* 17 (2003): 388–424.

Diefendorf, Barbara. *From Penitence to Charity*. Oxford: Oxford University Press, 2004.

Dziewicki, Michael H. "A Glimpse into a Jesuit Novitiate." Published in *Blackwood's Edinburgh Magazine* 146 (1889): 366–80; and in *The Living Age*, E. and R.S. Littel, eds. 182 (1889): 805–15. Both versions are available online through Google Books.

Elias, Norbert, *The Civilizing Process: The History of Manners*. Translated by Edmund Jephcott. Oxford: Blackwell, 1978.

Fierro, Alfred, and Sarazin, Jean-Yves. *Le Paris des Lumières d'après le plan de Turgot (1734–1739)*. Paris: Réunion des Musées nationaux, 2005.

Foucault, Michel. *Discipline and Punish*. Translated by Alan Sheridan. New York: Vintage, 1979. (French edition: *Surveiller et punir: Naissance de la prison*. Paris: Gallimard, 1975.)

——. *Naissance de la clinique*. Paris: Presses Universitaires Françaises, 1963.

Fouqueray, Henri, S.J. *Histoire de la Compagnie de Jésus en France*. 5 vols. Paris: Bureaux des Études, 1910–1925.

Fumaroli, Marc. "Introduction." *Lettres de Lord Chesterfield à son fils, à Paris, 1750–1752*. Paris: Rivages Poche, 1993.

——. "The Genius of the French Language." In *Realms of Memory*, ed. Pierre Nora. Translated by Arthur Goldhammer. 2 vols. New York: Columbia University Press, 1992. (French edition: *Lieux de Mémoire*. Paris: Gallimard, 1997.)

Garrigou, Alain, and Lacroix, Bernard. *Norbert Elias par lui-même*. Paris: La Découverte, 1997.

Goffman, Erving. "The Nature of Deference and Demeanor." *American Anthropologist* 58 (1956): 473–502.

Gordon, Daniel. *Citizens without Sovereignty*. Princeton: Princeton University Press, 1994.

Goyet, Francis. *Le sublime du 'lieu commun,' l'invention rhétorique dans l'Antiquité et à la Renaissance*. Paris: Champion, 1996.

Hamy, Alfred, S.J. *Galerie Illustrée de la Compagnie de Jésus*. Paris: By the Author, 1893.

Huppert, George. *Les Bourgeois Gentilhommes*. Chicago: University of Chicago Press, 1977.

——. *Public Schools in Renaissance France*. Urbana, Chicago: University of Illinois Press, 1984.

Ignatius of Loyola. *The Spiritual Exercises of Saint Ignatius*. Translated by George E. Ganss, S.J. St. Louis: Institute of Jesuit Sources, 1992.

Kelley, Donald R. *Foundations of Modern Historical Scholarship*. New York: Columbia University Press, 1970.

Lallemand, Paul. *Histoire de l'éducation dans l'ancien Oratoire de France*. Paris: E. Thorin, 1889.

Martin, A. Lynn. *The Jesuit Mind, the Mentality of an Elite in Early Modern France*. Ithaca: Cornell University Press, 1988.

Martin, Henri-Jean. *La Naissance du livre moderne*. Paris: Éditions du Cercle de la Librairie, 2000.

McCabe, William H., S.J. *An Introduction to Jesuit Theater, a Posthumous Work*. Edited by Louis J. Oldani, S.J. St. Louis: The Institute of Jesuit Sources, 1983.

Moisy, Pierre. *Les Églises des jésuites de l'ancienne assistance de France*. Rome: Institutum Historicum Societatis Iesu, 1958.

——. "Martellange, Derand et le conflit du baroque." *Bulletin Monumental* 110 (1952): 237–61.

Motley, Mark. *Becoming a French Aristocrat; the Education of the Court Nobility, 1580–1715*. Princeton: Princeton University Press, 1990.

Muchembled, Robert. *La Société policée*. Paris: Seuil, 1998.

Pagani, Catherine. "Clockwork and the Jesuit Mission in China." In *The Jesuits II: Cultures, Sciences, and the Arts, 1540–1773*, pp. 658–78. Edited by John O'Malley, S.J., et al. Toronto: University of Toronto Press, 2006.

Pantin, Isabelle. *Les Fréart de Chantelou*. Le Mans: Création et Recherche, 1999.

Pardailhé-Galabrun, Annik. *La Naissance de l'intime*. Paris: P.U.F., 1988.

Pillorget, René. *Nouvelle Histoire de Paris: Paris sous les premiers Bourbons, 1594–1661*. Paris: Diffusion Hachette, 1988.

Poisson, Jean-Paul, "Foi et au-delà dans les clauses religieuses des testaments déposés au sénat de Savoie au XVIIIe siècle." In *Notaires et société*. Vol. 2. Paris: Economica, 1990.

Quellier, Florent. *La Table des Français, une histoire culturelle (XVe–début XIXe siècle)*. Rennes Presses universitaires de Rennes, 2007.

Ranum, Orest. "Courtesy, Absolutism, and the Rise of the French State, 1630–1660." *Journal of Modern History* 52 (1980): 426–57.

———. *Paris in the Age of Absolutism*. 2nd ed. University Park, PA: Pennsylvania State University Press, 2002.

———. *Richelieu and the Councilors of Louis XIII*. Oxford: Clarendon, 1963.

Ranum, Patricia M. "« Feindre des poutres pour faire simettrie aux vrayes »: la rénovation de l'hôtel de Guise, 1666–1667." *Histoire et archives* 10 (2001): 5–60.

———. *The Harmonic Orator*. Hillsdale, NY: Pendragon Press, 2001.

———. *Portraits around Marc-Antoine Charpentier*. Baltimore: By the Author, 2004.

Rocco, Giancarlo, ed. *La Sostanza dell'Effimero: Gli abiti degli Ordini religiosi in Occidente*. Rome: Edizioni Paoline, 2000.

Roche, Daniel. *La culture des apparences, une histoire du vêtement, XVIIe–XVIIIe siècle*. Paris: Fayard, 1989.

Rochemonteix, Camille de, S.J. *Un Collège des Jésuites aux XVIIe et XVIIIe siècles: Le Collège Henri IV de La Flèche*. Le Mans: Leguicheux, 1889.

Saenger, Paul. "The Education of Burgundian Princes, 1435–1490." Ph.D dissertation, University of Chicago, 1972.

Society of Jesus. *The Constitutions of the Society of Jesus and their Complementary Norms*. St. Louis: Institute of Jesuit Sources, 1996.

———. *The Ratio Studiorum, The Official plan for Jesuit Education*. Translated by Claude Pavur, S.J. St. Louis: Institute of Jesuit Sources, 2005.

Stoeckius, Hermann. *Untersuchungen zur Geschichte des Noviziates in der Gesellschaft Jesu*. Bonn: Falkenroth, 1918.

Tchemerzine, Avenir. *Bibliographie d'Éditions originales et rares d'auteurs français*. Paris: Plée, 1930.

Vallery-Radot, Jean. *Le Recueil de plans d'Édifices de la compagnie de Jésus conservé à la Bibliothèque nationale de Paris*. Paris: Bibliothèque nationale, 1960.

Waquet, Françoise. *Parler comme un livre, L'oralité et le savoir (XVIe–XXe siècle)*. Paris: Albin Michel, 2003.

Wells, Charlotte. *Law and Citizenship in Early Modern France*. Baltimore: The Johns Hopkins Press, 1995.

Worcester, Thomas, gen. ed. *The Cambridge Companion to the Jesuits*. Cambridge: Cambridge University Press, 2008.

A newly discovered document (ca. 1755) reveals that François Sublet de Noyers' coat of arms decorated the vault of the Novitiate church and the white marble balustrade of the high altar; that his portrait hung in a room where lay people were received (*parloir*); that he and his family were buried in the crypt; and that there was an endowment for masses and services for the family. It asserts that Sublet "had the church built at his expense through the good offices of [François] Mansart," architect. Camille Le Fauconnier and Élie Haddad, "Une contre-généalogie imaginaire . . ., le destin social des Sublet de Noyers," in R. Descimon and E. Haddad, eds., *Épreuves de Noblesse* (Paris: Belles Lettres, 2010), pp. 194–97.

Index

This index can serve as a first step to exploring the *Instructions*. It pulls together information about daily life and activities at the Paris Novitiate, and it calls attention to some of the values and devotional tenets being inculcated into the novices.

The page numbers of the introductory material and of the appendices at the end of the book are italicized.

Only the English translation is indexed. Its page numbers (45–205 the right-hand pages), are in Roman type. To facilitate locating an entry in either the French transcription or the English translation, the page numbers are followed by the bracketed page number(s) of the original French manuscript. Where two or more numbers appear within these brackets, commas suggest brief allusions to the entry, while hyphens suggest a lengthier discussion. To find an entry, go to the designated page of the book and look for the bracketed number(s): the desired entry is near that bracketed number. To find the same passage in the French version, look for the same bracketed number(s) on the left-hand page.

abnegation: *8*, 47 [3], 59 [17], 155 [155]

abstinence: 53 [10], 55 [12], 113 [94, 95], 115 [97], 189 [92]. *See also* **fasting**

account of Conscience (activity): 169–73 [172–75]

action(s): 47 [3–4], 49 [5–7], 59 [17–18], 67 [26], 81 [44], 91 [61], 125 [115], 137 [135], 143 [142], 169 [171]. 193 [197], 195 [198]; ordinary vs. extraordinary, 47 [4]

admonition: 49 [7], 105 [80], 133 [129], 197 [200], 199 [204]

Admonitor, Brother (*Admoniteur*): *19*, 49 [6], 55 [12], 97 [69], 119 [103], 127 [118], 131 [125], 139 [138], 173 [176], 177 [179], 187 [190], 189 [192], 193 [195–96]

advancement, spiritual: 47 [3], 163 [164], 171 [173–74]

advice: 103 [78], 113 [94], 171 [172], 173 [175]

alms: *28*, 91 [60], 161 [161], 165 [166]

Aloysius Gonzaga, St.: 47 [4]

ambition: 167 [168-69], 201 [205]

angels: 61 [19], 81 [44], 91 [60], 103 [78], 147 [147], 179 [180], *207*

anger: 129 [123], 195 [199], 201 [206]

Anthony the Abbot, St.: 171 [179]

Aristotle: *213*

Augustine, St.: 113 [96], 185 [186]

Avancini, Nicola: 53 [12], 55 [12], 143 [142]

Ave Maria: 63 [22], 105 [81], 127 [117, 120]. 141 [139]. 143 [141, 142]. 147 [146], 161 [162]. 183 [185], 187 [188, 190]

bands of novices: *6*, *27*, 55 [12], 83 [47], 127–29 [117–21], 129 [124], 131 [125], 159 [159], 181 [183–84], 183 [185]

bareheaded: 63 [21], 83 [47], 87 [52], 145 [144], 149 [147], 197 [201]

bedchambers of novices: *5, 11, 16–17, 24–25*, 89 [58], 93 [62], 127 [118], 135 [132], 147 [146–47], 169 [185]; activities in, 51 [10], 55 [13], 59 [16], 61 [19], 63 [21–22], 65 [23–24], 81 [46], 89 [58], 93 [62], 105 [80], 125 [117], 149 [148], 165 [167], 181 [183], 183 [185], 201 [206]; manners in, 145–47 [144–47], 153–55 [154]

begging: 87 [53], 161 [161], 165 [166]

bells: *7–8*, 181 [183]

Benedicite: 105 [82], 107 [82, 83], 115 [97], 161 [160, 162]. *See also* **Grace at table**

Bernard, St.: 113 [96]

birette (*birette*), definition: *18*

Blessed Sacrament: *15*, 55 [13], 67 [25–26], 75 [37], 77–79 [40–41], 79 [43], 135 [132], 163 [164]; Benediction of, 57 [14]; visiting, *7, 14, 26*, 51 [9], 53 [10], 55 [12], 57 [15, 16], 59 [16], 61 [19, 20], 99–103 [71–79], 139 [138], 141 [140], 165 [167], 169 [170, 171], 189 [191, 192], 191 [193]

Blessed Virgin Mary: 125 [115]; commending one's actions to, 61 [20]; devotion to, 140 [139–40]; dispenser of graces, 141 [139]; intercessor, 127 [117]; name of, 71 [32], 83 [47]; mysteries of, 143 [141]; visiting; 51 [9], 57 [16], 63 [21], 83 [48]; womb of, 101 [76]. *See also* **Hall of Our Lady**; **Litanies**; **Office of Our Lady**

blessing: 61 [19, 20], 75 [37], 107 [82], 171 [174]. *See also Benedicite*

body of the Society: 45 [1]

bonnet (*bonnet*), definition: *18*

books: 49 [6], 53 [13–14], 59 [17], 63 [22], 67 [25,27], 77 [39], 93–95 [62–67], 97 [69], 113 [96], 137 [136], 143 [143], 145 [144, 145], 149 [148–49], 153 [153], 157 [157], 169 [171], 201 [207]

boredom: 59 [17], 133 [130], 147 [147]

Bretez: *see* **Turgot-Bretez map**

Brethren, definition: *16*

Brignon, Jean, S.J.: *32*

Brothers, definition: *16*. *See also* **coadjutors, temporal**

Canada: 157 [157]

Carafa, Vincenzo, S.J.: 131 [127], 183 (n. 56)

cases of conscience: 95 [66]

Cassette, rue: *10*

Cassian, John: 85 [49], 163 [164]

Castiglione, Baldassare: *213*

catalogues (lists): 87 [54], 139 [137], 139–41 [138–39]

Catechism: *26, 31*, 53 [11], 57 [15]

Cenobites: 163 [164]

chamber: *see* **bedchambers**

chapels of the Novitiate: St. Ignatius, (domestic), *11*, *38 (plan 1)*, 67 [27]; Congregation of the Novitiate, *28–31*; Montrouge, 187 [188], 189 [193]. *See also* **Church of St. Francis Xavier**

charity: 53 [48], 105 [80], 119 [104], 129 [121, 122], 139 [137], 147 [147], 155 [155], 163 [163], 165 [166], 167 [168], 171 [173], 177 [178], 179 [180], 181 [183], 197 [199], 199 [202, 203–204]

Charity (activity): *26*, 197–201 [199–206]

Charpentier, Étiennette: *31–33*

chastisement: 49 [6], 185 [186]

Church, Holy Catholic: 81 [45], 135 [133], 141 [141]

Church of St. Francis Xavier at the Paris Novitiate: *12*, *13*, *34*, *36*, *37*, *225* n.; activities in, *26*, 53 [11], 57 [15], 65–67 [25–26], 99 [71–73]. 135 [132–33]. 183 [185], 191 [193]; layout, *37*, 69 [30]; loft (*jubé*), *14*, *26*, 55 [13], 99 [72], 181 [183]; sanctuary, *14*, *15*, 67 [25], *225* n. *See also* **Novitiate of the rue du-Pot-de-Fer**

Cicero: *213*

civility: *15*, *21*, *23*, 109 [88, 89], 129 [121,122], 145 [144], 157 [156], 177 [180], 181 [183], 199 [204], *210–20*. *See also* **manners**

cleanliness, personal: *17*, *21*, 55 [13], 61 [19], 65 [23–24], 85 [51], 89 [58], 105 [81] 111 [90–91], 115 [97–98], 117 [101], 123 [111, 112], 153–55 [153–55], 161 [161], 199 [204]

Cleanliness Room (*Propreté*): *6*, *20*, 91 [58]

Clermont (Louis-le-Grand), college: *8*, *16*, *27*

clock: *7*, 127 [117], 133 [129]

clothing of novices: *6*, *17–18*, 61 [19], 67 [25], 81 [48], 87 [54], 89 [58], 107 [85], 125 [117], 141 [140], 145 [145], 149 [149–50], 153 [153–54], 155 [155], 157 [156], 161 [160, 161], 181 [183], 183 [185], 191 [193], 193 [196], 195 [199]

coadjutors, temporal: *1–2*, *16*, *17–18*, *22*, 123 [111, 113], 129 [121], 135 [132, 135]

cold: *8*, *17*, *20*, 71 [30], 79 [44], 89 [55], 157–59 [156–60]

colleges (*collèges*): *7–8*, 49 [5], 145 [144], 161 [162], 163 [163], *211*, *215–17*. *See also* **Clermont; La Flèche**

Colloquy (activity): *25*, *27*, 57 [14], 85 [50], 159 [159], 179 [180]

Communion: *33*, 53 [11], 55 [13, 14], 67 [26], 73 [36], 75 [37], 79 [41, 43], 81 [44], 167 [170], 171 [173], 193 [195], 197 [200]

Community, the: 99 [72], 113 [93, 95], 119 [104], 125 [113], 135 [134], 155 [154], 161 [161], 163 [164]

community rooms (*salles*): *11*, *20*, *23*, *26*, 53 [10, 11], 55 [12, 13], 57 [14, 15], 81 [46–47], 89 [58], 97 [68–69], 125 [116], 131 [128], 133 [131], 139 [137], 143 [142], 169 [171], 181 [183], 195 [199]. *See also* **halls, assembly**

companion(s): *33*, 145 [144], 179 [180–81], 181 [183], 187 [189, 190], 189 [191]. *See also* **bands of novices**

Conferences (activity): *25*, 83 [47, 48], 85 [50–51]

Confession: *19*, 127 [118], 131 [126], 145 [144], 163 [165], 165 [167], 167–69 [169–71], 179 [180]

Congregation of the Novitiate: *27–31*

conscience: 97 [69], 127 [120], 141 [140], 171 [173]. *See also* **account of Conscience**

consolation: 61 [20], 63 [23], 91 [61], 185 [187]

Constantine, Emperor: 177 [179]

Constitutions of the Society of Jesus: *3, 5, 19*, 45 [1], 47 [2]

conversation(s): 67 [27], 85 [50], 127 [121], 129 [123], 133 [129–30], 151 [152], 161 [161], 177 [179], 179 [181, 182], 181 [182], 187 [188], 191 [194–95], 193 [196], 199 [204]

Cook (*Cuisinier*): 117 [101]

Corneille, Pierre: *32*

correction: 149 [148], 163 [164], 197 [200]

courtesy: *210–20. See also* **civility; manners**

Courtin, Antoine de: 175 (n. 50), *212, 214*

Crasset, Jean, S.J.: *27–28*

cross, sign of the: 61 [19], 63 [21], 71 [31], 75 [37], 85 [51], 105 [82], 125 [115], 161 [162], 169 [170], *207*

crucifix: *26*, 69 [29], 75 [38], 181 [191], *209*

culpæ: see **Faults (activity)**

curiosity: 93 [64], 159 [158]

curitories (*curitoires*): *24*, 127 [117–18]

customs, customary: 61 [19], 95 [66], 109 [88]. 111 [93]. 119 [104]. 141 [139], 157 [157], 163 [165], 165 [167], 171 [172], 179 [181], 183 [184]

death: *28*, 101 [76], 135 [134], 201 [207]

declamation: *see* **Tones**

decorum: *5, 213. See also* **modesty**

delicate (daintiness, "immatification"): 95 [65], 155 [155], 157 [157], 201 [205]

desire(s): 83 [48], 85 [51], 103 [79], 105 [80], 127 [117,120], 163 [164], 167 [169], 171 [172, 173], 173 [175], 201 [205]

devotion(s): 59 [17], 99 [71], 141 [138, 139, 143 [142], 159 [160], 201 [205]. *See also* **Blessed Virgin Mary**

difficult, difficulties: *19*, 49 [7], 131 [126], 159 [158], 169 [172], 179 [180]

dining hall: *see* **refectory**

Diogenes of Sinope: 185 (n. 59)

dishwashing: *21*, 121–23 [108–112], 125 [114, 116]

dismissal from the Society: 47 [4], 49 [5,6], 93 [64], 149 [148]

Dozenne, Pierre, S.J.: *3*

drowsiness: 61 [19], 63 [22], 83 [47], 93 [63]

Du Tillet, Hélie: *9*, 137 [135]

Du Tillet, Jean: *9*

Du Tillet, Séraphin: *9*

duty, duties: 49 [6], 59 [18], 83 [48], 93 [62], 99 [73], 105 [80], 119 [105], 121 [107], 123 [111, 112], 125 [114], 127 [120], 141 [139], 151 [150], 153 [152], 171 [173], 173 [175], 191 [194], 201 [205]. *See also* **obligation**

Edict of Nantes, Revocation: *31*

edification: *19*, *33*, 83 [48], 93 [62–64], 95 [65], 129 [121], 133 [130–31], 135 [132], 153 [152], 155 [155, 156], 157 [158], 161 [161], 163 [163], 179 [180, 181], 193 [196], 199 [202], 201 [206]

elevation(s): 61 [19], 85 [51], 95 [67], 133 [129]

Elias, Norbert: *210*, *211*, *215*, *217*

Erasmus, Desiderius: *212*, *213*

Eusebius: 85 (n. 30)

evil: 59 [18], 151 [151], 171 [174]

exactitude: 47 [4], 59 [17], 149 [149]

Examens (activities): 63 [21, 22], 85 [50], 105 [79], 131 [126], 171 [173]; Examen of Prayer after rising, 51 [10], 63 [22]; general Examen of Conscience in mid-morning, 53 [10], 57 [14, 15, 16], 105 [79–81], 189 [191, 193]; particular Examen in early afternoon: 53 [11], 57 [14], 59 [16], 61 [20], 151 [150], 165 [167], 171 [172], 181 [184], 189 [192], 191 [193], 197 [200], 201 [206]; general Examen at bedtime, 55 [12], 189 [192]

exercises, bodily (*manualia*): *22*, *26*, 53 [10, 11], 87–91 [54–61], 125 [115], 189 [192], 193 [197]

exercises, devotional: *26*, 53 [11], 57 [15], 61 [20], 63 [21,22], 131 [127], 145 [145], 171 [173], 177 [178], 185 [186], 187 [189]. *See also* **Examens (activities)**; **Modesty**; **Prayer**; **reading, spiritual**

exercitants' house: *see* **Retreat**

Exhortation (activity): *25*, 51 [10], 53 [10], 81 [46], 83 [48], 85 [50], 171 [172], 189 [192]

experiences, the six: 125 [113]

eye(s): 67 [26], 75 [37], 83 [48], 85 [50], 87 [52], 105 [82], 107 [83, 84], 131 [126], 147 [147], 149 [149, 150], 153 [152], 155 [154], 165 [165], 183 [186], 195 [198], 197 [201]

faith, faithful: 47 [2], 59 [17], 65 [23], 81 [45], 115 [97], 141 [139, 141], 159 [158], 179 [180], 181 [182]

Falluère, François, S.J.: *220*

family: *see* **outsiders**

fasting: 51 [9], 53 [10], 57 [15], 107 [82], 115 [97], 135 [132], 189 [192] 193 [196]

Fathers at the Novitiate: *18*, *19 (n. 41)*, *32*, 83 [46–47], 115 [99], 125 [115], 127 [118], 161 [160–62], 167 [168], 179 [180], 193 [197]; lodgings, *15*, *22–24*

Fathers, first Jesuit: 65 [24], 87 [53], 91 [60], 101 [74], 141 [139], 153 [152], 193 [197]

Fathers of the Desert: 85 [49]

fault(s): *23*, 113 [96], 131 [126, 128], 133 [129], 147 [147], 149 [149–50], 185 [186], 195 [199], 199 [203, 204], 201 [206]; serious, 85 [43], 93 [64], 157 [158], 159 [158]; pointing them out, *7*, 83 [48], 105 [80], 151 [150], 197–201 [199–206]

Faults, declaring one's (activity): *21*, 53 [10, 12], 55 [14], 57 [15], 129 [123], 159–65 [160–65], 197 [200]

feast days: 51 [9], 55–57 [13–15], 121 [107], 127 [118], 151 [150], 163 [163], 191 [195], 197 [200]

feelings: 101 [76], 123 [113], 133 [130], 151 [150], 159 [158]

fervor: 81 [44], 131 [127], 135 [134]

fireplace: *20, 23, 26*, 119 [103], 123 [111], 129–30 [124–25], 157–59 [156–59], 181 [191]

food: *21*, 107–11 [85–91], 111 [93], 115 [97], 117–19 [101–102], 119 [105], 123 [112]

formulas: 161 [161–62], 165 [167–68], 175 [177]

Founders: *9*, 45 [1], 137 [135]

Francis Borgia, St.: 99 [74], 185 [186]

Francis Xavier, St.: *12*, 65 [24], 101 [74]

French language: *13*, 95 [65, 66], 137 [136], *212*

friends: *see* **outsiders**

friendships, particular: 127 [117, 120], 131 [128], 187 [188], 201 [205]

Fumechon, Father: 159 [158]

furnishings: *25*, 61 [21], 65 [23–24], 89 [58], 91 [62], 145 [145], 153 [153–54]

galleries: *15 (n. 31)*, 101 [74]. *See also* **Church of St. Francis Xavier, loft; walkways**

games: *6*, 187 [188–89], 189 [191], 191 [193, 195]

garden: *12, 13, 17, 19, 26–27, 28, 29*, 51 [10, 11], 55 [14], 57 [14, 15], 87 [54], 89 [56], 97 [68–69], 125 [116–17], 119 [137], 169 [171]

Gardener, Brother (*Jardinier*): *13*, 193 [196]

General Congregations: 171 [179]

God: blessings or good feelings from, 133 [130], 171 [174]; commending one's actions to, 61 [20], 107 [83], 125 [115], 167 [169], 182 [186], 191 [194]; dependence on, 185 [186]; elevations to, 61 [19], 153 [129], 155 [186]; empty of, 133 [130]; full of, 185 [187]; grace of, 65 [23], 85 [50], 91 [61], 127 [117], 177 [179], 185 [186]; glory of, 139 [137]; helpful, 85 [51]; indulgent, 191 [194]; judge, 49 [6], 59 [18], 91 [59], 135 [134], 141 [141], 145 [143], 157 [157], 163 [164], 167 [169], 199 [203]; man speaks to him, 61 [19], 95 [65], 101 [75], 135 [133], 159 [158], 195 [199]; occupied with, 99 [71], 193 [196]; pleasing him, 59 [18], 171 [174]; presence of, 63 [21], 99 [72], 105 [79], 113 [95]; respect for, 195 [199]; seeking him, 171 [172]; speaks to man, 85 [49], 95 [65]; suffering for him, 171 [173]; talking about, 175 [176], 179 [181]; tempting him, 181 [182]; thanking him, 61 [19], 165 [166], 185 [186]; watchful, 61 [19], 87 [52], 89 [58], 147 [147]; ways of, 47 [3]; winning souls for, 49 [6], 133 [130]; wishes of, 133 [129];

word of, 83 [48], 85 [51]; worthy of, 47 [3], 91 [61]

Gomboust, Jacques: *12*

Grace at table: 107 [83], 115 [97], 119 [103, 104], 161 [162]

grace(s): 61 [20], 65 [23], 81 [44], 85 [50], 91 [61], 95 [67], 99 [73], 101 [75], 107 [83], 127 [117], 131 [125], 133 [129], 141 [139] 171 [174], 177 [179], 185 [186], 195 [199], *207, 213*

Gracián, Baltasar, S.J.: *213*

Greek language: 95 [66]

Guise, Isabelle d'Orléans, Duchess of: *30*

Guymond, Henri, S.J.: *3*

habit(s), habitual: 47 [4], 49 [5], 61 [20], 147 [147], 199 [200–203], 201 [205]

halls, assembly (*salles*): *11, 25–26*; Hall of Our Lady, *26*, 53 [10, 11], 55 [12, 13], 57 [14, 16], 61 [20], 127 [118], 135 [133], 169 [171], 197 [200]; Hall of Our Lord, *26*, 53 [11], 97 [69], 127 [118], 183 [185]; Hall of St. Joseph ("great recreation hall"), *20, 26*, 55 [13], 119 [103], 189 [191]. *See also* community rooms

hallways: *10, 11, 23, 24*, 125 [117], 135 [132], 155 [154]

Harley de Chanvallon, François: *30*

health: *17, 19*, 91 [59], 97 [68], 113 [94, 95], 121 [109], 155 [155], 157 [156], 173 [176], 187 [189]

heart: 61 [19], 85 [51], 91 [61], 133 [129, 130], 151 [150], 171 [172, 173, 174]

Heaven: 90 [60], 101 [77], 145 [143], 177 [179]

Hell: 159 [158]

heretics: 99 [73]

Herod: 195 [198]

history: 93 [63], 95 [66–67], 113 [96]

Honoré-Chevalier, rue: *10, 27, 28, 29*

hospitals: 65 [25], 91 [60]

hourglass: 119 [103, 105], 131 [126]

Housekeeper, Brother (*Propretaire*): *20*, 87 [55], 91 [59]

housekeeping: *6, 7, 20*, 51 [9], 57 [15], 61 [19], 65 [23–24], 87–91 [54–61], 145–47 [145–46]. *See also* service rooms

Houses of the Society: *6, 32*, 45 [2], 49 [5], 69 [30], 101 [74], 157 [157]. *See also* Clermont; Montrouge; Novitiate; Saint-Louis

humbleness: 161 [161], 171 [174], 175 [177]

humiliation: 83 [48], 113 [96], 125 [114], 193 [197]

humility: *6, 19*, 111 [92], [165 [166], 171–73 [174], 197 [201]

Ignatius Loyola, St.: *2, 5*, 45 [1], 46 [2], 61 [20], 131 [127], 155 [156], 171 [173], 185 [187], 195 [197]

Imitation of Jesus Christ: *26, 31 (n. 7), 32*, 55 [13], 147 [147], 189 [191]. *See also*

Corneille; Thomas à Kempis

Institute of the Society: 171 [174]

instructions: 45–49 [1–7], 67 [26], 95 [66], 105 [80], 143 [143], 163 [163], 171 [173], 181 [182], 199 [204]; "body" of ("outer regulation"), *3–4*, 49 [6–7]; "soul" of ("inner guidance"), 3–4, 49 [6–7]. *See also* regulations; rules

Instructions for the Novitiate, manuscript: *1–2, 217–20*

intention(s): 97 [69], 141 [138–39], 191 [194], 195 [198], 199 [203]

interior, as contrasted with exterior: 49 [7], 65 [23], 155 [155], 191 [194], *214. See also* instructions, "soul"

James, St.: 85 [50]

Jean Casimir of Poland: *30*

Jerusalem: 198 [198]

Jesus Christ our Lord: *207*; intercessor, 101 [75], 103 [77]; model, 65 [24], 87 [53], 91 [60], 125 [115], 153 [152], 163 [165], 185 [187], 195 [198]; mysteries, 101–103 [77–78], 143 [141]; name of, 71 [32], 83 [47], 143 [141], 151 [151]; in the Blessed Sacrament, 73 [35], 99 [73], 101 [74–75], 103 [77]; in one's Brethren, 125 [114]; Passion, 67 [26], 91 [61], 101 [76], 115 [97], 159 [158]; prays for us, 61 [20]; quoting, 175 [177]; shut up with, 101 [75], 147 [146]; talking to, 101 [75], 103 [78]. *See also* Blessed Sacrament; litanies

John Berchmans, St.: 47 [4], 131 [127]

Joseph, St.: 125 [115]

Judgement Day: 151 [151]

kissing something: 61 [19], 63 [21, 22], 69 [28], 73 [33], 105 [79, 81], 161 [161, 162], 163 [165], 197 [201]

kneeling: *14, 25*, 63 [21], 67 [26], 71 [30, 31, 32], 73 [34, 35], 75 [37], 77 [41], 79 [43], 83 [46, 47, 48], 99 [72], 105 [79], 125 [116], 147 [146], 153 [154], 159 [160], 161 [160, 161], 163 [163], 179 [181], 187 [188], 197 [201]

labors, domestic: *see* exercises, bodily

La Flèche, college: *23*

laity: *see* outsiders

languages: *see* French; Greek; Latin

La Puente, Luis de, S.J.: *32*, 101 [74], 191 [194]

Latin language: *13, 20*, 95 [65–66], *216*

laughter: 83 [46], 91 [58], 93 [62], 125 [115], 129 [121], 135 [133], 149 [149], 151 [151], 153 [152], 167 [168], 181 [184], 201 [206]

law, natural: 47 [3]

letters: 139 [137], 143 [143], 173–77 [176–79]

Le Valois, Louis, S.J.: *30*

liberty: 49 [5], 93 [64], 131 [128], 149 [148], 157 [156], 175 [177], 199 [202], 210 [204]

library: *25*, 93 [63], 145 [144, 145]

lighting: *8, 11, 23, 25*, 55 [12], 61 [19], 79 [43], 93 [62], 117 [99, 102], 119 [103, 106], 143 [142], 155 [154]

litanies: *7, 19, 33*, 133–37 [131–35]; of the saints, *26*, 53 [10], 99 [72], 133 [131], 135 [133], 189 [193]; of the Holy Name of Jesus, *26*, 53 [11], 57 [14], 59 [16], 63 [22], 127 [118], 129 [124], 183 [185]; of the Virgin, *14, 26, 33*, 53 [11], 55 [12], 57 [14, 15], 59 [16], 63 [22], 99 [72], 127 [118], 129 [124], 133 [131], 137 [134], 191 [193]

Louis XIV, King: *30, 212, 217*

Luillier de Sainte-Beuve, Madeleine: *9*

manners: *4, 5–6, 212, 214*; during recreation and on walks, 129 [121–22], 181–82 [184], 187 [188–90], 191 [194–95], 193 [196]; in the bedchambers or community rooms, 63 [21–22], 83 [47–48], 93 [62], 97 [69], 135 [132–33], 145–47 [144–47], 149–50 [149–50], 199–200 [204–206]; in church, 67 [25], 99 [72–73], 135 [133]; in the refectory, *6, 21*, 86–87 [51–52], 107–13 [83–95], 187 [189]; in correspondence, 175 [176–77]; with the laity, 133 [131]. *See also* **civility; modesty**

Manuductor, Brother (*Manuducteur*): *19*, 93 [195]

Marie-Thérèse, Queen: *30*

market, going to: *7, 13, 18, 19*, 193 [195–99]

Martellange, Étienne, S.J.: *10, 12, 13, 35, 37*

Mary, Virgin: *see* **Blessed Virgin Mary**

Mary Magdalene, St.: 103 [77]

Mass: *14, 19, 26, 33*, 51 [10], 55 [13, 14], 57 [15], 59 [17], 65–67 [25–26], 85 [51], 99 [72], 141 [139], 189 [191]; serving Mass, *26*, 67–81 [27–45]

meals: *21*, 53 [10], 55 [12], 57 [14, 15], 59 [17], 85–87 [51–53], 105–15 [81–98], 131 [126], 185–87 [187–88], 189 [191, 192, 193], 193 [196]. *See also* **food; water, drinking; wine**

Meditation (activity): *25*, 51 [9], 53 [11, 12], 55 [12, 13], 61 [19], 63 [21, 22], 95 [67], 129 [124], 139 [138], 141 [140], 143 [142]

memorization: *17, 23, 25, 26*, 53 [10, 11], 55 [14], 95–99 [68–71], 99 [72], 133 [129], 165 [167]

Mérian, Gaspard: *12*

merit: 49 [7], 59 [18], 91 [61], 99 [71], 123 [113], 125 [115], 157 [158], 165 [166], 193 [197]

Mézières: hôtel de, *9–10, 12, 20*

Mézières, rue de: *10, 12*

Minister, Father: *19, 23*, 121 [106], 163 [163]

missions: 157 [157], 171 [173]

moderation: 113 [94], 167 [169], 181 [182]

modesty: *5–6*, 61 [19], 83 [47–48], 87 [52], 99 [73], 105 [81], 107 [84–85], 113 [95], 129 [123], 149–53 [149–53], 157 [158], 181 [184], 183 [184], 191 [194], 193 [196], *214*. *See also* **decorum**

Modesty (activity): 57 [14], 151 [150], 197 [200]

Montrouge, country house at: *13*, 183 [184], 185–91 [187–93]

mortification: *19*, 47 [3], 93 [64], 111 [91–92], 113 [94, 96], 125 [117], 157 [158], 167 [169], 171 [173], 177 [178], 193 [197], 195 [199]

mysteries: 101 [76], 103 [77], 143 [141], 185 [186]

Nancy, novitiate: *9*

nature, natural: 59 [18], 91 [59, 61], 125 [117], 131 [128], 155 [155], 171 [172], 173 [174], 175 [177], 177 [178], 201 [204], *214*. *See also* **supernatural**

Nazareth: 91 [60], 115 [97]

neatness: 51 [10], 61 [19], 65 [24], 145–46 [145–46], 153 [154]

neighbor(s): 83 [47], 97 [70], 107 [83, 84], 111 [92], 129 [121], 133 [128] 147 [147], 153 [152], 197 [199], 201 [204]

New Testament: 55 [14], 99 [71]

noble: 81 [44], 91 [59], 95 [66], 151 [150]

nonchalance: 95 [65], 99 [74], 151 [150], 201 [204]

novices: number of, *16–17*; two years' probation, *15*, 193 [197]; examinations, 139 [137]. *See also* **clothing; exercises; manners; Tertianship**

Novitiate of the rue du Pot-de-Fer ("the House"): *7–15*, 45 [2], 48–49 [5–6], 97 [70], 137 [135], 139 [136], 153 [153], 175 [178], 181 [183], 185 [187], 189 [191, 192, 193], 193 [196]; founding of, *8–10*; renovations of 1610: *9–11*; residence, *11–13, 20–27, 34, 35, 36*; floor plans, *38–39*; outside its walls, *13, 17*, 141 [140], 153 [153], 173 [175], 177 [178], 179 [180], 181–95 [183–99], 199 [202]. *See also* **chapels of the Novitiate; Church of St. Francis Xavier**

obedience: *19*, 45 [2], 47 [3], 117 [101], 137 [136], 139 [137], 161 [160–61, 162], 175 [177]. *See also* **abnegation; exactitude**

obligation(s): 47 [2, 3], 81 [45], 97 [69], 139 [138], 141 [139, 141], 143 [142], 171 [173], 177 [178], 199 [202]

Office of the Blessed Virgin Mary ("of Our Lady"): *27*, 55 [13], 143 [142], 167 [170]

Oraison: *see* **Prayer**

order of the day: *6, 7*, 51–59 [9–18], 137 [135], 189 [193]; waking, 51 [9], 57 [15], 59 [16]; bedtime, 55 [12], 101 [76]; free ("unassigned") time, 53 [10, 12], 55 [12, 13, 14], 57 [14, 15, 16], 59 [16], 93 [63], 97 [70], 99 [74], 143–45 [143–44]; no wasted time, 59 [17], 143 [143], 145 [144], 147 [146]. *See also* **meals**

outsiders: *6, 11, 13, 15, 20, 23, 27, 29, 31, 33, 38 (plan 1)*, 67 [27], 129 [121], 133 [131], 135 [133], 155 [154], 167 [168], 175 [178], 177–81 [179–83], 191 [195], 195 [198, 199], *225* n.; family, *4*, 173 [176], 179 [181], 181 [182], 193 [196], 201 [205]; friends, *4*, 173 [176], 193 [196], 201 [205]

pantry (*crédence*): *20*, 115 [98], 117 [100], 119 [104], 123–25 [112–16]. *See also* **service rooms**

Pantryman, Brother (*Crédencier*): *19*, 87 [52], 119 [105], 121 [107]

passions: 59 [18], 129 [123], 163 [164], 171 [172], 197 [201], 199 [202, 203], 201 [205]

Pater noster: 63 [22], 105 [81, 82], 115 [97], 141 [139], 161 [162], 181 [183] 183 [185]

Paul, St.: 91 [59], 103 [77]

pedagogy: *5, 23 (n. 54), 28, 30, 211, 215–17*

penance: 85 [50], 111 [92], 113 [96], 125 [114], 129 [123], 157 [157], 161 [160–63], 163 [164], 169 [171], 183 [185]

perfection, perfectly: 47 [2, 3–4], 49 [6, 7], 91 [60], 99 [73], 101 [76], 119 [104], 153 [153], 157 [156]. 171 [172, 173], 175 [177]

permission: *7, 11,* 53 [11], 55 [13, 14], 63 [21], 87 [52], 93 [64], 97 [68, 69], 113 [96], 121 [106], 125 [116], 137 [135], 139 [138], 143 [142, 143], 144 [148], 157 [156], 159 [160], 161 [160], 163 [163], 173 [176], 175 [177, 178], 177 [179], 179 [180, 181], 187 [190], 189 [191], 197 [200]

Peter, St.: 159 [158]

philosophy: 83 [49], 93 [63]

Pilate: 195 [198]

pilgrimage: 115 [98]

poor, the: *28,* 65 [24], 91 [60] 115 [97], 125 [114], 185 [187]

Pot-de-Fer, rue du: *10, 12, 13, 14, 29, 33*

Poussin, Nicolas: *12*

poverty of Jesuits: 87 [53], 89 [56], 117 [101], 153 [153], 157 [156], 163 [163]

Prayer, morning and afternoon (activity): *25,* 51 [10], 57 [15], 59 [16], 61 [20], 63 [21–23], 85 [50], 99 [71, 72], 101 [76], 105 [79, 81], 139 [137], 167 [170], 169 [170, 171], 171 [173], 179 [181], 183 [184], 189 [191, 192, 193], 191 [193]

prayer(s): *28,* 61 [19, 20], 67 [27], 83 [46, 48], 85 [50, 51], 87 [52], 95 [65], 99 [73], 101 [101], 125 [115], 131 [127], 135 [134], 141 [138, 141], 149 [149], 151 [152], 181 [183], 193 [196], 199 [202]

preaching: 91 [60], 167 [168–69]. *See also* **sermon; Tones**

pride: 163 [164], 173 [174], 195 [199]

probation: 45 [2]

Proclamation: 197 [200]

progress: 95 [66], 137–39 [136–37], 171 [172]

Province: 139 [137]

Purgatory: 141 [141], 145 [143], 159 [158]

Quintilian: *213*

reading: 55 [13, 14], 57 [16], 59 [17], 63 [22], 67 [25, 27], 101 [75], 133 [130], 143 [142, 143], 145 [144], 157 [157], 169 [171], 187 [189], 189 [191, 192, 193], 193 [196]; aloud, *5, 6, 21, 26,* 107 [83, 84], 113 [96, 97], 119 [103, 104], 121 [107], 165 [167]; instructions and rules, *5, 7,* 49 [7], 149 [149], 151 [150], 171 [173]

reading, spiritual (activity): 53 [10, 11], 93–95 [62–67]

recitation: *25, 26,* 53 [11], 55 [13], 61 [19], 97 [69], 99 [72], 135 [133], 137 [134], 139–43 [137–42], 165 [167]

recollected state: 83 [47], 99 [71], 101 [75], 107 [83], 131 [128], 135 [134], 143 [141], 151 [151–52], 161 [161], 177 [178], 183 [185], 195 [198]

Recollection (activity): 55 [13], 57 [15], 59 [16], 63–64 [21–23], 189 [191, 192]

recreation: *6, 23, 26, 27,* 53 [10], 55 [12], 57 [14, 15, 16], 59 [16], 63 [22], 85 [50], 101 [75–76], 125–33 [116–31], 135 [134], 141 [140], 143 [142], 149 [147, 149], 157 [156], 159 [159], 189 [191, 193], 191 [194]

Rector, Father: *3, 7, 19, 23, 32–33,* 45 [1], 53 [10, 11, 12], 55 [12, 14], 63 [22], 91 [59], 93 [62, 63], 97 [69, 70], 121 [106], 125 [116], 127 [120], 129 [122], 137 [135], 139 [138], 159 [159–60], 161 [163], 163 [163], 169 [172], 173 [176], 177 [179], 189 [191, 193], 191 [195]

refectory: *5, 6, 13, 20–21,* 53 [10, 11], 83 [49], 85–87 [51–52], 105–107 [82–83], 113–14 [96–98], 115–17 [92–100], 119 [103–104], 121 [106–107], 139 [138], 160 [160–63], 187 [189], 189 [192], 193 [196], 197 [200], 201 [206]; serving in, *20–21,* 115–21 [98–107]

regular, regularity: 59 [17], 99 [72], 113 [94], 151 [151]

regulations: *3, 5,* 45 [1], 47 [4], 49 [5], 171 [173]

religiousness: 47 [3–4], 93 [62], 99 [71], 111 [92], 125 [115], 127 [117], 129 [123], 131 [126–27], 147 [147], 159 [159], 163 [164], 175 [176], 191 [194], 195 [199]

Renty, Gaston de: 185 [187]

Repetition (activity): 53 [10], 81 [46], 83 [46–48]

resolution(s): 85 [51], 101 [75], 131 [125], 163 [164], 169 [171]

respect: 47 [4], 61 [19, 20], 65 [23], 69 [30], 83 [47], 95 [65], 99 [72], 113 [95], 115 [99], 119 [104], 129 [122], 135 [132], 153 [152], 157 [156], 163 [163, 165], 175 (n. 50), 199 [204], *211, 212, 214*

respect humain: 159 [158], 171 [172], 177 [178], 199 [203]; translation, 159 (n. 96), *219–20*

retreat, devotional: *28, 30,* 31 [126]

Retreat, lodgings: *27, 29–30,* 89 [56], 97 [68], 129 [121]

rhetoric: 165–66 [168], *207–209. See also* **Tones**

Richelieu, Armand Cardinal de: *12*

Rodríguez, Alphonsus, S.J.: 93 [62], 95 [66], 181 [182]

rooms: *see* **bedchambers**

rosary: 141 [140], 149 [149], 155 [155]

Rosary (activity): *27,* 53 [11], 55 [12], 63 [22], 99 [72], 129 [124], 139–43 [137–42], 169 [171], 183 [184, 185], 187 [189], 189 [192], 191 [193]

Rouen, novitiate: *9*

rubrics, Roman: 81 [45]

rules: *3, 4,* 45 [1], 47 [2–3], 59 [17–18], 81 [45], 105 [80], 113 [96], 133 [129], 141 [141], 149 [149], 157 [158], 161 [161], 163 [163], 171 [172–73], 179 [180], 199 [204]; common to all, *5,* 45 [2], 49 [6], 51 [9]; *re* specific rules, 91 [59], 113 [95], 121 [109], 125 [114], 127 [120], 131 [125], 163 [164], 179 [182], 183 [185], 195 [198], 199 [202]

Sacristan, Brother (*Sacristain*): 67 [27], 75 [37], 77 [40]

sacristy: *15*, 65 [25], 67 [26, 27], 75 [38], 77 [39], 135 [132], 149 [148]

Saint-Louis, professed house and church: *13*, *20*, *27*, [69 [30], 167 [170], 181 [183], 183 [185]

saints: 65 [24], 81 [44], 99 [74], 125 [113], 135 [133–34], 175 [177]

Satan ("Enemy," "Demon"): 61 [20], 185 [186]

scholarship: 97 [70], 129 [123], 195 [197]

schools of the Society: *see* colleges

Scripture: 99 [71], 145 [144], 177 [179]

senior novices ("seniors," *anciens*): *16*, *26*, 129 [124], 141 [142], 169 [170], 179 [180], 183 [185], 187 [188], 193 [195]; senior of the bedchamber, *16*, *24*, 49 [7], 63 [21, 22], 69 [29], 105 [80], 145 [144], 147 [146], 175 [177], 179 [180]; senior of Blessed Goto, *24*, 97 [63], 119 [103], 127 [118], 131 [125], 139 [138], 159 [159]

seniority: 115 [99], 117 [102], 121 [108, 109], 127 [119–20], 131 [125], 147 [146], 161 [160], 169 [170], 179 [180]

Sententiæ (activity): *23*, 55 [12]

sermon: 57 [14], 151 [150], 197 [201], *207–209*

servants: *16*, 65 [24], 123 [113], 125 [115], 141 [140], 165 [166], 175 [177], 177 [179], *207. See also* slaves

service rooms (*offices*): *20–21*, 53 [10], 87 [54], 115–25 [98–116], 143 [143], 149 [148], 195 [199]. *See also* pantry, refectory, dishwashing

Sewer, Brother (*Couturier*): *20*, 183 [186]

sewing room (*couturerie*): 143 [143], 149 [148]

silence: 55 [12], 81 [46], 87 [52], 91 [58], 99 [73], 105 [81], 125 [115], 129 [124], 131 [125], 139 [138], 145 [144], 149–51 [149–52], 157 [156–58], 159 [158, 159], 161 [162], 179 [180], 181 [184, 185], 183 [194, 185], 189 [192], 193 [196], 199 [203]

simplicity: 95 [66], 105 [80], 113 [94], 129 [122], 151 [150], 167 [168], 175 [176], 199 [203], 210

sins, sinners: 49 [6], 91 [62], 103 [78], 125 [114], 157 [157], 169 [170], *207*

slaves: 65 [24], 91 [61], 123 [113]. *See also* servants

Society of Jesus: *8*, *9*, *10*, *11*, *20*, *22*, *28*, *32*, 45 [1], 49 [5], 97 [70], 135 [133], 137 [134–35], 141 [139], 153 [152–53], 165 [166], 167 [168], 171 [172, 173], 175 [177], 191 [194], 193 [197], 195 [199], *211*, *213*, *216*, *217*, *220*; hierarchies within, *16 (n. 32)*, *20*, *22–23*, *24*, 47 [2], 117 [102], 121 [107], 161 [161]

Socius, Father (*Compagnon*): 177 [179], 189 [191]

sodalities: *27–28. See also* Congregation of the Novitiate

soul(s): 49 [6], 133 [130], 137 [135], 145 [143], 151 [151], 167 [168], 185 [187], *214. See also* instructions, "soul"

speaking audibly: *33*, 71 [31], 83 [47], 105 [82], 135 [132], 161 [160, 162]; speaking well, 165 [167], 177 [179], 179 [181–82], 201 [205]. *See also* silence

spelling: *2, 6*, 53 [11], 57 [15], 59 [16], 137–39 [135–37]

spirit: 63 [22], 85 [51], 91 [59, 61], 93 [63], 99 [71], 101 [75], 113 [96], 125 [114], 133 [129, 131], 137 [135], 143 [141], 151 [151–52], 171 [173, 174], 195 [198, 199], 197 [201]; inner, 49 [7], 67 [26], 125 [115], 163 [164], 193 [197]

Spiritual Exercises of St. Ignatius: *27, 30, 31*, 61 [20]

stairways: *12, 15, 22, 23, 24*, 101 [75], 125 [117], 127 [117–18], 149 [149], 193 [196]

Stanislaus Kostka, St,: 47 [4]

stove: *24*, 119 [103], 129 [124], 159 [159]

straining: *56*, 91 [59], 171 [173], 187 [189]

style of writing: *2, 41*, 95 [65, 67], 175 [176, 177]

Sublet de Noyers, François: *12, 225* n.

Substantials of the Institute (*Substantialia instituti*): 171 [174]

suffrages: 139 [137]

Superior, the: 49 [6], 117 [102], 161 [162], 163 [163], 171 [173, 174], 175 [177, 178], 177 [178], 179 [180, 181]. *See also* **permission**

superiors: *11, 18–20*, 47 [2–3], 61 [20], 97 [61], 113 [93], 133 [128], 137 [136], 141 [141], 161 [161], 163 [165], 175 [177], 197 [200]. *See also* **Society of Jesus, hierarchies**

supernatural: 91 [59, 61]

table of instructions: 49 [8], *204–205*

teaching: 59 [18], 145 [144]

temperance: 107 [83], 111–13 [91–96], 199 [204]

temptations: 103 [78], 171 [173]

Tertianship: 193 [196]

thanksgiving: 55 [13], 87 [52], 169 [171]

theology: 83 [49], 93 [64], 95 [66], 167 [168]

Thomas à Kempis: *32. See also **Imitation of Jesus Christ***

Tones, the (activity): *21*, 53 [11], *206–209*

Trent, Council of: 91 [60]

trouble(s): 103 [78], 167 [170], 169 [172], 171 [172, 174]

Turgot-Bretez map: *10, 13, 14, 30, 34*

useful: 47 [3], 59 [17], 67 [26], 97 [70], 101 [75], 129 [124], 133 [130], 143 [143], 165 [166], 177 [179], 195 [198]

vanity: 121 [109], 129 [123], 155 [155], 167 [169], 201 [205]

Versailles: *212, 215*

vespers: 57 [14]

vices: 151 [152], 155 [155]

Vitelleschi, Muzio. S.J.: 137 [135]

virtues, virtuous: *19, 28*, 95 [67], 151 [152], 153 [152], 155 [155], 157 [158], 159 [158], 191 [194], 195 [198]

vocation: 47 [4], 61 [19], 137 [135], 149 [148], 171 [172], 173 [176], 181 [182]

Voltaire: *214*

vows: 161 [161, 163]

walking: *13, 27*, 89 [58], 97 [68], 135 [132], 139 [138], 149 [149], 181–85 [183–87], 187 [188, 189], 189 [191], 191 [194]

walkways: *13, 14, 15, 27*, 97 [68]

warming oneself: *8, 20, 24, 26*, 79 [44], 117 [101], 119 [103], 127 [118], 129–30 [124–25], 149 [149], 157–59 [156–59]

water: drinking, 55 [13], 87 [52], 109 [87], 113 [95], 115 [98], 117 [100], 119 [103], 161 [161], 187 [190], 189 [192]; in household chores, *26*, 89 [55–56], 121–23 [108–12]

Weber, Max: *215*

wine at table: 87 [52], 109 [87], 113 [95], 119 [103], 161 [161], 199 [204]

women: *33*, 137 [136], 179 [181]

worries: 87 [53], 103 [78], 171 [173, 174], 175 [177]

writing: *2*, 53 [11], 137–39 [135–37], 143 [143], 173–77 [176–79]; as opposed to orality, *2–3*, 47 [2], 93 [64], 169 [170]

Xenophon: *213*

zeal: 47 [3], 81 [44], 85 [49], 97 [70], 125 [114], 139 [137], 167 [168], 171 [173], 199 [203]